George and Bridget Kane with Chloë Kane Gott, Victoria Kane, Felix Kane Gott and Georgina Kane

KANE FROM CANADA

ARIZONA CENTER FOR MEDIEVAL AND RENAISSANCE STUDIES

OCCASIONAL PUBLICATIONS

VOLUME 7

KANE FROM CANADA

EDITED BY
MARY KANE AND JANE ROBERTS

ARIZONA CENTER FOR MEDIEVAL

ACMRS

AND RENAISSANCE STUDIES

Tempe, Arizona
2016

Published by ACMRS (Arizona Center for Medieval and Renaissance Studies);
Tempe, Arizona
©Copyright 2016
Arizona Board of Regents for Arizona State University

∞
This book is made to last.
It is set in Adobe Kepler Std
and printed on acid-free paper to library specifications.
Printed in the United States of America

TABLE OF CONTENTS

List of Illustrations

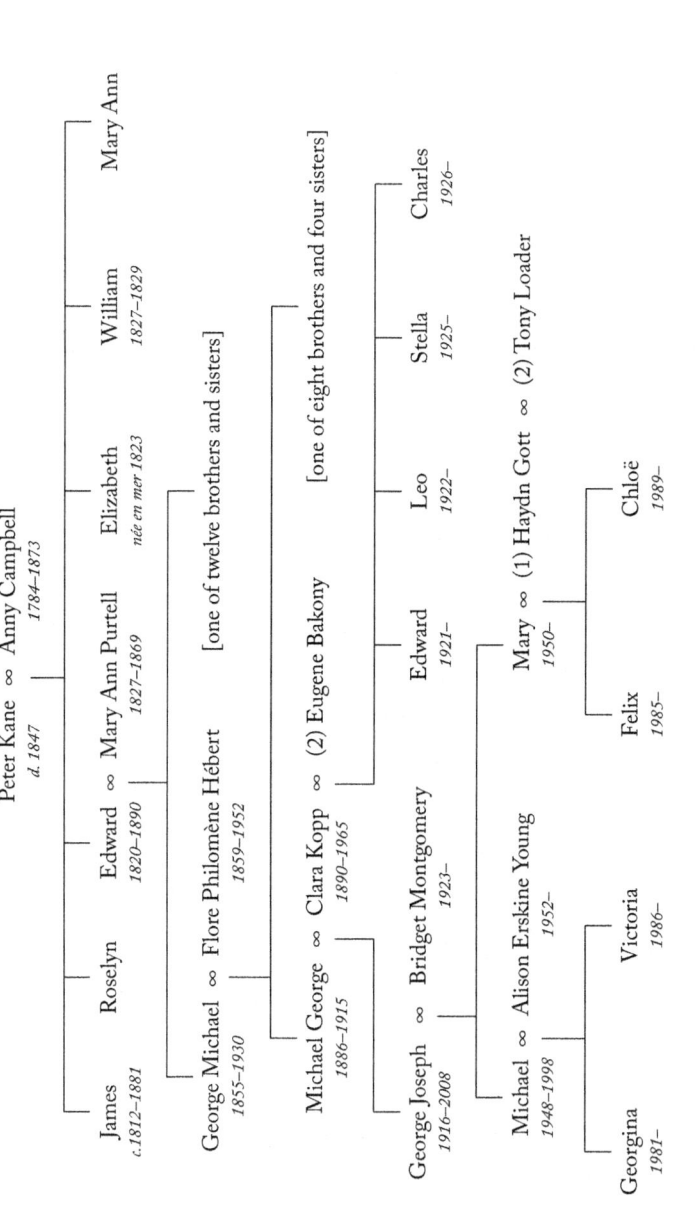

Peter and Amy Kane arrived in Quebec in 1823. A brief history of their descendants is to be found in *Sainte-Brigitte-des-Saults: d'autrefois à aujourd'hui* ([Sainte-Brigitte-des-Saults, Québec]: Municipalité de Sainte-Brigitte-des-Saults, [2001?]), pp. 396–97.

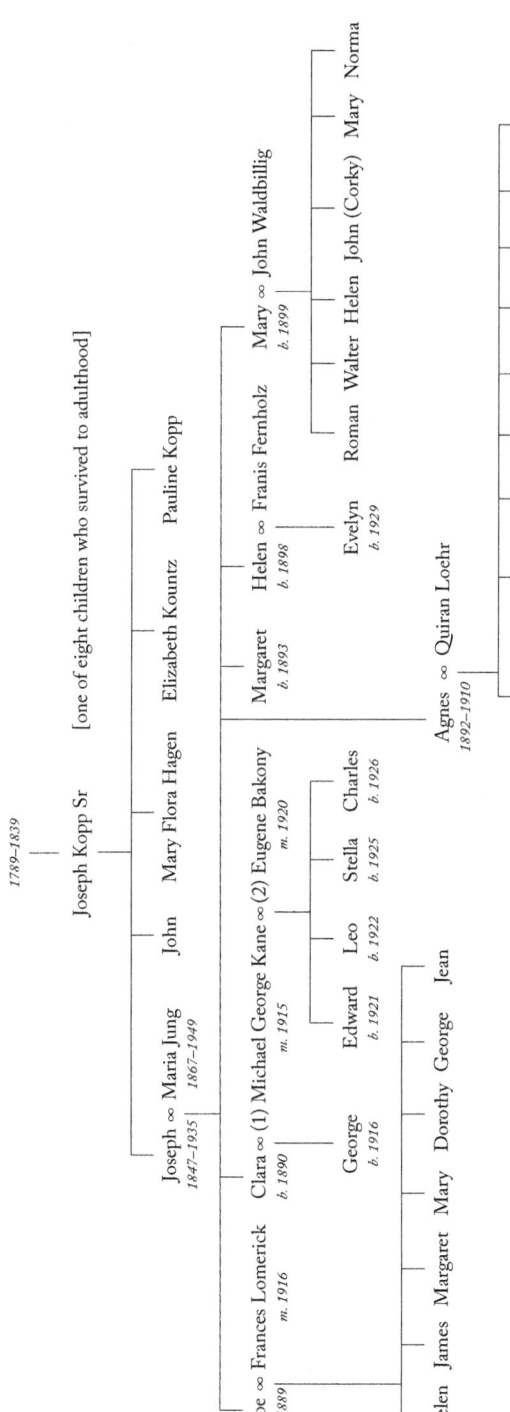

Grandfather
1789–1839

Joseph Kopp Sr   [one of eight children who survived to adulthood]

Joseph ∞ Maria Jung — John — Mary Flora Hagen — Elizabeth Kountz — Pauline Kopp
1847–1935 | 1867–1949

Joe ∞ Frances Lomerick — Clara ∞ (1) Michael George Kane ∞ (2) Eugene Bakony — Margaret — Helen ∞ Franis Fernholz — Mary ∞ John Waldbillig — Agnes ∞ Quiran Loehr
b. 1889   m. 1916 — *b. 1890   m. 1915   m. 1920* — *b. 1893* — *b. 1898* — *b. 1899* — *1892–1910*

Helen James Margaret Mary Dorothy George Jean

George Edward Leo Stella Charles
b. 1916   b. 1921   b. 1922   b. 1925   b. 1926

Evelyn
b. 1929

Roman Walter Helen John (Corky) Mary Norma

Josie (Fr. Philip) Margaret Helen Anne Jenny Monica Leo Eugene Gerald

In the previous generation Mary Flora Kopp m. Josef Hagen; they emigrated to Montana in 1882 with children aged nine years to nine months; Josef Hagen with his family moved on to Astoria, Oregon, where he died in 1888, leaving Mary with eight children to support. Mary Flora at some point went back to Bozeman.
Maria Jung from Goslar. After her mother's death (1882), her father emigrated with four young daughters; by *c.*1887 Maria was helping look after her sister's twins in Kansas

Acknowledgments

Many people have helped us in getting George Kane's memoir ready for press, and we hope we have remembered them all. First and foremost, we wish to thank Ron Waldron for scrutinizing the files so carefully and helping us to sort out details we could not otherwise have established. Fr Peter Novecosky, OSB, of St Peter's Abbey, looked back through 1930s issues of the *The Prairie Messenger* on our behalf. Kathryn Kerby-Fulton not only came on board to write a Foreword but press-ganged her mother, Doreen Kerby, into going to Muenster where they visited St Peter's Abbey and looked through the college's archives for photographs, together with Kathryn's cousin, Carol McLaren, the local school principal. Evelyn Chapuis, one of George Kane's cousins, has proved a mine of information on family history. Lt Col. Jan-Dirk von Merveldt (The Rifles) helped us with information about Kane's army years. Photographs from the archives of University College London were supplied by Neil Rodger and Kilian Thayaparan, and from Royal Holloway College by Sophia Haque. We also wish to thank the British Academy and in particular Peter Brown for allowing us to make use of materials in the British Academy memorial biography <http://www.britac.ac.uk/memoirs/11.cfm>, and for the help given by Joseph Wittig, Edward Kennedy and Patrick O'Neill (Chapel Hill, North Carolina) during its preparation. We have bludgeoned numerous friends, colleagues and relations into reading much of the contents of this book: Chloë Kane Gott; Felix Kane Gott; Paula Kane; Abigail Pierce; Tony Loader; Mary Chapuis; Rod and Lisa Bakony; Warwick Gould, Christopher Adams (Institute of English Studies); Ros Allen (Queen Mary University of London); Janet Bately, Trudi Darby, Chris Kenyon Jones (King's College London).

INTRODUCTION

The memoir, written by George Kane for his grandchildren, takes his life up to the end of his ten years at Royal Holloway College. At that point, his *Piers Plowman* edition (1960), awarded the Gollancz prize by the British Academy in 1963, had gained wide praise, one reviewer describing it as 'probably the nearest to a definitive text of the A version of *Piers Plowman* that human wit and diligence can hope to attain'.[1] He had published *Piers Plowman: the Evidence for Authorship* (1965), a clear and cogently argued analysis that was to quash the issue of authorship for the next couple of decades, and the Chambers Memorial Lecture of the same year confronted 'The autobiographical fallacy in Chaucer and Langland studies', complementing his analysis of the evidence for multiple authorship of *Piers Plowman*. He was already recognized internationally as one of the foremost scholars in medieval studies, and he was about to take up the long-established University of London chair in English Language and Medieval Literature at King's College. As a colleague from his King's days I feel cheated that the memoir ends here, and doubtless colleagues from his Chapel Hill days will share this feeling. Nevertheless, overall it is a satisfying whole, giving us many insights into the circumstances that went to form a Canadian boy from the plains into a scholar respected and honoured on both sides of the Atlantic. The memoir falls into three parts.

The opening chapters (§§1–6) cover the years that led up to graduate work at University College, London. Then (§§ 7–12) there follows Kane's account of 'the German war' or 'Hitler's war' — for his generation the First World War was still the 'World War' or the 'Great War'. For most of the Second World War he was a prisoner of war [p.o.w], a period that fills over half the pages of this book. Whereas many have written exciting tales centred on escape and adventure, here is a rounded picture of what life must have been like and how it was to be endured. There are of course stories aplenty of Kane's involvement in escape attempts, as was to be expected of any self-respecting officer, but as part and parcel of the daily life of a p.o.w. For Kane, 'one of the most horrifying experiences of the war, indeed of my life', was 'the newsreel of the first concentration camp liberated by British troops' and, as he tells us, that newsreel put an end to his 'self-pity about captivity'. In the last chapters (§§13–15) Kane faces up to hard decisions. Should

---

1. C. L. Wrenn, *Modern Language Notes* 76 (1961), 856–63 at 863.

he continue to seek an academic life? If so, on which side of the Atlantic? There are tantalising glimpses of the girl he would marry: he had seen a picture of her on her brother's bedside table in Spangenberg and when he met her 'she was all the photo had promised'; and of their children, Michael and Mary, born in 1948 and 1950 respectively. The importance to Kane of family and friendships is clear throughout the memoir, and we gain a strong sense of myriad individuals. Yet, in the end the memoir is very much Kane's view of his life, and somehow it is very private. Central is his coming to terms with Langland's *Piers Plowman*.

WHY LANGLAND?

In the autumn of 1938 George Kane entered University College London to work on his PhD. He had mapped out a thesis topic on Milton and expected to work with Professor C. J. Sisson (§6). On his third day in London he met Sisson, who listened to his outline of the proposed thesis and made no comment on it. Instead, asking Kane to follow him, Sisson straightway took him along the corridor to R. W. Chambers's office, where he introduced him with the words 'Here is Kane from Canada, whom we have been expecting' and, saying nothing more, left. It was a strange encounter. Chambers was welcoming, but in his turn showed little interest in the thesis topic outlined for a second time. After half an hour or so of general reminiscence, he gave Kane some books about Germanic heroes and dismissed him, telling him to return when he had read them. Sensibly, Kane betook himself off around the university in search of a supervisor more kindly disposed to his planned research, but without luck. Late in October he confronted Chambers. Kane presented his case, a thesis topic for which he had prepared himself as against the 'Germanic world of the dark ages' to which he could bring but a smattering of Anglo-Saxon. The reaction was inscrutable. Chambers offered 'a change of reading' and packed him off with a clutch of offprints about the authorship of *Piers Plowman*.

Had he been set up by Sisson? Was Chambers playing a canny waiting game? Kane could never decide, but, as he relates, the invitation to work on Langland with Chambers was both a challenge and a compliment, and he was now some months into the two years of his graduate scholarship. Chambers's view of his predicament was realistic: 'The time is yours to use'. And Kane saw that the new topic put to him could be completed within the time left, after which he could put Middle English aside and return to the field he had chosen. So, in the first week of November, he buckled down to collating his allotted Passus XVIII–XX of the B text. With Oxford, Bodleian Library, MS Laud Misc. 581, the manuscript preferred by Skeat in his editions, as his base text, he had, by the early summer term of 1939 collated all sixteen versions and an early print, and he settled down to pulling together the critical apparatus and to checking all his work. The end was in sight. But so was the war. In mid-August Chambers insisted on supervising the move of the college's rare books and muniments to Aberystwyth. His decision that Kane's draft thesis and all his working materials must also go into safe storage in Wales was a sudden interruption. Chambers's decision was fortunate. When he got back to London in 1945 (§12), Kane discovered that virtually all his belongings had vanished. Realizing that his incomplete thesis was safe in Aberystwyth, he headed to the Registry at University College, where he was welcomed with the words 'Mr Kane from Canada!' He did not then know that England would be his home for thirty years and more to come. The young graduate student of 1938 had confidently expected to go home in 1940. As things turned out, he was never to live in Canada again.

FROM CANADA TO LONDON

The first quarter of Kane's life left on him its indelible stamp. He was, through and through, Canadian, and proud of his heritage (§1). On his father's side he was an eighth-generation Canadian — his father's mother was a descendant of one of the original settlers of Nova Scotia, or Acadie as it was earlier called. The Kanes were more recent arrivals in North America: his great-great-grandparents, Peter Kane and Anny Campbell, emigrated from the north of Ireland early in the nineteenth century. On his mother's side, his grandfather, Joseph Kopp (1847–1935), was from Switzerland and his grandmother, Maria Jung (1867–1949), from Hanover, emigrants both to the United States, where their nine children were born. From 1902 Joseph Kopp was eyeing land across the border, first in Alberta, then in Saskatchewan, and in 1903 he bought land near Humboldt in St Peter's Colony and set about moving his wife and six surviving children north.

His father, also George Kane, was working for the Canadian National Railway Company when he married Clara Kopp on the 15th September 1915. That same year he died, suddenly, of heart failure, on the 28th December, and Clara went home to her parents. Before her marriage, Clara had worked as a librarian in Regina, and her parents encouraged her to seek work again, but nearer home, as a teacher, which is how George Kane came to be brought up bilingual by his German-speaking grandparents on their farm. His childhood was spent near Humboldt, where he was born, at first on his grandfather's farm, and later, when Joseph Kopp retired, in the village of Muenster. There he went to the local parish school, from which he went on with Fritz Weber, Ted Bergerman and his cousin Josie Loehr to St Peter's College (1930–1934), the school run by the nearby Benedictine abbey. Even though Kane ceased to be a practising Catholic soon after leaving school, his years at the abbey school left him with a sense of admiration for the religious life and a deep understanding of a life of dedication with its daily

ST. PETER'S COLLEGE

The first meeting of the St. Michael's Literary and Debating Society for the year 1932-1933 was held last Sunday evening. The Moderator Rev. Father Augustine, opened the meeting by explaining the purpose of literary societies, which, he said, was primarily to afford practice in public speaking, and secondarily to foster a spirit of good fellowship among the student body. He stressed the importance of the gift of eloquence throughout life and stated that a man was not a born orator, but acquired fluency through practice only.

The election of officers for the first semester followed. When the smoke of the electorial battle had cleared away, the following members wore the laurel crown of victory upon their brows: Mr. Bergermann in the vice-president chair, Mr. Kane with the secretarial quill behind his ear, Mr. Engele holding the keys of the treasury, Mr. Fred Weber wearing the badge of the Sergeant-at-Arms, and Messrs. Florentin and Francis Schwinghammer as the committee-on-programme.

The Reverend Moderator congratulated the society upon their choice of officers. Further, he promised the society a very enjoyable evening at the next meeting, to be held two weeks later, when the newly elected officers will speak.

* * *

Excerpt from the *Prairie Messenger*, 23 November 1932.

Gregorian chants. It was a highly academic school, at which the four local day boys flourished, remaining to take in their final year the First Year Arts course of the University of Saskatchewan. Games were played seriously too — baseball, handball, tennis, ice hockey. During his last two years at school Kane was the college's sports correspondent, writing reports for the weekly diocesan newsletter, the *Prairie Messenger*, which the abbey published. In winter there was tobogganing, and skiing in a nearby ravine, and the journey across country to and from school could be quickly made on skis. There were other extra-curricular activities. The *Prairie Messenger* for the 23rd November 1932 includes a report of the first meeting of the St Michael's Literary and Debating Society. Ted Bergerman and Fritz Weber are there, and 'Mr. Kane with the secretarial quill behind his ear'; both Kane and Bergerman are among the speakers at a second meeting on the 7th December.[2]

After Clara's second marriage in 1921 to Eugene Bakony, Kane spent his summers with his mother and stepfather in farming countryside sixty miles

2. I wish to thank Fr Peter Novecosky, OSB, today's editor of the *Prairie Messenger*, for sending me these references.

north-west of Muenster, as big brother to a growing family of three brothers and a sister — idyllic summers on the shores of Lake Wakaw spent swimming and messing about in rowing boats, mostly in a bathing suit. Kane looked back on those summers and the cottage at Lake Wakaw as his 'Walden, but better than Thoreau's'. Rather than take up the University of Saskatchewan scholarship he had won by his last year's work at school, in 1934 (§3) he moved west to Vancouver with his mother, stepfather and their four children, where he enrolled in the second year at the University of British Columbia. His choice of subjects — English, French and German — was not an available course, and he was offered honours in English and Latin instead. In his second semester in Vancouver, he joined the University Officers' Training Corps, undertaking a training that was to come in useful a few years later. The decision to weight his undergraduate work towards English came with his selection of the topic 'Critical Opinions in the Plays of Shakespeare' for the substantial essay required of all finalists. He graduated in 1936 with first class honours in English and Latin, and an application to the University of Toronto netted him a generous graduate fellowship that included fees and accommodation for his M.A. year.

The boy from the plains had first moved west, to British Columbia. Now (§4) he was to travel east across the continent to Toronto, by ship to Seattle and onwards by rail. The journey was so long as to make it impractical to go home for Christmas. At Toronto Kane concentrated his M.A. work in medieval and early modern literature, working in some depth on Ben Jonson and elaborating a future research topic on Milton and the theory of the epic in the renaissance. His year as an assistant warden at Massey College passed quickly, to be followed by a research fellowship at Northwestern University (1937–1938). He had, however, already decided that he wanted to undertake research in Britain and set about seeking funding. The year at Evanston (§5) he found academically challenging, 'a good year', even though he knew he was marking time. Taking courses without any examination pressures, he concentrated again on medieval and renaissance literature, adding Old French to his skills and enjoying reading *Beowulf* alongside the *Chanson de Roland*. The former, he discovered, more than repaid the chore of having to learn to read Old English for, in its 'greater sophistication', *Beowulf* outshone the 'crude execution and vitality' of the *Chanson*. But his two-year graduate studentship, awarded by the Imperial Order of Daughters of the Empire, beckoned and it must have seemed an academic career of promise would follow seamlessly.

THE WAR YEARS

There are many stories told about Kane's war years, mostly false. He was not at Dunkirk, though people talked confidently of seeing him lying in a ditch there. Nor did he collate *Piers Plowman* in Spangenberg, a myth built on the parcel of books R. W. Chambers sent to him in 1942.

Initially (§7) Kane enlisted in the Honourable Artillery Company, but he was posted to the Artists' Rifles, by then an officer training unit. From there he chose to move on to the Rifle Brigade. Towards the end of training he volunteered for a battalion to be made up of experienced skiers and mountaineers, the fifth battalion of the Scots Guards, newly formed to help Finland, which had been attacked by the Red Army—the unit was initially to be posted to Norway. This wild enterprise had to be aborted because Sweden refused the permission necessary to cross into Finland. Briefly, therefore, he served as a guardsman—like other officers, he had resigned his commission to join this special battalion. Eventually the unit was disbanded, but not before it had as its highlight a week's skiing in ideal conditions at Chamonix (March to April 1940). In the mean time Kane had missed his posting to Egypt with the Second Battalion of the Rifle Brigade, so now he proceeded to his first post as a regimental officer of the Rifle Brigade, Second Lieutenant, with the Motor Training Battalion at Tidworth. By May 1940 he was in Essex, in charge of C Company, digging entrenchments for the defence of England, and then in Suffolk. A call came suddenly on 21 May to move to Southampton, and next day he embarked for France.[3] There he took part in the chaotic stand at Calais. Leading a fighting patrol towards the end of the defence, he was hit by a bullet that went right through his body.

Left behind (§8) with other serious casualties, Kane was taken into Calais by the Germans as a prisoner of war, where he received treatment in a field hospital until fit enough for travel. The first of his escape attempts made while in hospital was foiled by an officious chaplain. In 1984, with his wife and daughter, he visited the place in Calais where he had been captured, only to find it was now the site of a large supermarket.

The journey to his first prison camp was not an easy one. There was transport on the 19th June as far as Lille, but after that it was a slow circuitous trudge through much of north-western France and Belgium. He spoke later of spending a night in a condemned cell, the only place with a roof, and of being given an omelette hot from the frying pan straight into his hands as he walked through Belgium. The column of well over a thousand prisoners reached Antwerp on the 1st July, to be herded into goods wagons and taken to a transit camp at Dortmund.

---

3. Cf. Arthur Bryant, *Jackets of Green. A Study of the History, Philosophy, and Character of the Rifle Brigade* (London: Collins, 1972), 343.

Kane was a prisoner first in Oflag VIIC (§9), once a country palace of the archbishops of Salzburg, near Laufen in Bavaria (July 1940 to September 1941). In January 1941 he was adopted into a tunnelling team, which gave some sense of purpose to his life until its discovery late in June. Otherwise the days were spent mainly in reading Tauchnitz fiction reprints (their purchase was arranged by the senior British officer, Major Charles Shears, who had before the war worked in a publishing firm).

Autumn 1941 (§10) brought a move to Oflag VIB at Dösselbei Warburg in Westphalia, a huge camp into which the Germans had poured most of the prisoners taken after the retreat from Dunkirk, some from the North African campaign and all from Greece, as well as RAF people shot down over Europe, some two and a half thousand officers together with 450 orderlies. An enormous amount of effort was put into tunnelling, but managed to get only three officers outside Oflag VIB. One tunnel with which Kane was involved was holed by a collapse in freakish spring weather.

From September 1942 to January 1943 he was in Oflag VIIB at Eichstätt, in southern Bavaria (§11). As a fluent German speaker he was much in demand and he was one of the group that escaped through a gate on 24 November, getting as far as Talmühle, about eight miles from Switzerland. His last prison camp was Oflag IXAH (§12), not the lower camp in the middle of Elbersdorf but the upper camp, Schloss Spangenberg, where he remained until its evacuation. Spangenberg, a small camp, even had a library that was well run by Charles Shears. Somehow Shears managed to arrange for good supplies of new books to be sent over, and others were given to the library from book parcels received by individual prisoners. Shears invited Kane to become assistant librarian, a role that gave him ready access to the books it became his duty to catalogue. At Spangenberg, he read avidly, and not just English books. He schooled himself through many French novels and he set about learning Italian well enough to read Dante without a facing translation.

On the 30th March the Germans evacuated Spangenberg, marching their prisoners out to the noise of gunfire. A few days later Kane was one of a small group who slipped away from the column and came across an advance troop of Patton's army. Their adventures were made famous by Terence Prittie who, in *South to Freedom* (1946), describes Kane as having 'exceptional nervous energy' and 'a remarkable determination which serves to keep him awake and alert long after physical exhaustion has claimed the average man'. For his part, Kane remembers rather differently detail of the escapes in which both he and Prittie were involved, and his account adds significantly to the published records.

LEARNING TO SWIM

Once back in London, Kane's time was his own until leave in Canada would come up. He was still in London for VE Day, but later in the summer sailed on the Queen Mary to North America, to travel across the continent and, for the first time in seven years, catch up with his family (§13). An unexpected interruption during his leave was an invitation to the University of Saskatchewan by John Lothian, who wanted him to take over and build up the English Department — it must have been a disorienting invitation for someone as yet to be demobilised and with a half-finished PhD. VJ Day he spent in New York, just before crossing back to England on the Queen Elizabeth. At Southampton Docks he was handed an order to report to the Rifle Brigade Regimental Training Battalion in Nottinghamshire, where there was so little for him to do that out of boredom he demanded a posting — and was told to take some leave.

By September 1945 Kane had applied to resume his PhD and he was appointed a Departmental Assistant (but without pay) at University College for the second year of his interrupted scholarship, with an Assistant Lectureship to follow on in 1946. His demobilisation came through in late February 1946, the month in which his collations and notes returned to London from Aberystwyth. So he set about writing up his PhD, an edition of Passus XVIII–XX of *Piers Plowman*, submitted in June that same year. He took up his University of London Assistant Lectureship in the autumn (§14), and was appointed to a tenured lectureship in 1948.

During the post-war years at University College Kane gradually developed confidence as a teacher. Ron Waldron, then a graduate student at Royal Holloway College, recalls being sent by his supervisor, Hilda Green, to sit in on his lectures, from which he learned a lot to supplement the medieval teaching he had had as an undergraduate. Yet, Kane writes of his struggles to get up teaching texts, at first feeling out of his depth. Careful preparation and background reading contributed to *Middle English Literature* (1951). A work of literary criticism at a time when historical and philological approaches were general, it was hailed by an early reviewer as 'one of the best books so far written on any aspect of Middle English literature'.[4] His direct engagement with romances, lyrics and *Piers Plowman* quickly attracted a wide audience, both in Britain and North America. The book remains in student use, being reprinted as recently as 2000. His department's generous recruitment of visiting professors meant that he was able to indent for Bloomfield and Donaldson as year-long colleagues. With determination, he decides there will be 'no more regrets for the unattempted study of the Renaissance epic', begins 'to find students interesting rather than formidable' and, with promotion to a readership, realizes that he has 'learned to swim almost anywhere'.

---

4. A. I. Doyle, *The Review of English Studies*, NS 4 (1953), 69–70.

In 1955 (§15) he became Professor of English Language and Literature and Head of Department at Royal Holloway College, still at that time a women's college at undergraduate level. He was, for a while, one of the very few men in the college. There he inherited the courses of his predecessor, Gladys Willcock, including two years of English poetry from Skelton to Herrick, the period in which he had originally planned to do research. It was a small department, and he was able to tutor each of the ten or twelve finalists every year. It was a good period too for research, for steady attention to the readings in the *Piers Plowman* manuscripts. (This chapter tells how Kane became the general editor of all three versions, and his account of others associated with editing is riveting.) These were the years in which the children were young: Michael, born January 1948, and Mary, born in the autumn of 1950, shortly after the family moved to Englefield Green. In 1961 they were to move to Shandon Cottage in Beaconsfield, their home for fifteen years. They managed a long summer visit to Canada in 1960, when Kane returned to the University of British Columbia to teach at the July summer school, an opportunity for them all to see his mother and many other members of his family properly as well as to catch up with old friends.

LATER LIFE

In 1965, Kane was teaching once again in central London. At King's College he managed to juggle undergraduate teaching and graduate supervision, a distinguished scholarly output and a heavy administrative burden with a kindly patience and quiet humour that made it all seem effortless. He had a remarkable ability to concentrate people's attention, evident also in his chairmanship of the University Board of Studies in English (1970–2) and he was, throughout his three decades as a teacher in London University, a force to be reckoned with in the dealings of the intercollegiate Board of Studies and on its examination boards. In addition to his departmental roles and many committee responsibilities, he was the University's Public Orator from 1962 to 1966 and Dean of the Faculty of Arts at King's from 1972 to 1974.

Kane's final teaching position was at the University of North Carolina at Chapel Hill, where he held the William Rand Kenan Jr Professorship of English, the only full professorship on the medieval side when he arrived. By 1976 the children were both in their twenties: Michael was training to be a doctor, and Mary was working as a solicitor in the West End of London. Bridget's mother and father were dead. The move to America was a new adventure. At Chapel Hill he carried on the strong tradition of teaching and mentoring graduate students vigorously, teaching courses in the Comparative Literature department as well as in English and energetically supporting and encouraging medieval studies across the liberal arts departments. Colleagues at Chapel Hill recall fondly the parties George and

George Kane, Ron Waldron and Ron's son Tom go fishing.

Bridget gave at the end of each semester, to which they invited all the medieval students and faculty with whom George's teaching and other activities brought him into contact. He served on many university-wide committees, and was for three years the chairman of the Division of Humanities (1980–83). He was elected to the American Academy of Arts and Sciences (1977), and he became a Fellow of the Medieval Academy (1978). After his retirement from North Carolina came two years at the National Humanities Center, an easy drive from Chapel Hill, and he and Bridget were able to enjoy two last years in the house they had built within walking distance from campus.

In 1989 George and Bridget returned to live in England, to be nearer their son Michael, their daughter Mary and their families. They lived at first in a tiny Georgian house near the British Museum. After Bridget had a fall on ice and broke her ankle, they moved to a house in Hampstead, round the corner from Mary and her family. Michael died of cancer in 1998. In 2002 they moved to West Sussex, again to be close to Mary. In these years Kane was a welcome figure at seminars and lectures in the University of London, and he continued to work steadily on Langland. To mark his achievement in completing the three *Piers Plowman* volumes he was awarded the Gollancz prize for a second time (1999). For Kane, however, the task he had undertaken was not complete until he got to press in 2005 his glossary for the English vocabulary of the three Athlone volumes. His *Oxford*

Michael Kane.

Dictionary of National Biography entry on Langland (2004) revisits fully the details known or surmised of Langland's life, now dated by him *c*.1325–*c*.1390. Placing the poet's putative birth in *c*.1325 lengthens his life, a change made in the light of recent discoveries about William Rokele, a cleric tonsured in the Worcester area by 1341 and, if the same man, beneficed within the jurisdiction of the Bishop of Norwich in 1353. Clearly Kane came to view the identification as attractive, but unprovable. This succinct overview of Langland's life demonstrates clearly the admiration and affection *Piers Plowman* inspired in him and which he communicated so effectively to others. The impact of George Kane's editorial and critical work was wide reaching, and his influence continues to be important in Middle English scholarship.[5] When the Athlone C version appeared, a century had gone by since Chambers and Grattan published the first results of their work on *Piers Plowman*. At last Skeat's parallel texts of 1886 had their true successor. The three volumes that comprise the Athlone *Piers Plowman* will continue to provide an unparalleled amount of invaluable textual detail for some time to come, even to readers who decry the authoritarianism of its critical editions. That they exist at all is down to the unflagging energy of their chief editor.

5. No attempt is made here to deal with the reception of the three volumes. An overview may be found in the British Academy memorial biography (2012) <http://www.britac.ac.uk/memoirs/11. cfm>, from which much of the material in this Introduction is taken.

George Kane's one hobby.

In 2008, George and Bridget moved into sheltered accommodation in East-bourne. Bridget had developed Alzheimer's disease and he and Mary were unable to care for her on their own. There he continued to work slowly at his typewriter, on requested articles and his autobiography, up to six weeks before his death. He remained interested in politics and academic gossip and delighted in being asked to look through and comment on his grandson's dissertation for his history de-gree, needless to say on the mediaeval period. He died in Eastbourne, on 27 De-cember 2008, survived by Bridget, his wife of sixty-two years, their daughter and four grandchildren.

Kane admitted to one hobby only, which he took up seriously in 1958. A keen flyfisher, the holidays spent wading in rivers or tumbling about in small boats on cold loughs were, apart from reading, his main relaxation, although fishing could be combined with seeking out little known and often isolated ruins of castles in Scotland and Ireland. His family was the centre of his life. This memoir doubtless grew from the interest in genealogy he developed with Michael while Michael was dying, when, before the arrival of the internet, they went to the Mormon library in London, to chase up links from Ireland, France and Germany leading to their family's various arrivals in North America.

Jane Roberts
University of London

FOREWORD

George Kane won every conceivable academic honour, but the memoirs of most such scholars, however fine, rarely reach press. Kane's case is different: the vision, penetration and monumentality of his editorial undertakings lifted him beyond the orbit of medievalists to the pantheon of great editorial theorists.[1] While a general Introduction to Kane's life and work precedes, this Foreword will focus on two key themes that he himself foregrounded for us: his Canadian origins and his editorial career, themes that intersected at the moment he was being introduced to R. W. Chambers, a Ph.D. supervisor he never intended to work with, hearing the enigmatic words: 'Here is Kane from Canada, whom we have been expecting'. Chambers was the man who would foist upon him the foreign field of Middle English, and the uncharted territory of *Piers Plowman* editing. Understanding the creative intersection of these seemingly unrelated strands of his life is my job here, because, by chance, I am both a Canadian from Kane's own prairie hometown, and, by trade, a Langlandian.

'KANE FROM CANADA'

As a fellow Langlandian, my admiration for the formidable editorial acumen of George Kane was already firmly established even before I read that we were from the same small prairie town: George was born in Humboldt, Saskatchewan in 1916, about 40 years before I was (by my time it had grown to a metropolis of about 2500–3000 people).[2] He grew up just outside the town at St Pete's (as locals call it), that is St Peter's Abbey and College, the school and junior college founded

I would like to thank the following people: Jane Roberts, for inviting me to take part in this project, one that I was entirely by chance born into; Derek Pearsall and Ralph Hanna for helpful readings; Paul Paproski, OSB, for gracious access to the St Peter's Abbey archives; and my mother, Doreen Kerby, and cousin, Carol McLaren, both, like me, natives of Humboldt, for pitching in to help sift through the enormous holdings of the Abbey archives, and Carol for accompanying me through deep snow of farmers' fields on a sub-zero Saskatchewan day in search of Kane's grandparents' house.

1. See Ralph Hanna's comment, 'one cannot overestimate the magnitude of George Kane's editorial achievement': 'George Kane and the Invention of Textual Thought: Retrospect and Prospect', *Yearbook of Langland Studies* 24 (2010), 1–20, at 1.

2. *Medieval English Studies presented to George Kane*, ed. Edward Donald Kennedy, Ronald Waldron and Joseph S. Wittig (Woodbridge: Brewer, 1988), xi–xiii.

St Peter's Abbey, February 2015, much as it was during Kane's childhood.

in 1903 by pioneering Benedictines from the distinguished St John's University in Collegeville, Minnesota. St Pete's was where the more academically gifted Catholic boys of the Humboldt area studied, especially those who might prove good prospects for the priesthood (Kane, too, records the moment he was asked the vocational question there). The hamlet that sprang up around the Abbey came to be called Muenster after its 'Minster' by the German settlers (pronounced 'Munster' locally). The beautiful murals painted at great cost by Count Berthold von Imhoff in 1919 for the abbey, and which George would have known, are today under restoration.[3] Just a few miles away on the Muenster side of Humboldt lies the small public school for the tiny Protestant minority that I attended. Religious difference was the key marker of identity in both our generations.

When, as a young Langlandian, I worked up the courage to meet George, he had just given the plenary lecture at the first *Piers Plowman* conference in Cambridge, 1993. When I told him that I, too, was from Humboldt, this formidable scholar threw down his walking stick and gave me a spontaneous bear-hug, melting into a bundle of boyish merriment before my eyes. Nothing would do but that we should sit down then and there in a quiet corner, ignoring the press of his other

3. For images, see <http://en.wikipedia.org/wiki/Berthold_Imhoff#mediaviewer/File:Berthold_Imhoff_remembered_2_(481919999).jpg>

Ice hockey at St Pete's, with a Benedictine monk coaching.

post-plenary questioners, and swap childhood tales of sun-filled prairie summers and glistening ice winters (these are described in the memoirs in delicious detail). We also talked earnestly of the strain of coming (as we both in some way did) from mixed Catholic-Protestant families in a locality zealously dominated by a Catholic majority — tensions to which we had both independently attributed our later interests in the religious complexity of *Piers Plowman*. In the generation before George was born, the Humboldt area had been settled as St Peter's Colony by a group of German Catholic immigrants who had originally fled religious persecution in their homeland. As the historic site plaque reads in English, French and German, 'Part of the rich cultural diversity forged in Western Canada by waves of newcomers, St. Peter's Colony was home to one of Canada's largest German group settlements and its first Benedictine Monastery. Founded in 1903 through a unique blend of church and economic initiatives, this colony was from 1921 to 1998, a rare Abbey Nullius, or independent diocese. The Benedictines, Franciscan Sisters of St. Elizabeth, and Ursulines of Bruno provided religious services, education, and health care and, despite anti-German sentiment during the two world wars, created a vibrant centre of German Catholic heritage on the prairies.'[4]

4. Historic Sites and Monuments Board of Canada, 'The Establishment of St. Peter's Colony and Abbey', sign beside St. Peter's Abbey.

As the Canadian historian Bill Waiser explains, while it was common to have settlement patterns in Saskatchewan created by distinct ethnic communities remaining together and continuing to recruit from their homeland ('chain migration'), nevertheless two colonies stood out as unusually exclusive: 'In a few cases there was a desire to create distinct enclaves. The St. Peter's and St. Joseph's colonies were German-American Roman Catholic settlements in the Humboldt and Trampling Lake areas respectively.'[5] As Father Paul Paproski, archivist at St Peter's, wrote in 2011: 'The colony was a religious jurisdiction in the Roman Catholic Church. It was similar to a Roman Catholic diocese, with the exception that the spiritual leader was a prior or abbot and not a bishop. [It] became home to approximately 18,000 Roman Catholics by 1930. The colonists lived in an area that stretched approximately fifty miles in an east-west direction and thirty miles in a north- south direction. The city of Humboldt lies close to the centre of the former settlement.'[6] In short, both George and I were raised in a patch of Canada that remained in many respects under Catholic church jurisdiction.

Though George and I did not know this historical assessment at the time, we had both lived with the result. Upon arrival, the Catholic colonists initially had tried to purchase the farms of the few early Protestant settlers and met resistance, thus beginning a tussle over faith and local politics that would enmesh succeeding generations down through the twentieth century. George's grandparents, who, along with the learned monks of the abbey, arrived as part of the German-American contingent, emphasized education and culture, and despised 'bigotry' (the term George uses throughout the memoirs for the local Catholic-Protestant tensions — indeed, George's grandmother had been Lutheran herself, before adopting her husband's Catholicism 'with Lutheran rigour' (7)). All this, George and I decided, must account for our life-long fascination with William Langland, the most 'reformist' and outspoken of the medieval English poets — the only one who could hold withering critique of the Church and love of Church tradition together under one big, inclusive roof. The Benedictines of St Peter's Abbey, whom George justly praises here for their learnedness in classical and Christian traditions, devout sense of community, and humanity, were locally distinctive. George says of this 'liberal attitude': 'While I am writing about religion, I record a remarkable feature of the teaching at St Peter's, its freedom from bigotry.... [In English courses] the spiritual anxieties of Arnold and Clough were presented as the problems of thinking men rather than the predicament of Protestant doubters' (34). But St Pete's was primarily a junior seminary, and when it came to be George's turn to be questioned about vocation, he writes, 'I could not see myself as a priest

---

5. Bill Waiser, *Saskatchewan: A New History* (Calgary: Fifth House, 2005), 67.

6. Paul Paproski, OSB, 'The German Catholics of St. Peter's Colony: 1903 – 1930', University of Saskatchewan Masters diss. (2011), p. 1.

. . . The parish priests had not impressed me: they were not personalities I would have selected as my intermediaries with a deity.' (32) Still later in life, encountering *Piers Plowman* he writes: 'My Benedictine schooling had based me soundly in practical theology . . . but I had everything to learn about the hostility between friars and regulars, the corruption of the monasteries, the worldliness of the papacy' (74). But what *had* prepared him for Langland, however, as we discussed in a handful of conversations, is the world he describes more indirectly here as the Catholicism he met with as a boy in the local parishes. So familiar he was with this parochial world that even as an adult who had by then studied at the University of British Columbia, Northwestern University, the University of London, and survived p.o.w. camps of World War II Europe, he still instinctively knew how to handle the local clergy: he tells of a crisis precipitated by his stepfather's death as a Catholic agnostic in nearby Wakaw Lake ('better than Walden Pond' in Kane's boyhood estimation). The priest being reluctant to give his stepfather a Christian burial, Kane writes 'With, probably, as good a theological education as he, I could have given him firm grounds for a Christian burial, but if he were to refuse to conduct the service I would be foxed.' So Kane secures the burial by negotiating a business transaction the priest had wanted (219). Kane's own father (who came from a long line of Northern Irish immigrants and via Quebec), had once called French Canada 'priest-ridden' (219). Kane was aware of the full spectrum of responses to Church tradition, which is great training for any Langlandian.

I hope Langland scholars, then, reading this book may now understand in part why George returns repeatedly to his Saskatchewan roots, even after his career and war experience had covered two continents, and his editorial fame exploded beyond the confines of medieval studies. The child is father of the man, but especially so in his case. This is underlined by another story I can add regarding his love of St Pete's and his home town. When the Athlone Press Russell-Kane edition finally emerged in 1997, and I had to send George a polite letter about a few transcription errors I had found in their Ilchester Prologue,[7] I also included, to sweeten the pill, an historical pamphlet published by St Peter's College about its early days, and postcards of its lovely, historic church with the Imhoff paintings, items I'd collected for him while attending a cousin's recent wedding there. George was so excited when he got the letter that he called me from England — briefly blamed the transcription errors on the use of computers (!), and wanted to talk of nothing but Humboldt — one of the longest trans-Atlantic calls I have ever had. Only upon reading these memoirs did I fully understand the reason for the trans-Atlantic call: looters had stolen all his personal possessions in the

---

7. These are corrected in the transcription published in K. Kerby-Fulton, '"Langland in his Working Clothes"?: Scribe D, the C-Draft Passages and the Nature of Scribal Intervention', in *Middle English Poetry: Texts and Traditions in Honour of Derek Pearsall*, ed. Alastair Minnis (Cambridge: University of York Medieval Press, 2001), 149–67.

Blitz, and though he had always intended to return to Canada to live, his marriage made that impossible. So ties to home were precious, and few and far between.

In yet other respects for a Canadian Langlandian, the memoirs proved to be a page-turner. George and I, despite the forty-year gap in age, shared an astonishing amount of geography, history and literature: from Saskatchewan's deep, crisp winters and canoe-filled summers, to studying English literature 'on the edge of the world' (beautiful British Columbia's coast), and in equally 'British' Toronto, or embarking for England as a young Canadian on an Imperial Order of the Daughters of the Empire fellowship (yes, there is such a thing, and we both did), and negotiating the English university system as a Commonwealth 'colonial'. Canadian readers will relish his portraits of Ira Dilworth as professor (visionary pioneer of B.C. artistic culture, and early mentor of the now famous Emily Carr),[8] the University of Toronto's magnetic A. S. P. Woodhouse (who excited George to become a Miltonist and to whom Northrup Frye dedicated *Fools of Time*),[9] and Earl Birney (a nationally famous poet, and a Chaucerian). Most of all we had shared what he calls 'the deep end' of English academia, and professional Langlandian scholarship — virtually too complex to be mastered by a single mind. Unless the mind was George Kane's.

KANE'S ADOPTIVE FIELD

Kane's memoirs, of course, are revealing for those many readers who want to come to understand how key and controversial decisions were made by the editors of the monumental Athlone *Piers* editions. Most compelling here is Kane's retracing of his editorial steps and philosophy in simple, candid prose that reaches across period and language boundaries to literary scholars in all fields. He explains in layman's terms how he sifted studies in multiple languages on the toughest editorial challenges: the New Testament, Classical texts, medieval French romance, and even medieval canon law. These taught him methods for recovering Langland's texts (which 'my ear', he says, had taught him was all the work of a *single* author — another of George's great contributions (268)). These studies also made him feel comfortable with his conclusion that the 'the state of preservation' of the A-text copies 'precluded the reconstruction' of a 'line of descent . . . or stemma'. From Kantorowicz's editing of canon law he learns of '*lebende Texte*, that is, texts particularly subject to change', texts that, like *Piers Plowman*, 'had lives' and were 'likely to be affected by changing contemporary issues' (269). From the classicist Paul Maas he begins to gather tools: *discriminatio* ('exercise of editorial judgment

8. On Dilworth as a famous CBC broadcaster, professor and literary executor of Emily Carr's writings, see www.thecanadianencyclopedia.ca/en/article/ira-dilworth-emc.

9. Northrup Frye, *Fools of Time: Studies in Shakespearean Tragedy* (Toronto: University of Toronto Press, 1967).

between rival readings'), and the virtually god-like and sometimes controversial *divinatio* ('scrutiny of readings unchallenged by variants but in some way . . . uncharacteristic of the grammar of the poet's style'). Together with Griesbach's belief that the 'harder reading' (*durior lectio*) is likeliest to be the original, Kane armed himself to revolutionize Middle English editing (270). Langland's standing as a great poet would be rescued, in Kane's view, from the incompetence of scribes, and his poem sifted as one of the *lebende Texte*. Though there is defensiveness, this magisterial and succinct account in the memoirs catapults *Piers Plowman* into place among the textual monuments of literary and sacred history, and its editor into the company of the great editorial theorists he admired: Housman, Lachmann, Maas, Kantorowiczz, Griesbach, and more. The reader is newly aware that Middle English scholars owe Kane so much: Middle English, which he poignantly calls 'the degraded language of a conquered people' (234), could now play with the big boys.

The story is the more remarkable for its unlikelihood: Kane had arrived at the University of London wanting to study Milton's *Paradise Lost* in relation to the Renaissance epic. Those who know Barack Obama's *Dreams of My Father* might notice a parallel here: a missing father, and a single object passed on from the father becoming central to the son's life: in Obama's case, a basketball, in this case, Kane's father's copy of *Paradise Lost*.[10] *Paradise Lost* (certainly a less usual choice for even a 'Catholic agnostic') comes up repeatedly in the memoirs, often in relation to his father's copy, whether he is reading it in bed prior to finals (48) or in relation to his lion-like mentor, A. S. P. Woodhouse, where we see Kane reading galley proofs of his influential *Milton, Puritanism and Liberty* in a graduate seminar there. Under Woodhouse Kane would discover the scholarly world of the Renaissance, and the 'pervasiveness of theological issues in English culture' (53) — perhaps a way to explore buried Protestant roots and satisfy his deep Classical underpinnings, but, more unpredictably, also this: 'His [Woodhouse's] course came alive for me two years later when I read *Piers Plowman* for the first time.' So for Kane, then, *Langland* helped him appreciate Milton anew (which can only mean that Kane saw *Piers* as an epic). He went to the University of London, on Woodhouse's advice, to study *Paradise Lost* as an epic, only to arrive and find that he was not free to choose his thesis topic: rather, it was assigned by Chambers, whose own interest in epic was purely medieval and Germanic, and who was — apparently — looking for free doctoral student labour to get *Piers Plowman* edited. At some level *Piers* was to become Kane's *Paradise Lost* (the latter never regained), and, I would suggest, it was both the salvational epic features of Langland, and his reformist spirit, that sustained George's interest throughout. In Langland's poem he saw

---

10. Barack Obama, *Dreams of My Father: A Story of Race and Inheritance* (New York: Three Rivers Press, 2004), pp. 70–71.

a great epic flawed by textual confusion and scribal meddling, and determined to set it straight. But not without a personal price: the last sentence he wrote before launching into his description of the war years is: 'Over half a century I have from time to time bitterly regretted the luck that put the larger part of the burden of *Piers Plowman* editing on me, denying me studies that I loved and would have revelled in. But I have never been moved to hold this against Chambers: to have known him enriched my life.' (79) Assigned to edit the last three passus of *Piers* B, a thesis interrupted by war, p.o.w. experience, and of which he writes that he was never proud, the memoirs record the loneliness, to borrow a phrase, of the long-distance runner. Kane realizes that Chambers himself had never edited texts that survive in multiple manuscripts, that apart from his more senior fellow student, A. G. Mitchell, there was really no one to advise him. Moreover, he would be expected to date and analyze hands in scripts, he disarmingly tells us, he could barely read, and in the unstable dialects of Middle English, which he had barely studied, adrift in a world without, as yet, professional palaeographers of vernacular texts: 'If aids existed to do that — this was well before the rise of Ian Doyle and Malcolm Parkes to authority, I did not, with the exception of Richard Hunt, find them, and I could not in conscience plague him unduly. Neil Ker professed ignorance of vernacular usage, as did Francis Wormald' (252).[11] While scholars today may justly debate the concept of 'vernacular palaeographies', Latin palaeography does not face quite the same issues (nor vice versa). In his inimitable habit of blaming inanimate objects for difficulties he encounters (like 'computers' mentioned above) he blames the bad lighting in Duke Humphrey's Library (74) for his struggles with MS Corpus Christi College, Oxford 201. But he is also remarkably honest about the flaws in his A text draft manuscript: it was Kenneth Sisam (255), the great Oxford philologist, who, as reader for the Kane's Athlone press edition would insist on the suppression of his lengthy attempts to describe and trace provenance for the *Piers* manuscripts, thus explaining the skeletal descriptions in the otherwise weighty volume.

For Langlandians, Kane's memoirs might even also prompt a reevaluation of something so fundamental as the base text of the *Piers* B text. Donaldson convinced him to switch the base text from Laud 581 to the now famous Trinity manuscript, and Kane, in awe of Donaldson's Middle English philology, agreed, but rather disarmingly also notes that Donaldson had no experience with working with manuscripts. Kane's philological training, by contrast, was all Latin — and good enough, we might note, to allow him to construct the evolution of Old French from 'the Vulgar Latin' backwards at Northwestern. Modern Langlandians, knowing more about the Trinity manuscript's London English and

---

11. He does indeed mention Wormald positively earlier on (p. 74) as being helpful when he was trying to read Add. 35287; apparently it is abbreviations that Wormald was helping him with.

its suggested connections with the scribe of the Hengwrt and Ellesmere manuscripts of the *Canterbury Tales*, would hesitate to follow Donaldson's project of making Langland sound like Chaucer (indeed, one recent edition of the B-text has restored the primacy of Kane's Laud 581 as a more likely vehicle of Langland's text and dialect).[12] But on Kane's most profound decisions and methods, he characteristically pulls no punches: '"Experts" in the theory of textual criticisms with no experience of large-scale collation have pooh-poohed what they call the "profiling" of scribes, which I take to mean identification of patterns of individual idiosyncrasies of unconscious or subconsciously induced and deliberate substitution. They have obviously not experienced identifying a change of scribe in the exemplar of their immediate copyist' (249).[13] But Langlandians will find his comments on the controversial Z text most riveting of all: he apologizes for not setting out his reasons for excluding it from the collations, but says 'To me it looked more like an attempt to restore a defective unbound copy of A from memory by a scribe who had copied A and copied or read B and C' (251). Fascinating here is the reasoning behind the now older theories of the interference of memory, which Kane relies upon so heavily (and usually without explanation) in his detailed explanations of emendations in the Kane-Donaldson B text. While all this needs some revisiting today in light of newer ideas about how memory does and does not function in manuscript culture, Kane's assessment of Z remains brilliant and incontrovertible: 'the restorer's response to the poems was enthusiastic rather than sensitive', often 'grammatically incoherent' (251–52). Right on the mark.

Kane did come to love his assigned text and his adoptive field. With his dry sense of humour he explains: 'I was 38 years old and very much aware of the time lost in the army. So I decided to finish editing the B text' [!] (248). But the job would prove enormous. Though assigned B, when it became 'plain . . . I would have to help Grattan edit the A poem. . . . [or] give up' (250), he does not hesitate. Still he concludes, 'in candour I must, I suppose, have become intellectually engaged in this poem, which stood out monumentally among other Middle English alliterative writing' (250).

The fact that Langland and Chaucer are now, in the words of Kane's famous article title, an 'Obligatory Conjunction', is owing to the courage, tenacity, and literary brilliance of a small boy from a slightly defensive German Catholic town on the prairies, a tenacity honed not only in the halls of academia, but in the

---

12. Elizabeth Robertson and Stephen H. A. Shepherd, eds, *Piers Plowman* (New York; London: W. W. Norton, 2005). I would like to thank Ralph Hanna for his advice on this.

13. For the most recent discussion of this still crucial point, see John Burrow and Thorlac Turville-Petre's Introduction to the *Electronic Edition to the B-Version Archetype of Piers Plowman* (Bx): <http://piers.iath.virginia.edu/exist/piers/restricted/crit/front/B/Bx/Front>.

challenging natural landscapes of Canada, and in p.o.w. camps across Europe.[14]
These memoirs are the story of this amazing trajectory.

Kathryn Kerby-Fulton
University of Notre Dame

---

14. George Kane, 'Langland and Chaucer: an Obligatory Conjunction', in *New Perspectives in Chaucer Criticism*, ed. Donald L. Rose (Norman, OK: Pilgrim, 1981), 5–19; also in *Chaucer and Langland: Historical and Textual Approaches* (London: Athlone, 1989), 123–33.

1
ORIGINS AND EARLY EDUCATION

My surname derives from the Irish tribal name Ui'Cathain or O'Cahan, nowadays also spelled Keane or Kane. The clan became prominent in Ulster in the thirteenth century after the killing of the Duke of Clarence, Edward I's viceroy in Ireland, by a fellow Anglo-Norman in a feud. Its chiefs claimed ascendancy in Ulster after the O'Neill. Their lands were in County Derry, in the lovely region of Limavady. But after 1601 because of the desirability of that territory it was gradually taken from them by various contrivances within a few years and those who held to Catholicism became in effect landless peasantry. Many exiled themselves in France; the Royal Irish Regiment was a notable element in Louis XIV's army, but on the other side a Sir Richard Kane was a Lieutenant-General in that of George II.

As for my more immediate descent, my great-great-grandfather Peter Kane was a plain man. He was certainly from Ulster; nowhere else on the island would a Catholic have a wife named Anny Campbell as he did, but this was before the foundation of the Orange Order and Presbyterian evangelism had implanted bigotry there. The first record of his name is in the Quebec Register of Births for April 1823 where he is cited as the father of Elizabeth Kane, 'née sur mer'. By this time he already had two sons aged twelve and five and a daughter of eight years. He appears to have brought his wife and family to Canada on the recommendation of his brother-in-law William Quinn, married to Anny's sister Bridget, who had already obtained a grant of land. Peter was not as quick off the mark; it was not until 1835, when he was granted 90 *arpents*, 70 acres in the Parish of Ste Catherine de Fossambault, that he considered himself established. It was poor soil north of the St Laurence, hilly and sandy but working it was preferable to being a labourer. In 1843 he moved with his family to better land in a *seigneurie* south of the St Laurence river on rich virgin land that had been bought by a retired officer of the 60th Regiment of Foot who was settling it with Irish and Scots tenants. The year before he died in 1847, only 55 years old, Peter made this land over to his second son, Edward who was born in about 1819 in Ireland and had in 1846 married Mary Ann Purtell, daughter of another of their English *seigneur*'s settlers. Their third son, my grandfather Michael Kane, was born in 1855. He evidently did not come into the land; in 1880 he married Flore-Philomène Hébert in Laconia, New Hampshire.

She was a sixth-generation Canadian, descended from Etienne Hébert, who was born in France in 1629, one of the original settlers of *Acadie*, Acadia, later renamed Nova Scotia. I do not have a record of his birthplace, but Marie Gaudet, whom he married in 1650, was from Martaize a few miles south of Loudon in the Department of Indre and Loire. They and their children were among the lucky Acadiens who escaped the transportation and dispersal in 1775 when the Crown and the Royal Navy decided that they needed their land and replaced them with Scottish settlers.

The second of their children who survived to adulthood, Michael George Kane, was my father. He was born in the parish of Ste Brigitte des Saults in the county Nicolet of the province of Quebec in 1886. I do not have a record of when my grandfather returned to Canada or came to own the land of the original grant which his uncle, Edward Kane had made over to his own son. It may have passed to him as next in the male line on that son's death, or he may have bought it outright; the system of seigniurial ownership having been abolished in 1854.

My grandfather, Michael George Kane, died in 1930 when I was a schoolboy. My mother was not drawn to him, and one of my female Kane cousins has written to me of him as a domineering husband and father. But to my male cousins, the grandsons who knew him, he is a kind of hero figure, and in Ste Brigitte to this day he is notable as having been mayor from 1895 to 1912, the choice (I read in a local history) of both 'les Canadiens français et les Irlandais', that is the descendants of a dozen or so other Irish settlers of about the same vintage. Somewhere between the extremes is the truth, I suppose. Certainly the progeny of that marriage have demonstrated that the gene mix, at any rate, was good. The ones I have news of are mainly American, some with houses in both Vermont and Florida, their grandchildren at Harvard or M.I.T or the University of California. French Canada in the twenties and thirties of the twentieth century was a poor country, and male emigration during the Depression to jobs in the Maine lumber camps is understandable.

As for my grandmother Kane, whom I met on my way to England in 1938, she was a charmer, even at 79. I have a formal photograph of her taken in her sixties; after bearing many children, and enduring, allegedly, an overbearing husband, she gives in her picture a strong impression of a happy personality.

My father was the first of Peter Kane's descendants not to become a farmer. Apparently his health was not robust enough: I remember being told by my maternal grandmother that his heart had been damaged by rheumatic fever. Like many young Canadians of his time he went west to make his fortune, apparently by land speculation as the railways had opened up the country for settlement. To that end, it appears, he learned Morse telegraphy, and then got a job as a station master for the Canadian National Railway Company, which was promoting land development as it extended its network in central Canada: he could travel free.

Michael George Kane (father).

I don't know where he met my mother, who was, at the time of their marriage an early 'career woman' on the staff of the Provincial Library at Regina, the capital of Saskatchewan. They were married at Muenster in Saskatchewan, where her family lived, on 15th September 1915. He took her east to meet his people and west and north to Hudson's Bay Junction in the middle of nowhere, the point where the C.N.R. would eventually strike a branch line across northern Manitoba to Port Churchill on Hudson Bay.[1] There he suddenly died of heart failure on 28th December 1915. That was the end of their adventure. He should probably not have married, but I am the last person in a position to find fault with him for that.

It is my great regret that when, eventually I met his mother in 1938, I did not learn more about him, but we only had two days and there was much to talk about. To his Kane nephews and nieces he is only a legend. I have a few photographs of him enlarged from snapshots, and his copy of *Paradise Lost*, apparently a school prize, elegantly bound in the limp black leather of those times.

He appears to have had great personal charm. My maternal grandmother, who thought the world of him, would speak to me as a child of how generally he was liked, and of his fine singing voice: this has missed me but has reappeared in all my grandchildren. How deeply losing him affected my mother, who found him dead at his desk, I gauge from the circumstance that it was only 1962, nearly fifty years after his death, that she spoke freely and easily to me about him. She was a beautiful woman and must as a widow have had many offers, but it was five years before she married again, and then only on an undertaking by my step-father-to-be to treat me as his own child; this she told me in 1962. He honoured the undertaking handsomely, though I must have tried him sorely at times, for I was a pestilential child until I went to 'big school'. He paid for my education there and at university when money was scarce, for which I am in his debt. As I grew to adulthood we became good friends, to the extent that his own three sons, my half-brothers, were given to saying that he favoured me.

My maternal grandfather, Joseph Kopp, was born in Hordern in the German-speaking canton Thurgau of Switzerland, on 1st March 1847, the elder son in a family of small landholders. He emigrated to America in 1872, followed next year by his younger brother John and in 1875 by his widowed father and two of his three sisters. The reason he gave me for the move is confirmed by family records, which abound. By Swiss customary law, land did not pass from generation to generation by primogeniture, but was divided between sons after provision of dowries for daughters. My Swiss great-great-grandfather (1789–1839) had eight surviving children, three of them sons; my great-grandfather five, two of them sons. By my grandfather's time, he told me, the family would have been reduced to peasantry. This was, apparently, a common situation at the time and the Swiss government

---

1. George and Clara Kane stood as godparents while in Sainte-Brigitte-des-Saults (southwestern Quebec) for a nephew, Joseph Marcel Bernard Kane.

The Kopp family, Switzerland, early 1870s. Back: Joseph Kopp Jr (grandfather), emigrated to America in 1872, and his brother John, who followed him in 1873. Middle: Joseph Kopp Sr (great-grandfather). Front: Mary Flora Hagen and Elizabeth Kountz, two daughters who accompanied Joseph Kopp Sr to America in 1875.

encouraged emigration to the United States, while taking the precaution of establishing resettlement centres at various points across the mid-west. Here the death of my great-grandmother is likely to have set off the move, and it looks as if the elder son, my grandfather, was sent over as a scout, so to speak, and that his report was favourable.

One of my many regrets is that I have never had the time to visit their part of Switzerland. My cousin Evelyn, with whom I grew up, reports that the records of that region for centuries back are intact. Had I spent time there I might now be able to sketch the outlines, at least, of the world he used to tell me about as a small boy. There was the family vineyard where he learned, he cautioned me, the consequence of eating too many grapes; what kind of wine did it produce? And what kind of farming did they practice? This is one of the regions of Switzerland suited to a mixed, virtually self-sustaining agriculture. Does his growing to manhood there explain why, after thirty-five years at another trade, he could return to farming and end up with a farm that was a model of management? The Swiss property would have grown its own wheat and rye to take to mill and market, made its own cheese when milk was abundant, beer when the hops were ready, pressed and fermented the grape, slaughtered at Martinmas. The original property cannot have been paltry: in the troubled years before 1870 and the Franco-Prussian war he was a cavalry trooper in the Swiss militia, providing his own charger and saddlery. The high quality of Swiss education which made its emigrants welcome was evident in his command of High German; it had unfortunately not extended to English, which he later learned to speak correctly, but all his life with an accent. Of course he had the local dialect, in which he readily instructed me upon request, and he would entertain me as a child with songs, some of which must from their content have gone back to the days of the fifteenth- and sixteenth-century mercenaries.

To go by what we know of his movements after his arrival in America, and by what I remember as his very wide knowledge of the Middle West, he was a restless man. So, it seems was his younger brother John, who joined him in 1873. They appear together in Bloomingon, Illinois, where the Swiss government had located one of its resettlement centres. Here they seem to have turned to advantage one of the various skills of their farming background by setting up as butchers in a 'meat market'. They are found, presently, in the same occupation in Iowa, first in Storm Lake and then in Cherokee. There is a tradition in the John Kopp family that in 1874 they prospected for gold (evidently to no great effect) in the Black Hills of the Dakotas.

The two brothers appear, in 1877, contracted as hunters to provide meat for a wagon train setting out from Sioux City, Iowa for mushrooming Montana mining camps. The distance as the crow flies is about 700 miles; by the modern highway it is over 900, the latter part through foothills and mountain country. Having to go by ways passable for wagons, the train is likely to have covered a thousand miles. My grandfather told me that he and his brother had visited the battlefield of Custer's defeat in 1876. There was some family scepticism about this, but in the eighties I learned that in the Bozeman pioneer museum there was a firearm from the Big Horn labelled a gift from John Kopp. I once asked my grandfather what was his most dangerous experience from those days: the answer was 'riding too fast into a ranch yard and nearly being beheaded by a clothesline'. What was the farthest he had ever ridden in a day? He was not out for records; forty miles was not unusual. What about the cowboys? (I was deep into pulp westerns at the time); 'there was one, once, who used to come into Bozeman on Friday night. We took his gun away from him and let him have it back on Monday morning.'

On arrival in Bozeman the two brothers got jobs in the Bozeman Meat Market, a log cabin notwithstanding its fine name. Within the year 1878 their father and two of their sisters joined them in Bozeman. In 1879 the brothers, probably with paternal support, bought out their employer and proceeded to develop a wholesale and retail meat supply business which grew and prospered until, no longer in their hands, it succumbed to the Great Depression. They owned this jointly until 1883 when my great-uncle John detached himself (the financial arrangements are not recorded) and, taking advantage of the newly-completed Northern Pacific Railroad, moved with a recently acquired family to Astoria in North Oregon. Here he turned another of his skills to advantage by establishing one of the first breweries on the north-west coast.

My grandfather's movements during the three following years are not recorded and the local newspaper does not mention him during this interval. Whoever was managing it, the Kopp Brothers' City Meat Market prospered even while one of them was brightening the life of the people of Astoria and the other, as it appears, was in Kansas.

Our next record is that he was married there, in Junction City, on 21st November 1886. When and how he met my grandmother Maria Jung is not recorded, and is regrettably not the sort of question a child thinks of asking his grandparents. He was thirty-nine years old, she nineteen-and-a-half. Her father had been a relatively junior officer in the service of the Elector of Hanover before 1871 — I seem to recall the term *Rittmeister* — with a small talent in music and versifying, who did not enjoy living in the Prussian *imperium*, and after the death of his wife in 1882 emigrated to America with four young daughters. This was not as foolhardy an action as might seem; their destination was Jefferson City, Missouri where there was one of the principal German resettlement centres.

Maria Jung married with her father's approval, and with one of her sisters as a bridesmaid and witness. Her father, she once told me, had said of her choice, 'Derjenige verlässt dich nicht', 'That man will not desert you'. I lived in their household throughout the year until I was six, and after that, throughout the school year until 1934, and I cannot recall either of them speaking disagreeably to the other, a rare affinity indeed by modern standards. There was unhappiness in their lives. They took poor advice about the education of their only son which did not do justice to his intelligence and aptitudes; they lost three beloved daughters to illness; and in their old age they were by no means as comfortable financially as they should have been because my grandfather could not bring himself to enforce payment of sizeable loans made out of kindness during the bad times of the early thirties.

My grandmother's home still stands in Goslar, a lovely old town in the Harz mountains southeast of Hanover. This was staunch Lutheran country: my grandfather's Catholicism went back to the Irish missionaries of eighth-century Sankt Gallen. She adopted his religion with Lutheran rigour, some of which marked my childhood, during which I spent a number of years in the belief that I was irretrievably damned for having made, at some time, a 'bad confession'. As if in compensation she had by heart a great many eighteenth- and nineteenth-century *Lieder*,

Joseph Kopp (grandfather).

Grandma Kopp and sister.

which she sang to me, first as lullabies and later for my pleasure. She too had a beautiful voice. When my grandparents were alone with me they spoke High German. In consequence I grew up bilingual, and constitute a living demonstration that the weak declension of the adjective can be learned by ear. When, later, I studied German at school, it seemed ridiculous to have to learn the rules, or indeed, the word-order. When I learned to write German she made sure I could also manage the pre-1918 script. This much later made reading Elizabethan hands easier, but in 1943 it got a fellow prisoner of war into deep trouble because I had signed his forged travel permit to such good effect that on his recapture after our escape the *Sicherheitspolizei* who interrogated him would not believe that it was a fake, and were determined to get the turned official whose signature it bore. My grandmother kept in touch with her sisters by correspondence in the old hand, writing on both sides and across as in the days before cheap postage; no doubt the letters survive in some cousin's attic. In 1903–1904 my grandfather sent her, with her eldest and youngest daughter, on an extended visit to Switzerland, where she made the acquaintance of his kinsfolk, and to Germany, to visit her own. Notwithstanding her severe religiosity she was a woman of delicacy and style. I recall her from the mid-twenties, when she had borne nine children, as still very beautiful. She played a large part of the formation of my character, to the extent that when as, not infrequently, I misbehaved, my worst punishment was her disapproval.

But back to her early life with my grandfather: they were still in Junction City in February 1889, but by November of that year had moved to Bozeman. The Kopp

Meat Market had evidently prospered in the absence of its two owners. In 1890 my grandfather bought three parcels of land in and around Bozeman. In 1891 he bought what in effect became a toy farm in an unspoiled nearby valley, to which my grandmother resorted in the summer. Winters they lived in a substantial house, still standing in 1982 I read, which he built in Bozeman in 1891. My mother was born in Bozeman in 1890, and my Aunt Helen, who taught me to read, in 1898.

But my grandfather was not settled. In 1902 he was looking at land across the border in Alberta and then in Saskatchewan, where in 1903 he bought land. There is no record of his reason for wanting to move, except one which he is said to have given to a daughter, that the doctor had ordered a change of climate; risible when one considers the Saskatchewan winters, but clearly indicating he did not want to discuss the matter.

He was born restless, I judge, for I know how cruelly bored he was in his later years when arthritis denied him movement. Indeed he did not decide to take American citizenship until 1894, long after satisfying the residence requirement. Even after he moved to Canada in his seventies his eyes were set afar; he took up options on land in the Peace River district of the Northern Territories offered by the federal government. I recall him 'letting them go for taxes' in the Depression. Some of the pressure to move was cultural; again I write from accumulated recollections over more than a decade listening to my grandparents' conversation. He did not find the often drunken and violent frontier society of Montana's mining country congenial. Then, simply his accent differentiated him from a social mix with a large element of misfits from the north-eastern states, embittered Confederate Army veterans, and nondescript rowdy miners, of which the values, to the extent that it shared any, were WASP. The accent and to some extent his religion exposed him to condescension by people who, except for the small professional class, had less education than himself — and chewed tobacco. Moreover the trade which he and his brother had adopted on coming to America, however profitable, was not stylish. Above all there was the matter of schooling for his children, the two eldest eleven and ten in 1900.

Just after the turn of the century settlement in central western Canada was being promoted by the Canadian National Railway, in territory north of the transcontinental line completed by the privately owned Canadian Pacific Railway in 1885; one of the reasons was to hasten the subsumption of present-day Saskatchewan and Alberta into the Dominion. The promotion evidently extended to the United States, touching the Benedictine Abbey of St John in Collegeville, Minnesota, today a respected centre of medieval studies, and awoke the order's historical urge to spiritual colonization. It appears that in 1902 my grandfather, on a reconnaissance by train to Saskatchewan, made the acquaintance of monks from St John's Abbey on their way to choose a site for a priory that would minister to the spiritual needs of an anticipated influx of Catholic settlers, German-born or

Aunt Helen.

first generation American, mainly from Minnesota, to central northern Saskatch-ewan. The outcome of this encounter was that in 1903 after the priory site was chosen my grandfather bought land in its shadow-to-be. In due course a rough and ready structure became the Priory (later the Abbey), one of the monks of the encounter its prior, and my grandfather, over the years one of its foremost patrons.

Meanwhile he had to sell the notion of resettling in Canada to his wife. She loved the Montana mountains and her summer home in the unspoiled valley of Sourdough Creek. In the spring of 1903 he bought her to Saskatchewan to look at the land he had bought. They must have travelled overland from Rosthern. The prairie, albeit gently rolling here, was smooth, eighty miles as the crow flies to the point on the railway's surveyed but as yet unbuilt permanent way where the priory and his land were located. My grandfather fancied good horses; they would have driven a pair in a 'democrat', a buggy with three seats, a hood for the passen-gers, and an open box at the rear where the tent, supplies and personal kit would be carried.

This must have been in mid-spring, when the Saskatchewan plainland shows at its glorious best. This I heard her admire many times in later years. But on that first occasion she was put off by the type of dwelling in which the earliest set-tlers before the railway came spent four months of the spring and summer, the sod house. In those days to promote settlement the Canadian federal government would grant 160 acres of crown land to any adult applicant on the condition that he dwelt on it and cultivated it for four months of the calendar year; after fulfill-ing this condition for a specified number of years (I forget how many) he acquired absolute ownership in the law. Where the right timber was available he would build a log cabin, but the trees in the region of my grandfather's land were mostly not suitable for that purpose. The settlers before the advent of the railway lived in what was virtually a pit roofed with sods of the densely rooted multi-millennial local turf. This kind of housing my grandmother would not accept; she would only move to a brick house. She loved her husband dearly; I cannot judge whether she thought this would put an end to the notion of moving. It was she who told me about it, not less than twenty-five years after the event. He answered, simply, 'You shall have a brick house'.

That summer he sent her with their eldest daughter, my mother, and their youngest, to Europe in style (again my grandmother's report) to make his fam-ily known to his Swiss kin, and for her to renew close contact with her own in Germany. To accommodate himself, the other children and the family household effects meanwhile he bought a house in Rosthern, a settlement at Nailhead by delicious irony founded by a strict Protestant sect called Mennonites from east Friesland. This was a sober and prosperous community with good schools. Sur-prisingly the town also had an office of the Catholic Settlement Society.

The family severance from Montana was now in effect both definite and complete. As to the family business, there is no record of the arrangements between my grandfather and his brother John, but they appear to have been amiable; the brothers were on many indications very close. But they were final. My grandfather was a farmer again.

The bricks for his wife's Canadian house came from Winnipeg in Manitoba or farther east to Rosthern by rail. Thence they were hauled by horse and wagon along a prairie trail the eighty miles to the building site; my grandfather had, along with the family's household effects, brought six horses, four of them heavy draught animals for this purpose. It was built in the south-east quarter of a 'section' of land, 640 acres, about 1000 yards north of the projected railway line and about two miles west of the site where, at length in 1920, the Abbey would be built. The family moved in 1905. That year the railway was laid.

The house stood on a slight eminence; to the west the land fell away to the barn, traditionally red, stables and byre below, a vast loft above to which the cured hay was hoisted from the wagons in great nets by pulley. To the east in a little natural dale my grandfather planted a grove of silver birches and poplars which, by the time I came on the scene, had grown enough to take hammock and a swing. Between the house and this grove were gardens for the kitchen and my grandmother's flowers; she had green fingers. Childhood memories of size are not reliable but a picture shows the house, of which I recall the ground floor plan, to have been large. Certainly the kitchen was, and I recall many windows in the dining room and the sitting room ('parlour'), where I was required to behave sedately. Of the first floor I remember only the room which I shared with my mother when she was at home, but there must have been at least four, probably five bedrooms. The house still stands; as late as 1982 it was occupied by the son of the man who bought it from my grandfather.

He was much respected in this new community, soon to be called St Peter's Colony, for his integrity and consequent unsought-for authority, a man who did not raise his voice in anger or debate, with no interest in prestige or power. A local history has it that he was very generous of help for newly arrived settlers, and lent money without interest. But from my long observation if one had put it to him that his was a personality of exceptional stature he would have been certainly surprised and probably amused. Living in his household I saw how, invariably, he received deference and courtesy not accorded to all in that community by men who were strong and resourceful and had little time for humbug.

We got on very well. While backing her up on all occasions when I had got into a scrape, he left disciplinary procedures to my grandmother. Only once I was the occasion of him losing his temper. Much too early, at the age of ten, I had been allowed by my mother to acquire a single-shot ·22 calibre rifle, and in due course, behaving foolishly with it, I shot myself in the foot. Neither of my grandparents reproached me; they knew my mother was wrong to sanction my having the firearm. My grandmother was full of immediate sympathy and care; he for his part without a word took the rifle out of doors to the nearest stout post and, holding it by its muzzle, with a single blow bent its barrel into uselessness. But back to the early days: in 1905 when Saskatchewan was incorporated into the Dominion as a province, he was the delegate sent from his community to meet the Premier, who was ceremonially visiting the new province.

My grandparents came to Canada with six surviving children, the eldest a son, then my mother, and four younger daughters. They sent their son to the boys' school of St John's Abbey in Collegeville; I have the impression that it failed to engage him scholastically: he came back wanting to be a professional baseball player. But his parents would have none of that, and he was never a happy person. They sent my mother to Mount Angel Academy, a Catholic girls' boarding school in Oregon which she loved. I can vouch for the excellence of the result, but one feature of it may not have pleased my grandmother, for my mother became an early 'career woman', not sensationally but to the extent that she was qualified as a trained librarian and in 1911 at the age of twenty-one was valued on the staff of the Provincial Library in the capital, Regina. In any event the younger daughters were not sent to Mount Angel. But the three aunts I knew, Agnes, Helen and Mary, were all very well read and until they married in constant demand as teachers in the local schools of the diocese. Where they went to secondary school I do not know.

My grandparents lost one of their five daughters to influenza in 1914. My mother married in 1915, her brother and her sister Agnes in 1916. Within those two years my grandparents found themselves in the big house with only two of the six children they had brought to Canada. Not that the house was quiet. The two girls, Helen now 18 and Mary a year younger, had many friends of their own age, and there was a family tradition of hospitality. Agnes and her husband lived only four miles away, and of course after my father died my mother came home. My grandmother, who already in Montana had brought up an orphaned nephew of her husband, took it for granted that I would be her next project, and appears, leaving natural affection aside, to have perceived that my mother would be less unhappy if she went back to work. So she did, in due course, but not to Regina which was too far for her to see her child often without difficulty; she moved into teaching nearer the family home. Her son never lacked for love, but the special occasions were her visits.

Some of my memories of living in the big house are particularly clear and vivid. One is being in trouble with grandmother, along with a cousin a year younger, Agnes's first son, for propelling ourselves at considerable speed around the spacious kitchen mounted on chamber pots. Another — I cannot have been more than two — is being taken out in an aunt's arms to see a newly acquired team of gigantic

Agnes and Margaret Kopp.

George Kane as child with mother.

shire horses, the brass on their harness dazzling, and of yelling my head off when I was put up on the back of the nearside one; another time being taken out on a beautiful late winter day to see the bloody spoil of a coyote hunt: they would be deadly enemies at calving time. To me that day the dead beasts seemed to be all blood and teeth. A more genial recollection is of the hammock in the birch grove, and being cosseted by my young aunts' friends, who treated me like a talking doll. I remembered how lovely they smelled as they petted and pampered me.

By the time I was experiencing those remembered moments my grandfather had passed seventy. He could have continued to run the farm without lifting a hand himself; the men who worked his land were devoted to him, and he was lively enough in mind and spirit. Indeed it was about this time that he took up the Peace River land options. But he had not realized when he built the big house how cruel winter could be in that part of Saskatchewan, or known that it was in for a phase of climatically extreme weather in the twenties and early thirties. The big house was proving hard to heat effectively during the worst months; its ceilings were too high. So he and his wife decided to sell the farm and retire.

A mile and a quarter east of the big house, and about a mile west of the eventually determined site of the monastery the C.N.R. had established a railway station. This attracted a post office cum grocery shop, a 'general store', a bank, a smithy, a timber yard, a livery stable, a hotel with a bar and petrol pump and a sweet shop that sold ice cream. This was appropriately named 'Muenster', monastery in German, after the Abbey less than a mile to the south. The population cannot have been more than five hundred, if that. The church and a junior parish school were about a mile north of the railway. After some havering about whether to build near the church, my grandfather bought a house which he enlarged and converted for his use on land about a quarter of a mile from the village that he planned to leave to the Abbey. Here I lived as a member of the household throughout the year until 1926, and thereafter during the school years until 1934. In 1921, when the cornerstone of the Abbey was to be ceremonially laid and ritually consecrated I was present. It was a miserable day in spring, and when I was told 'One day you will be going to school here', I could muster little enthusiasm in response.

But aside from its cause, my father's death, all this was great good fortune. I cannot pretend that I had a happy childhood. I was often too lonely for company of my own age. I probably had too much 'poor Georgie, poor fatherless child' in my upbringing. I was cheeky and interrupted adults. I often got into trouble. But I never lacked for loving care. For all my grandmother's strictness she lavished attention on me. And I probably had, by sheer good luck, as fine an education as was available in North America at that time.

It was impossible to live in my grandparents' house and escape education. By the time I was four my role as a talking doll for my young aunts was ended, and I became an 'if it moves teach it' object. Both were easy to love, sweet-natured and good-looking, as all the women in my family have been to this day. Both were certified teachers, and much in demand, but seem to have taken it in turns to be away from home, and the outlying schools of the Colony where they taught seem to have had some arrangement by which no parish would monopolize either. When away they would live with a substantial family responsible to my grandparents for their wellbeing. The effect of this was that there was almost always one of them at home.

I was read to from the earliest age. My German they left to their parents; indeed I think I was soon more fluent in that language than either aunt, though they understood it well enough. Already then, I shamelessly boast, I had an ear for words and speech. My aunts, for their own amusement, would tease me into repeating polysyllables: they admitted defeat when my grandfather taught me *Konstantinopolischerpfeiffenmachergeselle*, which for laughter they never managed to finish. By the end of my third year I had mastered the 'cat is on the mat' system; I moved on to learning words by contextual inference, which they called guessing, but encouraged. This was perforce: my Christmas present from Aunt Helen was *The Swiss Family Robinson*: big, I thought, and thick, envisaging many sessions of being read to. But I was mistaken. Aunt Helen and I settled down together in the big armchair and with some authority she said, 'Now, Georgie, I shall teach you to read.' That turned out to be fine, but very soon in the new year there was a teacher crisis in some parish of the Colony and Aunt Helen was called in to the rescue. The day after she left I settled down in the armchair with the book she had given me, resolved not to be deprived of its exciting extensions of experience: virtually every detail was novel. I found that, occasionally consulting a grandparent, I could follow the story. But at the outset there was one recurrent difficulty. Aunt Helen had taught me the phonetic value of many letter combinations, and to read words rather than puzzle them out, but we had not touched on one tiny detail, the phonetic values of initial *th*. There had been so much to take in that I had never given attention to it. In mastering that difficulty I taught myself to read.

That spring Aunt Mary taught me to write, which was easy to learn but hard to do neatly and prettily. As for arithmetic, I hated it. I could count and add and multiply well enough for my childish purposes, but the numbers made little sense to me. Aunt Mary, who was trying to teach me this mystery, was not as patient as her sister, and we never established a real rapport as teacher and pupil. I am doubtless unfair to her: I was fifteen before I encountered a good mathematics teacher, who, whether in so many words or not (I forget), showed me that algebra was a kind of language, which made it more interesting to me. Euclidian geometry was easy enough but the aridity of the theorems made them hard to remember. Algebraic geometry, which gave physical shape to abstractions, I actually enjoyed, but that was after what seemed many tedious years. More immediately in 1921 the situation became more acute when I was told that in the autumn I would be going to school where I would have to sit still and do as I was bid without asking why, as I saw it, without discussion.

I was five years and two months old that September. The parish school, at least a mile and a half from the grandparents' house, was staffed by Benedictine, that is Ursuline, nuns. It taught a 'baby class' and eight grades in preparation for a provincial Department of Education examination. Pupils who passed this could leave school or go on to high school; for those who did not take it or pass the leaving age was fourteen. There were two rooms; one moved after grade four, and took the government examination at the end of the eighth year.

For various reasons I did not enjoy most of my time there. In several ways I was a misfit. I was the only pupil who did not have a German name during my first four years at school. Even in 'baby class' I could read as well as most of the pupils in grade four. I spent a month there, and they tried to teach me how to

George with Aunt Mary, *c.* 1919.

hem a handkerchief, which I found humiliating and refused to learn, and a month in grade one where the other children were learning the alphabet. At Christmas there was a nativity play in German, and I was made to speak the Prologue: I was paralyzed and struck dumb by stage fright. And in grade two I came up against my bogey, arithmetic. One of the nuns in charge of the room, a childhood friend of my Aunt Helen, was very kind and tried to help this odd fish. Because I could speak German they tried to teach me German grammar: I could see no need for and thus no sense in this. To please my grandmother I did learn the angular *deutsche Schrift*. In grade three or four there were twins, Augusta and Henrietta, one very bright, both very kind, who spread their wings over me, which helped.

But in 1925 when I moved to the 'big room' and grade five, there were some very large (or so they seemed) boys of twelve or thirteen, serving their time till they could leave school. It amused them to tease me until I lost my temper, where-upon I was in trouble with Sister Clementine, a kind of sergeant-major nun in charge of the room. She kept the big boys in order in class if not in recess, but I irritated her because she could not teach me arithmetic, as well as because I had read more and more widely than herself. Grades five and six were not good years and one way or another I was often in trouble.

My escape was reading. At this time I began to work my way through the books in my grandparents' house. Many belonged to Aunt Helen, or had been bought by her for my benefit. There was Palgrave's *Golden Treasury*, the original edition of course, and a complete (sometimes puzzling) Andersen's *Fairy Tales*, and Lamb's *Essays*, and the *Tales from Shakespeare*, and an appropriately bowd-lerized Aesop. I suppose the *Treasury* was the most important single book in my literary education. To be sure, by the time I opened it I had all the pre-Opie nurs-ery rhymes by heart, along with a good many German ones, and took the distinc-tiveness of verse from prose for granted, but here, in the historical sequence that I had sensed with Mother Goose but here found pronounced, there was a strange magic. It constituted a challenge in the differences of language and sentiment be-tween the successive poems, the different presentations of aspects of experience, though obviously I could not have so expressed it. And much of the prose in the bookcase was American: here was another differentiating circumstance.

There were Washington Irving's *Rip van Winkle* and Fenimore Cooper's *Last of the Mohicans* and *Deerstalker* and Beecher Stowe's *Uncle Tom's Cabin* and Chan-dler Harris's *Uncle Remus* and Alcott's *Little Women*. Birthdays brought me *Tom Sawyer* and *Huckleberry Finn*. The English side was well if not strongly represent-ed by *Vanity Fair* and *Pride and Prejudice* — as I recall I found the latter difficult at that stage. But *Treasure Island* and *Kidnapped*, again birthday presents, put Irving and Fenimore Cooper in the shade. Thoreau's *Walden* puzzled me for I lived, in my judgement, as near to a 'wilderness' as he did and took it for granted.

George Kane in early school years.

Back to school: when it resumed in September 1926 the 'big boys' had left. My cousin Josie who had till then been educated at home for health reasons had joined my class, and I had made a friend, Ferdinand (Fritz) Weber. Except for an elder brother of the twins Augusta and Henrietta who was sweet-natured and not very bright, we were the senior boys. No longer teased I ceased to get into trouble, and a wary truce developed between Sister Clementine and me. As to arithmetic, I made myself take interest and managed, so to speak, to keep my head above water. There were some bright girls, and classes began to be competitive fun. In 1929 a somewhat older boy, Ted Bergerman, joined the class; he had left school at fourteen, one of two sons in a large family, to help on the farm until his brother reached the permitted leaving age. He proved a fine person and became the fourth of a close group with my cousin, Fritz and myself. Between the four of us the range of age did not seem to matter.

Moreover we had a new teacher. It had apparently come to the notice of the nuns and thus the school board that grade eight would be special material, and they engaged a lay person, a Miss Macdonnell, to teach history, English literature and composition, geography and a new course called 'Civics' about the mode of government and relationship of the provinces and the Dominion. She was unmarried, I suppose about thirty-five, slender, fine-featured, with the dark beauty sometimes found in the Western Highlands, from which, undoubtedly, her-not-so remote ancestors had been expelled during the enclosures. I soon fell in love with her, and I was lucky, for someone must have put her on to my grandmother, and she often came to the house for the coffee and cake which my grandmother gave her guests at teatime. She was a fine teacher, and we did not, as a class, disappoint the school board.

2
St Peter's College 1930–1934

My recall of the summer of 1930 does not include my grades in the final examination, but I do remember that I was given a bicycle on my fourteenth birthday, a handsome present far beyond the usual range of the depression years. In retrospect, I read this to indicate that my stepfather, who must have paid for it, had come to view me with more than amiable tolerance. At the time, as soon as I had learned to ride it I rejoiced in the freedom of movement it gave me. But I did not take it in that henceforward he would be paying for my education. In fact it was my grandmother who eventually told me that.

Summers in his household had become a part of my life. He was a Hungarian, Eugene Bakony, the only son of a merchant family in Eger who had emigrated to Canada and acquired Canadian citizenship before 1914. He had moved westward, pausing a while in Winnipeg before settling in Wakaw, about sixty miles northwest of Muenster. This was a railway station and a small-town market centre for what, until the Depression, was a very prosperous farming district peopled largely by first generation settlers and their families from Hungary and the Ukraine; in the town there was an element from Eastern Canada, mainly Scots-Canadian. Here he developed several businesses, notably a general store and a garage with the General Motors franchise. He employed managers to run these while, until the bottom fell out of the market for wheat in 1934, he played the Winnipeg Grain Exchange and golf. In the first game, according to my mother, he was worth a small fortune at one time and he did get out with his shirt, so to speak but no more, when the crash came. As to golf, he and the Hungarian manager of his garage business and an Ontarian, Basil Frith, manager of one the grain elevators, had founded a club and developed a very pretty nine-hole course on leased pastureland. He was a man of considerable charm and culture, and like my mother a book lover, but in the manner of Hungarians, indolent. For his superior education and style he was a figurehead in the local Hungarian community, much in demand for counsel or simply for a dispassionate talk about a problem. Like my grandfather's his English was correct but accented.

He and my mother had five children. The first were twins, born in August 1921, of whom one died very soon after birth. My grandmother had, I realized much later 'protected' me from my mother's remarriage. She need not have done so: my dead father was a cherished legend rather that a remembered personality to me, and in plain terms I had got used to my mother, whom I adored, being away. No doubt my stepfather found it more necessary to make adjustments in our developing relationship than I did. As for the bundle shown to me as my brother Edward — here my mother and my grandmother both showed excellent sense — he didn't look like much fun at the moment, but I had watched a female bundle born in 1918 grow to an agreeable girl cousin, and knew there was hope for this creature. In due course I acquired three siblings with less drama: a brother, Leo, born in 1922, a sister, Stella, born in 1925, and one more brother, Charles, in 1926.

When Edward was judged old enough to travel, in late 1921, my mother and her husband, taking him along, set out on a kind of grand tour, both to show her and their son to his parents in Eger where she was welcomed, admired and made much of, and for the pleasure of travel itself. They left Edward in the care of his Hungarian grandparents and a wet-nurse, and toured Italy, France and Germany, where my mother renewed contact with a friend from her previous visit, a second cousin, and bought literally a trunkful of books and toys to bring back for me. In the summer of 1922 I went to Wakaw to spend my first school vacation with my new family.

Before he took my mother and Edward abroad my stepfather had built a lovely bungalow (it was called 'the Cottage') on the shore of Wakaw Lake, after which the town, two miles away, had been named.

'Wakaw' means 'crooked' in Assinaboian Cree, and the lake is just that, an irregularly shaped fifteen-mile-long gash, made in the gently rolling countryside by a jagged rock formation embedded in a glacier moving south at the end of the last ice age and spring-filled; the lakeshore level fifty to one hundred feet below that of the surrounding land. Where the Cottage stood the lake was somewhat more than half a mile wide. On the opposite shore there was an osprey's nest in a tall lightning-blasted tree, and in the nesting season one of the pair of birds fished constantly, for handsome perch and young pickerel. All day the Arctic terns entertained with acrobatics; there were cormorants which, not yet a flyfisher, I had not begun to hate. In the evenings one heard the great northern diver, or loon as Canadians call it, but always at a distance. In the summer the lake harboured mallard and teal; they vanished during the shooting season. Across the lake the shore rose in a gentle bank of pasture land about a hundred feet to a long grove of aspen. The Cottage was set in a clearing among quick-growing Russian or black poplars, big trees with an eighteen inch diameter at full growth as they were in my time, but short-lived. Behind them where the land rose there were aspens and an occasional silver birch among thickets of brush willow and now and then a hazel bush. The willow was handy for making whistles and bows, and one August the hazels produced cobs which I picked green and dried until the nuts were ripe and edible.

Just by the door of the Cottage's screened veranda, in a huge black poplar, a pair of green humming birds nested each year. The summers in Wakaw quickly became in many ways an idyllic part of my life: this now was my Walden, but better than Thoreau's. Except for the occasional thunderstorm the weather was genial, summer wear for us young 'uns was a bathing suit.

I had only one responsibility, surveillance of my young siblings. This required organisation, but it was good for me to have to think of ways to keep them out of mischief. On the inland side of the Cottage close to the house they had a fenced-in woodland playground about the size of an allotment where, once I started Edward and Leo on some self-entertaining activity, I could safely leave them for a while. Outside this playground I had to keep a constant eye on them until they learned to swim which I taught each one as early as possible. It needed only one of them falling off the wharf while my back was turned to realize why my mother had taken such my pains to teach me my first summer at Wakaw.

The rules of the game were not quite the same as those at my grandparents' house. Offence there was viewed as against a principle, which seemed fair enough to me: my generation did not question the rule that children must obey their elders. My mother and stepfather saw good conduct in another aspect, as a matter of common sense, basic intelligence. Here is a typical instance from the time I was about six years old. Having heard mention that someone I admired was writing a book I decided that I would write one myself when occasion offered. It came when I was exploring a drawer in search of a pencil and found an elegant little book with only a few pages encumbered. This would do with those pages cut out. The book was, as it happened, my stepfather's new passport. He did not say a word to me when the mutilation came to light. My mother, however, who never in our lives together raised a finger against me, punished me cruelly by making me feel excessively stupid: 'I thought you could read!' Both possible answers were bad; I could read and had taken no notice of what I read. The implication was shaming.

Back to summer 1930 when I went to St Peter's College and my world was changed, again for the better. The College was an element of the Abbey, a boarding school which taught the four year course leading to Senior Matriculation, and, as a Junior College of the University of Saskatchewan, its first year syllabuses in English, French, German, Latin, Greek and Integral Calculus. My cousin Josie, Fritz Weber, Ted Bergerman and I were the only day boarders. I had known from childhood that I would be going there and for some years had haunted hockey matches, open days and suchlike where my presence seemed to be taken for granted. I did not know at the time the part my grandfather had played in its establishment as a founding patron and benefactor with considerable gifts of land. It is now, incidentally, a constituent college of that University.

It was a very good school. It suited me and I learned quickly how to get the best out of it. I found it easy to fit in, and increasingly enjoyed my time there. The

St Peter's College in the 1930s.

oldest students, in the fifth year and mostly intending to join the Order, were not called prefects, although they were a force for the control needed by the young male. That term was reserved for those teaching monks also responsible for discipline. These were wisely chosen, good at games and with agreeable personalities. The academic head of school was not the Abbot but the Rector, who would also teach. We day boarders arrived at 8:30, and usually stayed on for games, baseball, tennis, handball (a variant of fives played bare-handed against a winged wall) and in the winter ice hockey. After games the day boarders went home, the boarders to the Study Hall where each of us had his desk, with a prefect in charge. I was born left-handed and made to use my right hand by a well-meaning but mistaken grandmother; consequently I was a duffer at games, with a quarter-second slow hand-and-eye coordination. The good sense of the school management showed itself in arrangement for myself and other duffers. In tennis or hand-ball tournaments we were paired with good players; in ice hockey there were two leagues; in baseball my kind provided scorekeepers. I was in one particular privileged: during my last couple if years I was College sports correspondent for the diocesan weekly newspaper, *The Prairie Messenger*, published from the Abbey. That meant going off with our formidable ice hockey team to away high school tournament games in the evening.

All the teachers were monks, and all certified. All were competent, some very or exceptionally good. After forty years in the profession I would rate the average quality exceptionally high. There was only one I could not learn from, Father

"*Ut in omnibus glorificetur Deus.*" *That in all Things God may be Glorified.*
—*Benedictine Motto.*

ST. PETER'S COLLEGE
MUENSTER, SASK.

A BOARDING SCHOOL FOR BOYS AND YOUNG MEN
CONDUCTED BY THE BENEDICTINE FATHERS

Advertisement for the school.

Leonard Benning, the eldest of three brothers in the Abbey. He was what Chaucer would have called an *outridere*, the manager of the monastery farm which within a few years would become one of the model farms under the aegis of the provincial Department of Agriculture. Unlike Chaucer's *outridere*, Father Leonard was not only highly competent but also generally respected throughout the diocese. He taught algebra in grade ten when I was there, and found me dense. To go by his success with the rest of the class he was right.

In digression, his was an interesting family. His next brother, Father Xavier, was senior prefect of discipline and taught most of the Latin classes superbly. We had one contretemps, over the spelling of two near-homophones. I paid for being right: all had been very civil but I had put him down. Would I copy out the school rules twenty times in ink? I don't suppose this improved my penmanship, but it taught me that it can be expensive to score a point, a lesson that has stood me in good stead in committees over the years, mainly to the advantage of the outcome of the discussion. We became good friends over the five years I studied with him; he agreed with me that Caesar was dull and that in comparison Livy scored on every count and that Sallust was a better stylist than either. Monk and all he led me to see the vast differences between Catullus and Tibullus on the one hand and Vergil on the other, and deeply religious as he was, that artistic excellence and human frailty are not mutually exclusive.

George Kane (a school photograph).

The high school system of Saskatchewan of that time was designed to prepare for two successive sets of examinations. The Junior Matriculation examination was taken after three years in high school, that of Senior Matriculation a year later at the end of grade twelve. The syllabuses reflected the Scottish tradition of Nova Scotia. A good pass at Junior level implied a sound general education ensuring literacy, numeracy, some elementary science, Canadian and British history and geography. I cannot recall whether a modern foreign language or Latin was compulsory. Certainly for those intending to go on to the Senior Matriculation there were options. The subject syllabuses were prepared by the provincial Department of Education in consultation with the relevant departments of the provincial University in Saskatoon. I could not know at the time that the English Department was in the Grierson tradition, shaped in its early days by James Sutherland and in my time carried on by his student John Lothian.

My first year was both formidable and exciting. There was elementary algebra, of which I have written, and more complicated arithmetic, and plane geometry which made sense but did not set my mind afire: these I accepted as necessary evils to be endured. On the credit side was Latin, which had intrigued me ever since I was given a bilingual Roman Missal for my ninth birthday. I opted for German to please one grandmother and French with the other in mind. I opted for chemistry as requiring less calculation than physics; in the end I think I might have enjoyed biology more. The monk who taught history and geography was competent enough, and I did the class work adequately, but always with the feeling that I would rather be reading more widely, with less concern about the dates of treaties or the distances between places. I was restive about learning the German paradigms, but benefited from having to extend my vocabulary beyond family and domestic matters. The French class consisted of myself and a French Canadian whose attitude to its grammar was much like mine to German. Our teacher was from German-speaking Alsace, and used to tease himself and his Francophone pupil by referring to his own accent: 'Moi, je parle français comme une vache espagnole.' He was a very good teacher and we enjoyed his classes; and they gave me a medal, not for my accent, I am sure, but because I enjoyed memorising the grotesque irregular verbs. In English we were taught grammar, a new concept to me, by analysis of function with constant reference to the inflexional nature of the equivalent Latin which most boys were taking. I revelled in it — the idiom of the logic felt natural and obvious to me. We were taught how to shape essays, how to summarise, how to read poetry closely. As I recall I had read most of the verse in our textbook bar the Byron; I didn't particularly take to *Mazeppa's Ride* or *The Prisoner of Chillon*. There was some novelty in the prose; I admired Macaulay's; for a time I aspired to write like him, and even tried to read his *Trial of Warren Hastings* which I found among my mother's books. I recall reading Lytton Strachey's *Life of Queen Victoria* with puzzled interest, finding it hard to finish

The Mill on the Floss, being unable to stomach Carlyle's *Sartor Resartus*. In the third year we used an excellent anthology of Georgian poetry about which, until then, I knew nothing. Throughout the three years we would finish the week on Friday afternoon with a spelling bee; here I began to recover the confidence in my memory which algebra had undermined. My enjoyment of Latin began to mount in my second year. Here as in all our classes, competition was fierce, with a field of seven front runners, a pair of twins, George and Martin Brodner from outside the Colony, Philip Engele, whose elder brother had preceded him and joined the Order, and our four. We all got on well, but the competition was savage. A part of the teaching technique in Latin was to have a five-minute test at the beginning of each class on the prep assigned in the one before. The five minutes were strictly held to, and when they ended each of us marked someone else's paper: you could lose by missing an error as well as by making one; no quarter was given.

For me the sense of achievement came in the languages where, having read more widely than the other six, I was at an advantage. On the mathematical side I was confident of passing the geometry and arithmetic papers, even made some progress in algebra under a new and patient teacher, Father Francis, whom, many years later I had the pleasure of introducing to gin and fresh lime juice as a pre-dinner aperitif in my house in England. But in the third year algebra gave me an ugly fifteen minutes in the formal mid-session school examinations after Christmas. These were held in the study hall; each class had a block of assigned desks; one came into the room and found one's desk with the question paper on it. Come the algebra examination, there was my desk with a paper from which I could not answer a single question. I have no language adequate to describe how I felt except to say that this has remained one of the worst moments of my life. My sense of failure, of self-contempt, was absolute: after all my effort, nothing! I sat numb and desolate for what seemed like an ugly eternity. I looked around; what would other people think of me? There, deep in his Breviary at the Prefect's desk was Father Xavier with whom not long ago I had been sharing pleasure in the *O fons Bandusiae* ode. Somehow this stabilised me and I decided to have another try: the first thing to catch my eye when I picked the paper was 'Algebra Grade Twelve'. Father Xavier gave me a grade eleven question paper, half an hour over the three, and to my delight I made a B grade.

In June 1932 at the end of the school year my running mates and I passed our Junior Matriculation exams. I managed not to discredit myself in chemistry and the mathematics, did tolerably well in history and geography, and the best in languages, so that my average was par for the course and I could hold my head up high. In Wakaw my stepfather taught me to drive; on my seventeenth birthday I passed the driving test, and now all the younger children could swim, I acquired a boat. This was sheer delight, a twelve-foot double-bowed skiff, fitted for two pairs of oars, and very lightly built. When Josie came to visit, with practice we soon

George Kane, Francis Schwinghammer, George Brodner, Art Ehinan, Jerome Weber, Ted Bergermann, Philip Engele, Martin Brodner, and Father Al.

learned to shift it, and were able to match the speed of two girls our age in the cottage a quarter of a mile along the lake, who had the advantage in a Canadian canoe. One disillusionment came with the boat: now able to explore an island a mile up the lake where I had never till then set foot I found it fouled by cormorant nesting sites and overgrown with nettles.

As the qualifier for university entrance the fourth year at St Peter's was crucial. I cannot remember thinking of it in that light; taking a progression of examinations had become a sort of way of life. I had no plans; my mother had occasionally spoken of 'the university' in a very general way; that was all. For this examination, one offered nine subjects. In the mathematics algebra, algebraic geometry and trigonometry, one science, and European history were required; I made up my nine with the four languages. Our year, which had been about thirty strong at the outset, was down to half that number: this was normal. The farmers' sons who had been sent to College to acquire some polish and learning beyond grade eight had not taken the Junior Matriculation exam; a number of those who had taken it and passed did not go on. For teachers and students this was ideal. Our year was a happy one, and so far as my day-boarder's impression went, was the school. We were proud of the hockey team in which Fritz Weber and Philip Engele were stars; it was doing well in the High Schools league of that part of Saskatchewan. Our 'junior' (*sc.* 'duffers') tournament was lively. Unless there was a blizzard we were on the rink three afternoons a week from 4:15 to 5:30. There were toboggans and skis, for here in the plain another obliging glacier rock had gouged a three-hundred foot deep ravine with steep sides. I had a pair of skis on permanent loan and enjoyed the daily cross-country run to and from school. There was also baseball, weather permitting, for about six weeks in the spring, and also tennis and handball.

I finally came to terms with mathematics by exchanging coaching with my cousin. He was anxious about putting his essays together, and I capitalized on this to good effect. European history seemed all treaties and wars; it was easily accessible, but in the textbook we used, rather laboriously presented. The English syllabus was rich. There was *Vanity Fair* which I had read at home and was now taught to understand, along with *Pride and Prejudice* which I was now required to read and enjoy. I recall this year's reading as an experience of novels. In Wakaw there was a shelf-long set of translations of European novels, among them Tolstoy's *Cossacks* which intrigued me. Scott and Dickens I found in the Muenster parish library; my response was qualified; *David Copperfield* horrified me; I had trouble with the setting of *Great Expectations* but loved the story; I found *Pickwick Papers* incomprehensible; my experience of society did not extend to the world of the *Christmas Carol*. Of Scott's novels I enjoyed only *Quentin Durward*.

One personal rather than academic feature of that year I intrude here: the first decision of any importance I had to make for myself. This was the year — one bears in mind that an important function of the College was to educate boys for the priesthood — in which the Abbot would summon likely boys to discuss with them whether they had a vocation to the religious life. One knew that this would happen and had time to think about it.

First there were many things I loved about the Abbey. For several years I had been going to the chapel there for the Sunday high mass, having taken my grandparents to the eight o'clock service in the parish church which was also the cathedral. What attracted me, I now think, was the group of individuals whom I knew personally as my teachers, the monks and my friends among the lay brothers (for instance the operator of the printing press where the *Prairie Messenger* was typeset and run off) being translated by their community of devotion into a kind of transcendental unity that showed on their faces, and in the most commonplace teaching voice becoming in Gregorian music an instrument that expressed dedication, devotion. All this I found deeply moving, and I still cherish the recollection of it. But I could not see myself as a priest: I think I am a serious person, but I find it hard to take myself seriously. I do not have a talent for solemnity; I suppose I lack *gravitas*. And it was difficult for me, even at the early age of sixteen, to accept the actual concept of priesthood. The parish priests had not impressed me; they were not personalities I would have selected as my intermediaries with a deity. The religious instruction in College, about which I have not written, had other

Three who chose differently: the Brodner twins and Philip J. Loehr (Cousin Josie).

emphases than those of the parish priest's Sunday sermon, where the payment of dues was often prominent.

So when my turn for interview came I told the Abbot, with due courtesy but not wasting his time, that after careful reflection I did not think I had a calling to a life of religion. He was kind and understanding, and I left his presence with no sense of having failed him or of being devalued for my decision. As for the family, there had never been any talk of my being 'intended for the Church'. Moreover, leaving aside my grandfather's benefactions, there was no sense of my having a financial obligation to the Abbey. When it comes to that, my stepfather who paid my fees was an agnostic.

But I am deeply sensible of obligation to the Abbey as a religious institution for giving me, during my brief experience of its community, an understanding of the religious experience which I have been able to retain even though, not long after leaving College, I ceased to be a practising Catholic and came to find myself more comfortable as an agnostic in the Huxleian sense of that term.

While I am writing about religion, I record a remarkable feature of the teaching at St Peter's, its freedom from bigotry, for which the English syllabus gave plenty of scope. We were encouraged to read *Fra Lippo Lippi* and *The Bishop Orders His Tomb* and *My Last Duchess* and *The Haystack in the Floods* from a human rather than a moral standpoint. The spiritual anxieties of Arnold and Clough were presented as the problems of thinking men rather than the predicament of Protestant doubters. Some at least of this liberal attitude was owed, I judge, to Father Wilfred, who had been Rector when I came to College but stepped down to take over senior English teaching in my third year. He had read English at the provincial University; I am certain that books like Shaw's *Collected Prefaces* and Aldous Huxley's *Brave New World* and *Antic Hay* had been left in the school library by him. He was a quiet man but a fine teacher who enjoyed discussion and made me feel that my opinion was worth listening to.

That last year of high school was a heady time which I shall not attempt to describe in detail. I think that what I was experiencing was, in the abstract, the intellectual excitement conferred by a sense of focus, of being effectively engaged in an activity of unquestioned value both autotelic and practical, which conferred an enhancement of sense of identity. There would be a price to pay for this: not so engaged would induce a sense of drift, lack of purpose, but not yet.

Everyone in the class passed the Senior Matriculation examinations creditably, and we seven came back in the autumn of 1933 to 'grade thirteen', the First Year Arts course of the University of Saskatchewan. I do not recall even at this stage taking thought beyond this forthcoming year. There seems to have been a general assumption in the family that since I was enjoying school and doing so well I would continue. My mother and stepfather were more concerned about Edward and Leo, now in their last years at primary school in Wakaw, doing well enough but with the near prospect of going to a high school with an incompetent headmaster and a poor name for discipline. Before I went back to St Peter's my mother told me what I had already surmised, that they were planning to move to Vancouver, both because of the schooling problem and because my mother was finding the Saskatchewan winters increasingly trying. This was in 1933, the low point of the Great Depression, when wheat was fetching 36 cents a bushel and was not worth hauling to the elevators. I ought to have been thinking about my future, but my mind was on September when I would move into a world without mathematics, where I would study English, French, German, Latin and Greek. The year did not disappoint me.

Some of the excitement, and the main challenge, came from the Greek. This class was small; not all the seven had opted for it. The teacher was new, Father Fridolin, a saintly septuagenarian with the appearance and something of the personality of a superannuated cherub, infinitely patient and a fine grammarian, who had been brought out of retirement to look after us. Seventeen is a little old for an ordinary person to undertake a new dead language with a new alphabet and an immensely sophisticated literature and become highly proficient in it unless he can give it all his time. I did learn enough Greek to read texts that hugely enlarged my literary experience and texts that shaped my thinking in many respects, but never without Liddell and Scott handy. We started with an excellent school text of the *Anabasis*, an eventual advantage for me, though I never did become quite comfortable with Homeric Greek.

Latin continued wholly enjoyable, beginning dramatically with enough Ennius to make me aware, as Palgrave had of English, that Latin writing had a history. The syllabus was rich, and for those days, liberal. We read Ovid and the elegiac poets, Martial, more Livy, a good sample of Sallust, and some of Cicero's *Epistles*, which after his *Catiline* oration in a preceding year I enjoyed.

In the modern languages the prescribed texts at last became more interesting; fair enough, in high school the emphasis had to be on language, and on translation from English. I remember nothing about the high school German texts; of the French only that Corneille's *Le Cid* was easy enough to translate and essentially undramatic. In First Year Arts the German interest developed slowly. Here I started from a high base of the *Lieder* my grandmother had sung to me as a child and boy; I knew the *Lorelei* by heart before I went to school, and expected much. So when we started with Lessing's *Nathan der Weise* and went on to *Minna von Barnhelm*, which we read with Father Fridolin before Christmas, I was disappointed. Father Fridolin never told us that we ought to admire Lessing for anything other than being a pioneer, or that we were failing in response. He saw to it that we read and translated the two plays accurately; we had chosen to take the course. I suppose that if the intention of the syllabus was to awaken a sense of literary tradition in us Lessing was the man to start with, but one play would have done. Next semester we had another, younger teacher, Father Paul who also taught biology, probably in his mid-thirties, whom I had not yet encountered. He gave me an impression which I could not have named at that time, a blend of monastic distinction and urban sophistication. Certainly he was more suited to teach us the next two texts, Goethe's *Götz von Berlichingen* and *Faust* Part I. Certainly *Götz* was lively; the play brought Walter Scott to mind, and while I was told that Goethe was imitating Scott, I learned only recently that Scott had translated the play. As for

Faust, I had never in my reading encountered anything like the force with which the play communicated the pathos of Gretchen's situation. French by contrast was exciting from the beginning of the year: several of Montaigne's essays, as also of Pascal's *Pensées*, *Candide* as a counterbalance, Molière's *L'Avare* which rid me of the tedium of the preceding year's *Le Cid*, and just a sample of sixteenth-century lyric from Ronsard.

As to English, we read *Richard II* and *As You Like It* which Aunt Helen had put in my hands years before to show me what Lamb did in the *Tales*, and *Othello*, and Victorian poetry from an excellent anthology. Tennyson I had found among my mother's books, but Swinburne and Rosetti and Arnold and Clough were new, as was Morris, whose quality as a poet has been masked by his other activities. Here Father Wilfred was at his best.

The school year passed quickly; the only disaster was that I had to have my tonsils removed at short notice just before Christmas and was restricted to ice cream at Christmas dinner. I returned to College a day late with my mother's consent so as not to miss a party given by one of my Wakaw friends, knowing, as I did not, that the move to Vancouver next summer was a certainty. When I reported late to the new Rector with my excuse he handed me a sheet containing an ancient jingle of the Latin masculine nouns ending in *-is*. 'Come back when you know this by heart.' When in due course I went back to repeat it to him he laughed and sent me away. It was that kind of school.

We took the examinations in our stride; my cousin working out his calculus answers on the spot as he had said he would, and all passed without discredit. I made a B in German as I had expected but also in English, which dashed me; it did me good, no doubt. John Lothian, whom I met as a fellow external examiner about thirty years later, and still later came to know a little, claimed to remember my paper. I mentioned the B, but he said, as one does, that this was a high grade for him. In French and Latin I made an A, and so also, to my delighted surprise, in Greek. Even more to my surprise the University awarded me a scholarship. I did not take it up, for that summer we moved to Vancouver.

Looking back on my schooling after more than sixty years I see myself as having in four particulars been very lucky indeed. The first is my grandfather Kopp's restlessness and that chance encounter with the monks from St John's on the train, in consequence of which I came to be educated in the monastery they founded. The second is the uniformly good quality of the teaching there: I have not forgotten Father Leonard; I was his only failure. The third is the childhood circumstance that I was often thrown upon my own resources for entertainment, and with no other resources that the books in my house, many of which stretched my mind.

The fourth particular deserves its own paragraph: the young women of my immediate family. They were beautiful, and had style and taste: even very young

St. Peter's College Boys' Remarkable Showing

Father Matthew, Rector of St. Peter's College, has received a letter from the University of Saskatchewan in which are tendered to the staff of the College the congratulations of the University on the excellent showing of the Second Arts students.

The letter draws attention to the fact that three of the top sixteen students from all Junior Colleges of the Province (including that within the University) are St. Peter's men. A fourth St. Peter's College man fell just without the top sixteen. This is noteworthy, considering that at St. Peter's College only ten men were taking full Second Year's work. Two of the College boys were awarded scholarships.

Attention is called to the work of George Kane, top student of St. Peter's, who had "a very remarkable record.

'top student of St Peter's'.

children appreciate these qualities. And they were all very intelligent. Best of all, they were amiable, good-tempered and loving. They were responsible for most of the English books in their parents' house and taught me to read. As for my mother, I could not have wished her other. I valued her approval above all. She would talk to me about books, of which there were many on her bookshelves worth discussing. She showed me the world outside my school by sending me reading like *The New Republic* and *The Atlantic Monthly*, and on the lighter side *The Saturday Evening Post* where serial novelists and short-story writers like Scott Fitzgerald and Hemingway, soon to be canonized, practised their craft. She encouraged me to discover for myself the polarization of American society by suggesting such novels as Sinclair Lewis's *Main Street* and Marquand's *The Late George Apley*.

3
British Columbia 1934–1936

My last summer at Wakaw was one of mixed feeling: melancholy at the prospect of leaving my better-than-Walden Lake, where I knew every tree and rock along miles of shore, and excitement, paradoxically, at that of living in a city. My cousin Josie spent three weeks of July with us: he had almost made up his mind to join the Benedictine order, and this might be his last summer of running free. I would miss him too: we had been as close as brothers.

In mid-August, after much family leave-taking, we set off for British Columbia by car. The trans-Canada highway was still a dream. We drove west to the Alberta foothills, then south into Montana and over the Cordillera through Idaho and Washington to Spokane, where we turned north for Canada and Vancouver. Anyone who has grown up in plainland will know the excitement of the first sight of mountains. I recall most sharply, after that, clear running water, the fierce chill of a mountain stream in the heat of the day, the music of silence at high altitudes, the taste of tree-ripened peaches, the Pacific seen by glimpses from the northbound coast road.

Vancouver did not disappoint. We spent the first three or four nights in a motel in what is now West Vancouver, where the cabins were built of real logs and the smell of pine and spruce was pervasive. By that time my stepfather had bought a house for his family in a district where the schools were good, not quite big enough (I shared a room with my next brother, Edward), but only twenty minutes from Kitsilano Beach where there was a huge tide-filled swimming pool with diving boards and lifeguards. Presently my holiday afternoons would be occupied with taking my new siblings there. They were young enough to benefit from lessons, and became expert; I never did master the stylish new Australian Crawl.

But first I set out to find a job for the weeks remaining before the university term began. This was 1934. There were only door-to-door salesmanships, and those for unessentials, subscriptions to women's magazines, lottery tickets and suchlike: I quickly found that I was no good at that kind of persuasion. In fact I was no unluckier than most men my age without qualifications at the time. Among the male students I got to know in my first year there was one much envied: he had an uncle who was a tram driver, who thus had influence and could get him summer jobs with the city transport. Never mind, I got to know downtown Vancouver while I walked the streets looking for 'Help Wanted' signs in the windows. Now I ventured onto the still deserted University Campus, where I gaped at the Library, the most splendid building I had ever seen; I found the Arts Building and the Science Building and a mysterious structure called the Union Building. This would be my world for two years, but there was still a while to wait.

As not infrequently, my mother came to the rescue. By 1 September when the Primary and High School terms began, she had the children registered and ready, had settled us into the house, and begun to know her way around local and downtown Vancouver for advantageous shopping. She had also found and made her number with the Kitsilano branch of the excellent Vancouver Public Library. Now she took me there and taught me the mystery of call numbers and catalogues and subject bibliographies, and with a little direction set me on a reading binge that kept my impatience in abeyance until the beginning of my first term at the University. I discovered the travel book, already in those days an art form, and learned more geography than I had done at school to boot.

When at length the day for registration arrived my mother embarrassed me by announcing that she was coming with me. It was not her presence that bothered me — she was a stylish woman — but the implication I felt it carried, that I needed a minder. However, I knew her too well to resist: she seldom took a stand, but when she did she was hard to move.

Admission to the Faculty of Arts was no more than a matter of form. The difficulty came with the course I put myself down for, 'Honours in English, French and German'. As we were leaving the Registration Office I was called back to be told that, regrettably, the University did not offer such a course. I had better see the Dean. By the time we found his office my papers were on his desk. He began with civilities to my mother, which was just as well: I had been brought up standing by the disappointment, not having thought beyond a first choice. Then he looked towards me, as if waiting for me to speak. Without raising her voice, but coolly formidable, my mother spoke first: 'I want my son to read a subject that will get him a job when he graduates.' The Dean played it back beautifully. 'Ma'am, if he does well he will get a job whatever he reads.' But she had evidently put him on his mettle ; the suggestion he came up with, 'Honours in English and Latin', seems to me after forty years experience in the University world, to have been the right one, given my qualifications. Then and there it seemed to me an acceptable second best, and I accepted it. He picked up his telephone, spoke to the two heads of department concerned, and I became by that process the first student of the University to take that course. In retrospect it's just as well my mother came with me to register! And the Dean was shrewd. With a good English degree from a Canadian University and a classical background I would be marketable in any English Department on the North American continent.

The Dean sent me, then and there, to call on the two heads of department; they would plan my course. I fancy they discussed it during the ten minutes it took to see my mother to the campus bus stop. She liked the Dean; if I was happy with this course, so was she. My course had been called 'English and Latin', so I called first at English, where the Head of the Department, Professor Sedgewick, wasted little time on me. I would be taking three two-semester English courses each year. They would give me a calendar of courses in the Registrar's Department, where I would find listed the English courses available that year; having made my choices I must put my name down for them. By contrast the Head of the Classics Department, Professor Robertson, informed me that I would be taking two Latin and one Greek course, each of two semesters, in my second and third years, and specified those to be taken in the forthcoming one. The Campus bookstore had lists of required set texts.

What was left of that afternoon I spent exploring, first the Library where, as a second year honours student, I would have access to the stacks. This was overwhelming; for the first time in my life I would not lack for books. Then the Arts Building, where all my courses would be taught except, I discovered, in the summer term, where they might meet under a tree in the Library grounds. In the Union Building I found the Bookstore, and a cafeteria/refectory, and a huge theatre or auditorium and the Students' Union offices, and the office of the student newspaper, to me a shockingly irreverent weekly I presently discovered, but with a national reputation for producing notable journalists. Except for the Library these buildings were utilitarian and architecturally undistinguished, but functionally well designed. They would be replaced as money became available. The Library, built to be enlarged by the addition of wings, was a very fine example of Canadian University Gothic, the stone a light grey granite that would not darken in the clean air of the University Park, ten miles from the centre of Vancouver and 500 feet above sea level on the land's end between Vancouver Harbour and the Fraser River estuary. I swam in bliss at the thought of belonging to this world, at the same time aware of my rustic lack of sophistication and already sensible of my relative youth.

Settling in to work in this new setting after a relatively idle summer took my mind off such consideration. I did, however, become aware that there were two classes of student, those who had money in their pockets and belonged to fraternities, and those who did not. There was another stratification, of those born in British Columbia, and those whose families had moved there from the prairies, especially the dust-belt of southern Saskatchewan. We were not in that category, but still prairie folk. No one I met was ever unpleasant about either matter. As to money, I had my fees paid, and my tram fares and my books, and at home the means of making as many sandwiches as I could want for lunch. And I would not have had time for fraternity activities, for I was determined to do well. My sense of being a poor relation did not last long into the first term. A harder adjustment was to the weather; come late October it began to rain. With eighteen hours a week of lectures over five days Arts students would spend much of their time walking to and from the Library, and one's trouser legs from the knee down never really did have time to dry out. I had my own carrel in the stacks, and if they steamed as they dried, it was nobody's business.

That first year I made my choices from the available English courses in an attempt to satisfy a sense I had from earlier reading of the continuity of the subject. If that sounds precocious, I plead that in my grandparents' house it was impossible not to be aware that change was a feature of literature with the passage of time. The *Golden Treasury* had been for me a sustained exhibition of how this applied to poetry. Because of the way courses in English rotated it was not easy for me to fill my gaps systematically. And perhaps because I could not arrange this, I do not recall with real confidence the sequence of the courses I took.

There was a Chaucer course, taught by Professor Sedgewick. We read the *Canterbury Prologue*, the *Wife of Bath's Prologue*, the *Nun's Priest's Tale* and a book, if not more, of the *Knight's Tale*. The only background reading that I recall being recommended was Manly's *New Light on Chaucer*. In fairness to Sedgewick this was because he wanted us to see that the *Prologue* characters were typical enough to make Manly's argument about actual live models plausible. I don't recall that Sedgewick mentioned Rickert's *Chaucer's World*, or spent any time on the poet's cultural background; he certainly did not tell us about the Wife's prototype in the *Roman de la Rose* or about clerical antifeminism. It all seemed very remote to me; and I sensed that I was missing any amount of literal meaning. His teaching method was to read aloud from the text in hand, in what I take to have been the Harvard pronunciation of fourteenth-century London English, with intervening pauses in which he exhorted us to admire the poet for one or another reason. He did recommend a poem called *Piers Plowman* and, eager to improve my mind, I found it in the stacks that afternoon, five massive volumes (Skeat), and an anaemic Everyman paraphrase. This would have to do: having given it an hour without a glimmer of understanding what it was about I put *Piers Plowman* aside.

There were superb teachers in the English department. To 'place' Shakespeare I put my name down for a course on sixteenth- and seventeenth-century drama, taught by an ex-Rhodes Scholar with the splendid Viking name Thor Larsen. He wore an Oxford M.A. gown when he lectured. He happened also to be a natural literary historian as well as a man of fine critical sensibility, and, unlike Sedgewick, he did his 'homework' religiously. His lectures, without being at all formal, were models of organization and presentation. This was twice brought home to me. On the first occasion it was by the sense of shock at its lack of consequence when I read the draft of my first term essay for his course. It took me a day to reorganize the content in a cogent discussion, but he had taught me something.

The second was when, revising for the end-of-course examination, I found the reflection of his organized presentation in my notes of his course. I met him again in 1960 when my family and I spent the summer months in Vancouver. It was a melancholy occasion: he remembered, and was very pleased to see me, but had one of the afflictions of old age which impairs speech and movement, and we could communicate little. I would have liked to get to know him, but there was never time in the thirties.

The other fine teacher in the Department was Ira Dilworth, who lectured on post-Romantic nineteenth-century literature. He was Eastern Canadian and, with the name Ira possibly by way of New England before or soon after the American Revolution. He was not a public personality, and I don't recall ever knowing where he earned his higher degree. He lectured in a gown, but then so did my colleagues and I at King's London: it keeps the chalk out of your suit. One thing for sure, he was not the Rhodes Scholar type: he wore a rather large bow tie and admired Walter Pater. His critical faculty was acute and his sensibility fine, and again his lectures were well organized and delivered, conveying a sense of literary art as part of the culture from which it emerged, and best understood as such.

The eighteenth century and, of all combinations, Anglo-Saxon, were taught by Professor McDonald, the oldest member of the Department. He was a charming man whom we all loved, but shell-shock had left him with poor hearing and worse memory. Because I wanted to complete my sense of sequence I took his eighteenth-century course, and was taught why to read its literature, rather than how, and came away with a useful reading list. That leaves the one woman in the Department, Dorothy Blakey, an assistant professor just back from Oxford, where she had not learned how to lecture, either from good example or in reaction. She taught a required term's course on bibliography which might have been effective if we had had genuine specimens to work with, and another on Wordsworth and Coleridge which I took to supplement my knowledge from Palgrave. We were very kind to her, but she must have realized that she was not getting through to us. One day, Sedgewick came into class with her clutching his Wordsworth. He directed us to the 'One impulse from a vernal wood' stanza in *The Tables Turned* which we had been reading to no particular effect in the preceding meeting. 'Read it!' he barked. We put our heads down and did so. 'What does it mean?' No answer. Again the question, and the silence. This time he almost roared, 'Think!', at least twice, and stormed out dramatically. Both poor Professor Blakey and her students were very embarrassed; we did our best to help her through the rest of the hour.

Sedgewick had a very high local reputation as a teacher of Shakespeare, and fancied himself as an actor. I did not test the former for there was no time in my double programme. The legend has it that he once told his students how, although because of his size (5' 3") he could never hope to play Hamlet, it *was* his hope to give the part its definitive performance in heaven. Size aside, he did not look the part: in face and figure he was Mr Punch. His 'Shakespeare 100' course, where he so to speak played Romeo and Juliet, was the first choice of most undergraduates from the other faculties fulfilling their Arts requirement.

As a new student, callow and outside the gossip belt, I was unaware that he was homosexual, but I was also, this is true, unaware of the existence of that category of male. Such knowledge came with reading Plato, as good a source as any. According to the academic ethic of those days students were, for their teachers, sexually taboo. As far as I myself was concerned, when after my graduation he had established my lack of response, we became good if not close friends. Indeed, during my last long vacation in Vancouver before coming to England he would lend me his car to take out my current girlfriend. He was professionally very supportive, ready with letters of recommendation for his former students: there is unanimity about this. I learned to read fourteenth-century Italian from Longfellow's facing-page translation of the *Divine Comedy* which he first lent and then gave me. He was not a happy man, lonely and unfulfilled. His departmental colleagues appeared to respect him, but I did not sense — perhaps I had not learned to recognise it — the cohesion which I have felt in some departments.

But then I was there only two years as a student. There were people a year senior to me, but I did not get to know them except to greet. I made one good friend in my year, John Harrison, reading English Honours. He was very intelligent, but not scholastic by temperament. He was very popular in the fraternity world, and played rugger (very snob in Canadian context) for the University. His parents were English; the father, lately deceased, had been a High Anglican clergyman in Australia, upon whose death his mother had brought John and another son and a daughter to Vancouver. And there was Rodney Poisson, some three years older than me, who was registered as an M.A. student and taking make-up honours courses. He was likewise intelligent, but indolent.

The Classics Department, in fact a luxury in a university not yet fifty years old, was staffed by three professors and a graduate assistant. I recall about a dozen honours students, a very few graduates working for the master's degree, and a fair number of undergraduates from those departments where Latin was prescribed in the syllabus.

The Head was Professor Lemuel Robertson, a Latinist from the Scottish-settled east coast, one of the best teachers I have ever been privileged to learn from. I doubt whether he had published much, and never thought to enquire. He was immensely erudite. He excited one's imagination and made difficulties into challenges by bringing authors and their topics to life with a vast fund of anecdotes and gossip from the Greek and Latin minor writers. He held us to meticulous translation and close reading. He elicited questions, and gave direct answers or said 'I don't know!' He showed us Juvenal's third and fourth satires against Johnson's translation and when we read Seneca's *Moral Epistles* very gently indicated the elements of Stoic ethical thinking absorbed into Christian moral teaching. He showed us how Horace's *Ars Poetica* could be both dull and important. He enlarged my mind and forgave me my difficulty with writing Latin verse, which no amount of thumbing about in the *Gradus ad Parnassum* could reduce. And he agreed with me that Cicero's *Epistles* were better reading that his *Orations*.

The other professor of Latin was Col. Harry Logan M.C., with whom I read from Vergil's *Eclogues* and *Georgics*. He was much respected as a person. Although slight in build and quiet in manner he had been a Rhodes Scholar, and had shaped into a typical Oxford product. He unquestionably knew his subject, but failed to sell me Vergil. I got my only B grade as a U.B.C undergraduate from him: it was doubtless all I deserved.

That leaves the Professor of Greek, Otis Johnson Todd. He had recently published the *Index Aristophaneus*, still, I observe with pleasure, a standard work. He was, like Robertson, from the Maritimes, but by way of Harvard. At first encounter he appeared unforthcoming, but he was in fact very approachable. My first encounter with him was on the *Iliad*; everyone else in the class had had some Homeric Greek, but I had to begin sometime. I managed not to not disgrace myself, but the preparation took more time than I liked. After that came Plato, the *Ion* and part of the *Symposium*, where I was more at home. Todd's gentle guidance with the Homer, and when we were reading Plato, his evident response to the spirit of the text, modestly and quietly conveyed, made him a superb teacher. Like Robertson, he was hugely erudite and shared his learning and his time with equal generosity.

That Christmas vacation there was excitement, the heaviest snowfall in the memory of inhabitants of Vancouver. This ought to have been fun for the children of the city, but the snow was very dense and a thaw set in very soon after it ceased to fall. It brought down many flat roofs, and found a weak point in the roof of the University Library, threatening the bookstacks. A call was broadcast to local students to help move the books. A small number of us managed to make it there on foot — the trams were not running — and we lost no books. For us there was a bonus: one became *persona grata* with the two Deputy Librarians who handled the crisis, Hugh and Mary Lanning. What better reward could a student ask?

The second semester of my first year at British Columbia University passed quietly, swiftly and without event. I was orientated and knew I could compete, and I had made several friends and many acquaintances. John and Rodney were in a number of my classes, and I was getting to know Leonard Grant in Classics Honours, who became in effect my running mate for the rest of the course.

His home was in Victoria on Vancouver Island, where his late father, an officer in the Gordon Highlanders, had retired with his wife and only son upon disbandment in the twenties. He was three or four years older than me. After taking the First Year Arts course at Victoria College on the Island he had taught in a prep school in Victoria to finance completing his degree at the University. He was already a fine classic; when I measured my knowledge against his I realized my limitations.

Moreover he knew much more of the university world than I and was a shrewd social observer, the right mentor for a country boy. It was part of my education to walk, when the evenings were fine, with him the two miles to the gates of the University Park where our ways parted. After the first term he was often about the house. My mother and stepfather liked him, and he was evidently glad to get out of his digs at the weekend into a family ambience. I missed him badly during the long vacation of 1935.

Much of that vacation I spent haunting the Library stacks. In the Humanities sections the classifications system, almost chronologically based, encouraged a reading programme to match, and the carrel chairs were comfortable. Conscious of my deficiency I tried to teach myself Anglo-Saxon from Bright's *Reader* and made no headway, unsurprisingly, given the book. At the other end of the English section I found Eliot and Pound and Katherine Mansfield and Auden, and attracted by the name, discovered Thomas Love Peacock, intrigued by a suspicion as I first read him that he was up to something. The German shelves were not well stocked. I did find Hans Fallada's *Kleiner Mann, Was Nun?*; Brecht, in the same tradition, was yet to come. On the French shelves I began to make good sense of the early language with Villon, and fell in love with Ronsard's writings. The Renaissance, I was beginning to think, was where I wanted to work. All this was enjoyable in a desultory way, but it gave me little sense of systematic progress. I was glad when the session of 1935–1936 began.

The big experience of that last year at the University of British Columbia was a course under Todd on Aristotle's *Poetics*. This did not occur to me at the time, but he may have put it on for me. I was aware of the *Poetics* from Larsen's lectures, where the meaning of 'catharsis' and the question of the unities in Renaissance vernacular drama had come up. We were a small class, Leonard Grant, a couple of formidably bright women finalists whose names I have forgotten, and myself. We spent the whole of the first semester on those few pages. Our prescribed text was austere, without glossary or commentary but with textual variants, a novelty to me, at the foot of the page. Larsen had named a couple of facing page translations. We could use these, Todd observed, but at our peril. They had to make sense, he said, which the received text sometimes failed to do. Todd described the theories of the origin and quality of the text, showed us the unities in a setting of Greek classical tragedies as descriptive, not prescriptive, and from both broad and close knowledge, the varieties of emotional experience possibly comprehended in Aristotle's meaning 'catharsis'. I asked him about the concept of the 'sublime' which had come up in an English lecture, and he treated us to a remarkable impromptu on the applicability of the classical rhetoricians' analyses of language to the linguistic structure of canonical poetry, what Gustave Cohen and after him Jakobson would be making capital of when at length linguisticians began to look at poetry.

That semester I acquired an extra-curricular subject by joining the University Officers' Training Corps. We met three times a week in a large basement room of the engineering building. The commanding officer, Col. Sherwood Letts, a disabled veteran, professed that subject; our instructor was Company-Sergeant-Major Smith, seconded from the Canadian army. He was interesting: quiet-voiced and intelligent, with a sardonic sense of humour. I asked him, one break, whether he had come out of the Great War with any hate: 'Yes Cadet Kane, a strong one, for Libby, Mc Neill & Libby's corned beef!' That taught me not to ask silly questions. I met a different type of student which was interesting and made several friends whom I regrettably lost over the years. One in particular I would miss, John Logan, the Professor's son. We came to England together in 1938, and we saw each other occasionally in Oxford. He was colour-blind, but lied himself into the Canadian Army and was killed in Italy in 1945.

By mid-semester I had to decide in which of my two fields I would write the substantial essay, called a thesis, which was required of Humanities honour students and had to be submitted by March. The choice was effectively made for me by having begun my Greek late. I would miss my Latin authors, but not writing Latin verse. There was further consolation in a subject which my two interests, vernacular drama and classical theory, had suggested to me: where better to examine their interaction than in Shakespeare, whom I needed to read? I formed up to Sedgewick with it, and he approved the title 'Critical Opinions in the Plays of Shakespeare'.

So I spent the fortnight of the vacation, my last family Christmas as it turned out, reading the thirty-seven plays of Shakespeare canon of those days in E. K. Chambers's sequence at the rate, I recall, of about two a day. At the end I had a huge sheaf of notes, and an insight (already implied, of course, in Sedgewick's title) that the opinions of dramatic characters were not necessarily those of the playwright. When the essay was in longhand draft I submitted it to Sedgewick, as he had required. He began to read it immediately, and I sat quaking, uncertain whether to go or stay. After about ten minutes he stopped reading and held the manuscript out to me: 'If you were listening to a lecture on this subject, how would you like it arranged?' Without thinking I answered 'According to topics and subheads'. 'Take it away and don't come back'. Luckily by that time I had heard enough about his manner to translate this into a direction of amendment. The adventures of the essay were not over yet. The kind woman in the university bookstore who typed it for me modernized all my quotations. There were not many days left to the deadline for submission and I had no money to pay for a second typing. The kind woman retyped it for nothing, and in time.

Sometime in March it dawned on me that after graduating I would be without occupation. Leonard Grant and I had often talked about postgraduate study. He had his career mapped out: he was going to take a Master's degree in Vancouver and then apply for a graduate fellowship at Harvard, probably on Todd's suggestion. If I was going to do graduate study in English I did not wish to stay in Vancouver. Encouraged by Grant I went to Sedgewick for advice, only to learn that the closing date for application in Toronto, where he would have recommended me to apply, had passed. I must have looked pretty desolate, and he may have been sorry for me, or he may have realized that it was the Department's business to give timely advice in this matter. For whichever reason, he undertook to write to Woodhouse, the Head of the English Department in Toronto, about the possibility of a late application being accepted. A favourable answer came, with an application form. I filled this in and sent it off with the names of my referees.

There was no time to be anxious about it. Finals were looming, among them a three-hour General Knowledge paper in each of my two fields, along with the six other papers. I did not, to my relief, have to submit a specimen of Latin verse. But I had read no Milton, beyond what was in Palgrave, and was aware of deserts of vast ignorance about the classical world. For the Milton I divided the number of lines in *Paradise Lost* by the number of days before the first finals paper, and read the answered number in bed each night, in my father's copy. I would have to chance the Classics paper. But, doubtless by the kindness of Robertson and Todd, this turned out to be the last of all my examinations, and I prepared for it by spending the night before reading the entries for A to C in a classical encyclopaedia. I slept or dozed for the best part of a week after that last paper, and woke with delight, so to speak, to a letter from University College Toronto awarding me a year's graduate fellowship, worth $500, a princely sum in those days, with fees and accommodation.

The summer of 1936 seemed long. To have nothing to do but wait, however agreeable the awaited end, does not suit me temperamentally. To be sure I had a good degree — in fact I missed the highest average grade among new graduates by ½ %, beaten by a physicist. This made my mother, who had spotted it in a newspaper indignant — but I knew there was luck, one way or another, in such matters, and anyway the examinations were a rapidly receding past. Len Grant was at home in Victoria working on his Master's thesis, John Harrison in the Library, less enthusiastically applied to his English Honours graduation essay. The weather was glorious, the beaches attracted for a day or two. Then I found myself drifting back to the Library, but there I found it hard to settle down to systematic reading. I did not understand then, that such anticlimax after sustained effort is normal, and that I was simply very tired. But things soon improved. In the last while before the examination I had made the acquaintance of a congenial honours finalist in maths, called Ivan Niven, who was going on to a research fellowship at

George Kane, 1936.

Chicago University. When, after graduation, we met on campus I grumbled about how long the summer seemed. He had a remedy, hill-walking in the mountains on the north shore of Vancouver harbour; he would take me out. One crossed the harbour by ferry, then rode the bus westward along the coast road to the point where the first trail set out onto the spur of the Coast Range called The Lions from its silhouette. Where we walked was not true climbing country, but it took us into the rarefied air that taxed the lungs, where the ringing stillness of high places can be heard. We would have gone more often but for the cost of the fares; and Niven was as penniless as I. And I did not like to borrow from my mother.

She was a remarkable woman, intensely practical when she had to be, but with some freak of genes that had made her reject the life of a farmer's wife. To the limits of possibility of her situation she was an emancipated woman. I have written about the extent of her reading. She was a sensitive pianist and an opera fan, and had a collection of early H.M.V. records of Caruso and Galli Curci and Melba which she used to play for me as a child. Now in 1936 my stepfather and his golf-and-chess companion Basil Firth were not finding it as easy as they had hoped to re-establish themselves in business on the Coast, and my stepfather was still commuting, while she managed the household, the children and the family finances on a monthly cheque never more than just adequate. To be sure the house was easier to run than either the Cottage or the apartment in Wakaw where they wintered, but there she had domestic help, farmers' daughters whom she trained. My stepfather would come as often as he could get away, invariably with a trunk full of goodies for the family, but she must have found the intervals of his absence lonely. I had a sense of guilt at leaving her to cope. Yet as long as I can remember in our association she had spoken of the importance of travel.

Come the moment, Niven and I left for our respective universities, travelling by ship to Seattle and then by the Great Northern Line to Chicago, where he detrained and I continued to Toronto. As we came through the mountains I had seen what I presumed to be one reason for my grandfather's move to Canada, the still evident ruthless devastation caused by mining in his part of Montana.

4
TORONTO 1936–1937

It cannot be more than 600 miles from Chicago to Toronto, but what with changing stations and numerous stops on the way it was late morning before I arrived in Toronto. Term started in three days, and I was a little anxious, but things went smoothly. I checked my heavy luggage, armed myself with a map of the city, and by 3:00 was in the Registrar's Department, where I found to my surprise that I was expected. I was already on the books; I would be living in a University College hall of residence which would open the next day, was given the address of a recommended lodging for the night, and sent to call on the Principal of the College, Dr Malcolm Wallace, a gracious and charming man who was also the senior professor in the College's English Department, where he taught sixteenth-century literature when his duties as Principal allowed: he had, I later heard, a very good name as a teacher. Graduate Registration, he told me, was informal: I should make an appointment for the next day with the teachers whose courses I planned to take.

Next morning I moved my luggage to the hall of residence. The Warden, possibly five years older than myself, was an Assistant Professor, of economics if my memory is correct, engagingly named Wynne Plumtre and not at all formidable. To my surprise he told me of my status: I was to be one of the two junior wardens, the other — I probably knew him — was John Harrison, also from Vancouver! On later consideration I decided that there was contrivance here, and suspected Sedgewick of the thought that John and I might be good for each other in different ways in his mind. More likely it was an accident.

The Hall had been a rich merchant's stately mansion about the beginning of the century, given along with its grounds to the College by his family. John and I shared a suite consisting of a very spacious study-sitting room (customarily borrowed, we were to learn, by our fellow residents for their dances) and a double bedroom which must once have been a conservatory, its glass walls high enough above ground level to preserve the decencies. The walls being glass alarmed me from Saskatchewan, but come winter it turned out that the heating system could cope, and we had a window open most nights.

The Hall had no kitchen, but was only a short walk from Hart House, effectively a club for all male students of the University founded and endowed by the

Massey family in memory of a much-loved dead son. There they could breakfast, lunch and dine at subsidized prices, and the kitchen was good. The Hall also comprised a fine library with all the major reference books, formal reception rooms which served as lecture halls for special occasions, a gymnasium, a swimming pool and squash courts. Sunday dinner was a formal occasion. John and I rarely dined there; breakfast was quicker at a drugstore up the street; one picked up lunch wherever one happened to be. We were very comfortable, and both housetrained enough to get on as roommates without friction; the young people in the Hall were amiable, and our duties nominal.

Academically my year at Toronto was anticlimactic. Still intent on improving my sense of an English literary tradition I signed up for three seminars, on Chaucer and his school, Shakespeare, and Milton and Seventeenth Century literature, as well as a one-semester undergraduate course on Old English.

The biggest disappointment was the Chaucer course. It could have been good; the Chaucer section of the University library was very well stocked, and the group was not too big for real discussion. The trouble was the teacher, Professor Clawson, who was in plain terms very dull, and — worse luck for him — seemed to realize this. He had studied under F. N. Robinson and knew his way around the literature of the subject, but made little attempt to evaluate or correct past opinions and interpretations and seemed to have none of his own. My seminar paper — I thought this clever at the time — was a spoof. Clawson had great respect for German Chaucer scholarship, and I offered a review of this as my project. My paper was twice a mistake, first in the agonising boredom of reading it, and second in no one seeming to realize, when I presented it, that it was meant as a take-off. When Clawson praised it I was embarrassed. Moreover, like Sedgewick, he seemed content with Robinson's glossary, so once more I learned very little Middle English. But his undergraduate Old English course was rewarding. The class consisted of very bright senior honours students who had had some instruction in the language and I had to sweat to keep pace, which was good for me. I emerged able to read Old English to about the level of my Grade Eleven Latin. Regrettably I came away with a distaste for historical phonology studied for its own sake, which I still have to suppress.

The Shakespeare seminar should have been good. The teacher, Professor Knox, a Scotsman of the dryly intelligent sort, knew the plays. He, again, failed to arouse group discussion. It may have been our fault as personalities. I kept finding myself wishing I could discuss a play or character with him *à deux*. On occasion, when he put two opposed critical views and I succeeded in pressing him to give his own, he was very stimulating. And his recommendations of reading were invariably judicious. I must have been irritating at times, but he was patient and good natured, and happy enough to come to my home in London for dinner in the sixties.

Professor Arthur Sutherland Pigott Woodhouse was physically large and seemed to overshadow the other staff of the College English department, and appeared to be its head, though I do not recall hearing him named so explicitly. He was very much an Eastern Canadian, but with a Harvard finish, and he had written and was in process of bringing out *Milton, Puritanism and Liberty*, a weighty book in several senses. A big feature of his seminar was to read from the galley proofs, elaborate on what he had just read, and invite discussion. Thus he elicited questions and gave direct and clear answers or admitted ignorance. I learned readily from him, first how extensive my ignorance of the seventeenth century and its literature was, and after that, the pervasiveness of theological issues in English culture throughout most of its history, notably, of what he called 'the problem of evil' as the main theme of *Paradise Lost* and *Regained*. His course came alive for me two years later when I read *Piers Plowman* for the first time. This was a lively group with some more senior graduate students in it, and I learned the term Metaphysical Poets and first heard of a poet Donne. Woodhouse was not enthusiastic about him; I suspect that he found the style too baroque for his taste. He did not require a seminar paper of us, but we paid dearly for that remission in the final examination. This began with assembly in the seminar room at 9:30 with any books or texts we cared to bring. Woodhouse swept in at 9:35, and announced that we could write on any topic we chose related to our subject as long as we liked, using any aids, with intermissions as we pleased. It was a bad day, beginning with choosing my subject. I wrote very little, and eventually quit at 9:00 p.m., as did John Harrison and several others. We made for the nearest 'beer parlour'.

A main requirement of the M.A course was a thesis. It was early obvious that mine would not be on Chaucer, and that if I chose a large seventeenth-century topic I would not finish in the year. From my reading for the Shakespeare seminar Ben Jonson emerged. I had in mind my 'Critical Opinions' graduation essay, and the engaging differences, the distinctiveness of Jonson's plays, his aura of classical erudition, the miscellany of opinions expressed by or attributed to him personally, his presidency, so to speak, of the literary circle in the Mermaid Tavern. Knox approved of the general subject, and with him guiding we fixed on 'Jonson's Criticism: a Study of Its Controversial Basis and Distinguishing Themes'; it seems pretty pretentious in retrospect. Knox proved a very helpful supervisor but I found it hard to be satisfied with what I was producing. Obviously I did not have enough background knowledge to form and set down opinions confidently; moreover, seeing myself in retrospect, I had too little experience of personalities to 'place' Jonson. That thesis is not something I wish to be remembered by. Nevertheless the examiners at my oral were complimentary about it. Just as well that Harold Jenkins was not of their number![2]

2. Harold Jenkins (1909–2000), a distinguished Shakespearean scholar and London University colleague.

I did however emerge from writing the thesis with an earned insight into the relation between 'creative' writing and critical theorizing about it, how it was by nature complex in the first instance, and particularly so in the case of the writer and his own composition. I caught a glimpse of a doctoral dissertation here, relating to the renaissance vernacular epic and classical or neoclassical theories about the kind current at the time. Woodhouse had looked at *Paradise Lost* in this aspect, and I probably owed the notion to him. I could read the Latin and the French and Italian, so why not. Woodhouse did not discourage me and the dissertation I never came to write would be called, on his advice, a study of the critical theory of the epic in the renaissance with particular respect to Milton.

John and I did not go home to Vancouver for Christmas. The transcontinental fares were a consideration, but the main reason was the three nights travel there and back that put us off. We both had work to do and would need that time. John still had his graduation essay to finish off before he would get his degree, having respectably satisfied the exam requirements; and I was discovering the difficulty of finding any system or cohesion in a 'whole' that Jonson's expressed or alleged opinions I hoped might constitute, and to get to know his plays thoroughly.

We two got on pretty well, having regard to the extreme difference of our backgrounds and temperaments. John was socially poised and in most respects self-assured, though never with a hint of arrogance. Many of John's Vancouver friends were first-generation Canadians. He was not shy of girls as I was, very conscious of being younger than my group, and with the farm boy inferiority complex common in North America. Wynne Plumtre's parents (his father was an Episcopalian canon in the Toronto diocese) invited us to spend Christmas Day with them; they were engagingly hospitable, observing without ostentation elaborate English food rituals that were new to me. I did get the basic reading for the Jonson thesis done during the vacation, which was just as well, since putting the first draft together proved much harder than I had anticipated.

Living with John ensured that I 'grew up' socially. Living in the Hall contributed: it amused my undergraduate hallmates, many of them older than me, that I was called a 'warden'. By the spring we had shaken down into a community, and would make a point of sitting together in hall at Hart House, or going out for a glass of beer in the same group. It began to feel good to be confident and orientated, and at the same time independent. I recall the excitement of having a suit made for me, admittedly at a cheap tailor's, but never mind! Whether I was good for John's work I would not know. He was not by temperament scholastic.

Meanwhile there was still hard reality, the next year, to think about. I had assumed that my fellowship would be renewable and that I would work for my doctorate under Woodhouse. When I approached him, later than I should have done, it turned out that the endowment for my fellowship was specifically for one year's tenure. I had already missed the first flight of applications, for Harvard and

Yale and Princeton or Cornell, where he would have recommended applying. But there were still the American state universities, for instance Illinois and Wisconsin with sound English Departments, and there was Northwestern University, privately endowed, on the shore of Lake Michigan just north of Chicago. I applied to the three and received an offer from each, the most attractive from Northwestern, a fellowship without duties worth $800 and all fees, more than the pay of an assistant lecturer in London at that time. According to Woodhouse this was academically the best choice. He was, as not infrequently, right.

My thesis was finished and typed with its seventeenth-century spellings intact, examinations, written and oral, completed, and another new experience in prospect for the coming year. I had made some friends in Toronto whom I would see again, a hallmate, Kenneth Macalister, an undergraduate law student, and Claud Bissell, a graduate student of my vintage working on twentieth-century English literature. I had met, and got to know a little, Earle Birney, somewhat older than me, one of Sedgewick's students, who later made a name for himself in the first flight of Canadian poets and novelists with a half-whimsical, half-satirical war book called *Turvey* after its hero; he would be seen by mid-century as the doyen of Canadian writing. Teaching in the States in the depth of the Depression he had become a Communist; during a period in London he had acquired an English wife, and the two were developing into Trotskyists. There were interesting to watch and listen to, very different. I understand them better now than I did at that time.

John and I set out by rail for the west coast in the company of two English graduate students from Vancouver, a pleasant engaged couple. I left them and broke journey in Saskatchewan to visit with my stepfather. It was good to see him: the last time had been Christmas 1935. He had a small flat in Wakaw but we camped nights in the cottage, which was in good order. The lake was as lovely as ever, but I noticed, the first morning when I plunged off the jetty, that it was shallower; being spring fed it was suffering in the dry years. My boat was still afloat. He had a surprise for me: on the second day he produced my schoolmate Ted Bergerman, married, with at least one child, and headmaster of the Wakaw high school, where, in a couple of years, he had achieved an absolute improvement in the discipline and teaching. It may have helped that Ted was over 6 feet tall, strongly built, and although mild of manner, disinclined to stand any nonsense. I stayed several days, but it was still term time for Ted. I regret not having had more time with him. We never met again. He died in 1990.

Mother and the young ones, markedly larger, were at the station in Vancouver. She was pleased with me and not reticent about it, which I enjoyed, the more so when I told her about the Evanston fellowship, which I had kept as a surprise for her. They had bought a larger house, this one within a stone's throw of the bay, albeit on the landward side of the street. It was good to be home and among kin.

But life was not all plain sailing. The garden at the back abutted on a small park with tennis courts, and one after another my brothers Edward and Leo took me there and beat me roundly. I could not imagine why they should want to play with a duffer like me until mother let it slip that their father had been holding me up to them as a model. They did not crow about beating me and I did not have it in me to grudge them the restoration of their egos.

It was not long before I gravitated to the University Library, beautifully quiet during the vacation. John was there, resolved at length to finish his graduation essay, and Rodney Poisson drifted in occasionally. Leonard was away at his master's thesis. For the moment I was enjoying desultory shelf-sampling, became acquainted with Eliot and Auden, sensed an element of humbug in Pound for all the talent. I was just beginning to think that this would not be much of a way to spend a summer, when I ran into Professor Todd, who after exchanges of civilities and congratulating me, asked, 'How would you like to read a little Greek this summer?'

We met twice a week in his departmental study. I would go prepared to translate; he would listen and improve or correct, and at difficult points, of which there were many, show me how to proceed. At times he would talk, quietly and with what seemed to me uncalled-for diffidence, about the culture that what we were reading expressed and constituted. We began, as I recall, with the easier choruses from the *Orestia*. This involved an introduction to Greek metrics. He read the poetry quietly but with feeling, so that from listening to him I began to understand how the interaction, interplay and counterpoint so to speak, of vowel quantity and word stress and pitch and dramatic emphasis created and constituted an intensifying music. Then we turned to the plays he decided I should sample first *Agamemnon* and then, appropriately, *Electra*. The summer seemed not long enough. This was hard work for me, but there was no stress and the reward was rich.

I also learned something completely different. Rodney and his father had just finished building a twelve-foot sailing dinghy; he took me out in the eight-mile long harbour and showed me the first elements of seamanship. He was skilled himself, and a good teacher. I took to it, and as with mountaineering, still wish that the way of life I fell into had given me more time for this activity. Rodney and I had one 'adventure' which I set down here for my great-grandchildren.

We two had set off early on a fine Friday afternoon in mid-August, planning to cruise among the cluster of largely uninhabitable small islands off the mouth of Vancouver harbour. There we would put in each evening at some handy bay with a sandy beach, pull the dinghy up well beyond the tide mark, and them comb the beach for the main course in our evening meal, mussels and clams and if we were lucky a crab. These would go into a tin pot of seawater — this was before the days of pollution — and the contents would obligingly open when cooked. There would always be fresh water to drink (there was), which we would touch up from our half-bottle of Canadian Rye. After dinner we talked till night fell and the fire was dying out, then rolled up in our rugs and slept till dawn on the comfortable adjustable mattress of fine sand.

But late Saturday afternoon it came on to blow from the east, so instead of running up onto a beach we sailed up an inviting little inlet, a kind of miniature fjord, with a tiny beach at the end. Here we passed a relatively quiet night, and it did not rain. But next morning, although the wind had dropped somewhat, there was in the open water, as we could see, a considerable swell and it was by no means calm. Still, we were expected home that night, with about fifteen miles to go and the breeze not in our favour.

So Rodney decided we must get out into the open water and tack our way to North Vancouver. We waited for the ebb to begin. Then Rodney began to row the dinghy out while, my slacks in the boat, I walking beside it to steady it and keep its weight down until we were out of the shallow water. This went well; I had barely climbed aboard before we were in open water. Now was the moment to hoist one sail. 'Take the tiller, George; hold her as she is while I manage the sheet'. This went well: the sail went up, we were under way and sailing clear of the island.

What happened next neither of us remembers clearly. It was time to set course, for which Rodney must have the tiller; we must change places. To this day he blames himself; I for my part am conscious that as a duffer I may well have done something clumsy. For whatever reason, the dinghy jibed, went broadside to the wind, and slowly but relentlessly capsized. The retractable centreboard slid gently into the deep, and clinging to the boat I watched my slacks being carried away on the swell. This was still some 20 feet high, but well spaced and subsiding. The water was comfortably warm, and in our kapok jackets we were in no immediate danger. Moreover it was Sunday and no later than 9:00. In a couple of hours the pleasure boats would be out.

In fact one appeared before we had done more than assess our situation. The dinghy would not sink, but she was held on her side by the sail, now full of water. We would have to get this in and somehow stowed before we could think of righting the dinghy. The boat that spotted us was an antique, what in Vancouver was called a 'putt putt maru', that is a two-stroke Japanese commercial fishing craft, scarcely twice the length of the dinghy, and evidently sold off as obsolete by its owners, for its crew of two were Caucasian, and the boat from its look and performance had seen better days. They spotted us from the crest of a swell and came down into its trough, where they wallowed dangerously close to the foundered dinghy: they had a line ready to tow us to safety. Rodney told them with many thanks that they did not have the power to budge the waterlogged dinghy and sail. But they would not take no for an answer, so Rodney accepted the line, and made it fast to the dinghy and advised them to put some water between the two craft before they started to tow. Paying out line they made it to the next crest and rope became tense. Within a second they were in danger of capsizing, but careful Rodney had made their line fast with a single-bow knot for instant release. It worked, which was just as well, for their boat with a heavy cast-iron-cased engine, would probably have sunk, and I don't recall that they were wearing life jackets. We were relieved to see the last of that kind but misguided pair.

It took about two hours of hard, awkward work to get the sail furled after a fashion and inboard, and the dinghy righted, but she was full of water, and of course, the bailer had gone. At least the oars, stowed and tied under the thwarts, were safe. And our timing was lucky. Just as we had finished righting the dinghy we heard a hail, this time from a more powerful craft, which took us aboard and towed our dinghy, water and all, to Gibson's Island in the mouth of Howe Sound. Here while I lurked in my boxers with the dinghy, Rodney borrowed a bailer from a summer cottage. We dried out, so to speak, and braced ourselves for the now ten-mile row to Rodney's home on the North Shore: without a centreboard and with a contrary wind, we had no option. Once more, on arrival there, I sat trouserless in the boat while Rodney fetched a pair to lend me; he also lent me the fare home — my money was in my trouser pocket — and after embarrassed civilities to his parents, whom I had met only once before, I made my way home, by bus, then ferry, then tram, in a garment sized for a man six inches taller than me, to face my mother, whom Rodney would have telephoned and forewarned that I would be late. Other considerations apart I had lost one of her favourite rugs. And my legs were shockingly sunburned.

Thus the summer of 1937 was variously richer than the one before it. Earle Birney, whom I had met in Toronto, and his wife were in Vancouver. There was also Roy Daniells, much later Head of Department at British Columbia, just back from England. Both were five years older than me, and their talk was all about London, and theatre and art galleries and the Reading Room of the British Museum Library, a world with unmistakably larger horizons. It struck me that this larger world was what my mother had in mind when she spoke of the importance of travel. I had heard of two-year scholarships to Great Britain, one awarded annually to a Canadian from each Canadian province by an organisation called the Imperial Order of Daughters of the Empire, and while I was aware that my Northwestern fellowship, awarded in the first instance for one year, might be renewable, I knew nothing about its English Department, or whether I would want to stay on for doctoral work. I would look at the situation.

In the Registrar's Department I was told that I.O.D.E was represented in the University by the Dean of Women, Dr Mary Bollert: I should make an appointment with her secretary to see her; she in turn named one for the next day. In the male folklore of North American universities Deans of Women were formidable, overprotective ogresses. This Dean, however, proved a charmer. She did not discourage me from applying, and kept me in conversation for some time. This, it later dawned on me, was the interview mentioned in the information packet. For my part I applied with some hesitation; I did not see myself as the type. In any event I would learn in November whether I had been awarded the scholarship, in plenty of time to make other arrangements. I was pretty confident of getting something good in the States if it came to that.

My dear mother was very pleased for me with the prospect of having two years in England, remembering how much she had enjoyed and learned from her two long visits in Europe. At the same time she did not care for the notion of my being away for so long.

5
NORTHWESTERN UNIVERSITY 1937–1938

This time I travelled East through Canada as far as Winnipeg, crossing the Cordillers by a new route through the mountains and thence after changing lines and stations, south to Chicago where Northwestern University occupied a large part of Evanston, the first suburb to the north of that city on the western shore of Lake Michigan. Evanston was a trim, neat community governed by the Women's Christian Temperance Union, a last bastion of prohibition after its federal repeal. The University was a very wealthy private foundation, known nationally for its Economics Department and Business School, the latter not yet eclipsed by that of Harvard. It was efficiently run. The University Information Service was excellent, the Bookstore adequate, the Library very promising. It was unitary, not collegiate. Most undergraduates lived in fraternity or sorority houses.

By the end of my first day on campus I was a member of the University with a library card, a bank account and accommodation, this a room in a lodging house kept by Mrs Cady, the widow of a missionary to the Chinese. The room was a trifle Spartan, but adequately furnished and spotlessly clean, the bed was comfortable, the water hot. We were half a dozen lodgers, civil and agreeable enough, a senior medical student, one undergraduate with a Polish name who did not belong to a fraternity, three graduates and a young lawyer in a local firm. Mrs Cady did not provide meals and the University had no cafeteria, but there was an excellent lunch counter in a drugstore a block down the street, a Greek restaurant where, once you knew the menu and were known, you could eat tolerably well, and a Chinese laundry.

Registration for graduate courses took place the day after I arrived, at tables along three walls of the university gymnasium. You identified yourself at the door and were sent to a numbered table with your designated advisor's name in prominent view on a card. Mine read 'Professor W. F. Bryan'. The man had a strong featured but agreeable face; he looked about 50, which seemed old to me. All my data were in his filing basket. He wasted little time: 'Welcome Mr Kane; we are glad to have you in our graduate school. Here are the courses I would advise you to take.' This was clearly not a prescription, but it had an authoritative ring. He named a course on *Beowulf*, one semester, and Old French and Medieval Literature, each two semesters. It was up to me whether I registered for more. I had a sense that I ought to do as he said, but the Old French worried me and I asked why he advised it: the answer was a brisk three minute lecture, very casually delivered, about its influence in the formation of Western European culture. This was not like Toronto.

It turned out that Bryan himself taught the *Beowulf* course. He had been a student of Friedrich Klaeber, and for his part knew the text of the poem virtually by heart. He taught translation much as Lemuel Robertson had, with meticulous concern for exact meaning, reminding us that we were not poets, but students learning a language. He explained how the structure of the poem was designed, functional rather than casual, and as we read showed us something of the sophisticated rhetoric of the best Old English poetry. We translated about half the poem in class during the semester, but were responsible for the whole in the examination. Competition was friendly enough, but relentless. I soon realised that the low opinion of Old English as a subject of study among the Vancouver students was a consequence of poor Macdonald's teaching.

Old French was new ground. Nothing in the excellent French teaching at St Peter's had prepared me for the dry-as-dust phonology of M. K. Pope's book with which our excellent professor, whose name I am ashamed to have forgotten, opened the course. In Clawson's Old English course I had developed an antipathy toward 'sound laws', historical phonology as a theoretical subject, and in the Old French instance my ignorance of Vulgar Latin depressed me. I came to terms with this problem by applying Pope's laws in reverse, so to speak, and when one day the professor actually commended me on the range of my Latin, I 'came clean' and he was amused. Presently we began to read the *Chanson de Roland*, using the current Oxford edition of the time; the glossary was adequate, and the professor made up for its indifferent annotation. To read *Beowulf* and the *Chanson* side by side, so to speak, was exciting. The greater sophistication of *Beowulf* and the remoteness from the time of composition of the culture it preserved was set off by the combination, in the French poem, of crude execution and vitality, potential for growth. In the second semester we read extensively under another professor: his selections, which later on, reading the whole works, I recognised as judicious, were from *Ywain* and *Cliges*. I was not sorry to have taken Bryan's advice.

Much of my teaching to this point had focused on the uniqueness of the personality in individual writers. But I was beginning to appreciate how much understanding of that unique personality was enhanced if time and place and cultural circumstances were accepted as prime factors in all particulars of its formation and thus of its literary expression of itself. The third of my recommended courses, Medieval Literature, was certainly to that effect.

It was taught by John Webster Spargo, whose *Vergil and the Necromancers* is still a standard work. His manner of proceeding was quite new to me. The course was minutely planned. Spargo would sit with a small file box of cards before him, and begin by naming the topic of the day: to give extreme instances, the Desert Fathers, Irish monasticism, Icelandic oral composition. Then, taking a card out of the box, he would give us author, title and date of a book and its library reference number. Next he would sketch what the book had to offer, specify what we should read, whole or part, and invite questions. At the end of 50 minutes he would have treated thus a variable number of books, depending on their scope and importance, on subjects relevant to the understanding of Western culture from the collapse of the Empire to, say, Duns Scotus's day, leaving the Anglo-Saxons and post-Carolingian French to their departments. We met twice a week; at the end of each class he would specify recommended (*sc.* required) reading from the book or books discussed that day, and it quickly became apparent that it was advisable to keep up with the reading. The books were lodged on reserve shelves behind the desk in the huge Main Reading Room of the University Library, to be read there but available on weekend loan. This worked very well; we were virtually the *Beowulf* group with one addition, a mature student back from teaching for an M.A.

I liked Spargo and found him easy to learn from. In other circumstances I might well have stayed at Northwestern to work for my doctorate under him, but sometime in November I learned that I had been awarded the I.O.D.E scholarship for British Columbia for 1938–1940. I indulge myself with a story about him. He wrote very favourably about my first-semester examination paper, but graded it A-. I suppose this was cheek, but I called on him, paper in hand, and asked him most civilly what I had done wrong: why, if as appeared, he had liked it he had given me a minus. He looked coolly at me for a moment, the murmured 'NO dates' and grinned broadly. I observed, quite fatuously, that dates interrupt the flow of discourse. His 'one pays for elegance' put me in my place. For the second-semester examination I prepared a list of dates and memorised it. In the examination I set it down on the first pages of the answer book, but also took pains to put some dates in my answers like currants in a bun. This amused him, but he was right of course. Many's the time when it has irritated me to read a complex historical account which runs, page after page, without a single date.

These three courses were intellectually the most rewarding of my graduate student years. It was worth learning Old English to be able to read *Beowulf.*

I had learned the difference between phonology in the abstract and its practical use; and I was aware of a horizon of cultural history which embraced the Desert Fathers and *Njáls saga*, with a reading list to map it. I took two other courses, of one semester. One was a graduate lecture-course on the history of literary criticism in English by a professor engagingly named Zera S. Fink This was a superbly organised performance. Fink could have made a book out of his lectures without much labour, but then he would have had to put together another set. He was an interesting subject as an academic: I sat in for a couple of weeks on an undergraduate course he was teaching on the Romantic poets, hoping to improve my attitude towards them, and learned about the level of intellectual content thought appropriate for sorority girls whose fathers made endowments to the University. The second graduate course, a seminar on Coleridge and Wordsworth taught by George G. Fox, not more than thirty-five and a 'full' professor, was first rate and I learned to respect its two subjects.

I have lost the friends I made at North Western, inevitably, I suppose, by the intervention of the Hitler war. One was a somewhat older lodging housemate, Erich Mueller, an assistant professor of German from the University of Alberta working for his doctorate on a year's leave. He was in his early forties, had a wife and one child whom he could not afford to bring to Evanston; he had been caught up in the last months of the Great War. A quiet shy man and a fine person, but I had trouble with him for wishing to speak German: we had to come to an arrangement about this in which we shared the time for each language. Another was a friend of his in Germanic graduate studies, a Swede named Sten Gunnar Flygt, my first experience of someone from that nation who was not a Minnesota farmer. Then there was Claude Henry, my running mate, so to speak, in class. He was very pleasant quiet company; the two of us used, when the library closed at 10.00, to slip down by the elevated railway to Howard Avenue, the southern side of which was in Chicago, for a drink or two. Then there was Carl Bode, a junior graduate student whom I met in Fox's seminar. Erich I saw once more in September 1938 on my way east. He brought his wife and young son to the station in Edmonton where my transcontinental train stopped for water and fuel and catering stores. We had a good half-hour together and I was glad to learn that he was going to get his associate professorship. But the reunion was sombre, for the Munich crisis had begun to mount. Carl Bode I met again in Senate House in the sixties, when James Sutherland was about to introduce him to me as the American cultural attaché and Carl brushed the introduction aside with, 'Professor Kane won't remember me of course but I admired his seminar paper on Wordsworth and mysticism'. He was liberal with invitations to embassy receptions. Claude I never saw or heard of again. I suppose he was swallowed by the war.

So back to Vancouver after a good year. This time I travelled by car with a Canadian engineering student, Bill King, sharing the driving and paying half the cost of the journey. No more affluent than me, Bill had bought the car, a Ford roadster, in Chicago for a good price and would recoup by selling it in Seattle for considerably more. This was fine, and so, I hoped, would be sending my trunk home as unaccompanied luggage. The drive, for which we took a leisurely week, was interesting and Bill was agreeable company. But my trunk did not arrive until mid-August and then only after much fuss.

The summer was far from boring. I read more Greek with Professor Todd, notably from *Prometheus Bound* and *The Frogs*, which latter I found very difficult, as I had found Terence. Pindar, whom Todd thought me about ready to tackle, was even harder. All this was both taxing and rewarding. Ivan Niven whom I had occasionally seen in Chicago had stayed there to work through the summer, so there was no mountain walking, and I did not dare disturb Rodney, who had at length settled down to serious academic work, with talk about sailing. John and I played golf occasionally, but neither of us was much good at it. And John, for that matter, had not yet finished his graduation essay.

I tried to write but found it difficult to settle down, probably because I had nothing to say. Fox had casually spoken about the possibility of making my seminar essay into an article, but the subject did not really attract me; I had been getting that 'One impulse from a vernal wood' episode out of my system and the catharsis was successful. I must have been subconsciously aware that a phase of my life was coming to an end.

Two years seemed in prospect a long time to be out of my by now quite comfortably oriented world, to be away. I had the Canadian advantage of being at ease in the States, of having no sense of being a stranger or standing out. All Canadians are said to feel innately superior to the 'great republic to the south of us'. England was different, especially when seen from the West Coast, where the financial refugees from Britain had set the tone. Would I match up in England to the required standards of the Daughters of the Empire? Moreover that alien, potentially exacting world had sinister undertones in the progress of Hitler, of Franco and his vicious war, of Mussolini's jackal foray into Abyssinia.

And I had academic misgivings about graduate study in England. To have studied in England was vogue in the Canadian university world, but when it came to deciding *where* to study the decision was not simple. Oxford was not recommended. 'They make you take another B.A. there!' The Cambridge English school was gnawing its own entrails in feuds. London? 'At least they leave you to yourself there'. Roy Daniells had been at King's where Jack Isaacs's brilliant comet was in transit, but his interests were to me ultramodern. That left University College with R. W. Chambers about to retire from the Quain chair, whereupon C. J. Sisson, the Lord Northcliffe Professor, would take over the department. Woodhouse had spoken well of Sisson, whose field was the seventeenth century, and I had applied there. But British Universities did not seem to publish calendars, and I had no notion what to expect. It was necessary to suppress uncomfortable misgivings.

Taking leave of the family, especially my mother, was not easy. We had come to be very close since the move to Vancouver. I knew she wanted me to go abroad for the experience and was suppressing her concern about the ugly situation there. As for the children, they would be different people when I came home in 1940 and I would have to get to know them again.

I arranged two stopovers on my journey East. The first was in Saskatchewan with my stepfather. We drove from Wakaw to Muenster, where there was a considerable gathering at my grandmother's home. My grandfather had died in 1935,

George Kane before leaving for England.

two months short of his eighty-ninth birthday. It is in my mind that he was glad to go; he had been a very active man and in his later years, indeed already in 1934 when I saw him last, was virtually chairbound and very bored.

In two snapshots I have from that occasion my grandmother looks well, the many young cousins already grown out of recognition, my almost-brother cousin a novice in a Benedictine cassock. The second stop was in Montreal, where one of my father's sisters lived. I stayed four days with her and her husband, during which time my grandmother Kane, with whom I had been corresponding for almost twenty years (grandmother Kopp had been very punctilious about this), came up from the country with another aunt. I liked them all, as my mother had when she was taken east by my father to meet his family during their few months of marriage. I wish there had been time to get to know them a little. We spoke of a meeting in the spring of 1940 when I would be coming back, but when at length in late June 1945 I did go home I was not my own master and travelled on a service warrant by way of New York.

I never saw my grandmother Kane or those engaging aunts again and it was more than fifty years before I spoke to another Kane kinsman, a first cousin, this time also called George Kane, so named after my father who had become a legendary figure for the next generation. This was a cruel trick of luck.

From Montreal it was a short journey to Quebec, where there had been a large element of Kanes in Montcalm's army when he fought and was beaten by General Wolfe — not that I had any notion of this in 1938. The immediate present was exciting enough. For one thing Kenneth McAllister turned up on the station platform in Montreal, also bound for England. For another, the setting was dramatic, climaxing in our arrival in Quebec, where the train crawled along the foot of a cliff with the Citadel towering above it, dwarfing even the liner we would be boarding. For the third that liner, the Canadian Pacific Empress of Britain, would carry almost no passengers except eleven male students with scholarships of one sort or another. Another passenger I knew was John Logan. The I.O.D.E. scholar from Ontario, Bobby Allan, was going to Oxford to read English. The others, but for a French Canadian Law student going back for a second year, were first timers, I.O.D.E or Rhodes Scholars. In first class there were possibly a dozen British business men going home.

By the second day the Captain had learned of us. We were invited to spend a morning on the bridge, where we watched with great interest the tricky navigation through Cabot Straight out of the St Lawrence mouth into the Atlantic. To top this the Captain gave us the run of the ship; it would simplify catering if we fed in the first class dining room.

The crossing was by no means smooth, but I found that I did not get seasick and revelled in being on deck in rough weather. The dining room stewards were a living lesson in English to us; it had to be English because they came from

Liverpool which we knew was in England. They for their part would challenge us to eat our way through the yardlong lunch and dinner menus. We did not talk about the international political situation. When we disembarked at Southampton searchlights were playing over the harbour. It was only an exercise but ominous enough.

6
LONDON 1938–1939

Everything in England, on arrival, matched expectation, the tiny locomotives and carriages, the foggy platform at Waterloo, the miniature taxicabs, the Edwardian furnishings in the Imperial Hotel in Russell Square where we stayed at the recommendation of the 'old hand' in our party, the hot milk for the breakfast cornflakes, the abominable coffee. This was the real thing.

The hotel was handy to University College; I was in the Registrar's Department by 10.00 next morning, and made an appointment to see Sisson the following day. The College did not have a list of recommended lodgings, but there was one in the Senate House in Malet Street. Here I learned that there was little accommodation left. From that little I chose a bed-sitting room in Hampstead in an elegant-fronted Edwardian mansion. The room was of grand proportions, but scantily furnished and heated by a minute gas fire that one fed with shillings. I should have known better. In my ignorance of London I decided not to breakfast there, but to pick something up on the way to work, as I had often done in Toronto and always in Evanston. That was my second mistake. I was miserably cold in my huge room; there was no place in the vicinity of my lodgings where I could pick up breakfast, and nothing but one wretched Lyons in the Tottenham Court Road where the best bet was tea and toast and a roll, and the college refectory did not open until 'morning coffee' time. I felt sorry for myself, but it was my own fault. Had I made enquiries in Vancouver before leaving I would have learned of London House in Bloomsbury, a sort of residential club for Commonwealth male graduate students, founded and endowed by the William Goodenough Trust. Naturally there was no vacancy at that time of year but I put my name on the waiting list and eventually I got a room in the spring when the Antipodeans tend to go home. In the meantime I shivered in Hampstead until Christmas, after which, at intervals, I worked in Bodley and the Cambridge University Library or shared a flat in West Hampstead with a Canadian doctoral student in the Chemistry Department in U.C.L. where we were warm enough and got our own breakfast. I was learning about life in England.

My third mistake became evident during my interview with Professor Sisson. Hitherto all the academics I had met except Clawson, who was unnaturally shy, were outgoing personalities who seemed to enjoy the company of students and gave freely of their time; Sisson was different. Woodhouse, who was no fool, had spoken well of him, in effect had sent me to work with him. In all the years I knew him at University College I never once saw Sisson lower his guard. He comes into this narrative again. But I labour the account of that first interview because there is a certain amount of fiction in print about how I came to work on editing *Piers Plowman* under R. W. Chambers.

Woodhouse had coached me well for that first interview on how to present my proposal. It was at the project stage only. I would undoubtedly have to narrow the field, etc. I spoke my piece carefully with all Woodhouse's caveats in mind. Sisson gave it scarcely a moment's consideration. He carefully pinched out his home-rolled cigarette for further use, rose to his feet saying 'Please accompany me', and with no more ceremony led me down the passage to the study of the Quain Professor, R. W. Chambers. He knocked, ushered me in, and said 'Here is Kane from Canada, whom we have been expecting' and left. In my cynical old age I rephrase this into a candid 'Here is Kane, etc. I know nothing about his subject and ought probably to have discouraged him from coming to us. But since you have a book at press in which Milton figures prominently I pass him on to you. Please get me out of this box.'

I came to know Sisson pretty well during my time at University College London. He was a complex personality, less malicious than on the defensive, as if he sensed himself under threat from persons abler than himself. Yet he invariably spoke with admiration and great respect of Chambers, whose intellect was unquestionably superior to his own. Possibly this was because Chambers did not demand respect and could give a disarming impression of other-worldliness. Chambers was not at all physically impressive, small of stature and without any striking facial features. But that ordinariness hid an inner strength that had expressed itself in late middle age during his time as a stretcher bearer in the mud of Flanders.

His students and his colleagues worshipped him. A year or so before I met him he had been gravely ill and recovery left him with little physical energy. But I was to find his mind sharp and deep, albeit deliberate. Before he was translated to the Quain Professorship in 1922 he had been College Librarian for eleven years, during which time he published extensively in the Old English field. All the while the scope of his interest and scholarship was broad; his 1935 life of Thomas More is still respected. When I met him in 1938 I was not aware that his *Man's Unconquerable Mind*, a kind of spiritual call to arms against totalitarianism, was at press.

He was cordially welcoming, but it was soon apparent that he was not too interested in my carefully prepared description of my thesis plans. He listened very civilly but did not respond by revealing his own general interest in heroic poetry. Indeed his response was a half-hour anecdotal reminiscence that would have been fascinating in other circumstances. I left his room with an armful of books

R. W. Chambers.

on the Germanic Dark Ages and an injunction to come back when I had read them. This was to be my treatment for the next while. Reading about Widsith and Odoacer and Theodoric was not altogether without interest, but plainly there was in the short term no thesis subject for a student whose ignorance of the field was almost total, and knowledge of Anglo-Saxon language and culture trifling.

By mid-October the implication of my situation was becoming clear to me, and I did the rounds of the English Departments of the other colleges of the University of London cap in hand, so to speak, for Sisson had my letters of recommendation. Even without these I found everyone I addressed very kind and understanding. But all, regretfully, they said, and regrettably, I thought, professed themselves not competent to supervise the project. I did not know of Professor Willcock of Royal Holloway College, who was interested in renaissance critical thinking. From what I came to know of her later she might well have taken me on. So would E. W. M. Tillyard, to whom Woodhouse should have sent me in the first instance notwithstanding the disarray of English studies in Cambridge. So here I was, faced with the dismal prospect of returning to Vancouver without a doctorate and forfeiting the remaining five terms of my scholarship. No doubt I would 'find something' for 1939–1940 somewhere in the States, but there would be a gray, if not a black mark on my record.

In the last week of October I spelled out my predicament to Chambers. My Milton project was a good one. I had the languages, some knowledge of Renaissance theory from my M.A. work on Ben Jonson, and all the energy in the world. The Germanic world of the dark ages was unquestionably interesting, but I was not equipped for research there; even my Anglo-Saxon was the merest smattering. He let me talk, and when I stopped there was a pause.

I can recall Chambers sitting sidelong at his desk so as to face me. His back was to the window; I could read nothing from his expression. At length, and it seemed a long while, he swivelled on his chair to fetch from a drawer a handful of what looked like pamphlets, checked their titles quickly, and handed them to me. 'You might like a change of reading. Take these away and come back to me when you have read them.'

Back in the English Library I found that the pamphlets were what I would learn to call 'offprints', excerpts from learned periodicals. Scanning them I found that they were elements in an evidently sustained controversy between Chambers and a person named Grattan on one side and a variety of opponents who wrote in support of an article in the *Cambridge History of English Literature* by J. M. Manly — I knew that name — proposing that *Piers Plowman* was by several authors. I fetched volume one of the *CHEL* from its shelf and settled down to read the Manly proposition. It was unquestionably written as if asserting a certainty. This *Piers Plowman* was the poem I had been sent to read by my teacher as an undergraduate, and found unreadable. Back in the offprints I began to get some sense of the scale of the disagreement. I did not have an opinion. Of the two parties I found Chambers and his collaborator the more temperate in their conduct of the argument, indeed the more effective debaters. They favoured single authorship, but wrote of a need for better texts of the poem before the issue could be settled.

Among the habitual readers in the Library was a man a little older than myself (I judged) who sat, day after day, working at an impressive-looking file. We had reached a nod and smile acquaintance, no more because he was evidently very busy whereas I, with no substantial undertaking in hand, tended not to stay until closing time. This man must have noticed my comings and goings, and that on this occasion I returned with offprints that sent me to the shelf and *CHEL*. At the end of the morning when I stood up to break for lunch he followed suit and as he closed the library door behind me he said 'I see Chambers is after you'. We lunched together.

He was Alex (A. G.) Mitchell, an Australian graduate of Sydney with a scholarship who, in consequence of Antipodean rhythm, was in the fifth of his six terms of residence for the Ph.D. He had come to U.C.L. without a subject, but with a good basis of Old and Middle English, and had promptly been put to work by Chambers, who had assigned him editing Prologue and Passus I–IV of the C text of *Piers Plowman*, some 2000 lines of verse from what seemed to me a great many manuscripts. He planned to submit his thesis and take his oral at the end of the Easter term. Not far into our conversation that first day he asked — I forget the apropos — 'Don't you realise that Chambers is recruiting you?' He may have been right; or, as is conceivable — when Sisson received my letter of application and the papers went with it, he took the lot to Chambers with 'Here's one for you' or some such words. Even the medieval courses Bryan at Evanston prescribed for me may have been a factor.

Having very carefully read and reread Manly's *CHEL* piece and the offprints and the periodical articles I was very much of two minds about getting involved. Unquestionably Mitchell's circumstances were enviable. Chambers was pleased with his nearly finished thesis; he would go home with a doctorate to a job. But he had come with a solid base of Old and Middle English. To acquire that asset I would, early in my five terms and two months, have to learn to read Middle English in a real sense, to read fourteenth-, fifteenth- and sixteenth-century book hands, and hardest of all, how to go about 'editing'. Of this last I knew only, from my *Poetics* course, that it tended to be a controversial procedure, and from my Oxford *Chanson de Roland* textbook, that it was difficult. I had learned of the labour of collation and the tedium of checking from Mitchell. Beyond those details, unknown territory lay. Mitchell listened patiently to all my concerns; his counter was not helpful: Chamber's invitation was both a compliment and a challenge. I was left to weigh up all those near-impossibilities against the consideration that if I succeeded and had that degree I would be a free agent again and could go back to Canada and my beloved Renaissance. But for the last consideration I put my concerns to Chambers. His answer was cruelly to the point: 'The time is yours to use'. So I gave in, and he did not delay in setting me to work.

The doctoral project he assigned without discussion was a critical edition of the last three passus of what Skeat had called the B version of *Piers Plowman*, about 1300 lines of text preserved in sixteen early copies and a black-letter print made from a lost manuscript. The object was to reconstruct the presumptive exclusive common ancestor of those copies from the evidence they afforded, to present all that evidence systematically, and to support my interpretation of it in an introduction and notes. My work would begin with collation of sixteen of the copies with a seventeenth, the latter selected because it appeared to have been the least corrupted in transmission. This, the base text, was to be MS Laud Miscellany 581 in the Bodleian Library, already singled out by Skeat and printed in his editions.

For this work Chambers put at my disposal his photostats of all the B copies not in London and wrote the magic letters that made me a reader in the British Museum Library and Manuscript Room. There was a stationer in the City who would provide foolscap ruled and squared appropriately for collation. With Skeat's B text beside me the Laud hand was easy to learn. By the first week in November I was well under way.

The second copy in the collation series recommended by Chambers (on the finding of an early graduate student, Elsie Blackman) was BM Additional 35287. The hand of this copy was vastly more difficult, a cursive anglicana of various degrees of formality and proportion, much corrected, moreover, by both the main scribe and two other hands. I combed the shelves of the Manuscript Room and found nothing to help me. Johnson and Jenkinson's *English Court Hands* was not to the point and if the Manuscript Room had a copy of Cappelli's *Dizionario di Abbreviature latine ed italiane* I did not find it. In the Manuscript Room there was a sort of glass booth secluding a young man with a severe expression whose head was almost always immersed in a book or manuscript. If one stood in front of him long enough he would eventually look up and be very helpful. His name was Francis Wormald; in the course of years of my bothering him we became good friends.

When the Manuscript Room closed at 4:45 it was back to the College Library and reading first *Piers* B, then A and C. As background reading Chambers recommended Jusserand's *English Wayfaring life in the Middle Ages* and Owst's various books, notably *Literature and Pulpit.* They were not without interest, but at that stage I would have learned more about *Piers* from Dorothy Owen's *Piers Plowman and some Medieval French Allegories* and de Deguileville's *Pelerinage de Vie humaine.* Neither of my Chaucer teachers had said anything about the importance of the dream-vision genre in thirteenth and fourteenth century vernacular poetry; it did not figure in my Old French courses, and while Spargo must have shown us the great Latin instances, I do not recall his relating the genre to the vernacular. I had never heard the term 'estates satire'. My Benedictine schooling had based me soundly in practical theology, especially the eschatological side, but I had everything to learn about the hostility between friars and regulars, the corruption of the monasteries, the worldliness of the papacy. As for the politics in Passus II–IV of all versions, McKisack's *Fourteenth Century* volume in the Oxford series, only just out, would have made them meaningful at first reading.

Except for a misguided Christmas visit to the Lake District where I saw nothing but snow I spent the vacation in Oxford, where I took over Tommy Allen's digs in Merton Street while he went to France. There I lived in pampered comfort; his landlady went to the unusual extent of providing dinner. By day I checked my collations of Laud and Rawlinson Poetry 38 against the manuscripts, and struggled in the indifferent light of Duke Humfrey with Corpus Christi College MS 201, which was kept in Bodley. Rawlinson and Corpus afforded my first experience of variants strikingly different from Laud, the base text. But the Corpus copy was even harder to read than Add. 35287, not because of its hand, which was easy, but because of blur from the writing on the other side of leaves. It was only in the 60s when Duke Humfrey was closed for refurbishing and one read manuscripts in the New Bodleian that, in good summer sunlight, I acquired some confidence in my collation of that copy.

The new Oxford term drove me out of Oxford to my chilly Hampstead room. To escape I made for Cambridge where Mitchell had recommended lodgings. He must have stayed there in summer, for without being actually cold my room and bathroom were damp and depressing. The landlady's breakfast was adequate but she did not provide dinner. When I had discovered that every one of Cambridge's tearooms and cafes closed after teatime she directed me to a fish and chip shop 'down the street'. I was not long in Cambridge on that visit, but long enough to acquire a profound dislike of fish and chips. My luck was out in another respect: the day before my arrival in Cambridge the central heating system of the fine new University Library failed. I worked there in my greatcoat just long enough to collate its three B text copies and then made for Oxford; the Trinity and Newnham copies would have to wait until spring.

Here luckily Tommy's landlady found comfortable digs for me with a friend who did not however provide dinner. Here I was further lucky: by arrangement between Tommy and the Principal of Postmasters' at Merton I was allowed to dine there regularly, formally as Tommy's guest, provided we two took care of any financial adjustments without bothering him. I was in Duke Humfrey mornings the moment it opened, for I needed a place with a good light, and worked there until it closed, but I fear I did not spend many evenings reading *Piers* in my digs during that Oxford stay.

Back in London when my Oxford collation and checking was done, I gave up my chilly lodging and shared a flat in West Hampstead with a Canadian postgraduate student in the Chemistry Department at University College until a vacancy at London House came up. The flat was adequately warm and we got our own breakfast, but neither of us knew much about cooking, or indeed had much time for it, and although we parted amicably I was glad to move to Bloomsbury.

It was possible now to foresee that after another short visit to Oxford and a longer spring stay in Cambridge, I would have finished collation and a first check against the actual manuscripts, except of course the important copy in the Huntington Library in Pasadena. For this copy excellent photographs made for Chambers at the Huntington would have to do. I could fairly assume that my data would then be solid enough for the next stage, putting together the critical apparatus. For this the only model I knew of in Middle English was Skeat's with, of course, Mitchell's development of this.

At this stage I did not feel myself ready to think forward about decisions about 'good' and 'bad' readings. Apart from what I had noted in the controversy literature, most of it pretty obvious argument from contextual appropriateness, I had only preferences formed during collation and checking. I was acutely aware of my inexperience of the language, my ignorance of the metrical form and, above all, of any larger overall meaning of the poem.

Such supervision as I received was over tea in the Refectory when I happened to be working in College. Chamber's own editing, apart from a revision of Wyatt's edition of *Beowulf*, had largely consisted of erudite and judicious commentary on cruces of detail in Old English poems that survived in single copies, critical of the handling of those cruces by predecessors and proposing improvements. I do not recall his discussing theoretical points beyond expressing the opinion that Greg's *Calculus of Variants* was a complicated substitute for common sense. He had no great opinion of McKerrow, which is not surprising. His recommended reading for me was Housman's preface or introduction to his editions of Manilius and Juvenal's *Satires*, Westcott and Hort's introduction to their 1881 edition of *The New Testament in the Original Greek*, and Moore's 1889 *Contributions to the Textual Criticism of the Divine Comedy*. After reading Westcott and Hort I formed the opinion that the New Testament cannot be edited to general satisfaction. I learned nothing from Moore. But one of Westcott and Hort's footnotes sent me to Griesbach's 1796 *Novvm Testamentvm Graece* where I learned the first of the game rules, 'Difficilior lectio potior'. In my experience of editing and teaching, learning how to apply that principle is a good beginning. Another helpful beginner's book would have been Havet's *Manuel de critique verbale*. Maas's *Textkritik* and Pasquali's *Storia della Tradizione e Critica del Testo* had only recently come out, and what with his illness and *Man's Unconquerable Mind* it is not surprising that Chambers missed them. They would have given me some sense of orientation. But I put my concerns about later procedures aside and set about assembling a critical apparatus, a straightforward practical undertaking.

Life was by no means all work. My patron the I.O.D.E was in liaison with a British institution, the Victoria League. I first learned of this from receiving an expensive looking invitation to an At Home in what my *London A-Z* showed me was the Belgravia of the English novelists. My first inclination, in ignorance of the term 'At Home', was to decline. But curiosity got the better of me, and having accepted I found that the object of this League was not to preserve the memory of the Queen Victoria whom I had read about in Lytton Strachey's biography but to make Commonwealth students feel at home in Great Britain. I don't know about making us 'feel at home'; that was a tall order. There was one quite personable man of my age, from Toronto of all Canadian cities, who told me that he could not stand any more of England and was going home next week for good. But the League certainly knew how to make one feel welcome. At such receptions and the dinner parties and weekends in country houses to which one was asked the mix of age and genders by the hosts was very skilful. One did get to know the English a little, and the England outside London. There were competing attractions in the theatre, opera and ballet, all affordable, the excellent English and French films and always the museums. There were pilgrimages: two, not conventional, come to mind. Alex Mitchell wanted to see Limehouse, the setting of detective stories he had enjoyed. It took some finding, but the weather behaved by providing a thick fog. In return I made him climb the Monument with me. I got to know London a little; one evening I took a girl who lived in South Kensington home after an evening at a West End cinema, only to find the iron gates of the Underground closing when I had seen her home. It was a long walk to my lodging by the only route I knew then, ending in a weary climb of Chalk Farm Road and Haverstock Hill with the pubs closed and only a cup of tea to be had from the very occasional street stall. It would not have cost much more than a pound to take a taxi, but I was not aware of this. One long weekend I made an excursion to Paris to see an Evanston girlfriend who had been in my Old French seminars. She was being 'finished' by a season in the home of an aged countess with a very old house on the Île de la Cité. I was to be inspected by the Countess, who invited me to lunch. The inside of the house was a period piece, the Countess elegantly frail and gracious. To my inner glee my St Peter's French served me well enough; the Countess commented that it was 'accenté' but she added with a smile, not so gravely as that of a pair of girls from Montreal whom she had had with her the previous year. Nowadays I am gently mocked if I say *j'irai* rather than *je vais aller*, and my imperfect subjunctives are labelled *très chic*. There is no justice. In Oxford Tommy Allen had made many friends and during my second stay there I saw something of the lighter side of undergraduate life, to which latter almost all the overseas scholarship holders were consigned. Indeed I can claim to have climbed out of a number of colleges. If it had a more serious side I did not see this, for I was in Bodley every day until it closed, and the other readers there did not look like undergraduates.

Early in the summer term of 1939, having drunk to Mitchell's doctorate and seen him off at Tilbury, I went into retreat in the London House library, which as often as not, I had to myself. It was not easy to shut out the unmistakeable likelihood of war with Germany, but I did manage to put together a critical apparatus that combined completeness of information and clarity with economy of space, and to begin the checking process. But in mid-August I was brought to a stop.

Already in autumn 1938 in consequence of the September war scare, the governing bodies of the constituent colleges of the University had begun to consider emergency measures. University College in Central London, as one of the most vulnerable, was to move its undergraduate Arts component to the University College of Wales in Aberystwyth. Whether on his own initiative or as part of a larger plan, its quondam Librarian Chambers had prepared a list of the rare books and muniments that must be moved and stored in the Aberystwyth vaults. He complained to Hugh Smith that some were so precious that he was concerned about not being able to see them into safe-keeping personally. This was no problem for Hugh; he would take Chambers and his parcels by car. I was not party to the

George Kane in Kew Gardens, 1939.

project until Chambers remembered my collations and apparatus; he had had a glance at the latter in rough draft. In the end all my *Piers* materials and Chambers's photocopies and photographs went to Aberystwyth. And for good measure they took me along.

Roads and cars those days were not what they are today, and we took two days for the journey. Chambers, who did not drive, did not conceal that he was enjoying the expedition and cast all formality aside, speaking very freely in my presence of departmental matters. It was his plan that Hugh Smith should succeed him in the Quain chair. And, out of the blue, he was sorry that what the College could offer me as an assistant lecturer was probably less than my scholarship. This was very complimentary, but I kept my mouth shut. I had no intention of staying in England once I had my degree. It would have been crassly offensive to tell him that.

I recall the journey with pleasure. On the way there we called on Allan H. Bright, an eccentric Langland enthusiast, and broke the journey each way at Hugh's house in the Gloucester village of Dulverton. The vaults at Aberystwyth were deep and grim, and I was conscious of absurdity in committing my papers to their care. But the house where my belongings were stored during the war was first firebombed and then looted in 1942, and but for Chambers my draft dissertation, for what it was worth, would have gone with my other effects.

As it turned out the department did not move to Aberystwyth until, at the end of the Blitzkrieg, the German armies and air force reached the Channel.

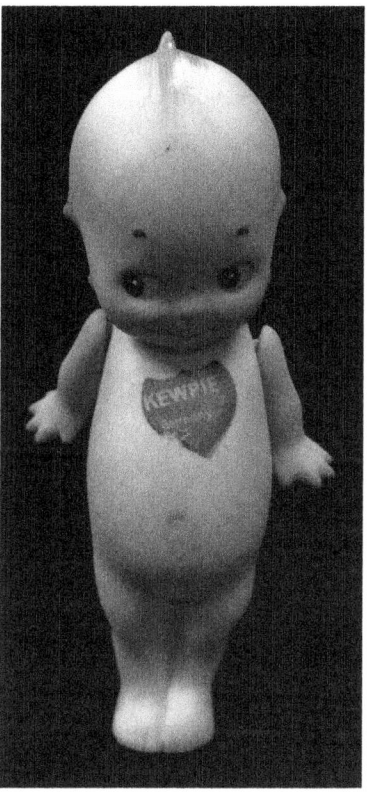

Kewpie doll.

I did not learn of that deferment until I was in uniform. But twice, on week-end leave, I was bidden to his house in North London where, to use his description, he 'lived very simply' with his sister and her companion Elsie Hitchcock, herself a scholar and member of the Department, cared for by an excellent cook, a housemaid and a handyman-gardener. The women addressed and referred to him as 'Q.P', ostensibly after his title, but mercilessly calling to mind at the time a chubby doll called 'Kewpie'. Although he drank little himself he kept a good cellar. The three made a great fuss of me as, I suppose, was natural of childless people in the circumstances, and although somewhat embarrassed I found it impossible not to be touched by their concern, that of 'real people' in the fullest sense. Over half a century I have from time to time bitterly regretted the luck that put the larger part of the burden of *Piers Plowman* editing on me, denying me studies that I loved and would have revelled in. But I have never been moved to hold this against Chambers; to have known him enriched my life.

7
SEPTEMBER 1939–MAY 1940

At various times the war-time years have seemed to me a regrettable interruption in the course of my life. But as they have become more remote they have acquired the aspect of a broader education. It has become impossible for me to conceive of myself as not having experienced the war. It is a feature of my generation, one way or another. Len Grant, flat-footed and with indifferent vision spent five years in Canadian naval intelligence; John Harrison flew Catalinas over the North Atlantic hunting submarines, Rodney Poisson was in a destroyer in the extreme North-East Pacific, Tommy Allen survived the Italian campaign where John Logan, colour-blind and all, was killed; Ken Macalister, physically unfit for service, was shot by the Gestapo in Northern France, where he need not have been.

We grew up in the receding shadow of the Kaiser's War, listened as children to 'Tipperary' and 'Keep the Home Fires Burning' and 'The Yanks are Coming'; we read the Boys' Own Paper for its stories of heroism. As we grew to manhood the shadows formed again, the occupation of the Rhineland, the Spanish Civil War, Mussolini in Abyssinia, the Anschluss, and in the last while Czechoslovakia. Now Poland was in peril. This could not go on.

In the event, when war was declared I went to Canada House in Trafalgar Square to be told by the solitary major who represented my country's armed forces in Great Britain that there were no arrangements for enlisting in the Canadian army overseas; they would doubtless be glad to have me if I went home. At London House we were restless and impatient. The few native British residents, intended, one supposed, to be the leaven that leaveneth the whole, knew about enlistment. The vogue unit was the Honourable Artillery Company, a City-based territorial battalion with a history going back to the seventeenth century. I went to their armoury, was medically vetted, and was told to go home and wait for orders. And I wrote the requisite letter to Dean Bollert, but also, after some procrastination, a more difficult one to my mother, who was not pleased.

The weeks that followed were among the most tedious of my young life. Having nothing to do has always affected my morale badly. One after another my friends went off. I took to reading military history of which there was a fair selection in the House library; I could pretend that there was some purpose in this.

In what follows I go into some detail because, again, some fiction has developed about my 'war'; for instance, I had been 'at Dunkirk'; my experience had been 'harrowing'. The actualities are prosaic enough, and of quite another order: 'my war' was an extended education, unplanned to be sure, which for better or for worse imposed a new identity on me.

The first lesson was to discover what it is like not to be a free agent and to come to terms with that condition. My posting orders came. I was to report on a specified day at a specific time at a specific barracks in Shorncliffe, Kent, having travelled by a designated train from Victoria station to Folkestone where there would be transport. I was to bring the following items of kit and clothing. I was posted not to the Honourable Artillery Company but to the Artists' Rifles. My initial disappointment about that was brief: this unit had been founded in the mid-nineteenth century by the President of the Royal Academy; many of its first recruits had been pre-Raphaelite painters and poets.

On that specified train there were quite a number of men of about my age with noticeably short haircuts. At Folkestone we were met by half a dozen Army Service Corps trucks in command of an irreverent corporal who unceremoniously herded us into the transport for the five-mile drive to Shorncliffe. The barracks proved to be a geometrically arranged set of undistinguishable brick structures with large rectangular areas of grass or tarmac interposed. All was enclosed in a high fence, of which the gate was controlled by a guardroom. The individual barrack buildings contained, as far as I can recall, four long rooms on two floors, these divided by a staircase, several smaller rooms, showers and washrooms and latrines. Our truck was first in, and pulled up before one of these buildings, where we were formed up in groups of thirty. Mine made for the ground floor on the right. A glance showed it austerely furnished with fifteen beds down each side, long trestle tables down the middle, benches not chairs, a locker by each bed, and a coal burning stove. Some instinct made me head for a bed under the window at the end of the room farthest from the door, which I claimed with my kitbag. So far so good.

The next stage in the education process, levelling out, now began. A sergeant-major from a foot guard's regiment appeared on the scene and took our names. Henceforward we constituted a platoon of thirty officer-cadets. One was addressed formally with 'Cadet' before his surname. After the sergeant-major had had called our names once to check his list, he handed us over formally to another guardsman, Corporal Jackson. He lived 'on the premises', so to speak, in one of the single rooms, and would be our mentor for the duration of the course. The first day was the worst. Jackson formed us up and marched us to the Quartermaster's Stores. This in itself was an experience for any of us who thought we had learned to march in the school or university corps. Jackson had the gift of being scathing while preserving the formal courtesies. I wish I had a tape of his commentary on

our movement that day. At the Stores, except for the boots which were carefully
fitted, our uniform was issued by eye; almost all of us came away with at least
one garment that had to be taken back for another size. We broke rank to carry the uniform to our barrack building, and then reported to the barber's where
we learned about military hairstyles. At 1:00 we were marched to the mess hall
for dinner. This was a grim experience, and we were not surprised to learn that
the cooks were beginners too. They improved a little during the month they were
with us, but not much. By 4:00, however, we found ourselves shorn, with mostly
fitting uniform, and ready for our first Jackson lesson.

He taught us how to store our kit in our locker, how to black our boots, how
to polish our cap badge, a silver head of Athens in a helmet, how to blanco the
white band around our forage caps which set us apart as cadets, how to make up
our bed (the mattress consisted of three 'biscuits') for the night and to ready it for
morning inspection, in particular how to fold the blankets, and so on, in effect
how to conform. Lights out would be at 10:00, reveille at 06:00. At 06:15 we would
parade outside the barracks as a platoon in shorts and singlets; we knew for what
purpose. At 06:30 we would break off P.T. and 'perform our ablutions'. Breakfast
would be at 07:15, by which time we would have made up our beds for the day. At
08:00 Jackson would show us how to lay out our kit for inspection. It sounded a
tight schedule, but feasible, and in any case was self-imposed. I don't recall supper
the first night — there was always plenty of cold food, the cheese was good, and
milk to drink if one disliked tea. I do recall, still, the agreeable weariness at lights
out, such as I had not in my adult life until then experienced.

Nor shall I forget the shattering shock with which the bugler, sounding reveille just outside my window, awoke me, or how I knew, the moment I emerged from
the barrack door in my shorts and singlet, immediately, why he had sheltered
there to sound it. The east wind was bitter. So was the P.T. that followed. None of
the exercises we were put through, I later came to realize, was particularly difficult or strenuous but I suppose I must have been as unfit physically as a man
otherwise in good health could be. That morning they seemed a hellish torture,
and it must have been a fortnight before I ceased to dread them or to hate the instructor, as indeed the cold shaving water and the cold shower and a breakfast
with only tea to drink.

After breakfast the instruction proceeded. Once Jackson had shown us how
to have the room ready for inspection, which included sweeping it and polishing
the stove, it became military; we were marched off to the Armoury to collect our
webbing equipment and weapons, the latter a ·303 short muzzle Lee Enfield rifle
mark three, the materials to care for it, and a bayonet or side arm. Back to barracks
where he showed us how to put the webbing equipment together, more complicated than this might sound, and to wear it, how to dismantle and reassemble the
rifle, how to keep the inside of the barrel clean, how to tell when a soldier's rifle was

not clean. There was much detail, and it quickly became apparent that the best way to cut any such boring instruction short was to master it. This attitude came to characterise our platoon and made our relation with Jackson easy.

Then came arms drill on the main barrack square under the sergeant major who had met us on arrival. He appeared mercilessly critical, but I anticipate myself to say that within days we found him, off the parade ground, an affable and reasonable man. Drill is not as senseless as might seem. The precise coordination of group movement, like certain kinds of dancing, has a weird primeval attraction. By some means it bonds a group; the component persons come to be proud of belonging to this, and therefore the group functions more effectively as a unit.

It soon became clear that the non-commissioned officers at Shorncliffe had been hand-picked. The two Guards, n.c.o.s doubtless, had Sandhurst experience but were also shrewd enough to appreciate the difference between boys fresh out of school and a somewhat older group, many of them graduates, all with experience of independence and in some cases responsibility.[3] The one exception, Company Sergeant-Major Dawkins at Headquarters Company was, as far as we cadets were concerned, *vox et praeterea nihil*; I do not recall an instance, all the time I was at Shorncliffe, of a cadet up before the Commanding Officer.

As for the officers, there was one, Captain Greenwood, kept over from Territorial Army days, whom I apparently irritated; I for my part found him a pompous ass. As a student I had been conditioned to ask the question 'Why'?; I learned best by knowing the reason for what was being laid down. Greenwood taught from the manuals, expecting us to learn by rote. At the end of the first month he was replaced by Lieutenant Brian Mulvaney who had been both English Master and in command of the Cadet Corps at Eastbourne College, a genial man who enjoyed teaching us. I remember nothing about the officer commanding the training unit during my first month. He was replaced by a major from a Dogra regiment of the Indian Army who had come back to England so as not to miss the war and professional advancement, so people said. I liked him; he came on field exercises whatever the weather, and like Brian Mulvaney was a good teacher, and he had a sense of humour.

By the end of the first month we had learned to live with the system. The apprentice cooks were gone and the food became edible. We had made friends of our two guardsmen. The n.c.o.s who taught field training and marksmanship were quite a different type, all from the Rifle Brigade, originally seconded to the Artist's Rifles and kept on when that became an officer training unit. Here the attention was to the subject in hand rather than disciplined uniformity; they dominated, if that is the word, by expertise.

---

3. An n.c.o. was a non-commissioned officer.

One feature of the Shorncliffe experience which struck me was how an accidental assemblage of twenty-nine people of about the same age as myself should have produced such a congenial and in some instances interesting group. We worked hard and well together and got on without friction. Each week there were a different cadet platoon sergeant and corporal, whom we took seriously to the extent of supporting them where it mattered. We competed fiercely with the other two platoons over smartness on guard duty. Our rugger team which happened to contain two Cambridge blues and an England cap appropriately named Mickey Rooney repeatedly beat the team of a company of Woolwich sapper cadets doing an accelerated course in a nearby barrack. We could be out of barracks from 17:30 until midnight on weekdays unless our section was on guard duty, similarly on Saturdays from 13:30. Folkestone was about half an hour away on a good bus service, and a two mile walk south of barracks was an unspoiled country pub called the Star, where I drank some of the best beer I have tasted to this day. If one had a weekend pass there were good trains to Victoria Saturday afternoon and to Folkestone Sunday night. There was always a room for me at London House and a welcome from the Warden, Commander Crofton and his wife. Leaving serious considerations aside this wasn't a bad life, and certainly good for me in its absolute difference from the academic ambience.

The Victoria League continued to be generous with invitations. As Christmas approached I received one from a family in Kent with a son my age who had just been commissioned into the regular Army. They could not have been more welcoming or hospitable, and but for the weather which kept us indoors it was a very good Christmas, almost as if I were at home, my last in a household until 1945.

When I returned from Christmas leave Shorncliffe was virtually snowbound. Training did not effectively resume until we had established a routine of shovelling snow to keep the camp streets open for the daily provision of fuel for the stoves and rations. When the snow eventually ceased to fall worse followed: a vicious type of influenza ran through the camp. It got almost everyone in the end, and because the Medical Officer insisted on sick leave for all those affected training as good as came to a standstill. I was one of the last to go down, and did not return from leave until well into February.

The point in the course came where the cadets were allowed to express their choice of regiment, a privilege of the volunteer. Whether a man was posted to that regiment depended, we were told, on an interview by an officer from outside our training unit and on his report from this. Almost everyone I knew had some reason for his choice, regional or family in most instances. With nothing else to go by I chose the Rifle Brigade, so named because when it was founded in 1795 it was the first regiment in the British Army to be equipped with a rifled firearm in place of the smooth bore Brown Bess musket. I had much admired what I had found in my September reading, of its conduct during the Peninsular War when it covered the retreat to Corunna, and on the left flank at Waterloo. I was somewhat disconcerted, when my turn came to be interviewed, that the officer from 'outside' came from the Rifle Brigade. I did not think I had done well in the interview; nevertheless when we learned of our postings I found that I had been accepted.

With the snow gone and the sick back on duty the course more or less resumed its normal routine, but it would terminate on the original date. Not long before its close there was a flurry of excitement. A War Office paper appeared on the notice boards inviting volunteers for a ski battalion designed to serve in Norway, to be called the fifth Scots Guards. Commissioned officers who volunteered would resign their commissions on the understanding that when the skiing battalion was disbanded these would be restored without loss of seniority; cadets due to be commissioned would be treated correspondingly.

Along with two or three other cadets from our platoon I put my name down. Within a few days we found ourselves in barracks somewhere near Aldershot, with different badges and no white bands on our forage caps, armed now with a modified Lee Enfield of less weight but otherwise, we judged, inferior. We were as near as no matter 500 strong. After a few days of 'shaking down', getting to know each other, our n.c.o.s and company officers and the new rifles, and crawling about the local heathland on elementary field exercises, we entrained for Chamonix where we would be equipped with skis hired, so the talk went, from the French army. In the event they proved long and heavy, not suited to the cross-country movement we could expect. At Chamonix, for little more than a week, we practised downhill runs in conditions ideal for a winter holiday. Then without notice, presumably because a crisis situation had developed in Norway, we entrained without skis for Cherbourg, crossed the Channel crowded, all 500 with our kit, onto a little ferry with no more than eighteen inches of freeboard, made a night journey to Greenock, where our train pulled up on the docks at midday and we sat the afternoon through waiting for orders. I slept through most of it. Next morning we were back in Aldershot and by noon disbanded.

From all possible points of view this operation was grotesquely misconceived. The notion that one lightly armed infantry battalion without automatic weapons or artillery support could seriously interfere with the highly organised German invasion of northern Norway was to prove typical of the quality of leadership in the War Office at the time. The plan, it became known, was a brainchild of Lord Lovat and a Scots Guard officer, Captain David Stirling, misconceived in haste and without reflection.

What I learned from my first six months in the army has obviously no direct bearing on my professional life, but since this memoir is written in the first instance for my grandchildren, I will tabulate the lessons.

First I learned not to volunteer without due consideration; in fact the lesson had immediate application: even as we were packing up, Andrew Maxwell our platoon corporal (actually a captain in the regiment and David Stirling's cousin) asked me whether I would like to be kept in mind for any future adventures of the kind we were just emerging from. I suppose I might have felt complimented by the enquiry, but the answer that it was probably a good idea to serve with my regiment for a while came to me without reflection.

Further I learned, never having been any good at ball games, that there are useful physical aptitudes besides throwing or hitting or kicking a round object worth cultivating. With that I discovered, after a chair and desk bound youth, the sense of well-being that comes with physical fitness. I learned a new kind of human association called comradeship, generated by joint undertaking of a venture made serious by an element of serious danger. I learned about good natured accommodation, how eight grown men of recent acquaintance, with weapons, packs and kit bags, can travel amicably from Aldershot to Chamonix and by way of Chamonix to Cherbourg and on to Southampton and Greenock and back to Aldershot in one third class railway compartment, provided that two of them are small enough to sleep in the net luggage racks above the seats. I learned how to obey orders sharply given without a sense of personal degradation and how to give them in a tone that did not arouse resentment. I learned some elementary tricks of teaching from the Rifle Brigade n.c.o. instructors at Shorncliffe.

I learned above all about the absoluteness of the chance factor in one's life. But for the freak impulse that prompted me to volunteer for the skiing battalion I would almost certainly have been posted to the Second Battalion of my regiment in Egypt, in which case, were I writing a memoir today, it would go quite another way. Or, to see chance in another aspect, if another 'guardsman' who happened to sleep next door to me on the floor in the school gymnasium in Chamonix had bedded down elsewhere, he would probably not be alive today. But that story must wait.

Now I was about to learn how to become a regimental officer. From Aldershot I was sent on leave with instruction to await orders. They were quick in coming, and after a frenzied ten days of sessions with the regimental tailors and outfitters I set off for the regimental Motor Training Battalion at Tidworth on Salisbury Plain.

Here I moved into another world. The driver who met me at Tidworth saluted me, which took me by surprise. In Camp he drove me to Battalion Headquarters where I reported to the Adjutant who took and introduced me to the Commanding Officer, and then handed me over to the Orderly Officer of the day who took me to my quarters where my soldier servant, called my batman, was waiting and we left my luggage; then on to the Officers' Mess, where he explained the routine of meals, the bar and so on. He was very brisk, efficient and friendly. Back in my quarters I found my kit unpacked and my 'service dress' uniform laid out for me to change into for dinner; the batman wanted to know how hot I liked my bath, which he was waiting to run.

My roommate was there as well, a 'full' lieutenant called Adrian Buxton, an easy man to live with if one accepted friendliness combined with reserve. I was not at Tidworth long enough to get to know him and do not know how he fared in the war; his name does not appear in the Regimental History.

Back to the anteroom, that first day: this is the term used for the social or common room. 'Mess', originally signifying a group of soldiers who eat together, came to mean the building containing the dining room, anteroom, kitchens etc. and other appurtenances. Here there were numerous brother officers to meet, the majority of them, since this was a training battalion, subalterns like myself. The first thing I learned was that, within the regiment, officers addressed each other by their given names unless on formal duty: I had to forget the rigid prescription we received at Shorncliffe that field officers, that is majors and above, were invariably to be addressed as 'sir'.

Dinner was an impressive occasion. The mess hall was a beautifully proportioned room. The lights bore candlesticks on one long table or obliquely lit the walls and sideboards where the regimental silver gleamed. The Mess president, an elected officer, led us in. The Colonel, or a more senior guest, sat facing the door at the middle of the single long table; opposite him the Vice-President, in normal times the junior subaltern. Otherwise seating was casual. The mood was informal and sociable, but quiet until the ceremonial toasts, to which the Vice-President responded, were proposed. We newcomers to the Regiment were conscious of the mess waiters, mostly grey-haired veterans.

Junior officers, that is second lieutenants and lieutenants not on duty, turned out in battle dress before breakfast for half an hour's parade-ground drill under the Regimental-Sergeant-Major, who was courteously merciless, on the principle that an officer could not reasonably exact standards of performance from his men which he could not match himself. Here I had quickly to learn the drill of rifle regiments, which did not slope arms, but trailed them and marched at a much quicker pace than the 'heavy infantry', which had different words of command. Luckily I was not the only one. After breakfast the training was largely on new tactics; the regiment had only recently become 'motorized', that is equipped with its own transport, and armoured scout cars and tracked 'bren carriers'. Its rôle would be to operate in support of heavy armour, namely tanks. A new scale of independent judgement would be required of junior officers.

In late April or early May, along with several other second lieutenants I was assigned to the First Battalion, of which the headquarters were at Blandford in Dorset, specifically to 'C' company whose headquarters were in the picture village of Milton Abbas. The troops were billeted here; David Fellowes, also fresh from Tidworth, and I were billeted in a big house about three miles from the village with a branch of the Hambro banking family. A company truck would take us there after duty each evening and pick us up early the next day. Our batmen came with us and became effectively domestic servants in the household; our four ration cards went into the domestic pool. The War Office, we presumed, paid for our keep.

The Hambros, second-generation anglicised Norwegian and immensely wealthy, seemed to see the billeting as an affront to their affluence and standing, and had evidently not assimilated the customary traditional hospitality of English country houses which I had admired and enjoyed in my Victoria League experience. They were distinctly cool in their manner; David and I were uncomfortable with them and crept about like mice.

Otherwise the following ten days or so, but for the maps in the daily paper, were agreeable enough. David and I took over platoons that had been commanded by platoon-Sergeant-Majors, warrant officers of a rank created especially, I believe, to economize in peacetime. To David's and my relief, when we took over they did not stay with the platoons. My riflemen and I got on very well.

They were kind to the novice and very efficient. Almost all were serving professionals; the calling up of reservists was only just beginning. Almost all, if not all, had qualified as marksmen, as was traditional in the Regiment. Again traditionally, they were recruited mainly from East London, especially the Tower Hamlets, and from the mining districts of north-eastern England. The platoon sergeant, Headley, was quietly efficient; the corporal, Stacey, something of a wag but very much in control of the men and good to work with. It was he who told me that Dawkins was considered a blowhard by his comrades. My dispatch rider, Rifleman Eagle, whom I was later able to recommend successfully for a Military Medal, was brave enough to try and teach me to ride his motor bicycle contrary to all common sense and army regulations. I began to feel that I was getting to know my soldiers, getting to know my job.

I was apparently wrong. One afternoon the platoon exercise was to 'dig ourselves in', that is to say, prepare a defensive position. The ground was hard and chalky, and when the time came, had it not been for those disturbing maps, I could have called a halt even though our heads were still, so to speak, above ground level. I put it to the men that this was dull work and we didn't want to come back to it tomorrow; half an hour would see the job done. There was no dissent and we finished in that time. But next morning when I was on the point of moving the platoon off to the day's training I was called to the Company Office where the Commander, Major Vernon Knollys, told me that one rifleman — I forgot his name; his comrades called him Jeep after the entity in the Popeye strip cartoon — had formed up to the Company-Sergeant-Major and complained that Mr Kane had kept the platoon at work after quitting time. I agreed that this was the case and waited for Vernon to go on, but he seemed to have no more to say, so I came to attention, saluted, about turned and dismissed myself. Poor Jeep! When after the war had ended I met Sergeant Headly again and I asked after Jeep I was told he was the first casualty in the platoon. I sometimes wonder whether his comrades put him up to complaining. My experience was too limited at that time to know that the C.S.M. should have sent Jeep away with a flea in his ear, that union rules do not apply in wartime, or failing this, that Vernon should have checked him for not doing so. At the same time it may have been coincidence that I was within days assigned as Liaison Officer to the newly assembled headquarters of Thirtieth Infantry Brigade, of which our battalion and the second battalion of the Sixtieth Rifles would be components, while Platoon Sergeant Major Burman resumed command of what I had come to think of as 'my' platoon. That the Brigadier needed a liaison officer will have been a War Office decision; he would have asked the commanding officers of the two battalions to provide one; as a newcomer, not yet 'settled in', and able to speak French, I may have seemed an obvious choice.

Before my appointment became effective the German war machine had moved with alarming speed through Luxembourg and the Low Countries. One response of Higher Command in the War Office was to move our two motor battalions, at that time the only fully equipped units in Great Britain, to the Eastern Counties, first to Essex and then presently to Suffolk, presumably in anticipation of a German seaborne invasion! I travelled to Essex with C company, spent a night at Battalion Headquarters, and then with my own 30-hundredweight truck and driver, Rifleman Knight, to Brigade Headquarters.

Battalion Headquarters reminded me of a large family just after it has moved house: disorder, nothing in the right place, but the faces familiar and everyone knowing what to do. Brigade Headquarters, in a requisitioned sparsely-furnished house, was small and without evident cohesion, in no sense familial. There were five officers: the Brigadier, Claude Nicholson, the Brigade Major, Captain Talbot, his military assistant, a Staff Captain Coxwell-Rogers, for general administration a Signals Officer, Lieutenant Millett, and the Liaison Officer. The brigade was to be completed by a third battalion, the Queen Victoria's Rifles, a reconnaissance unit equipped with motorcycles, at this time training in Kent. There were n.c.o.s and drivers, and presumably signallers as well. I do not recall that there was a mess. At night you rolled out your valise and slept on the floor.

The Brigadier was an unusual professional soldier in that, although a cavalry officer, he had not merely passed through the Staff College but had been an instructor there before taking command of the regiment to which he had originally been commissioned. The Brigade Major, Captain Talbot, was in his early thirties, a very ambitious professional soldier; his eye was never off the map as it became progressively more depressing. I had a sense that because there was virtually nothing for me to do he found me a nuisance: fair enough. Coxwell-Rogers was affable and charming, and Millett, not much older than myself, was easy to get on with. It could have been an interesting posting. But within a week I was sent or called back (I don't know which) to the Regiment and C Company where, to my ironic satisfaction I was in put in charge of the activity which may have cost me my platoon, digging the entrenchments in which, if it came to the crunch, C Company would be defending Essex and England. The weather was fine, I had something to do, and I was billeted with John Surtees (who had the scout bren-carrier platoon) in a pleasant pub with a good breakfast menu and good beer.

But one evening, I had the gravity of the situation brought home to me. I was viewing the day's dig when an n.c.o. from Company Headquarters brought along a strange subaltern in a Scottish looking headdress. 'Major Knollys wishes you to show this gentleman around the defensive position.' His unit, a territorial battalion of a Scottish regiment, would be taking over our position; they had actually marched down from the Border because there was no transport, albeit not quite so fast as Harold Godwinson had from Stamford Bridge. I took him around with some pride. When we came to the weapon pit where I had sited the Company's one 'Boys' rifle because there was a good field of fire, he thought I was making fun of him: he had not heard of, let alone seen, that weapon.

I had seen one but not fired it, a heavy long-barrelled ·50 calibre single-shot piece with a bipod, allegedly armour piercing and with a kick like a mule in its prime, named after the designer.

We moved to Suffolk the next day. The drive is memorable for me from the sight in Ipswich of the red sails of barges moving serenely above dock warehouses and factories, and the sudden clamour of voices and clatter of clogs on the cobblestones as hundreds of fresh-faced factory girls poured out onto the street for their lunchtime break. By evening the battalion troops were encamped among the Suffolk villages under canvas and the four subalterns of C Company, John Surtees, Francis Reed, David Fellowes and myself, were billeted along with Vernon and his second-in-command in a fine old vicarage where we were much cosseted. I recall us sitting, after a day setting up road blocks, in deckchairs under flowering apple trees with long, cool drinks in our hands. But that was a single occasion.

On the 21st May at about five o'clock I had taken a truckload of C Company riflemen on pass to the swimming baths in Needham Market: we would reassemble at seven-fifteen. For an hour I explored the lovely town; then I made for the Bull Hotel to sample the beer of East Anglia. On its very doorstep I found the Brigade Signals Officer, who told me that the Brigade had orders to move that night to Southampton for embarkation overseas. By amazing luck there was one of our sergeants in the bar; between us we managed to collect all the men on pass with me, and we reported back within minutes of the receipt there of the order to move. The entire battalion was under way by eleven-fifteen.

It came on to rain as we set out, the Sixtieth as senior regiment in the lead in a long column driving by sidelights only. We moved around London, by way of the North Circular Road, then Staines and Winchester. It was still raining at first light when the column halted somewhere in Hartfordbridge Flats on the Southampton side of Camberley. The cooks brewed a drink called 'gunfire', a strong tea heavily laced with Nestlé's condensed milk; a spoon would have stood in it. I had been obliged to stay awake all night to keep Rifleman Knight, my driver, not much above eighteen, awake; in 'gunfire' I found something to be said for tea. By midday the sky had cleared; we reached a rest camp outside Southampton where the troops were fed. Here we parted with our vehicles, which were driven to the docks loaded as they were, leaving each man with a rifle and forty rounds of ammunition, and the battalion with only eight of its bren guns. After lunch we marched through Southampton to the docks, the Sixtieth again in the lead.

There the situation was chaotic. Two small ships were assigned to move each battalion, one for vehicles, the other for personnel. The senior officer of the dock transport staff had simply overridden the orders of Colonel Euan Miller in command of the Sixtieth about loading them, and weapons that should have travelled with the men were loaded without system on the vehicle ships, and weapons that belonged with vehicles, such as the bren guns of the bren-carrier platoons, onto the personnel ships.

None of us, as we embarked, knew our destination, not even (I read in the histories) the Brigadier. Neither, it appears, on the afternoon of May 22, did high command in Whitehall, which had very poor intelligence of the rapidly developing situation in France. Unbelievably, it seems that by 21 May the German armour had already cut off the French Seventh Army from the British Expeditionary Force, and that a German Panzer Division had reached Noveles just south of Boulogne. In the night we moved up the Channel to Dover. There in the morning the Brigadier learned that his brigade was being sent to Calais, and received orders to move on disembarkation southwest to the support of the twentieth Guards Division in Boulogne. But early in the afternoon when he disembarked at Calais that order was countermanded; he would provide armed escort for a convoy of lorries standing on the docks loaded with 350,000 rations, to the B.E.F. at Dunkirk. This was after the Sixtieth, whose vessel came in first, had taken up positions west of Calais in readiness to move to Boulogne. Accordingly it fell to the Rifle Brigade to provide the escort. But the regimental vehicle ship had docked second after waiting for the tide — the tugs had fled days ago — and before the half of its essential cargo had been unloaded, it had been commandeered by a transport control officer on the docks and sent back to England with a deck cargo of wounded, from a hospital train on the docks, to be sure, leaving the Regiment poorly equipped to mount and arm the escort: what had come off the ship belonged haphazardly to various platoons and sections of its four companies. The order had been to move off by midnight, but assembling its escort by that hour was manifestly impossible. In the event it did not set out until about first light on Friday the 24th, by which time elements of a panzer division to the right of the one that threatened the Guards in Boulogne had bypassed Calais and were moving north across the Calais-Dunkirk road. About the time the convoy set off Whitehall added to the Brigadier's predicament by a signal that evacuation of the British forces in Calais 'had been decided on in principle but not yet'. This was becoming black farce: already by the morning of Friday 24th May disengagement and withdrawal, street by street to the docks which, as such, invited air attack, would have been simply lethal. The Sixtieth on the west and south of what was becoming a defensive perimeter was fully engaged; pressure on the east, where the Regiment had taken up defensive positions, was developing, and all around the perimeter, wherever main roads entered the town there were elements of the Queen Victoria's Rifles; one of five had landed on 22 May without their vehicles and, accordingly, their wireless, and been sent there by the Town Commandant, Colonel Holland. They would have to be brought in. When Churchill learned of the decision 'in principle' he was furious. In due course the predictable order to hold to the last came to the Brigadier at some time Saturday 25 May. By that time he had twice declined German invitations to surrender.

I have sketched the circumstances in which the battle of Calais was fought because in one aspect it shows warfare as a wicked farce directed at the highest levels by incompetence, and thus puts my trivial experience of it in proportion. It has also another aspect: military historians who concern themselves with the 1940 campaign seem now in agreement that Thirtieth Infantry Brigade's four days stand at Calais bought Gort the time to organise the evacuation of the B.E.F. at Dunkirk.

In England I had been made a liaison officer when there were, apparently, as yet no specific duties, handy so to speak, for chores as they came up. In the deployment at Calais, C Company was ordered into reserve and assigned to the extreme northeast of the defence perimeter, from the Channel beach to the eastern end of a reservoir called the Bassin des Chasses, a front of about 500 yards. When at length John Surtees's carriers came off the ship they were sent to another part of the regimental sector. In the course of Friday 24 May Francis Reed and Platoon-Sergeant-Major Criss would be sent with their platoons to reinforce a part of the Sixtieth sector, and David Fellowes with his men to I Company. For my part I felt a need to establish my identity by acquiring a job. I addressed Vernon, who suggested that now Brigade Headquarters might have something for me to do. But he had no notion of its whereabouts. I went to Battalion Headquarters, where Tom Acton the Adjutant likewise did not know. (I read that the Brigadier was mostly on the move until the 25th.) I decided to ask around, and was lucky at B Company Headquarters, where I found Captain Talbot standing by while the

Company Commander, Major Hamilton-Russell was putting together from available resources the escort for the rations convoy. But I had no need to establish my identity; Talbot got in first with 'I have a job for you.'

Tony Rolt of A Company with his carrier platoon had been sent out some time before to establish an advance picket on the Calais-Gravelines-Dunkirk road that the convoy would be taking, and was not responding to wireless contact. I would make my way to the designated point of his picket and ascertain why he had not reported and did not respond. I asked for transport: there was none. A map? 'There are no spares; have a look at mine.' The route was easy. The regimental history puts Tony's picket seven miles to the east of the perimeter; I don't think it was more than three. I set off on foot at about 19:00 hours and there was still some daylight left when I found Tony. I tried to check the field in 1985, but the area had become a high-reach industrial development.

The terrain was flat and dull, all pastures and grazing with patches of brushwood. My main concern as I walked was that Tony's platoon might be so well camouflaged that I would miss it in the deepening half-dark. There was no local traffic, and there were no lights in the few houses along the road. But presently to take my mind off camouflage and lightless houses I saw approaching me a large lorry which proved to be a British Army three-tonner carrying soldiers of a Royal Artillery searchlight battery. It bristled with rifles and moved very slowly behind a man on foot, a second lieutenant like myself. I stepped out into the road and the rifles converged on me. He was taking his men into Calais; what was I doing? I suppose my being alone was suspicious; it was a little time before he accepted my explanation. For my part I found him unimpressive; he was stocky, acneous, and looked just as nervous as I felt. Many years later I established that this was Airey Neave from his book *The Flames of Calais*. It does not mention our meeting, but from his description of his route I can pinpoint it on the map.

With my next encounter my evening walk took on a picaresque quality. Approaching me on foot was a very large man in an unfamiliar but not German uniform carrying a rifle with a very long barrel and walking, in Quaker parlance, not as steadily as he might. He as good as fell on my neck, rifle and all. 'Ah Dieu, merci! Anglais! Allons, cher camarade, allons démolir les sales Boches!' A Belgian private soldier, and it seems that he saw in me the advance guard of a force come to recover Belgium from the Germans. It was impossible to disagree with the sentiment of his proposal and anyway he was much larger than me. But there was the matter of camouflage and failing light: I had no time to cultivate the *entente*. Moreover he waved that long firing piece about alarmingly — it was visibly loaded — and he was very drunk.

A mile or so east of the crumbling bastions of old Calais, in the middle of nowhere at a point named Le Beau Marais on the pre-war map I have by me, I came upon what to go by its advertisements was a roadside pub. I was thirsty — my own fault for having failed to fill my water bottle either in England or on the boat. I pushed open the door and entered what on later experience I would call a cross between a *zinc* and an Irish bar where they sell groceries, a stalwart woman in her forties presiding over it. She would not look at my English money and I came out as thirsty as I had gone in. There had been no provision for that situation in my training.

Tony's platoon was where it should be, but its wireless was malfunctioning; he proposed to stay put until either the convoy or the Germans showed up. The platoon was in good order but the riflemen were grousing because they did not have the means of 'brewing up', making tea. As Tony and I talked we noticed lights, as of campfires, appearing in the middle distance. We attributed them to refugees; they would prove to have been German armour laagering for the night.

At B Company Headquarters to which I got back without incident somewhat before midnight when the convoy was initially due to start but still far from ready, and the Brigade Major had gone, without, so to speak, leaving an address, Major Hamilton-Russell took note of Tony's problem but had nothing for me to do, so I dismissed myself and returned to C Company. I had not slept at all on the drive down to Southampton, and not too soundly on the boat after an initiation party given on board by the senior non-commissioned officers with war experience for the green subalterns. The night was warm and dry and I soon fell asleep under the stars. Not long before first light I was woken by the sound of heavy firing to the east and a display of pyrotechnics, flares and Verey lights. This was the convoy escort engaged with German armour on the road to Marck and Dunkirk. Tony and his men came to mind; I was glad later to learn that although his platoon was surrounded he managed to extricate it without loss.

Meanwhile the undercurrent of black farce persisted. About the time of that engagement, in which the Regiment lost good men killed and wounded, the Brigadier received the preposterous signal about evacuation being decided on 'in principle but not yet', and then, within hours, an order to place his Brigade under the Regional French Commander, General Fugalde, who ruled out evacuation. Both were in ignorance of the collapse of French High Command.

On May 24 I was still an odd job man. Here too there was an element of farce, though less outrageous. Not far from C Company Headquarters there was a structure called a blockhouse, a small coastal fort, the walls about ten foot high and stoutly built. It was garrisoned by French marines who would presumably man a mounted piece of artillery facing out to the Channel. They did not seem pleased to have C Company nearby. It could attract trouble.

Early in the day we made a connexion between a German reconnaissance plane, a Fieseler Storch, reputed to be able to fly backwards, and occasional local mortar bombardment. We could expect this when the plane circled above us, however high. It was becoming evident that the performance of the mortar teams was improving as the observer in the plane called their shots by wireless; it occurred to me that they might not have had much practice in their race across northern France and the Low Countries. In any event presently one of them got our range and put a bomb in the blockhouse compound. Within seconds of its explosion there was a clamour of voices and within minutes a rush of men in blue uniforms with suitcases, shouting as they made off.

Now C Company had a fort. Vernon rightly decided not to man it; with only one depleted platoon and his headquarters staff he could not have done so effectively. Its single piece of artillery, albeit formidable, could not have been trained inland or along the coast. But he sent me to look it over. The barracks smelled like the guardroom at Shorncliffe. But in the kitchen and storeroom we found cases of tins of *singe*, French style bully-beef, and we were hungry. We brought away a case containing a couple of dozen cans, such vegetables as we found and a big cauldron. The fort provided fuel, and I handed over the provisions to the company cooks, who would make a stew. Presently it began to smell promising; my last meal had been breakfast on the boat. As we waited I remembered the Storch, and sent a couple of riflemen to look for spades in the fort. They were back within minutes with half a dozen. Eagle, no longer my dispatch rider and without his motorbike, was watching. I handed him a spade and with that galling afternoon in mind said 'Let's see how fast we can dig a weapons pit.' We were just finishing when a runner from Battalion Headquarters appeared: 'Mr Kane to report to the Colonel'.

I had met the Colonel, Chandos Hoskyns, only a couple of times, but had very much liked what I saw. He was a man who inspired both respect and affection, brave and as mild mannered as Chaucer's Knight, much cherished by the soldiers. At headquarters I found him surrounded by a couple of dozen apparently agitated French Officers, both army and navy, and pretty senior from the amount of gold braid on their caps and sleeves. They had apparently got wind of the possible evacuation and were concerned about the arrangements for important people like themselves. They had no spokesman; those who had English seemed all to speak at the same time. The Colonel, when I reported, came straight to the point in a quiet voice: 'George, for God's sake get these people off my neck! And disarm them if you can; they're a menace!'

Looking back on how I set about this I see myself in the role of a priest preaching for reasons of expediency a doctrine of salvation in which he did not believe. Among my reading at London House before reporting to Shorncliffe had been histories of the Peninsular War, of which one sensational episode was the retreat to Corunna. A consequence was that I did not believe in the feasibility of extracting our brigade from a battle which had already then, by the sound of it, become street fighting, the most intimate form of combat, by way of an awkward tidal harbour with no anti-aircraft defences. But I could see no way of getting those French staff officers off my Colonel's neck except by simulating faith and hope.

So I made the only speech in French of my life. Would the gentlemen please accompany me? I had indeed heard of the possibility, and if they would permit me as a very junior officer to express my opinion, the best place to await this was the beach: it would be insolent of me to tell them that the harbour invited both shelling and air attack; one damaged ship and it was blocked. There seemed to be a consensus of agreement about this so I went on. I would take them to a point on the beach nearby from which the harbour was in full view: since no one knew when evacuation would take place it was important to observe the movement of vessels at the harbour entrance. Evacuation from the beach would necessarily be by small craft; weight therefore was important, and would they accordingly please leave their weapons at my Company Headquarters where they could not possibly come into hostile use? None of this was false, only the underlying premise that evacuation was feasible. They agreed. At Company headquarters the Sergeant Major watched them dumping their pistols onto a growing pile with surprise. It was a dazzling May day. I settled them on the beach edge of the dunes where they had a fine view of the docks less than half a mile to the west. They would, the next time the docks were strafed, see the advantages of waiting on the beach.

I was about to take leave, having assured them that I would keep them informed of any evacuation plan, when one of the half dozen or so less senior officers who had attached themselves to my charges spoke up. Pointing to a man in a rather shabby brown cassock sitting uncomfortably between two other latecomers, he said 'That man is a fifth columnist. Please take him away and have him shot.'

Unquestionably fifth columnists had been active in Calais for days before we landed, although I did not know at the time. Some wore civilian clothes; others, once infiltrated, changed into uniform, Allied or German. The latter took up positions on rooftops or attics from which they operated as snipers; the others spread rumours and false information among a populace understandably in a high state of panic. It was certainly possible that the accusations against this man were well founded. But my French was not up to conducting an interrogation. At the same time I did not think I should either leave him with his accusers or release him. So I took him with me and handed him over to the Regimental Sergeant Major. If he was an innocent man of religion — I guess he was wearing a Franciscan habit — he will have been able to establish his identity.

This was ugly; the farce to counterbalance was not long in coming. When at length Eagle and I got back to Company Headquarters we found that 'they' had forgotten to keep back any bully stew for us. And while we were adjusting to this deprivation our mortar team to the southeast began to search for C Company.

Being mortared is not as violent an experience as being shelled by field artillery. But it is disconcerting because, from the physical character of the process, you participate in it. You hear the unmistakeable bang of the mortar being fired. Then because the trajectory of a mortar bomb is relatively high, there is silence (its length depends on the range) while the bomb mounts to the apex of its flight; then follows the shriek as it comes down, finally the detonation.

The mortar team was evidently becoming expert. The first bomb was on line but fell short of target, the next crept closer. By then Eagle and I were running flat out for our weapon pit. We were half a dozen yards from it when we heard the bang of the third bomb being fired and found that our pit was occupied. We hugged Mother Earth, as the saying goes. The seconds that followed seemed like an eternity to me; then there was a dull thud followed by silence. I lifted my head cautiously and there lay the object, gleaming, elegantly shaped, intact; its image is still vivid after sixty years. So is Eagle's face a second later with a cheeky grin on it. Meanwhile the two figures who emerged from our refuge, dusting themselves down, proved to be Vernon and the Company Sergeant Major. Neither had anything to say about the bomb, which lay between us and the weapon pit.

There were no labour problems on Saturday about digging a crude defensive position from the beach to the eastern point of the Bassin. But that position was never actually defended. Vernon and his remnant of C Company were moved east in the late afternoon into the dunes, where the German probing attacks on Sunday were checked; they did not like operating without armoured support, which could not be given in the loose sand. I read that on the Friday they were held at many points on the perimeter, and even driven back at some. It appears from the war diary of the Tenth Panzer division that already by midday Friday its commander was asking for corps artillery and Stuka support. His own artillery was active enough; many parts of the city were on fire and there were palls of black smoke from burning fuel tanks to match the huge one visible at extreme distance hanging over Dunkirk, which we took to be the B.E.F. destroying its fuel reserve.

I would like to have been able to write or imply, with due modesty of course, that I played a significant part in the defence of Calais, but that would not be true. By the time I was sent into battle the outcome was settled. Baldly put, I did as I was ordered and no more. Before that happened Vernon did not put me to use. He puzzled me then as he still does; it was not possible to know what might have been in his mind: he had become very abstracted. He was very much a family man, so it was said, and must have found the prospect of virtually certain defeat and at best a prisoner of war camp hard to accept.

As for me, I needed to have something to do. In the middle and later afternoon of Friday there had been sporadic local sniper fire, and it was sometimes possible to make a fair guess about the direction it was coming from. There were half a dozen soldiers from other regiments who had collected around Company Headquarters; they were ready enough to come sniper hunting with me, and although not surprisingly we never caught one I like to think we kept them from settling down to business.

On the night of Friday 24 May I cannot recall whether I had a meal or exactly where I slept, except that it was out of doors. My recollection of early Saturday morning however is very clear. I awoke not long after first light to the sound of aerial activity at a very high level. A Headquarters Company truck with a Bren gun on a swivel mounting and seats for the gunner and his loader had moved to a position not far from me. The two were watching the dogfight directly above us well beyond the range of their gun. We had barely exchanged good mornings when I heard the noise of a very low-flying plane. Without thinking I shouted the order 'Look in!', which in civilian speech means 'Align your sights on a possible target'. They must have been just as jumpy as I was; they not only aligned their sights but also let off a long burst, and the plane made a gliding descent into the Channel about 1000 yards offshore. I suppose I would have done the same. The roar of its engine was overpoweringly loud, it cannot have been more than fifty feet up, and it looked as big as a house. The plane was certainly not R.A.F.; its colour was wrong. Now it lay in the water at such an angle that we could not see its markings. I like to think that it was German. Otherwise it must have been French; if that was the case and the pilot, to go by his direction, was making for England, why was he flying at such low altitude over a combat zone? I must take responsibility, for although I did not give an order to fire I alerted the riflemen, and the half-second of warning did the trick.

By Saturday morning it was becoming clear that the perimeter defence was, however slowly, being driven in. There were just too many Germans and they had tanks and artillery support; the defenders had no heavy weapons, not enough automatic weapons, and for most of the battle only smoke bombs for their mortars. We did not know that the notion of 'evacuation in principle' had been abandoned, and that the Brigadier had already dismissed a German attempt to negotiate a surrender with the reply 'If the Germans want Calais they will have to fight for it.'

My recollection of the greater part of Saturday afternoon is vivid but not serial: being shelled, being bombed from the air, the stench of burning oil tanks and old buildings, the sirens of the Stukas. What took me away from C Company I cannot recall. I was certainly not in personal combat, for next morning the magazine of my pistol was fully charged and the six rounds in my belt pouch were untouched. But I must some time have been a target, for my handsome green and black lanyard was severed at the knot under my left arm, and a week later, searching my battle dress jacket pockets for money, I found two Schmeisser bullets embedded in the army pay book in my breast pocket. I do recall a sense of self-reproach for not being active, 'doing something', rather than simply observing a battle from within. My detailed recall takes up again with being on my way back to C Company Headquarters and meeting Francis Reed, and David Fellowes with a bloody face and a hole in his tin hat, with the same intention. This would have been late in the afternoon. We found it unoccupied. The word at nearby

Headquarters Company was that Vernon had been ordered to move eastwards to a new position. David we sent back to look for a dressing station; Francis and I found what was left of C Company without difficulty.

As I remember the light this was about eight o'clock. There was not much Vernon could do about a defensive position except post lookouts; the dunes, formed haphazard by winds of variable strength and direction, some more than man-height, offered poor fields of fire. He was out of contact with the perimeter defence in his right flank. I think he had only one Bren gun. If we were attacked, this was hand-grenade terrain, and we had no grenades. Needing the physical activity that distracts from contemplating ugly situations, I risked rebuke for insolence and asked Vernon for leave to reconnoitre. This he gave, so I collected Eagle and we made our way discreetly east to a point where the dunes ended in salt flats with occasional tufts of coarse sea-grass, just enough cover, presently replaced by poor pasture with occasional scrubby trees, and some 500 yards east what looked like a quite substantial farmstead. We lay for some time watching this by turns with the elegant Bausch and Lomb binoculars I had bought to celebrate my commission. It was unoccupied.

Vernon heard my report of the lie of the land without comment. I was thirsty, as was Eagle, who had told me that the company had no water. Farms had wells, buckets and suchlike. Vernon of course agreed to my taking a party to fetch water from the farm. I played favourites and did not take Eagle this time; water weighs ten pounds a gallon and the carry would be at least half a mile. There was no problem about volunteers. I took four riflemen.

We moved cautiously to the farm, which proved empty of humans, beasts and fowls. Within the farmyard the house formed one wall; there were a stable, a byre, fowl houses, a granary and, yes, a well with a hand pump. Best of all, we had vessels to carry the water; near the farmhouse door stood two gleamingly clean ten gallon milk cans of the sort one used to see standing by the roadside in Irish country lanes. I showed the men, townsmen, how to prime a pump and we filled the cans to carrying capacity. On with the tops and we were ready to return to C Company.

But as we passed the kitchen door, in fact the main entrance to the house, I had an impulse to look inside, to see how this farmhouse would match in detail an unsorted accumulation of impressions from years of reading and looking at genre paintings. The door was not locked. The room into which it led was exactly as it should be: I could trust the painters and the novelists.

The men had followed me in and were gaping; what they saw will certainly have been different from Northumbria or the Tower Hamlets. As I watched them they spotted, on the side-plate of the *four*,[4] a complete roasted chicken. They looked at me; I made the officer's face that means 'I do not see you' and

4. 'oven'

looked about me while it vanished. Sensing the need now to reassert command I gave the order 'Get carrying', and took a last fond look around at what signified peace, order and continuity. My eye was caught by a bottle on a shelf beside the door among plates and cups, the cork two-thirds out, not labeled but full of a pale golden liquid. Without scruple — the Germans would drink this if I did not — I downed the bottle, a plain white country wine, drinkable in any circumstances, eminently so at that moment.

We delivered the water to the Company-Quartermaster-Sergeant; it actually made a sentence in the regimental history. Vernon I found deep in conference with the Adjutant, Tom Acton. Vernon saw that I was back, so I did not interrupt them. Darkness was falling and I was weary, so I skipped my report, found myself a comfortable patch of fine sand and was quickly asleep. Once in the night I was awakened by light rain; I covered myself with my gas cape and went back to sleep. Daylight woke me at about five o'clock.

It had rained again in the night and the sky was overcast. I moved among the motionless shapes to find Vernon, who was awake and sitting up. He agreed that it might be a good notion to fetch more water before things livened up as was bound to happen. So I took four men and the cans and set out.

Short of the end of the dunes I left the men and crawled forward to check whether my farm was still clear of Germans. It was not: on open ground in front of the farmstead there were three armoured cars, with men in the wrong uniform busy attending to them. There would be no more water: back in cautious haste to Vernon to report.

He would have known without me. Almost the moment I reached him we came under fire from the east, at fairly close range by the sound of it. This lot must have moved west, almost certainly from the armoured cars, along a more northerly line closer to the shore than that of my water fetching. We were lucky not to have run into them. It looked as if the Germans, of whom there were necessarily more than I had seen, were probing to find the strength of the northeastern defences of the town perimeter, which until then had not been attacked because of the impossibility of bringing tracked armour of those days onto the dunes.

Vernon's only sound move was to fall back on the town and make contact with the perimeter defence before he was fully committed. He did not have enough men to make a stand, but the dunes were ideal for a fighting retreat. If he stood his ground his little force would easily be outflanked from the south and cut off. That is how my inexperienced thinking ran, remembering Company-Sergeant-Major Smith's sand table lessons in Vancouver. But not so Vernon's: I was to take out a fighting patrol.

There are two kinds of patrol, my instructors had taught me. One, which bears no adjective, has the sole object of gathering information and returning, intact and undetected, to its unit. The strength of this would be three or four men at the most. The fighting patrol, generally somewhat larger, is designed to bring back prisoners for interrogation about the enemy's force and disposal. My abortive water-fetching mission that morning had accomplished the first — immediate enemy strength: the crews of three armoured cars, almost certainly a reconnaissance force. But a junior subaltern does not debate tactics with his seniors. And anyway it was my turn to go out: Francis Reed had had a couple of rough days on the southern perimeter.

About the size of the patrol my memory is not confident. Having no noncommissioned officer of my own I asked for rifleman Eagle, and I know that the Company Sergeant Major detailed half a dozen Company Office personnel, all seasoned veterans and marksmen. I have an impression that there may have been more. I would have liked a rifle, but was told that there were none to spare. The trench warfare mentality prevailed: a subaltern leading an attack picks up the rifle of the first casualty in his force. As it happened the first casualty on my patrol was German, and the sights of his rifle differed radically from those of the Lee Enfield; it took me half the magazine to learn how to align them to effect. And of course I had no ammunition to reload it with.

We moved east along the line of my water expeditions until the dunes began to level off and then struck north for the Channel until we picked up the footprints of the Germans heading westward in the wet sand. It was a gift, for we came at them from the flank or rear. I don't know how many casualties we had, beyond one rifleman, and of all people, Platoon Sergeant-Major Burman who had taken over 'my' platoon. He was on the ground, bleeding at the throat, but when he saw me his face broke into a large grin. I am glad to record that he survived the war. He must have volunteered to come.

The regimental history describes this patrol as 'most successful'. Not having seen it out I am not in a position to judge whether that expression overstates: I was out of action before it reported. But if we disposed of three machine gun sections — if that is correct — they were the personnel of the armoured cars I had seen in front of the farm, except for the drivers. But I will indulge myself, because this points to the farcical side of war, with one correction of the regimental history. I was not, as it reports, 'wounded by a German non-commissioned officer who appeared from behind a knoll at the wrong moment', but by the single-striped number three of a machine gun section which I came upon unexpectedly around a dune. The gunner and his number two were quick enough to put their hands up when I shouted 'Hände hoch!', but he lagged a little, and when I pulled the trigger there was an embarrassing click. So he shot me with the pistol in his hand. When I told Alex Allan this, the senior surviving officer of the battalion, on whose report the history is here based, he shook his head with dry disapproval: 'failure to count the number of rounds!' With this little fiction he was covering up for the Regiment; it must not be thought that one of his officers, however green, could commit such a beginner's error. As for the machine gun team, they packed up and made off after the man who shot me had relieved me of my binoculars and the empty pistol.

When I could straighten my thoughts I found that I was lying on my back and that the bullet appeared to have gone through me: my back was soaking wet. From the pain when I tried to move it seemed to have damaged a rib. I lay and listened to the intermittent local firing, offset by the heavy but distant sound of battle from the town. After some indeterminable period — my sense of time was not lively — I heard English voices. It was Francis Reed with Eagle and a couple of riflemen looking for me: Vernon was moving and they proposed to take me along. They bandaged me as best they could and then began to pick me up. This hurt unbearably, and much to their distress I sent them away. I could not bear the thought of shaming myself by screaming, and it might well have come to that. This was somewhere between six and eight o'clock on the morning of 26 May 1940.

8
INTO THE BIG BAG CALAIS

It would be gratifying to be able to write how on that Sunday morning Socrates's pronouncement in the *Apology* that an unexamined life is not worth living came into my mind and prompted me to examine my own life up to that point. But I recall no thinking beyond assessing and coming to terms with my situation, which was serious enough. It became clear to me that by my cowardice over the pain of being moved I had cut myself off from medical care, and that loss of blood, dehydration and exposure would take care of me in due course. Through a very long day I passed in and out of consciousness. I recall the noises of battle in Calais with Stuka bombing while the sun was still quite high, afterwards mortar and small arms fire, the occasional aircraft, sporadic automatic fire, and by late afternoon the noise falling off into quiet. Throughout the Sunday night I was either asleep or unconscious; I do not remember awakening or coming to my senses until well into midmorning. I could hear a distant rumble of gunfire which I took to be from Dunkirk; the smoke pall, I could see as I lay, was still there.

My mind was clearer now. I realised that I would be reported, eventually, as 'missing believed killed', and I hated the thought of what that would do to my mother. I cursed myself for having got too far in front of my men; one of them beside me with a rifle and fixed bayonet and we would have had that machine gun team. I wondered where in the dunes I was and tried to remember how far I had followed their tracks toward the east before coming upon them. I do not recall thinking about the state of my immortal soul.

I found that, if I moved very slowly, I could sit up without unbearable pain. I managed to get to my feet and staggered a couple of paces before my knees gave. I just managed to sink slowly rather than pitch forward. I was no better off.

I must have gone into a coma, because it seemed much later when I heard voices, German voices but out of my field of vision. The speakers came nearer: 'Da ist noch ein Anderer'. 'There's another one'. 'Tot?', 'Dead?' 'Wahrscheinlich'. 'Probably'. This was not to be endured, and without turning my head, which would have been very painful, but with as much voice as I could muster, I said 'Ich bin eigenlich nicht tot!' 'Actually I am not dead!'

They were a pair of private soldiers from a reconnaissance unit who had ridden their motorbike and sidecar into the dunes as far as the terrain allowed, and were wandering about looking for souvenirs. They were delighted to have captured an officer, and determined to take me in. Like most German combat troops except the Waffen SS they could be friendly, indeed kind. They had no water, which I asked for, but one of them offered me his bottle of ersatz coffee with an apology; I was thirsty enough to enjoy it. And then the other fetched a substantial slab of chocolate out of his pocket and offered it to me. One has no pride in those circumstances. I thanked him warmly and wolfed it. They brought their vehicle as close as they could. Getting me into the sidecar would have been hard for them to manage, and ironic for me, since it boasted a mounted machine gun for the use of its occupant. So I rode on the pillion seat behind the driver. The cross-country ride to my farmhouse and the road was agonizing, but I managed not to scream, and I was glad of it pain and all. The prospect, not so much of dying as of dying alone and slowly had not been good.

In the city they took me to a large church of which I did not learn the name, a collecting point for strays and wounded not yet cared for, and found me a place to lie on the floor. Then beaming at my expression of gratitude they took their leave. I hope they did not end up in Russia. I never knew their names.

There was no British medical officer or orderly in the church. At one point a French Officer with a Red Cross armband and a nurse in tow put in an appearance. I asked him to look at my wound; he replied 'Nous sommes ici pour les Français'. But there must have been some organising process that I missed, for about midday a number of us who could walk or stagger were identified and helped into a civilian Model A Ford truck manned by two French marines. There were no seats or benches, but I was lucky and had the back of the driver's seat to hang onto. The drive was memorable in one particular. The engine of the Model A Ford of those days was vacuum-fuelled from the tank by way of a covered glass cup mounted on the instrument board. In our truck the cover of the cup had been shot off, and the driver's mate was feeding the engine by delicately pouring petrol into the cup from a champagne bottle. It improved my opinion of the French immensely to watch him, and I cherish the recollection.

At the hospital where I was put down I remember nothing of my arrival except a young British medical officer cutting my shirt off, cleaning my wounds front and back, congratulating me on my luck — no fabric in my wound at point of entry and my spine missed by half an inch at point of exit — sticking on dressings, giving me a white tablet, and putting me to bed. This was Monday; I slept until late morning Wednesday.

The room I awoke in was long and narrow for its length, with about twenty beds each long side, heads against the wall, a six-foot aisle down the middle, and tall windows along the side which my bed faced. It was obviously an improvisation;

there were no visible fittings for attaching medical apparatus. Nevertheless it had been put into medical use — in peacetime it was a parish hall — within two days, and that must have been by the good burghers of Calais who had nothing to thank us for.

My sheets were gleaming white, albeit rough and starchy. I was wearing a clean nightshirt which I don't remember putting on. My filthy jacket and trousers and my pathetic haversack were on a chair by my right side. Someone was asleep in the bed that side, the last before the end wall. The bed on my left was empty. There were no signs of indoor sanitation, only, I was to learn, a standing tap in the compound outside. But the hospital functioned effectively under Surgeon Lieutenant Waind, R.N., not much older than myself, aided by a few Rifle Brigade bandsmen who by army custom had paramedical training. During the battle Waind, who had come ashore from a destroyer, had run a crucially important dressing station on the docks, and had stayed behind, heroically, to care for the wounded who were not taken off. In our hospital he had with little equipment carried out several serious operations successfully.

When I awoke there was no one in the bed on my left; presently a man with chaplain's badges came down the room and sat on it. My tag which made me an R.C. must have been checked while I slept for he was a Jesuit, come to see 'if I needed him'. I liked him and we chatted; I told him about St Peter's College. But I did not waste a lot of his time.

When he left I saw that the man in the bed on my right was awake, and we introduced ourselves; he was Joe Bennett, a second lieutenant in a territorial anti-tank artillery unit. He had a leg wound. A very genuine person, easy to get on with, he proved a good companion. While we were talking an orderly brought our lunch, a bowl of the sort one drank *café au lait* from in those days, containing a stew of meat and pulse, and a chunk of bread. I made my excuses to Joe and set to my meal; I barely noticed the taste but was greatly heartened. The thought of a second helping came into my mind, with almost at once, a sense of its unlikelihood, and I turned to Joe, intending to apologise for my unmannerly greed. To my surprise he had left his meat in the bowl: was he not hungry? In a very broad Yorkshire accent which, I later learned, he used mainly for emphasis, he said that he was indeed bloody hungry but nevertheless would not eat the bloody stuff. I must have looked puzzled because he exploded 'Horsemeat'. Great hunger subdues pride, and I asked, 'May I have it please?' He gave it without grudging or comment, and for the rest of our stay in hospital I ate his meat ration. Horseflesh, which of course I had never eaten before, seemed to me like the moose that my grandfather's friends who had been shooting 'up north' sometimes used to give him, coarse in fibre and rather sweet. The pulse in that invariable lunch was also new to me: lentils; later when we were lucky they appeared in our soup in the camps.

There were two other officers in the hospital, Joe's battery commander, Captain Woodly, and Bobby Allen, a second lieutenant in the Queen Victoria's Rifles, both walking wounded. Woodley's sense of humour was ponderous, but he was amiable enough, and readily accepted being treated with less than Olympian respect by us juniors; Bobby and Joe in their several ways were very entertaining. Not that any of us was minded to be cheerful, with the alternatives of an unfavourable peace and an indefinitely prolonged war in prospect. We found it hard to conceive of an absolute defeat and bitterly accepted the likelihood of long captivity.

Our situation was brought home to us one afternoon when a party of three or four German officers, apparently checking on prisoners in hospitals, swaggered down to our end of the long room and 'inspected' the captured officers. I kept my German to myself, but at least one of them spoke English and harangued us about the guilt, not to mention the folly, of declaring war on Germany. This was a topic we would be exposed to on many occasions until after the Wehrmacht's first winter in Russia. We were glad to see the back of them. Another day a couple of French medical officers looked in. At Waind's request they examined me, and advised strapping my chest in plaster of Paris bandages. Luckily Waind did not have the means and I escaped at least that confinement.

Most days a little French civilian of seedy appearance did the hospital round with useful objects, flint and tinder cigarette lighters, Gauloise cigarettes and suchlike. I found enough English money in my jacket pockets to buy a cheap razor and soap, and a toothbrush and tooth powder (new to me) with a little left over for chocolate and cigarettes. It seemed an accepted feature of going into battle at short notice that the Paymaster's Department would not arrive until much later. Joe and Bobby were soon broke like me. But Captain Woodley, as an officer in command of a unit going overseas had the cash value of his battery's Imprest account in his pocket. We put it to him in hospital that in the interest of the well-being of the Service he should release some of this; his answer was that he intended to take the money back to England intact; we were after all, being fed every day.

After about ten days or so, that would be about the 10th June, I found that I could get around without undue pain; indeed I had little option, for the sanitary arrangements were of the most basic military outdoor kind. The hospital boasted a bath of the sort described in army equipment lists as 'bath, folding, canvas'. With Waind's permission I asked an orderly to set it up by the standing tap and set about becoming clean again; what with the ungainly bath and my being virtually one-armed it was an exhausting operation. But I felt vastly the better for it. I had of course, no shirt — a socially reductive circumstance — and my hospital nightshirt, originally off white with a blue stripe, was shading into grey by the day. I found an orderly in good mood, and he attempted to wash it, but the colour was unaffected.

As I became more active the days became drearier. The weather was dry and often fine, which would have been heartening, but we were unmistakably confined. There were no guards, but the compound wall was unscalable without a ladder, and there were huge locked iron gates. Our hospital had been built as a parish hall in an anticlerical age and was designed for defence. Joe and Bobby and Woodley rightly favoured their wounds. For myself, once I could get about I could not bear lying abed; I am not good at staring at the ceiling. If we talked, as often as not it was about how long the war would last; one avoided adding 'and we go home'.

There were two books. I never learned whose they were: a Penguin volume of Munro's Saki stories and Erskine Childers's *Riddle of the Sands*. I read each one twice. After that I was on my own.

I often found myself standing at the compound gate, peering through the wrought iron structure at the street outside. Occasional passers-by greeted me with unmistakable friendliness. One afternoon, a girl of fifteen or sixteen with two lads, evidently younger brothers, actually stopped at the gate. We exchanged greetings; I added that I was sorry we had brought such desolation on their city and inflicted the horror of being caught up in a battle upon them. The girl was sorry for me as a prisoner and brushed my apologies aside; it was not the fault of the English. Such meetings tended to recur, until they became a regular occurrence. One day as we talked I said without thinking how much I hated being confined and wished I could escape. 'But we will help you to escape'! This alarmed me; the girl was barely out of her childhood, and there were the two brothers, eyes suddenly gleaming with excitement. I glanced at the younger of them and he read my mind. 'Moi, je suis discret!' And with outrageous cheek he turned his head to indicate his elder brother, 'Et lui aussi!' To go by their sister's face she believed him. Here I had nothing to lose except self-respect, but I salved my conscience by making the girl — I had no notion of her name — promise to consult her parents about what she was proposing, which she did. We arranged to meet at a given hour the next day. They evidently had access to the key of the great gate!

Even today I am bitter about what happened then. Next day they came early, and caught the attention of a Welsh chaplain of the Methodist persuasion who by chance was in the hospital, saw them waiting expectantly at the gate and asked them what they wanted. They asked for me, and he sent them away. They must not come back! Then he came to rebuke me for even thinking of attempting to escape from hospital. For the record, a number of successful escapes were made from hospitals in the course of the war. The conditions our senior officers laid down were that no officer must sham illness or disability to gain admission to hospital for the purpose of escaping, and that the senior British medical officer in the hospital must be satisfied that the would-be escaper was sufficiently recovered to make an attempt. In plain terms the chaplain was exceeding his duty; although he carried the courtesy rank of captain, his only authority was spiritual.

I am happy to dismiss him as the only padre in my experience whom I had no respect for. Otherwise the chaplains I know of in the British Army deserved their rank and earned their pay: they risked their lives beside the combat soldiers, comforted the wounded in battle, and helped many a man to die without anxiety. I kept my temper with the little busybody, but it was *the* opportunity of all my time as a prisoner of war to escape.

That disappointment I date from memory at about mid-June. On the 18th June the excellent Surgeon Lieutenant received German orders to prepare his walking wounded to move. He passed the order on to Woodley, Allen and Bennett, from whom I learned of it. The last thing I wanted was to be the only officer left in the hospital, and I begged Waind to add me to his list, arguing that I had in fact been more active than the other three. This he could not dispute, and he gave way. He put new plasters on my wound with a stern injunction not to touch them under any circumstances, and I was ready.

On 19th June we four were moved by truck to a collection point in a French military barracks commandeered by the Germans for the purpose. Regrettably there was no water supply. Here we spent the afternoon and night. My disappointment about not having a real bath disappeared when a fifth British officer, Major Peter Brush of my Regiment, joined us for what was clearly going to be our trip to Germany. He had been three times wounded and — I later learned — had to be restrained in the dressing station after the third occasion. He bore the good news that John Surtees of C Company had survived, severely wounded but now making a good recovery.

Next morning to the sound of much shouting, both Gallic and Teutonic, the five of us were loaded into the back of a truck with a couple of dozen French officers and driven to Lille, which we reached in late afternoon. Here we were herded into the walled grounds of a boys' school and seminary already enclosing what seemed like thousands of French prisoners. There was barely standing room, it seemed, but we found a main building unlocked, and within it the rector's study with armchairs, a sofa, and a good rug on the floor. We took this over and no one challenged our occupation. If the Germans fed the multitude we missed the meal, but there was comfort in finding a bathroom where the plumbing was in order and we could wash, albeit without towels, like civilized creatures.

We were not greatly surprised, next morning, to find that there were no rations, but it was a shock to learn that there was no transport. There was no German officer to protest to, only a *Feldwebel,* a sort of sergeant-major, who took no notice of my complaint and brushed aside the argument that we were only just out of hospital. We found that we were the only British prisoners in the column, which seemed interminably long when the Germans held us back to march at the end, whether to humiliate us or for better supervision I do not know.

At first I was very sorry for myself. Luckily I had almost nothing to carry, only the smallest of military haversacks, and that empty but for my shaving kit and toothbrush. Luckily too most of the French had apparently surrendered with foresight and were heavily burdened with loaded knapsacks, some even with suitcases, and moved at no great pace. And when I reflected that each of my four companions had a leg or foot wound I was ashamed of my self-pity. The day began overcast but soon cleared, and the road had the customary line of trees along it to provide shade. But I did not care for its cobbled paving. Otherwise except when we passed burned-out British vehicles by the road side it was beginning to feel good to be physically active. And it was not wise to think of our eventual destination.

In the course of the morning we crossed the Franco-Belgian frontier: there was of course no *douane*. The French civilians had not been unfriendly, but the Belgians, especially the country folk, were remarkably friendly in the hamlet we passed through and by the roadside where they gathered to watch the dismal procession. We found it heartening to be singled out for kindnesses, of which not the least was the buckets of drinking water they put out as the day grew hot. This last irritated the German sentries who were not offered any, and inclined to kick the buckets over. When I shamed them one or two took note, but since the locals merely refilled the buckets, they left off spilling them in the end. As the only French speaker in the party I did the thanking and became the focus of the kindness, notably five raw eggs, which we ate as we walked — quite a feast — and another time a freshly cooked omelette, very hot, which had my comrades literally eating out of my hands; it delighted those who watched. Yes, I had some too: without any arrangement or discussion we were sharing everything.

The way the French were shambling along with their loads we found ourselves, presently, at the head of the column. This was not in competition, but simply because we found it easier to keep in step, almost as if this were a source of strength. The French did not seem to mind and made way for us willingly, but it infuriated the *Feldwebel*, who several times held us back to the tail of the stragglers. But presently he got tired of this, and next morning we started at the head.

The first day we halted in Tournai, about 12 miles east of Lille. I do not recall what kind of pen or enclosure we were in, if any. Peter and I took over a room in a picturesque empty house of the old town; it had two bedsteads but no mattresses. We were almost too tired to care. I was sitting moping on my springs when my eye was caught by Peter very carefully pulling off a boot and emptying blood from it; one of his wounds had reopened. I tried to persuade him to come with me or let me go and find someone who could dress it but, no, he was not moving.

Not long after that a great outcry of French male voices broke out below our window. There, when I looked down, stood a horse-drawn French field kitchen, a four-wheeled stove with a cauldron, and two cooks dishing from the cauldron with ladles. It looked too good to be real. Like any true soldier Peter had a mess tin at his belt; this I commandeered. Downstairs and outside I thrust my way toward the men with the ladles. There was still plenty, and when I said 'It's for two' they believed me. The food was neat macaroni. When I asked for the sauce or relish the cooks gave me the compassionate look kind people reserve for idiots. We were too hungry not to eat some of it; I remember thinking how much difference a well seasoned cheese *fondue* would have made to it. I also remember sleeping like a log that night, ribs or no ribs, on those bare springs.

The next day we walked farther, about 18 miles east north-east to Ath. This day passed much as the one before but for the absence of even macaroni at the end. We five were bedded down in an enclosed tennis court with a clay surface of which I remember that even the slightest breeze stirred up dust that got in one's eyes. The days began to fall into a pattern of walking, being heartened by the kindness of the people along the way, the amazing good will, who fed us in passing, finally sleeping in strange conditions — the only real novelty of the day. Such a day was the one we slept on shelves in a factory warehouse; that day was otherwise special in there being a tap where we could wash, and in the bread and cheese and sausage the manager's son brought us. On evenings when we were penned in an enclosure with a gate I would hang about there until a likely person, usually a boy, or a girl who had had a British soldier friend, stopped by. They would usually as an errand of kindness go off with such money as Major Woodley released for the day and buy food for us. I am afraid we subalterns gave poor Woodley a bad time for being careful with the Crown's money. Peter Brush, by military etiquette, could not interfere, although he told me privately that Woodley would not be expected to account for Imprest Account money spent in our circumstances.

The best day for me was the one when, in the fine morning, I saw a pair of young nuns standing a little back from the road watching us with evident compassion. By good chance the column was halted within sight of them for a rest. I left it, inspired by grace, one might almost say, and went to ask them to write to my mother in Canada that they had seen me. Certainly they would; I gave them my name and address without much confidence that she would ever get their letter. Bless their pious hearts, she did — although she did not tell me this last until 1945 — a couple of days after the grim War Office information that I was 'missing believed killed'.

Another incident verges on black farce. I can't give the place or date, for my diary was presently taken from me.[5] This day we halted somewhat earlier than usual, and were locked up in the grounds of an empty civilian prison. We five were slow off the mark getting a cell; the straw in the unoccupied ones, their only furniture, was foul — with one exception; this had a sign CONDAMNES on the door, and fresh clean straw. We moved in and I was sent to the gate to do the marketing,

5. See p. 115.

so to speak, clutching the Woodley allowance. As I stood looking out for a likely errand boy or girl a spotless British Army 30-hundredweight truck pulled up. A German soldier got out of the cab and went round to the back and helped four French generals down. Despite all the gold braid they had a distinctly unmilitary air and looked sadly dejected. Then after a small interval, a craggy faced British major-general in battle dress followed. The guard and his driver shepherded them to the gate; the sentry there unlocked it, let them in and locked it behind them. The Frenchmen shambled off to the prison building, the British general hung back as if he wanted to dissociate himself from them. I was standing to one side, ashamed of my dirty uniform, without a headdress (lost in Calais), unpolished boots, needing a haircut. But I had no option: I stood to attention as smartly as I could and uttered the greeting 'Sir!' in the best military tone I could command. (Whatever film directors may make him do the British soldier does not salute bareheaded.) The General had in fact not noticed me until I spoke. 'Thank God! A British (slight pause for a quick glance at my shoulder straps) officer!'. I reported myself and the presence of four others in the prison building and led him to our CONDAMNES accommodation, which amused him. This was Victor Fortune, Commander in Chief of the Fifty-first West Highland Division on the Somme. He had heard of Calais; we had not heard that Higher Command had planned a stand on the line of the Somme, with the Highland Division holding the western sector, and that the French Seventh Army, intended to continue the line of defence from its eastern flank, had collapsed and surrendered *en masse.* Victor Fortune was not left with us more than an hour or two before being taken away to resume his journey into captivity by road and rail. His news made our eventual return seem utterly remote.

From Ath we walked 20 miles northwest to Renaix, then 15 miles northeast, skirting Brussels, to Ninove, then 12 miles to Aalst. After that the next stop I can name confidently was Turnhout, about thirty miles east of Antwerp. To get there we would appear from modern maps to have marched east for a day on a line a few miles north of Brussels, thereafter by two stages northeast for about 35 miles, leaving two easy marches to cover the 30 miles westward to Antwerp. As the crow flies the distance from Lille to Antwerp is about 90 miles; our route was more than twice as long.

Opinion in the prisoner of war camps was that the prisoners captured in May, whether B.E.F. or from Calais or Boulogne, had been brought out of France by such roundabout routes to show the extent of German triumph to the conquered populations of France and Belgium. A more likely purpose will have been to keep the main north-south routes free for German motorized traffic, and to gain time for preparing camps in Germany for an unanticipatedly large number of captives, both British and French. Keeping a column of prisoners on the march was eco-nomical of both food and personnel, let alone transport; in any case the railway system in north-western France had been much damaged in the fighting. Our column, which I would estimate at about 1500–2000 French prisoners, was guarded by about a platoon of second-line infantry with a single senior non-commissioned officer in command.

On that last point in retrospect I think that if we five had refused to march without food the Germans would have made at least a show of providing it. But we were battle-weary and did not know the ropes. It took me about a year to discover the force of uttering in best High German, 'Solch eine Behandlung hätte ich von einem deutschen Offizier/Unteroffizier/Soldat nicht erwartet', 'I would not have expected such treatment from a German officer/non-commissioned officer/soldier'. Admittedly I never had occasion to try it on the Waffen SS, but it very rarely failed with Wehrmacht personnel.

On the second-last day of our march the column, to my amazement, was virtually unguarded, with an n.c.o. at its head, another at the tail, and not more than half a dozen guards down its whole straggling length. The route was, to be sure, through flat, fairly open country, but there was occasional cover. The sun was hot; the marchers, and the guards like them, trudged along with their heads down as if half asleep. I put it to Peter Brush that the two of us should leave the column; with reasonable luck I could talk us into unoccupied France, where security would still be imperfectly organized, and thence into Spain and home. He was unwilling, citing the lecture the officers of our Brigade had attended in England, where a successful World War escaper had strongly recommended the newly captured prisoner waiting until he was in an officers' camp, where 'everything' would 'be organized'. That was the theme of all the books about successful escaping in 1914–1918 but it did not apply, as must be obvious, in 1940, if at all in Hitler's war. In our case there were half a dozen occasions that day when we could have dropped out, no line of trenches to get through, and an as yet overextended occupying force.

It was a good dream, which faded as we marched through the streets of Antwerp to a large railway station where we were herded without ceremony into goods wagons of the *huit-chevaux-quarante-hommes*-sort; there were certainly more than forty in ours. The doors were padlocked, ventilation was minimal; there were no sanitary arrangements. To this day I recall the journey that followed with horror. Our train lay in a siding for much of the afternoon. There was not really enough floor space for all the occupants to lie down. The French were surly and uncooperative, and they had evidently not gone out of their way to wash. When they slept they snored. It seemed a tedious age before we moved, but the night was worse.

We had no notion of our destination and no means of observing our route. But mercifully in the midmorning of next day we detrained, stiff, bleary-eyed and feeling squalid in what we were allowed to know was Dortmund, about 150 miles northeast of Antwerp. From the station we marched two or three miles out of town to a complex of large pens with high barbed wire fences enclosing rows of huts. They looked fairly new, and anything at that moment was preferable to the *huit-chevaux* arrangement. This was the 2nd of July.

Here, in what I suspect was an unauthorized search, I was deprived of my diary. It was no great loss, containing little more than telephone numbers, except for the detail of our march. Presently our five were almost civilly ushered into a separate hut, which proved to be entirely unfurnished and somewhat dusty, but we were delighted to be on our own. We chose a room and 'settled down', that is to say took off such luggage as we were carrying and went out to look around.

What followed was not a good experience: the shocking realization of captivity as a total absolute. It was the barbed wire: you could see freedom through it. The sense of being confined was the more acute for that. None of us said anything about a reaction which we must have been sharing. But for the moment at least we did not want to be alone.

The pen was more than big enough for our trainload. As we explored we could find no kitchens or feeding arrangements. There was a crude outdoor stand of taps and basins where one could wash effectively, but of course no hot water. Even so it was better than anything we had experienced on the march. The latrine was primitive, a long deep ditch with a pole to perch on. I thought of washing my nightshirt, but wondered whether without soap it was worth the effort.

We spent two nights in this pen, sleeping on the floor of our hut. The days were long stretches of tedium not marked off in any way. There were no rations. But unquestionably although we were certainly very hungry we were not starving; we did not feel faint. I suppose that we fed better on the march than it had seemed at the time, a splendid recommendation for a diet mainly of sausage, cheese and bread.

For me the big event was acquisition of a shirt. How I came by it I feel morally obliged to reveal. Drifting aimlessly about the pen on the morning of the second day, I noticed a Frenchman hanging three dripping khaki shirts on an improvised line. With the one he was wearing that made him four times luckier than me in the matter of shirts. I waited until they looked almost dry and then, with a deftness that surprised me, appropriated one. I cannot claim that before I took it the lines in the last passus of *Piers Plowman* which proclaim that 'nede at gret nede may nymen as for his owene | Wiþouten conseil of Conscience', with indeed specific reference to articles of clothing, 'þou3 he come so to a clooth and kan no bettre cheuyssaunce | Nede anoon righte nymeþ hym vnder maynprise' came to my mind, but they most certainly suited my case.[6] And in taking only one of the man's

6. 'if he is in dire need, Need (the needy person) may take (what he needs) as if it were his own property, without permission from Conscience ... and if he should acquire a garment in this way and can find no better expedient, Need immediately goes bail for him': *Piers Plowman: The B version: Will's*

shirts I followed '*Spiritus temperancie*'. My comrades, affected not to note, or did not note, the improvement in my dress.

The next day, 4th July, was my twenty-fourth birthday. In the course of the morning a German n.c.o. with a guard appeared in our pen, sought us out, and took the five of us on foot to another compound half an hour's walk away. This proved to contain exclusively British officers, mainly from the West Highland Division captured at St Valery. Here our group broke up. Bobby Allen was spotted as we entered by a couple of Queen Victoria's Rifles officers hanging about the gate, Woodley and Joe Bennett went in search of gunners, and Peter, taking me with him, set out to find a senior staff officer to report that we had seen Victor Fortune en route and that he was in good order. In the course of the morning Bobby, who knew it was my birthday, appeared with a very handsome present, four squares of chocolate, at least half, I am confident, of what his regimental comrades must have given him. That was no trifling gift; I was moved by his generosity and thoughtfulness.

About midday we all entrained, this time in style in third class carriages. Because of Peter's rank the two of us travelled with officers of the divisional staff, only six in the compartment, which was luxury. One of those officers was the divisional Quartermaster-General. To go by their luggage they had come up from St Valery by rail or truck. Once we were on the move they set about having lunch by getting down one of his suitcases from the rack and very seriously discussing what to have that day while Peter and I salivated. It took a while. But at length they became aware that we had nothing to eat and shared with us, albeit sparingly. A night on the train, and in the early afternoon of the 5th July our journey ended at a small station in Bavaria called Laufen. Here a new set of guards took over and marched us about a mile to our prisoner of war camp Offizierlager, briefly Oflag, VII C.

visions of Piers Plowman, Do-well, Do-better and Do-best, ed. George Kane and E. Talbot Donaldson (London: Athlone Press, 1975), XX 1–22.

9
LAUFEN JULY 1940–SEPTEMBER 1941

By the time our consignment arrived at Laufen the German staff there had developed a system of 'processing' new prisoners quickly. We were first admitted to an outer compound which held the Kommandatur where the guard room was located. From here, after searching, batches of a half-dozen were passed on via a guarded gate, into the inner, actual camp compound where in what must once have been a coach house, and subsequently a vehicle shed, they were briskly shorn by British orderlies. This took about five minutes, during which an English-speaking German in an officer's uniform but without badges of rank, a *Sonderfürher*, we learned to call them, explained that this was necessary because British officers were very often lousy, as well as syphilitic. To the best of my knowledge both allegations were baseless, but the shearing was intensely demoralising, as was probably the intention.

From the shearing shed we were moved to a larger building which looked like and was in fact, a gymnasium, with a stage at one end. As we sat there on the floor we were given, again by British orderlies, a largish loaf of dark bread, a small object they told us was a cheese, a small quantity of what looked like jam, and a pat of margarine. I forget how the last two were packed; I was so hungry that I began to eat without more ado, until a kind person nearby said, 'That's the coming week's ration by the way.' Less than half the loaf remained.

Presently in little groups we were conducted to the rooms where we would live and be assigned to messes. My room, called 'Room Sixty' because of the number of bunks in it, was on the third, the top floor, of a large grey stone building across a yard from the gymnasium. It might once have had pretensions to stateliness but now it looked pathetically seedy; its age showed in the worn stone staircase. Room Sixty proved bewilderingly full of bunks in tiers of three. There were two untenanted at the end farthest from the door. While I was debating with myself there was a joyous shout from behind me. Joe Bennett who had followed me greeting a brother officer from his battery who was dozing on his bunk. He took the empty bed in that tier, and, as it turned out I did better, getting one against the end wall. Its mattress was a straw palliasse of coarse hemp sacking with a pillow to match. On the palliasse there was a cotton sleeping bag in lieu of sheets, a similar pillow case, a blanket and a small towel. My guide told me that if I had been wounded I should report to the medical officer in the sick bay, wished me luck, and left. The medical officer took my plasters off, asked me the date when I was wounded, exclaimed 'Amazing', and declared me a very lucky man and quite fit. He was Major Hadley, R.A.M.C.[7] I remembered his name when I met him in the 60s, fishing the Lodden in Berkshire. Then there was a hot shower, bliss, albeit soapless. Back in Room Sixty I was assigned to a mess, the table nearest to my bunk, provided with a mug, bowl, plate and cutlery, shown the locker I would share, and left to orientate myself. This would be my home for the foreseeable future.

Most of the floor space in the room was taken up by the three-tiered bunks head to the wall along the sides of the room, without regard for the windows, as I recall, with about two foot six between the tiers and about eight foot down the long middle. Here were the mess tables and our stools. Between capture and spring 1944 I rarely sat on a chair. Toward the door end of the room there was an iron stove for which presumably there would be coal come winter. Along the walls between the tiers and in the hall outside there were lockers, one for two men. Down the hall there were latrines, kept in good condition by the orderlies and of adequate number as long as the bowels of all of us were in good order.

In what was left of the afternoon those of my messmates who had not been lounging on their bunks when I came drifted in; Joe's brother gunner Gordon, whose name I have lost, introduced the two of us. In the bunk immediately above me was a very young sapper subaltern called Quincy whose given name I never knew, above him John Vickers from a territorial battalion of the Ox and Bucks Light Infantry, otherwise Jack Hales not long out of Sandhurst, an older man from the Sixtieth named Ashford, Ray Snowden, a Q.V.R. who had his nose broken at Calais by his helmet, knocked forward by a shell fragment, and a dour but sound Edinburgh solicitor, Douglas Cairns, with whom I would share a locker. They were all well mannered and we got along smoothly without a great deal in common.

About 5:30 a pair of orderlies brought up a large vessel of soup from the kitchen, our basic evening meal, and the *Zimmerfürher*, or room commander, nominated by the Germans as in charge of the room, dealt out a portion with the ladle provided into our bowls. My messmates fetched their loaves from their lockers and cut a careful slice to go with it: I savoured the bitter lesson about taking thought for the morrow. There would now, normally, be a parade to be counted, called *Appel* in German, but it was omitted that day to give the Germans time to work out the new muster roll called for by our arrival. So I lay my on my bunk and listened to people. Mostly they talked about *their* war; it took a month or so before that topic lost interest.

---

7. R.A.M.C. = Royal Army Medical Corps.

As darkness fell the occupants of the bunks by the windows put up blackout boards; the sentries tended to shoot at windows with light showing at this stage of captivity. At about 9.00 a *Sonderfürher* and two guards appeared with a cry of 'Achtung!', literally 'Attention'. This one, with the unteutonic name of Kofiata, was particularly unpopular because he stood on his honour as an officer, the Kommandant having decreed that *Sonderfürhers* were to be saluted, contrary to the Geneva Convention, which required that honour only to officers of superior rank. We did not, I was pleased to learn, oblige the Kommandant; indeed we stood up only casually to be counted when our room commander reported all present. After this little farce our lights were turned off. That first night and generally as a prisoner of war I slept like a log. There is nothing like a month of sleeping rough to accommodate one to a palliasse.

Next morning we were roused at 7:00. At 7:30 the orderlies brought up a vessel of hot liquid called by convention 'coffee'; it varied in taste from day to day but invariably made the drink given to me by my German friends at Calais taste like coffee. At 8:30 we formed up for *Appel*, the counting process. It took a long time that morning. We were formed up in companies according to rank, I forget how many to each, and an officer of that rank put in 'command', that is, to call his company to attention while it was being counted. Here it paid to make a show of conformity; this speeded the process. After an hour or more the German *Lageroffizier*, Camp Officer, had a figure which appeared to satisfy him and we could dismiss. The next event of the day would be soup and potatoes at 12:30. So I set out to explore.

Room Sixty was in the oldest building of the camp, originally a country palace of the Archbishop of Salzburg. It now formed part of a rectangle of masonry enclosing a cobbled courtyard. Opposite the palace was the 'New Building', joined to it by a row of smaller structures which now housed the sick bay and orderlies' quarters; and on the fourth side by a blank wall some 30 feet high that shut us off from the town. The entrance to our 'Old Building' gave onto another cobbled rectangle, bounded on one side by the wired off *Kommandatur*, on another by a wall, and on the fourth by the gymnasium and vehicle shed. Between these there was access to a small piece of open ground where we had paraded for *Appel*. This ground looked south toward what appeared to be an orchard and east to the River Slazach. At the outside its area was a quarter of an acre. On three sides it was bounded by a double nine-foot fence of barbed wire, the yard of interval between filled with a tangled roll of the same, high lamp-post lights outside the wire at intervals, and the wire overlooked by open-sided sentry boxes on twenty-foot towers with movable searchlights; if these were like those in my next camp the sentry was armed with a light machine gun. Around the perimeter of this area walkers for exercise had worn a ten foot wide path subsequently gravelled. At a point on the eastern side the ground inside and outside this wire fell away to a few feet above river level; here was another open space. Too much sloped for walking, bounded on three sides by the wire fence with its security measures and on the fourth by a stone parapet reaching to the main level of the camp. A man could sit here and watch the river through the wire. Here at one point there was an island created by a fifteen-foot channel, about a quarter of an acre, long and narrow. Opposite this island there was a formidably secured gate in the perimeter wire; a wooden bridge spanned the channel there. Talk was that presently this was to be a recreation ground for fine afternoons.

Here was the setting of my life for the next fourteen months; days punctuated by 'coffee', *Appel*, soup and potatoes, *Appel*, and lights out at nine, all permeated by a bitter sense of the interminable. It did not help me that across the river lay a glorious panoramic silhouette of the Alps.

One of the stipulations of the Geneva Convention for the Treatment of Prisoners of War was that officers, who were not allowed and could not be required to work, were to be fed at the nutritional level of the captor's garrison troops. With meals the only notable occasion of our day, we were interested in food, and acutely aware that this stipulation was not being decently honoured, in our camp at least. We could not grumble about the bread, a 2 kilogram loaf per week, dark and heavy, just over 285 grammes per day. It tasted pretty good, even though as was often the case, if a man was hungry and had nothing else to eat; so much and no more can be said of it. A modern dietician would describe it as having a high residual component. The week's cheese, with the appearance of a miniature camembert, 3 inches in diameter and ¾ inch in depth, we ate because we thought it might have some food value; the taste was nondescript. Our jam ration, a composition of turnip fibre, colouring and saccharine, was too small to matter. So was the margarine ration, but this was better in taste and texture than what the Red Cross later sent us; they had not yet learnt to make it at home. In the summer of 1940 the soups were watery and insipid, without any discernible solid content. The midday potatoes, usually a couple the size of billiard balls, got progressively worse; on my grandfather's farms they would have been considered unfit for the pigs. Our medical officers calculated that the daily ration in 1940 was worth considerably less than 200 calories per day. The Kommandantur staff disregarded their persistent complaints. Everyone I knew was always hungry, and remembered meals soon displaced 'my war' as an obsessive topic. I recall dreaming about the lunches of beer and bread — a hunk of the farmhouse kind — and cheese John Surtees and I ate in our pub billet. Climbing the three flights to Room Sixty demanded a conscious effort, with pauses when you felt faint.

But a moment came when the Kommandantur's disregard of formal complaints was no longer possible. About a fortnight into August the quality of the potatoes deteriorated to the point where certainly all the officers on our floor, some

200 in number, and apparently the whole of the camp were stricken with severe and prolonged diarrhoea, actually disabling in some cases.

Investigation revealed that there had been extensive collusion between the British camp quartermaster, a Captain Goodrich, and his German counterpart, by which Goodrich accepted potatoes past their date of use and signed receipts for meat and vegetable supplies that were not delivered in return for goodness knows what favours or privileges. These were not revealed to us. But the Kommandant, Oberst Frey, apologised to our Senior Medical Officer and sacked his offending subordinate. As for Goodrich, I don't suppose he enjoyed the rest of his time in captivity, at the end of which he was court-martialled and ignominiously dismissed the service. And Colonel Holland, the 'Senior British Officer', that is the senior officer responsible to the Germans, was replaced. This was the man who, as Town Commandant at Calais, had sent the Queen Victoria's Rifles, with none of their vehicles and barely half of their arms, let alone heavier weapons or wireless, to defend the five main roads into Calais on the 22nd May. His place was taken by a formidable six-foot-six battalion commander of a highland regiment who could outface Frey, and life improved. The cellars were cleaned out and disinfected, the potato ration improved in quality and quantity, the soup now contained recognisable elements of meat and vegetables. We were no longer quite so hungry.

We were allowed to write two letters a month on forms made to be closed but not sealed: they were of course censored. My first to my mother reached her a little before Christmas, third in order after the predictable War Office message and the kind reassuring Belgian nun's letter. My messmates were busily writing to friends, in Switzerland and Spain or Portugal or Sweden. A few of the early arrivals were already getting food parcels from friends in the neutral countries. I thought of my cousin in the Benedictine College in Rome. If this was possible he would have been called or sent home when Italy entered the war in June, but just conceivably he might still be in Rome by some arcane ecclesiastical arrangement, even if virtually interned there. Writing to him was worth a try, and if he was gone my letter would certainly be read and probably answered. A big event in our mess was Douglas Cairns receiving a food parcel from Switzerland in late September; to his great credit he shared some of its contents with us. As the near-starvation time became more remote, so sharing food above the rations came to be general practice in messes.

Again by the Geneva agreement officer prisoners received a part of their pay in the form of camp currency, *Lagermarks*. There was nothing you could buy with it except shaving kit, toothpaste and suchlike, and unbelievably thin beer available in a cheerless canteen, of which the only advantage was that it was heated in winter. Even in deep winter and 300 feet above sea level we had coal enough for only about three hours of fire a day in our stove.

Morale, at its all-time nadir for me in July and August, improved a little with the improved rations, and was generally boosted by the defeat inflicted on the Italian Army in North Africa, so devastating that even the *Völkischer Beobachter*, the Nazi Daily Mail, so to speak and of course the only paper we got to see, could not conceal it. And now we had a Senior British Officer who could face down Oberst Frey. This last showed in small but important ways. He had lost a great deal of face through the dishonesty of his quartermaster, and it was by so much the harder for him to refuse requests for a recreation room where one could sit and read in quiet, or a few pieces of furniture and better lighting for the camp theatre. We were even allowed to buy a good piano with money levied on our pay, by our ready consent, I must add. Then by a brilliant insight of a Major Charles Shears, in peacetime on the board of Hutchinson's, who saw that they would not have much sale for the duration of the war, we bought all the fiction titles on the list of the Tauchnitz Library, after which Frey could not decently refuse us room space for a real camp library. In any event it seemed to have penetrated his Prussian head that a prisoner reading a book was less trouble than one at a loose end.

Before Tauchnitz a prisoner without a book was in a poor way. If he had come to camp with a book, once finished with it he looked about him for another equally lucky man. If neither had read the other's book they negotiated an exchange, either on the spot or as soon as both were ready. I was lucky; I had 'borrowed' André Maurois's *Les silences du colonel Bramble* from the Rector's shelves in the seminary at Lille. I admit with shame that I have failed to return it, pleading in extenuation that I have returned all the other books I borrowed in my life. I read *Les silences* several times before I parted from it; it started my pre-Tauchnitz borrowing from a high base. For my first exchange, if I recall aright, was for Graves's *I, Claudius*. I made some good friends on the exchange circuit, notably John Buxton, who honoured me by asking my opinion of his love poetry, and Reynold Higgins of the Q. V. R. Tim (A. N. L.) Munby of that regiment I knew to greet, but he was very reserved and a captain; I wish I had got to know him.

Notwithstanding the joy of having books in abundance I was essentially very bored. I sensed that this was dangerous; it was evident from observation that the borderline between boredom and damaging self-pity was very lightly drawn. I made a private ritual of counting my blessings: how lucky I was to be alive at all. Unlike Quincy and Jack Hales, barely more than senior schoolboys, I had had my nose in the trough of life for three full years, whereas being taken had deprived them of one of the best parts of theirs, those first heady years of independence. Unlike John Buxton I had not been separated for an evidently indeterminate period from a woman with whom I was deeply in love. I had not (this was a very private thought) had to put my hands up in surrender. My problem was an aggravated sense of the slow movement of time. Reading was fine, but now it lacked a focus, could be no more than a palliative. That summer of 1940 seemed very long indeed. It does not, I reckon, once its quality has been described, make much of a story. Only a few features mark that summer off.

One such was getting to know Major Alex Allan, the second in command of our battalion, who assumed command late on Saturday afternoon when it appeared that Colonel Hoskyns's wound was too severe for him to carry on. Alex, before long one of my favourite people, I had first observed in the officers' mess on the morning after our arrival in Essex complaining about the quality of the breakfast. He was, in an engaging way, something of a dual personality, perfectly cast for the role of crusty major, which (aware of this or not) he would on occasion play to perfection. Under the crust, I came to realise, were a soft heart and absolute integrity. Before appointment as second in command he had C Company; he was much cherished by the riflemen because while he demanded first class soldiering from them he looked after their welfare like a loving father. Likewise under the crust and pepper there was a highly intelligent and perceptive mind, albeit imperfectly educated as was often in my observation the case in wealthy English families.

As senior surviving officer of our battalion it would be his duty when we got home to submit an account of its actions at Calais, and presently it became my turn to report. This I did by word of mouth while we walked the round of the exercise ground or, if we were lucky and found one unoccupied, on a bench on its perimeter. I told him about my patrol and how well the riflemen, especially Eagle, had behaved, suggested that Eagle might be recommended for a Military Medal, and that the patrol had from the sound of it carried on after I was wounded. He duly rebuked me for the beginner's error of not counting the number of rounds. Then he questioned me at length and closely about Vernon's defensive arrangements and whether I had any notion of his intentions and plans. In the end he had to believe that I did not know what was in Vernon's mind. He particularly wanted to ascertain why, late on Saturday, Vernon had not fallen back on the shortened defensive position dictated by the day's casualties. Apparently the Adjutant, Tom Acton, whom I had found with Vernon when I came back from the farm with water, had been sent with an order for him to do so. Alex knew that battle-memory can be selective, but after another couple of longish sessions of questioning he accepted that I had no notion of the order, that he had all my information.

I can understand his concern. But I did not feel called upon to speculate for him about Vernon's reasons. At that time I would not have known what to think about them. Over the years I have come to the opinion that Vernon was a little old for a fighting command, a condition as much to do with personality as with the calendar of years, and that Tom Acton, not many months older than myself, was too young to carry the responsibilities of an adjutant as the commanding officer's agent. Vernon was a very 'nice' man, but although we were in the same camps for three years all told I never got to know him. I last heard from him in 1947 when he wrote asking me what I thought of the notion of his emigrating to Canada: he did not like the way things were going in England. Alex and I however became close friends over the years.

Toward the end of September I was told on morning *Appel* that Brigadier Nicholson would be obliged if I would meet him in the canteen after lunch, an unmistakeable order, however courteously put. I made myself as presentable as I could without tie or lanyard or boot polish or clothes brush and duly reported. It was a fine day and the canteen was as good as empty. He motioned to sit at the table beside him, pointed to the *Völkischer Beobachter* open before him and asked me to translate the war communiqué of the day. By convenient luck I had already read it; my German military vocabulary was growing. When I had finished he amazed me by asking for my opinion about how the war in Tripoli was going. While I was giving thought to my answer he called up beer for both of us; the barman, surly with one-pip lieutenants, brought it smartly. I could not conceive why he should think my opinion worth anything, but I answered that the view of all the subalterns in our mess was that on present form we could deal with the Italians if we had the tanks and vehicles, but that supply of these by the Mediterranean was hazardous and around the Cape was very slow. If this was a test it was too easy. I was relieved not to be asked my opinion about how long the war would last. He put me on translation duty another couple of times, a very agreeable man, able to make easy conversation notwithstanding the difference of rank. It was plain that he was deeply concerned by the military prospect, and I suspect that he regarded his command at Calais as a failure, which was unjust to himself, for he was faced with a task that had no options. It never entered my mind that this would drive him to suicide. Some time before Christmas he moved to another camp.

In November the weather turned cold, but to my good fortune a number of parcels addressed to the Senior Officer, the Rifle Brigade, arrived from Budapest. It appeared that the British Military Attaché in the Budapest embassy was a Greenjacket. It was a fine surprise, Alex appearing in Room Sixty with a huge grin and an armful of clothing for me, a second shirt — oh joy! — warm underwear, pyjamas, soap, and cigarettes. These were of Turkish tobacco from Iraq, strange but vastly preferable to the fierce Belgian stuff sometimes available in limited amounts. My morale soared: to be able, in Dr Johnson's terms, to shift my linen rather than wait for a warm day when my shirt and smalls would dry while I went about with battle dress fabric next to my skin restored self-respect.

Soon after that I had my first food parcel from Rome, with various goodies, notably a whole globular cheese about six inches in diameter, a tin of Nestlé's condensed milk, a quantity of quite delicious ship's biscuit, chocolate and tobacco. I paid my debt of honour to the mess by dividing the chocolate; we had not yet come to the point where one shared everything. An engaging note came with the provisions: the American monks had recently heard from my cousin in Canada;

would I accept these tokens of their pleasure at having had him in their community? Life was improving as long as one did not look forward. Winter came suddenly. One day the orderlies brought up our first daily ration of coal, enough to keep the room temperature tolerable in the afternoon and evening. How this came about I don't know, but someone had the splendid notion of flooding the inner part of the exercise ground and — there will have been a connection, doubtless — the Germans were able to find skates for us to hire. Here, until it snowed and covered the ice, we even played hockey with makeshift sticks. One or two of the senior officers were expert figure skaters; that art had not reached Saskatchewan in my time there.

Early in December there was a rumour that distribution of British Red Cross food parcels was in prospect; at last there was to be a delivery! These parcels, funded by contributions to the British Red Cross and packed in Great Britain by volunteers, were dispatched on a scale of one prisoner of war per week by way of Portugal, France and Switzerland, and distributed to the camps from Geneva. Certainly they were less urgent freight in German-controlled France. We did not think the German authorities would steal or countenance stealing them, but they never reached the camps at the rate laid down in the convention, even after the German capitulation in Tunisia, when almost the whole Afrika Corps was bagged and sent to Canada and the U.S.A. and there was an incentive to reciprocity. In December 1940 the issue at first was one parcel per mess per week. This we assigned Douglas Cairns to divide. Things got gradually better in this respect until 1945 when the Allied air forces turned their attention to the German railway system, but at no time, to my knowledge, was there ever in any camp an issue of a parcel per prisoner per week, although I heard of much luxury in other camps. The parcels were of good sustaining fare, but the margarine, if kept too long in its tin, tended to be rancid. In some camps it was used to fuel lamps for tunnelling.

One more notable event in that 'term', for me at least, was the delivery of a Red Cross shipment of British battle dress uniform and boots from Geneva. There had been rumours of this and I was looking forward to the day when I might have a clean jacket; nothing could get the mix of blood and dirt out of the one I had gone to war in. So I did not object when to my surprise I was made interpreter to the British Quartermaster who had been put in charge of distribution, with a German n.c.o. by his side. This was Captain McIntosh, inevitably 'Tosh', a charming little highlander. We soon had the German assigned to us tamed, and after the first rush my duty was about an hour a week. Before that rush I was the privileged first served, thereafter a new man. Not by any means least, I rated a pair of the army's excellent boots and would now have dry feet on parade. The Belgian cobbles had ruined the 'officer's boots' I had bought on being commissioned.

Christmas was pretty dismal. The next issue of Red Cross parcels was two per mess, and the Germans conceded a second blanket, which was welcome. It

was good to be warmer and less hungry, but the season of the year enforced realization that nothing had really changed. The best a man in our situation could
do was put 1940 behind him. It has not been good to remember those first six
months in the bag. Yet seen in the sixty-year perspective of our time they were
soft and easy.

Seen in my immediate perspective at the time, things improved in January.
Being a prisoner of war in our circumstances at that time was like being in a civil
prison with no charges against you, no foreseeable term of release, and not even a
system of justice to rage against — we were, at that stage of the war, all volunteers,
thus with only ourselves to blame for our plight. There was one difference: a man
could, just conceivably, end his confinement by his own effort. It had been done. I
had heard one successful escaper describe his effort, and read books by him and
others with the same achievement. Even I had had two good chances, one spoiled
by an officious busybody, the other neglected because of regard for advice not applicable to our situation. That could not be all.

During the summer, whenever I could muster the energy, I had studied the
possibilities at Laufen. They did not look rich. The front gate of the prisoners' area
of confinement opened into another, the forecourt of the Kommandatur, high
double wire everywhere, every gate locked and guarded. The sentries at all points
were trigger-happy, reflecting Oberst Frey's choler. The towers covered the double
wire, apparently along its entire length. In daylight it was an absolute barrier; at
dark we were locked in. As for the gates, at this stage in the development of escape
techniques they were simply impossible. The only informal way out of the camp,
all too obviously, was by tunnel. Even here the restriction was severe. Any tunnel
from the New Block would emerge in the actual town, and seemed ruled out by
this. As for the Old Block, we did not have free access to its ground floor. A tunnel
demanded a concealed starting point, and that for a long period. After all this, a
tunnel was an engineering project that required organization; simply disposing
of the spoil, the excavated earth, undetected was a major undertaking. Above all,
a tunnel was a team project; how did one set about forming or joining a team?

There was one point on the perimeter of the camp defined by the wire where
the ground inside and outside this fell away to a few feet above river level, and it
looked as if, just possibly, there might be a blind spot between two sentry towers.
Here, I judged, was the only place for a tunnel to emerge. The closest place in the
camp to this with cover of any kind was the north-east corner of the gym, the end
actually farthest from the stage about forty feet away. But within the gym at that
corner there was no hope of secrecy or security; it was simply floor and wall. People came and went constantly, threw medicine balls about, did fitness exercises.
Strolling sentries looked in at irregular intervals.

I was standing in that corner one day in January, peering hopelessly at the
walls and floor, when I sensed a presence near me and turned my head. It was a

Newspaper cutting of three p.o.w.s sent to Clara (George Kane in middle).

subaltern in the Welsh Guards whom I had not yet met. I became conscious of the absurdity of standing inactive in a corner apparently contemplating a wall in a room full of active people. There was even a bustle on the stage in preparation for a rehearsal later in the afternoon. I am sceptical about telepathy, but we looked at each other and said almost simultaneously, 'I know what you're thinking'. His name was Charles Janson. He had been in the rearguard company of the Welsh Guards covering the withdrawal of the 20th Guards Division into Boulogne for evacuation on 22 May 1940: that was his route into the big bag. We talked about the possibility of escaping and where a man made a beginning. There was a brother officer in his company who might know. He would speak to him.

This was Captain Archie Noel, one of the people I noticed busy on the stage. Charles spoke to him to good effect and next day took me to meet him. Archie looked me over and noncommittally said he would be in touch. There was probably some sort of vetting process. The first effect was that I was moved from Room Sixty to Room Ninety where I was assigned to the mess to which Charles belonged and told to report to Archie as a stagehand.

The change of mess was probably a security measure. Before I joined it consisted of only four people, one of them the room commander, Edward Rae, a two-pip lieutenant of about 35 in the Royal Sussex Regiment, in peacetime headmaster and with his wife owner of a preparatory school at Seaford in Sussex. Anything but solemn, he carried remarkable authority. He would see to it that Room 90 did not get a bad name with the German n.c.o.s and *Sonderführers* responsible for the 9:00 count by baiting and poor cooperation, for this might provoke an impromptu room search when even a pair of trousers with grubby knees would be a disaster. And my new messmates would know from his example not to ask how 'things' had gone after I had been absent, indeed not findable, for an afternoon.

All that apart I was greatly the gainer by the companionship of four excellent men. Ed, who concealed great common sense under an ebullient, sometimes almost buffoonish exterior, was kind-hearted and generous to a fault, a serious man without solemnity, which I admire. Then there was Max Duhamel, an odd fish whom nevertheless it was impossible not to like and respect. The oddity was his frame of mind. He was anything but stupid and could argue very shrewdly in a quiet way if you accepted his premises. He was, in short, deeply religious, and, unlike many such, a model of Christian meekness. Now here is the oddity: he had an *idée fixe* that Charles was ineffectual and helpless, needed looking after, and went so far as to wash his dishes and cutlery after meals. Charles meanwhile was anything but ineffectual and resourceless; one of his resources consisted in making people want to wait on him. Max was occasionally teased for having once said, apparently, that he was kin to Winston Churchill. There was no reason why this should not have been true, but nobody believed him except the Germans, who, later, included him in a group of *prominenti* and sent him to Colditz for safekeeping, and in spring 1945, to the Bavarian Alps where such people might come in handy for bargaining or as hostages. Then there was Mike Wittet, a large, well-featured, quiet young man not long out of school and into the City. He had a fine sense of humour and, in an indefinable way, a lot of style, although he never asserted his presence. His family, with strong Channel Isles connexions, had been merchants in the Levant since the seventeenth century. That leaves Charles. I reserve him for later description; he will not be lost. We became close friends, and if we were both not now so arthritic, would see each other joyously and often. This mess was already sharing absolutely when I joined it, and I was much relieved that before long I had an Italian parcel to contribute.

The tunnel enterprise which I had been allowed to join was indeed based on the gym, not, of course, from the too obvious nearest point to the wire, but from under the stage at the far end of the gym. This would call for almost twice as much digging, about sixty feet instead of thirty. There were two compensations; it was unlikely that the German security officer and his team would look for a tunnel there, and the surface members of the tunnel team could legitimise their presence by taking on the roles of stage manager, lighting expert and stage-hands. Their being busy was actually good cover. Archie Noel was in charge; the stage electrician, Sid Helm of Royal Signals, something of a wag but a superb im-proviser, provided the luxury of electric light underground: just as well for at that time we did not have enough rancid margarine for fat lamps. The engineer was Jim Rogers, a sapper major; he was too tall and conspicuous for splendid musta-chios to be a stagehand. But he was a good instructor. The digging was done by 'face workers', small and agile enough to cut out the earth and get it past their bodies into a box on sledge runners with a cord on either end behind them. When this was full they signalled to Number Two, in the vertical shaft from which the actual tunnel chamber proceeded. Number Two thereupon pulled it back to the shaft, emptied it, and signalled this by a reciprocal tug. While Number One dug he packed the spoil for lifting to the surface and disposal. At half time he and Num-ber Two would exchange jobs. A shift was three hours long; on good days when the timing of *Appel* was not disturbed there might be two, depending on disposal and the weather.

The dimensions of the tunnel were dictated by the material available for shor-ing, which was provided by our bunks in the form of the wooden cross slats which supported the palliasse, about two foot six longs. These bed boards were contrib-uted over a period of time by every room in the camp; such a levy was not all that brutal; a man could sleep comfortably on half the number originally in the bunk.

Because of my stature — I was all of five foot nine-and-a-half in those days — I was a face man. My first time down was with Jim Rogers as instructor. I wore my disreputable old battle dress trousers. Under the stage floor, a part of which was lifted as if by magic, there were about eighteen inches of headroom. The cover of the tunnel was open and a light coming up from the shaft. Jim sent me down this ahead of him. At the bottom I peered into a rectangular excavation shored up at its beginning and at intervals by those bed boards, and a light about ten foot ahead at the face, then shoring and beyond it blank brown earth. Here I found a kitchen knife, blunt of course, and one of those little shovels that used to go with domestic coal scuttles. Jim, six foot six and all, crawled up behind me pushing the sledge ahead of him. Over my shoulder he showed me how to maintain direction and angle of incline needed both to ensure ventilation and to emerge at the right height above river level at the end. For half an hour he watched while I dug; then crawled backwards to the shaft, I following similarly. There we changed places, and I worked as number two until he called me to the face. Now he showed me how to fit a piece of shoring. We changed places; I fitted the shoring as he had shown me, and he told me I would 'do'. That ended the lesson.

There were a number of face workers; my 'mate' was Pat Sherrard, a subaltern in the 60th, like me taken at Calais. Before we joined the team we were casual ac-quaintances. But we found each other congenial to work with, and in that sense had a close relation, but without any particular intimacy. One day in Germany I asked him, half mockingly, what he might be thinking about when he gazed, as he often did, into the middle distance for long periods. 'Nothing, George, absolutely nothing.' We worked together on two tunnels, were in the same much smaller room and mess in two camps after Laufen, from September '41 to November '42. I did not see him again until 1946 when I was on a very dull, waiting-for-demobilization posting in Nottingham and he took the trouble to look me up. He was best man at my wedding, and I was one of four fellow prisoners he invited to his own. Doubtless he found me as much of a freak as I did him; he was certainly different from both the Eton and Winchester stereotypes in our regimental messes. There was money in his family; his father occupied himself breeding daffodils. A very comfortable and unexciting friend: we lost touch with him and his wife when we moved to the States in 1976, which I regret.

Pat and I would do a three-hour shift underground every second day. My filthy old battle dress came in handy. We would turn up at the gym in good time, stand by and on the word that it was secure, be on the stage and under it within two minutes. The soil was just about ideal for digging, impacted fine river silt with just enough clay component to hold it together so that it could be cut away, no stones bigger than pebbles. Because of the incline and the slight warmth of the electric light the air was sweet; the temperature pretty constant at about 55° Fahrenheit. Working every second day you were aware of progress, accomplishment. Out and up by a succession of 'all clears', a shower, albeit cold, and clean clothes induced euphoria, a rare and precious state in our community.

At the outset the spoil from the theatre tunnel was simply 'lost' under the stage, buried among the mix of earth and sawdust and builders' rubbish. But this could not go on. The earth we dug out was much the same colour as the gravel on the perimeter of the recreation ground, if not the same texture. It would blend and disappear there if thinly spread. There was plenty of willing labour to get it there; the method of distribution devised was absurdly simple and ingenious. By processes I had nothing to do with some dozen helpers were recruited, equipped and trained. The kit was their older pair of battledress trousers with the right hand pocket slit. As security permitted they picked up, at the stage door so to speak, an army-issue sock which had a drawstring governing a hole at the point of the great toe and another at the top. A helper fastened this sock, drawstring tight, filled with crumbled spoil, inside his right trouser leg, strolled out and onto the exercise ground, and once on the gravel surround, released the toe-drawstring, and controlling the rate of fall, plodded around until the sock was empty, and then collected another full one. Other helpers, too senior for that undignified exercise, shuffled around the course working the spoil into the gravel. Pat and I would do our spell at disposal on 'off' days; Charles, who was too tall for underground work, emptied many a sock when he was not on sentry duty, curiously called 'stooging'.

On rainy days the method could not be used, and if we dug, the filled socks had to be stored, risk notwithstanding, under the stage.

In my new ordered existence that began in January 1940 time, seen in terms of our objective, acquired a physical dimension measurable by the length of the tunnel chamber as this grew. There were two regulators of progress: the need for care about precise direction and slope, and for security in the process of disposal. It was easy enough to measure the chamber; this we knew. But establishing precisely the distance from the shaft to the wire, and then to the riverbank, was another matter. The tunnel route lay almost exactly under a sentry tower; there was no question of pacing it out. It looked, unverifiably, to be between fifty-five and sixty yards from the theatre to the river, but this could only be a rough guess. The only certainty was that we were making progress.

As a concomitant life seemed richer. Charles, a notable exception to what I have written about the children of the rich being undereducated, broadened my experience and deepened my understanding of music as a listener. He was an accomplished pianist himself and was willing to play for my pleasure. The Tauchnitz and subsequent library acquisitions steeped me in the works of the British novelists and essayists active between the wars, whose writing I had already spotted and begun to collect in the Penguin series: here they all were. I came upon Hemingway and got him out of my system by discovering that I could write like him but did not enjoy the exercise because his style did not survive abstraction from the unique combination of crudeness and sensibility in his work. I learned not to be an intellectual snob as I observed the abundant talent in music and other arts, notably graphic, in my unacademic brother officers. The camp orchestra and jazz band could fill the theatre/gym to the point of standing room only at the back for Germans. I observed Tim Bailey, an agreeable subaltern from a cavalry regiment reckoned to be officered by pinheads, turn a second-rate thriller, *No Orchids for Miss Blandish*, into a stylish three-act social comedy. A captain in the Welsh Guards, Henry Coombe-Tennant, could hold a packed gym for two hours improvising to classical themes on the piano, with naughty excursions into what we called 'vamping' that brought down the house. This was a talented regiment; a second lieutenant, Mike Edwards, one night lock-picked his way into the *Kommandatur* and back out undetected as a prank. Life, with the prospect of finishing the tunnel, was not too bad, even though the war in the desert had taken an ugly turn with the arrival of the Afrika Korps in Tunis at the end of March.

Meanwhile we dug at the rate of about a foot a day. This may not seem much, but the control was disposal. A foot of progress produced in fragmented form what when compacted had been 6 ¼ cubic feet of earth. As the chamber lengthened so it took longer to get this to the shaft, and it had to be disposed of in the day; the space under the stage would take no more without increasing the danger of discovery.

But even at the rate of a foot a day, by the middle of June we reckoned the face to be not far short of the wire; we might be able to break out in August. There was now a camp Escape Committee from which we could expect help with maps, compasses and concentrated rations; such contraband came into camp by various 'informal' means in personal, not Red Cross, parcels. Thus when Pat and I began to come upon larger stones as we dug we were not depressed, much as these slowed down digging and disposal. But we decided that Archie and Jim had better know about this. Jim went down for a shift, a long belly-crawl there and back for such a big man. He reported that in his view we were approaching the foundations of a very old wall. There was no option but to work through it; we did not dare change the course of the chamber. He would, for the time being, take over the face work. But he warned that getting through the stone was not the problem: if the sentry towers had ground microphones, that is percussion sensors, as was likely, they might well pick up the unavoidable sound of metal pinging on stone. And so they did.

I suppose it was about a week later that the security staff were certain, and then they wasted no time on shortest distance thinking but made straight for the stage. We learned of our loss from the orderlies who brought us our 'coffee' at 7:30. They brought more details in the course of the day: the Germans moved in on the theatre at daybreak; when they had taken up enough of the stage and found our shaft cover the Security Officer had to use his pistol to persuade the smallest member of the guard company to take a cord to the face and measure the chamber. Of course Archie and his stage hands were marked men, but for whatever unfathomable reason nobody was sent to solitary confinement, as was permissible for escape attempts within the Convention. They simply gave the Senior British Officer a bill for the cost of the repairs to the stage floor.

I prefer not to dwell on the depth of my disappointment. But it speaks for the resilience of the human animal that all of us were heartened by the distance we had taken the chamber of our tunnel. Given the chance we could do it again and, after all, we had known all along that our operation was never not at great risk.

Meanwhile the summer was not over. There were two more escape attempts, one successful and that by a means so outrageously impossible that it proved effective. The Germans had, in June, honoured their undertaking to give us access to the little island as a recreation ground. They activated the gate by the twenty-foot wooden bridge across the fifteen-foot channel that created the island, and for three or four hours, I forget how long, on fine days, we could enjoy what was in effect an idyllic park, grass and occasional trees set off by swiftly flowing water. Here we could lie staring at the sky, or, across the main river to the west, the silhouette of the distant Bavarian Alps, without the depressing intervention of barbed wire. We could ignore the sentry tower high above the gate — very likely the one that picked up our digging. At the given hour we were shepherded off the island and two dog-handlers with Alsatian shepherd dogs would clear it, come back into camp by the double gate and secure it. As long as we were on the island the swift current of the broad river on its way north to the Danube, and the field of vision of the nearest sentry tower effectively penned us in.

So, apparently, the Germans believed. But over the summer two field officers, Lieut. Col. Hugh Swinburne and Major James Murray-Grant, with the help of a superb team, demonstrated that the apparently impossible can be accomplished. In an open space on the island, away from any trees, a half dozen or so prisoners lounged on the grass around a rug on which they played card games of kinds unlikely to interest any occasional strolling sentry who might be on the island while beneath the rug they somehow excavated a coffin-shaped pit big enough to accommodate Swinburne, a big man, and Murray-Grant, to dispose of the spoil, and make a cover topped with the original turf that successfully concealed their dig. I knew about the scheme only because as a German speaker I was on distract-the-sentry duty. But I had no notion how they went about the undertaking. Come the day, Swinburne and Murray-Grant stayed behind on the island while the rest of us were shepherded off; those of us in the know went indoors so as not to show any interest in the dogs clearing the island. All went well. The runners had chosen a moonless night, and when total darkness could be presumed they emerged, put back the cover of the hide as best they could by touch, tiptoed across the bridge with boots in hand, crept along the bank until they were well clear of the sentry tower, and headed for the Schaffhausen salient. Except for the virtual impossibility of digging the pit undetected it seemed so easy next day, especially after the team during another afternoon at cards had successfully finished covering the roof of the pit. Moreover the absence of the pair had been successfully covered on parade: the guards who counted us often had difficulty with their arithmetic.

A few days later, much to our surprise, Pat and I were offered the use of the hide, apparently as reward for our work in the theatre tunnel. Of course we accepted. Then followed several days of frenzied preparation while we were 'kitted up' by the escape committee that had taken shape early in 1941. We were going across country. Pat having no German might not have been an obstacle to travelling by train, but escaping techniques had not reached the sophistication of civilian clothes and false papers. The moon was still right and, our pockets loaded with chocolate and concentrated food and maps, we were buried alive. I will not prolong the story here; we were both very excited and found it hard to believe that this was real. We went under at about 3:30 and would have a long wait for complete darkness. Breathing through rubber tubes, we could not have talked had we had anything to say. We listened to the island being cleared, and then the footsteps, doubtless of the dog handlers; they approached and then went on. I remember thinking, 'Now we are clear', when Pat gripped my shoulder and hissed, 'He's tugging at my tube!'. There was a joyful, excited yelp, then barking, and we knew we were finished. Much later, in cold blood, we concluded from the sound of the footsteps receding, that the dog had picked up the scent on a random shift of the breeze after his handlers had decided the island was clear.

What passed through the mind of the sentry in the tower above the bridge I don't like to think. Unless he had only just come on duty he was in trouble. For the handlers this was a coup. They would probably be allowed to keep the chocolate and other goodies we had on our persons. They encouraged the dogs to smell us, praising them the while. That the dogs did with a certain aloofness; I hope they got some of the chocolate. I kept my German to myself.

We were taken, sheepish and dishevelled, with earth in our hair, through the camp to the *Kommandatur*, while our brother officers stared at us in surprise, with expressions of sympathy for our rotten luck. The German Security Officer whose English was good treated us civilly, but we had to endure a homily to the text of 'Why do you want to go home, when for you the war is over?' We gave the simple answer that we considered it our duty as officers, and that he would do the same in similar circumstances, which ended the discussion. After that we were ushered back into camp, no cells, no punishment. A few days later Swinburne and Murray-Grant were picked up well on the way to Switzerland. This was in early August. It would have been a dismal month but for being told that we would be moving in September to Oflag VIB at Dössel bei Warburg in Westphalia, which had previously held Polish officers. Our team flexed its muscles, so to speak. We would do it again.

Warburg is about 300 crow-flight miles north of Schaffhausen, twice as far from the salient as Laufen and five times as far as Oflag VB at Biberach in Swabia, from which, in the early summer months of 1941, five of our people had escaped to Switzerland. When we were settled in at Warburg and found that the camp held all but a few hundred officers of the 1940 bag, and unlucky R.A.F. pilots brought down over enemy territory to boot, we set this down to a Wehrmacht attempt to simplify the administration and security problem by concentrating a large number of prisoners of war in a single camp. In one sense they may have succeeded, but in the course of the year at Warburg more than fifty tunnels were dug, there was a successful front gate escape, and a fabulous wire assault that got twenty-seven men out and three home, albeit not by way of Switzerland.

We travelled from Laufen to Warburg by goods train. Some of my friends have made pilgrimages back to Laufen in better times; I have never been moved to that. In retrospect I find that my first three months there were the most miserable of my life, because only then the realization of a captivity without foreseeable end came home to me; and of course the low diet contributed. Recovery came in the form of activity, the digging with the possibility of a supremely desirable reward. It was as if in my own mind I had recovered status. In one sense, in Room Sixty, I had been living alone, now I had friends and identity. Childish, to be sure, but that is how it was. So when the slow train journey to Warburg in goods wagons came it was exciting; I suspect that I was not the only one in that frame of mind. I must confess to having enjoyed the journey. There were only about twenty of us in each van, and by the instinct that, unless hampered, governs such groups, all congenial, friends or close acquaintances. The Germans had learned that the less they shouted at us the less trouble we gave. The train made frequent stops, when we could take the air through the open truck van door, so to speak, and look out (over a sentry's head). That reduced claustrophobia. We had enough to eat; the Germans had actually issued travelling rations of bread and sausage for the two days the journey would take. There was no chance of running; there must have been at least two sentries for every van. The long tunnel and the successful island break had ensured that. The next chance, Pat and I agreed, would come at Warburg.

10
OFLAG VIB WARBURG
SEPTEMBER 1941–1942

Oflag VIB was a very large camp; Foot and Langley say it housed 2500 officers and 450 orderlies.[8] It covered a lot of ground. The map in my friend and brother rifleman Terence Prittie's book *Escape to Freedom* is out of scale: the walk around the inner perimeter was the best part of a mile. The camp held most of the 1940 catch, some of the North African, all that of Greece and a leaven of R.A.F., mostly bomber crew shot down since 1939.

The camp was set in almost featureless terrain that sloped gradually eastward, mainly when we arrived stubble fields or plough land. The wire enclosed about fifty huts of various obviously standard sizes; complemented outside the wire by another dozen or so that housed the guard company and command structure. The perimeter fence was the formidable standard nine-foot double wire, with an interval of about four feet between filled to three-foot height with tangled rolled wire, the whole topped with a two-foot wire net canting inward. Nevertheless, for me at least, the place by its diversity and sense of space was not as oppressive as Laufen. You could be out of your hut in twenty paces, and after that could range — up to a point only, of course, but that small difference seemed to matter.

On the journey to Warburg Charles and I had arranged to stay together; the ritual search on arrival did not depress us since we had no contraband. Once inside we found the immediate prospect, a long view with no wire before us, inviting and set out to explore, to get as far from the gate we came in by as we could. This proved to be the southeast corner of the huge compound, where there was a hut no more than ten yards from the perimeter wire. We knew that Archie planned another tunnel, and agreed this was the obvious place to start it from.

I took it for granted that I would be on Archie's team, but Charles and I agreed that a room from which a tunnel started would not afford peace for reading and music: we were determined to acquire, by whatever means, a gramophone. We would if it could be managed lodge in the hut just before the one we

---

8. M. R. D. Foot and James Maydon Langley, *MI9: the British secret service that fostered escape and evasion 1939–1945, and its American counterpart* (London : Bodley Head, 1979), 125.

had earmarked as the handiest place. We found it empty, and at one end a small room with two two-tier bunks which would do us very well. We staked out our claim with our luggage and blankets, found the mess hall where we were fed soup and bread, and turned in, postponing decision about whom to invite as room-mates until tomorrow.

Next day it was taken out of our hands. Archie had moved fast and already had the Escape Committee's authorization, and would have a room in the hut we had chosen for his tunnel, along with choice of occupants. As a face-man I was in it, but Charles, too tall to work underground and not good with his hands, was not. Pat was there, to my relief, Sid Helm the electrician, Cecil Tress, a Laufen stage hand, two professional actors whom Archie had got to know in the theatre world, two brothers, a lieutenant colonel and a major, professional soldiers from a north-country regiment, almost certainly nominated by the escape committee, three Laufen roommates of Archie's, Henry Coombe-Tennant the pianist Guards officer, a miniature major who in civil life had been starter in the Newcastle races, and a melancholy second lieutenant named John Sinclair who had stalked me at Laufen until he met Pat and I was freed of his shadow. I don't know how he got in, but his father was big in the Civil Service.

This little world was about as far as could be from the university ambience I had lived in most of my adult life. I was the odd man out; the peak of literary in-terest was James Agate's reviewing in the Sunday Times — the actors, of course. I learned my lesson, so to speak, after challenging his quality as a Shakespeare scholar. Henry Coombe-Tennant was talented and well read, thoughtful not talk-ative in general company. Nevertheless my social horizon was enlarged by the talk after lights out at the absurdly early hour of 9:00. And three or four evenings a week there was three-card poker, which five of us played for *Lagermarks*, keeping a book account. It has never been my luck to hold good cards, but one cannot read too much in indifferent light, and my year of gambling at Warburg cost me under £10. One way and another I was getting to know a little about the British male.

It is hard to compare Laufen and Warburg, but I was certainly less miserable there. Rereading Terence's book it seems to me that in Hut 11 we were lucky. The roof did not leak; we had electric light; our room was louse- and bedbug-free. To be sure the latrines and 'ablutions' were some distance from the hut, but they were roofed and adequate. You could have a shower, albeit cold, if you had a mind to. The orderlies, who knew how lucky they were not to be in a labour camp, brought us coffee in the morning and tea about 5:00, pooled from the Red Cross parcels; there was a tolerable soup-and-potatoes meal in the mess hall at midday, and the German rations were honest, if Spartan. By the time we were in Warburg a month those Red Cross parcels were coming fairly regularly, about once a month, and so, at length, were our personal parcels from home, even from Canada; I seem to remember four a year could be sent by one's family or friends under Red Cross sanction. If a man was affluent enough in those terms he could have his laundry done by one of the two room orderlies.

A tedious feature of life was the morning and afternoon *Appels*, musters for counting. For that purpose we were paraded in six 'battalions' at the same time in various parts of the large compound. At Laufen our senior officers had seen to it that the parades were orderly, and thus as brief as possible. But at Warburg the six counts had to be consolidated and checked; if any battalion count did not tally all six might find themselves standing for an hour or more while German n.c.o.s scurried about between the formations. On a number of occasions when it was cold and windy the Germans had real difficulty in maintaining control, especially in the case of our battalion's German minder, Hauptman Hager, unquestionably both stupid and ill disposed. Once, notably, the *Appel* of our battalion broke up in disarray; as I recall, someone lit a cigarette on parade, and he saw fit to punish us by not dismissing the battalion. There we stood, while the rest of the p.o.w.s made for their huts. All, that is, but some of our friends from another battalion, who fetched the band's musical instruments and marched around our formation playing Sousa's *Colonel Bogey*, which all soldiers of my day knew as the music for a 'lyric' very abusive of the Nazi rulers while, roaring with laughter, we stood to attention, if the combination can be imagined. Hager lost his temper and drew his pistol, whereupon the impromptu 'band' closed in on him and surrounded him with music. He had at least the sense not to shoot anyone. Some other German officer called out such of the guard company as were not on sentry duty; they came and seized the instruments, and disappeared through the gate carrying a trombone or some such incongruous object in one hand and a rifle in the other. Legend is that the smallest soldier in the guard company was left with the big bass drum. We got the instruments back before long: the Germans enjoyed the band concerts and the jazz band's performances too much.

Ordinarily there would have been some form of punishment. But the state of the war may have had something to do with an improvement in the German attitude. By Christmas it was clear that the Russian campaign, in the throes of its first winter, would not be quickly over; there was little preaching, any more, about the folly of the British in opposing German domination. Now it was, 'You should be our allies!' At Laufen, before he lost face over the potato ration scandal, Oberst Frey arrogated the right to order that any p.o.w. seen looking out of a camp window risked being shot at; here, during a wire escape which I shall presently describe, a sentry fired to miss, as a warning shot.

The *Kommandant* at Warburg scarcely figured in our lives; the S.B.O. could negotiate with him. Our enemy here was the security staff. With a mile-long perimeter and two single barrier gates Warburg was by no means as secure a pen as Laufen, which had very few vulnerable points. Within a month of our arrival at Warburg the security staff here was effectively employed, activated by some early abortive escape schemes. Its commander was a superb ham actor, Hauptman Rademacher. Terence's book makes him out to be something of a hysteric: my perception is that his rages and pistol-waving during room searches were designed to put its occupants off guard while his men watched their faces for anxious looks by which contraband hides could be given away. His second in command Hauptman Klau meanwhile went about his business quietly and was much more dangerous. The sentries, moreover, were specialists. Those in the tower posts had binoculars, a light machinegun and a searchlight which they played up and down the wire at night, when it was patrolled by guards on foot as well. The most dangerous of the German security team were the 'ferrets', three soldiers in grey overalls who spent their whole day crawling about with torches and probes in the 18-inch space under the hut floors looking for the disturbed surface that would indicate a covered tunnel trap, or for signs of crawling, or for differences of texture or colour that would indicate disposal of spoil. What saved us was that there were only three of these for many huts and a brick block holding a whole battalion of p.o.w.s. Finally, inside the camp, were the strollers who drifted aimlessly, as they hoped it would appear, on no predictable course, and would visit a room without warning.

These were particularly dangerous because escaping of any kind called for much clandestine preparation, mapmaking, preparing emergency rations, tailoring of civilian clothes or disguises, preparing documents; all such activities would involve giveaway material certain to be confiscated in a sudden search.

To combat such loss we developed a sentry system called 'stooging', an unkind term for indispensable helpers who would not take part themselves in the attempt. They bore a heavy burden of responsibility. During 'working', that is escaping hours, between the *Appels* in particular, there would be a chain system of stooges in the huts along the main camp roads and the bounds of the open spaces in the camp. Every German who came into the camp would be marked by a stooge reading a book in a window, or sketching, or just sitting like the Mexican in the story enjoying the sun. He would signal to another stooge by elementary means, a violent sneeze, slapping at a fly, angrily closing his book, a languid stretch. In the huts where there was forbidden activity the sensitive materials would be whipped out of sight into a ready hide. There the warning was the cry 'Goon up!' For young readers, 'goons' were the weird, shapeless and slightly sinister otherworld creatures of the *Popeye* cartoon strip, and 'up' meaning 'approaching' went back to the third floor at Laufen, where room searches were frequent. Then there was Hauptman Klau, whose mode was to drop in as for a visit. I don't know what kind of intelligence came to Warburg with the stage tunnel team, but he quite often looked in on us. He was easy to like and I took it upon my junior self to suggest to my roommates, including the very senior, that we should cultivate him rather than appear uneasy at having him there.

Within a month of arrival at Warburg, as soon as camp routine was established, and the camp no longer swarmed with workmen repairing huts Archie activated us. For quick access and ready communication our tunnel would begin immediately under our room. Its location would necessarily put it under particular security surveillance. But, we reasoned, there were plenty of other huts not much further from the wire, and the Germans would assume that nobody would be fool enough to dig from under Hut 11, such an obvious starting point. We were right; the ferrets did not give the under floor area of our hut more than routine attention.

Each hut had an entrance to its under floor space, generally in full view. That obviously was not to be used for access to the tunnel; this had to be through our room floor. But because a tunnel was most exposed to discovery at the start of digging, the trap for the shaft, the wooden frame around its upper edge and its fitting cover, had to be prepared before the trapdoor in the room floor. Here is where the colonel and his brother major whose surnames I have forgotten came in. They built this of bed boards within days, and we stored it unassembled under our palliasses. I only got a glimpse of their work, and spent my time by one of the hut doors ready to hold an approaching goon in conversation. Their work on the floor trapdoor was even more elegant. This was the most dangerous operation in the whole process, when the evidence could not be hidden quickly. Every room in the hut had a little iron stove for which, come winter, we would get a coal ration, enough for a fire in the evening. This stove stood on a metal plate about 30 inches square, screwed to the floor; the stovepipe was the usual set of tubular light sections of thin metal. This was disconnected, the stove moved to one side. Then the artists unscrewed the metal plate, and lifted it to expose the wooden floor beneath it. From this they neatly cut out a two-foot square section of floorboards, joined them on the underside with battens, and screwed the metal plate the stove would stand on to the product, so that the metal plate projected about six inches on each side, and when replaced, would be strong enough to support the stove. The stove replaced, the stovepipe reassembled, the room-floor first trap was secure. Where the Escape Committee acquired the screwdriver, the brace and bit and the keyhole saw needed for the operation I do not know; I do know now that the German sentries at Warburg had early acquired a taste for Virginian cigarettes and their local girlfriends responded favourably to real coffee and scented soap.

We were set to go. Except for a small room like the one Charles and I had spent our first night at Warburg in, ours was the southeast room in the southeast hut in the southeast corner of the camp enclosure. Here the ground sloped on that axis very gently to a small gully; along the far side of this was a barely perceptible ridge. We aimed the tunnel to pass diagonally under the gully and break ground just beyond that ridge. This would reduce the risk of silhouetted figures at night until we got out of range of the searchlights. At the outside the finished tunnel chamber would be no longer than the one at Laufen was when discovered.

Sinking the shaft did not take long. Pat and I, the right size, and with training and experience, would dig the chamber; Sid would see to the lighting; Archie and Cecil Tress would take care of covering up underground. In all respects it seemed a good setup. The two of us would go down after morning *Appel*, change places at half time, and come up in time to get ready for evening *Appel*. Our roommates would take care of our lunch ration, which would be heated for us as 'supper'. We did not plan to break cover until late spring. There was no urgency, and we progressed at a rate calculated not to tax the disposal problem beyond security. The soil seemed of good consistency and there was no shortage of bed boards; the air below was sweet.

It was a huge relief to have a sense of purpose again and to realize it actively. The digging was also a very welcome distraction from the war, which was going badly in the desert. The German paper was full of statistics of the shipping being destroyed by submarines and the progress of the war in Russia. In that respect we were lucky. The camp now had a secret radio, brought in by a medical officer in a medicine ball, and each evening a summary of the BBC foreign bulletin was read to us; this kept things in some proportion. And the RAF officers in the camp were full of stories about the Battle of Britain. Even when the news was very bad, as it presently was from Malaya and Singapore, it was above all heartening to learn how the Japanese attack on Pearl Harbour improved the American attitude to the European war. Now, however bad the news, especially in the East, we could see an end to the war, even if it would not be soon. The camp library was improving; there were concerts of very high quality in all kinds of music, musical evenings with Henry Coombe-Tennant solo at the piano. But best of all for our lot, there was the tunnel.

The weather that winter was generally foul. From 21 December there was a long wet spell, after which followed snow that made walking disagreeable and then in late January a freak thaw. I was glad of the exercise afforded by digging, but because the line of direction and rate of slope had to be carefully watched it was not relaxing. One good feature of this period was that my mother's letters were becoming more cheerful; moreover she was learning the tricks of having a son in the bag: she was in touch with the Agent General for British Columbia in London and a splendid woman in Victoria active for the Canadian p.o.w.s from Dieppe, who put me on her list.

In the room we began to talk quietly about plans for 'outside'. There was no reason, if all went well on the night, why the number who went from our room should be limited. It would have to be cross-country running, for I was the only German speaker in the room. As the Escape Committee became better informed train travel began to seem worth considering, but none of my roommates had the right appearance or manner to impersonate a foreign workman, and I kept quiet about the possibility of 'carrying' one. None of them suggested it.

In any case we never got to that point. About mid-February a freak cold front moved down from the north. I remember the night it reached Warburg. We had a window open, and the beats of two foot-sentries bounded just outside it. I heard their boots crunch in the snow as I lay awake, and one of them saying to the other, 'Hū lāt is hit?', what is the time?' best Oldenburger dialect for 'Wie spat ist es?', but also good Anglo-Saxon. The cold front lay upon us for a good week; then came very warm weather and a freakish thaw. Everyone took this for the advent of spring and put up with the camp roads becoming seas of mud. But in our room, one morning as we were getting out of bed and dressing to go on *Appel*, someone with a top bunk by the window let out an anguished yell, 'Jesus! Look at that!'. We crowded to see, and there at the point where our tunnel would pass under the little gully was an ugly gaping hole. Pat and I looked at each other; one, I forget which, said bitterly 'Third time lucky!'

The Germans, in no hurry to fill the tunnel in, let more of it collapse, until it came to look like a ditch with pieces of awkward scaffolding in it, pointed accusingly toward Hut 11. The ferrets, had they tried, could not have failed to find what had been done to the floor under our stove. It was not worth their while; Hut 11 was out of action. The farmer who ploughed the stubble next spring probably filled in the tunnel. We did not watch him or take note.

We were in effect now unemployed. Opinion about the number of tunnels attempted at Warburg differs. Bill Edwards, who wrote the second part of *Escape to Freedom*, gives sixty as the number discovered by the Germans, adding that only five of these broke ground and only three got officers outside. I soon found that tunnels had a waiting list. Archie, not a man to sit in idleness, went back to 'straight' stage-managing, easily arranged by our actor roommates who were producing a play at the time. I turned up for a few days, but did not find it fulfilling and quit.

There was in fact a tunnel involved here too, not under the stage but in the coal cellar of the kitchen where the soup was served when the theatre was a dining hall. It sounded promising, but of course had a waiting list. The camp milieu did not lend itself to systematic reading. It was easy to be glum; the war looked like going on for a long time. German pressure on the Soviet armies had resumed with the warmer weather; Britain had lost its hold in Southeast Asia, along with a couple of its navy's flagships; India and Australia were under threat. There was some comfort in the now total American involvement. But manifestly the war could not end without an allied presence on the European mainland and the prospect of this seemed remote. Life improved with the advent of fine spring weather in April when the surface escaping season opened. It began with a resounding victory for our side when seven p.o.w.s, a trio and two pairs, escaped in daylight in a single day through the wire not far from our hut. The trio cut a passage through first the inside fence, then the tangle of obstacle barbed wire, and then the outside fence, put enough wire back in good order for the gap not to be noticeable to the casual German eye, and disappeared over the horizon, followed after an interval by the first pair.

This was a very elegant and hugely risky operation, a masterpiece of timing and coordinated distraction of the sentries, the latter managed by a complex but unobtrusive signalling, in each instance keeping two tower sentries occupied for a considerable period. We lost some points because the sentry on duty when the second pair went through spotted them making off. He was sporting and only fired over their heads, and of course the pair were caught within the hour. The other five, however, had a good run before they were retaken. The mastermind of this attempt was Major Tom Stallard, one of the unsung experts of the escaping world, brilliant at identifying weaknesses in the camp security system and organizing their exploitation. For instance in this one the absolute essential was a pair of efficient wire cutters, about the least likely instrument to be available to prisoners of war: he made them out of the blades of a pair of skates. It was a cruel feature of the game that Tom never had luck on the run himself.

I had a very small part in that wire 'job' which was good for my morale, as a second actor in a distraction at a crucial moment. I lounged on a blanket in the sun about 20 feet from the camp perimeter trail at a point where there was a key sentry box. Down from Number 3 battalion area came Wing Commander Douglas Bader, walking rather less well than usual on his two artificial legs. At a signalled moment he stumbled and the legs came adrift. He sat there like a clown, waving them and swearing. The sentry, leaning over the edge of his box, dissolved in laughter. At this I rebuked the German; 'he was not ashamed to make fun of a wounded war hero? I would not have expected such behaviour...' It was chancy but proved more effective than I had dared to hope. As I spoke a couple of walkers, on programme of course, came along and helped Bader strap himself up again while the sentry watched them anxiously.

Then there was the gate. At Biberach, Oflag VIB, several 'gate jobs' had been successful, among them by Peter Brush and Terence Prittie dressed in workman's overalls and carrying electrician and plumber's kit. There were still the odd workmen in the Warburg camp then, about the end of October 1942. Terence, who spoke German albeit with a foreign quality to it, Stewart Walker who could speak it with a Bavarian accent, Tony Rolt and Bill Cheyne, who had no German, prepared a similar scheme. They had observed that the workmen mainly used the west gate, where control was not as full as in the eastern one beside the *Kommandatur*. They would go in pairs, a German speaker in each, one pair before and one after a change of sentries. Terence and Tony lost the toss for the first go, obviously the better, for the sentry then would be ending his tour of duty and likely to be less alert. So it proved; worse still the relieving sentry, sharper than his predecessor and keen, quizzed Terence about what part of Germany he came from. Then he turned to poor mute Tony and the game was up. There were other gate attempts that autumn, but no successes.

Nevertheless escape by the camp gate was clearly worth attempting, subject to certain requirements. The first, namely luck, was common to all escapers' efforts. The gate job needed, further, good disguise, good German, good papers, that is exit permits, and a plausible story, that is reason for having been in the camp: along with these it helped to have some acting ability. In that case the two deciding factors were clearly luck and language.

After this Terence joined a tunnelling team run by a couple of Old Etonians, Hector Christie and Brocky Mytton, the latter a descendant of the famous Georgian duellist. Like ours this came to grief in the rains of the late winter, collapsing along its extent. Terence from his account was relieved; I don't think he had the tunneller's temperament. But then a gate scheme planned for early summer became available. Two Highland Division officers, James Murray-Grant who had escaped from the island at Laufen, and John Logan, a fine German speaker who had tried the gate there with an inadequate German uniform, had spotted a very promising occasion for an attempt at Warburg, namely a periodic visit by the Swiss Red Cross Commissioners. The scheme would be to act their departure at the end of such a visit: two civilians accompanied by a courtesy escort consisting of a strange German officer and n.c.o. from outside the camp; they would set off on foot to the railway station a mile or so away. Papers could be prepared in advance, leaving only the date to fill in. But before this plan could be developed Murray-Grant, who was a field officer and over 35, was moved with others of a similar rank or age to Oflag IXAH at Spangenberg in Hesse-Cassell. Needing support, John offered the scheme to Hector, reserving a place for himself. With his excellent German and a good presence, he would be the senior of the two German officers; the other would be an even better German speaker, Lance Pope, and the n.c.o. Terence Prittie. Tony Rolt and Bill Cheyne would play the Commissioners.

In costume production there had been remarkable advances. Bill Cheyne, who had so far occupied himself with giving a civilian look to pieces of British uniform, proved to have considerable aptitude as a cutter, the man at the centre of the tailor's craft, and was teaching Tom Acton who proved a ready learner. Tobacco, coffee and soap procured illicit dyes and bleaches. German uniform bore various insignia and much silver braid. The three German uniforms involved a mass of detail down to the buttons of silvery metal, the unusually peaked officers' headdresses with an elaborately plaited cord, actually a vestigial chinstrap, of plaited silvery wire, oak leaf cap badges. The civilians, by comparison, were easy to dress; they had merely to look well paid and important. Means had to be contrived to conceal civilian clothes for the uniformed Germans in the party to travel in, and at least three days rations for a period on foot to get clear of the local stations, which might have been made sensitive to p.o.w. attempts. Finally there was to be the unknown, the date of the next visit by the Commissioners. This was thought to be due 'about the beginning of July'.

Having in mind Terence and Tony's experience at the gate in 1941 and that various gate attempts in the interval had sharpened gate security, John Logan and Hector decided to hold a dress rehearsal. For whatever reason I was asked to play the part of the sentry. I was surprised, for although I knew John Logan I had never met Hector or Lance, and although Terence and I were in the same regiment, he had left Laufen for Titmonning before I arrived there; I scarcely knew him. The rehearsal was interesting. I played the role straight and hard. Nothing bogus caught my eye about the uniforms. The civilian clothes were good. John and Lance spoke *echtes Hochdeutch*, real High German. The gate passes, like all John Mansel's work, were superb. And they had the answers to all my stalling. In the matter of appearance or behaviour the only thing that could go wrong was for a sentry to recognize Terence or Tony. I kept the passes; obviously a sentry would hand them in to the guard commander at the end of his tour at the gate. In this matter they were lucky at the actual attempt where the sentry returned them. If he had passed them to the guard commander the hunt would have been up within hours.

As things were they got out smoothly and soon found cover for the soldiery to become civilians. In three nights they walked about 20 miles over most difficult terrain to Münden where they entrained. The walk had been taxing: Lance wore light shoes, unsuited to rough going; Terence's boots did not fit. They made the mistake of eating new potatoes gathered in a field where the farmer had, I suppose, been using cesspool sewage as fertilizer; these gave Terence a gastric upset for a day and a night. Then Lance was incapacitated by stomach pains. He recovered and they pressed on, but he had another attack when they returned to camp. They failed in the first essential, luck.

For me the dress rehearsal meant an immediate anticlimax and with it depression. To rid myself of this I accepted, as did Pat, an invitation to join a tunnel scheme that had started in the washroom, which was very seldom visited and certainly not visited by the Germans. The digging was very easy, but I disliked the project from the first because the shaft and chamber were damp and clammy, which I took to be a bad sign. I worked at the face two days; on the third I escaped by inches being covered by a fall of earth from above and beyond a shoring I had just fitted; I found myself with a pile of loose earth in front of me and sort of vault above this, where what was needed was a good earthen roof. It was evident that there could be no further digging without a roof of continuous shoring to the height of the 'vault'; for this the standard timber, our bed boards, would not be long enough. I came up and found the leader of the team to report this, adding that whatever he might decide to do I would not push my luck by going down again. Whatever he may have thought of me at that moment, having gone down himself to look he decided to abandon the project. And wisely; within a month the past wet winter took its toll. In the ambitious kitchen coalhole tunnel the face worker, John Dupré, a fine young man whom everybody liked, suffered a severe electric shock caused by damp wiring, and was dead before he could be brought out and resuscitated.

Soon after I left the washhouse tunnel to my delight I was approached by John Logan with an invitation to join Hector Christie's team; I suppose I should have asked to join it earlier. There was now a grand scheme to move a large number of p.o.w.s, a dozen or more, escorted by two German officers, an n.c.o. and five soldiers, to another camp: that was the scenario. It might have worked; one party of officers had recently been moved, and the camp was full of talk about the possibility of further transfers. The scale of the preparation underway was formidable. The uniforms, except for the insignia, were tailored and sewn within three weeks of the return of the 'Red Cross Commissioners'. The plan was to be quite ready by the end of August. It was set back at least a week by one successful room-raid in which braid and insignia were lost, and the production of so many civilian outfits for the 'Germans' was taking longer than expected.

Presently it was confirmed that we would be moving to another camp in September. There would have been time for one more gate attempt but, quite fairly, another grand scheme had priority as next in turn.

This was a plan again conceived and designed by Major Tom Stallard, who had organized the successful wire-cutting escape. This time it was to go over the wire at the moment of nightfall when we were still at large, that is not confined to our huts, but dark enough for the perimeter lights to have been turned on. This tricky condition was imperative and there was another which, where right weather and light were a matter of luck, this was a matter of one man's judgement. This was a captain in the Royal Signals who claimed to know how to fuse the lighting system of the entire camp. The tower sentries would be nearing the end of their tour of duty; the foot patrols outside the wire would not be mounted until we were in the huts. Otherwise it would be a matter of timing; according to Foot and Langley ninety-four people were involved; even the organization of that was complicated.

Tom was lucky with the weather. The day came, August 30th, and the team went into position. German speakers manned all the key points on the camp roads. In the library building what appeared to be shelves became two ladders with hinged bridging boards at one end. In a hut near the chosen point of attack a man-size Jumping Jack at the end of two long poles was put together; the ladder teams stood to. The perimeter lights went out. The Jumping Jack was pushed into the wire 20 feet from a tower box. The sentry opened fire on him. The ladders went into place. The escapers, forty-one according to Foot and Langley, were over and away, having jumped nine feet from the bridging boards into the stubble field. Nobody broke a leg, but one officer was wounded in the foot by a stray shot. He was caught some miles away next day. We faded away into our huts; the lights came on again conveniently just in time. I read that the whole operation took three minutes.

The men who went over the top that evening had been chosen by the Escape Committee, many because of their contribution to escaping activity without having had the chance to go themselves. Three got back to England, one of them Henry Coombe-Tennant. Foot and Langley credit the Escape Committee with its success. More accurately, the Escape Committee's credit should have been for supporting Tom Stallard in his brilliantly devised and executed scheme. It was dangerous from start to finish for those who made the attempt, but also for three heroes who did not go, the man who lay activating the Jumping Jack while it was under fire — I never knew his name — and two friends of mine, Bill Rawlings and Allan Kirkwood who held steady the feet of the ladders while the escapers swarmed over and out.

I have written of luck as the first requirement of a successful escape. Henry Coombe-Tennant is a case in point. He and his two companions, unmistakeably English in appearance and wearing uniform, with few words of German between them, made for occupied Holland, about ninety miles distant at the nearest point. They were gambling on making contact with its Resistance, which was said not to be easy in the Netherlands. But literally as luck would have it, the first person they came upon proved to be pro-British and to speak English. The evening of the escape Henry and I were sitting on our top bunks waiting to go into action, he over the wire and I to my goon blocking post. I was going over German weather lore and terminology as a topic of conversation in my mind when he broke the silence: 'I'm tired of this whole escaping business, George! I've been trying to get out for two years without ever coming near to being on the other side of the wire. If nothing comes of this show tonight I shall give up, and sit down to compose music till the war ends.' In our poker school he almost always held the best cards.

Soon after the ladder scheme we learned the exact day of our move and its destination, Oflag VIIB at Eichstätt in southern Bavaria. Our team had to hope that its store of contraband clothing and objects could be successfully smuggled through. We were told to leave this to the escape committee.

11
OFLAG VIIB EICHSTÄTT
SEPTEMBER 1942–JANUARY 1943

Our journey to Eichstätt, luxurious in third class carriages, was without event. Morale was high. For the first time in our captivity we could see a term to the war, and with the Americans now inextricably committed, a favourable one at that. Reason now reinforced the blind faith that Britain would not be defeated. And in our own artificial world 'our side' had scored many points with the ladder as with the earlier wire scheme. Pat and I had come through the departure search with our personal contraband undetected. And we were leaving a camp where the landscape, dreary in its absence of vistas, and the mud, were oppressive. For me individually the great thing was to have been taken on by what might fairly be called a first division team. Above all, there was the prospect of something new. In this last Eichstätt did not disappoint.

The town was baroque in the best seventeenth/eighteenth century sense, a delight after the drabness of Warburg. Our camp, about a quarter of a mile to the southeast, lay beside a road cut out along a lateral slope of a wide valley through which a swift river called the Altmühl flowed northward, inevitably, to the Danube. The camp itself was on two levels, one with the road, perhaps thirty yards wide, the other the natural level of the river valley. It had originally been a *Gebirgsjäger* training camp. At the north-eastern end were the *Kommandatur* and guardroom and troops quarters, and the main gate to the prison enclosure, with a second small guardroom and an n.c.o. in charge. From that gate to the southwest corner, the long dimension of the prison enclosure, ran a paved street. Along its four hundred yards six three-story stone buildings stood between the wire and the street; at the southwest end of this there was a second gate, manned by a single sentry on the ground, but with a tower sentry box almost directly above it. These buildings had well-lit rooms, running water and modern sanitation. The one nearest the lesser gate was used as a storehouse, the next along was the camp hospital, then a cookhouse and mess hall, and finally three fine blocks of prisoners' quarters. On the river side of the camp street the ground fell away naturally to a level where there were a parade ground, a running track, a football field and what must have once been tennis courts. At the southwest end of this level stood five large brick barracks in which about 1800 of the prisoners from Warburg would be housed.

When my friends and I arrived there, in the second consignment, so to speak, the camp looked idyllic. There were the ridges along both sides of the valley, the playing fields, and the river. We were admitted into camp without much ceremony and herded to the football ground to await assignment to our quarters. Then a group of a couple of dozen were marched off to a point on the field where they were just within sight and there, for the rest of us to view, subjected to a most thorough body search. Of course we set to burying our personal contraband under the springy turf of the field; presently we were ourselves taken off and searched and after that guided to our assigned rooms. When the lot of us were through this process guards with sniffer dogs moved onto the field and picked up our compasses, waterproof maps and what have you. It was humiliating to watch this haul. We had lost points at the outset.

By some procedure I made no effort to discover I once more found myself in a room of which the core was an escape team. All were civil, and most of them highly agreeable people as well; the mix was quite different from that at Warburg. There were two captains from cavalry regiments if I recall aright, Hector Christie and his running mate Brockie Mytton, a third, Roger Mortimer and guardsman, and Hector's tunnelling expert Freddie Corfield. The first three were racing buffs and great gamblers; nothing elementary like poker for them, they favoured chemin de fer, faro and roulette. Freddie was more serious. Unlike the gamblers, whose talk after lights out was of another world for me, Freddie was a reader: we could talk about books. There was Tony Rolt, indispensable for his fieldcraft. So was Lance Pope, with whom came two friends, Ernest Edelman and Dick Tombes who had both been outside. Tom Acton and Bill Cheyne of course were 'in', as was Terence Prittie, very much an activator with gate experience. Two of his Warburg roommates came with him. Then there were a professional actor, Desmond Llewellyn, whom years later I saw on the London stage playing 'heavies', grave and reverend signors, a passionate birdwatcher caller Peter Conder, Pat Sherrard as a good man on a team, his shadow Sinclair ('Might as well put him on the list, he'll be in the room all day whether we do or not') and myself the avid observer. However odd the mix may seem in retrospect, the mood in the room was uniformly good.

When I called on my friends in the brick barracks on the lower level I was shocked by their accommodation. The rooms were huge and poorly lit by day and night. The washrooms and latrines were in another building. Where my room, albeit overcrowded, was cheerfully bright, theirs were dismal; there is no other word for it. People made an amazing best of it, helped by the fact that a sixth building on the upper level was being developed into a library and study room. For instance, Charles Janson set to learning Russian and over the next two years acquired an excellent command of the language; after the war he became something of an authority on Russian post-Revolution thinking. And a somewhat older Cambridge law don captured in the Greek debacle set up, by arrangement with cooperative powers in the U.K., a highly effective law school; his students, junior and less junior officers, took (again by arrangement) and passed professional qualifying examinations. 'Overeducated and over-specialized', I felt no urge to study, whether from sloth or from a healthy corrective reaction to that condition. Probably the latter is the better explanation: in retrospect I now see that my education, in a broader sense, was continuing.

Meanwhile, with a gate scheme in early prospect, I was finding it hard even to settle down to reading. By now I had read all the Waugh and Greene in the camp library; we had, of Charles Morgan, then in vogue, only *The Fountain* and *Sparkenbroke*. The flow of new books at this stage of our captivity was thin. I turned to the nineteenth century. Someone mentioned Baron Corvo; I tried, but found him a tedious poseur. I remembered being struck by Peacock when browsing in the stacks at U.B.C. I did not know enough to penetrate *Headlong Hall*, but intrigued by the evident presence of satire, persisted with *Nightmare Abbey* where I could identify the subjects. By good fortune I chanced on Borrow's *Romany Rye*: a family of gypsies I had seen as a boy acquired a new dimension from this book. I followed it up with *Lavengro*, which I ought to have read first, and reread *Romany Rye*. I continued to find Borrow a puzzling character.

It took all of six weeks for our heavy camp luggage from Warburg to reach us. I suppose in one sense we were lucky to get it at all. These were the last days of October, and although it turned out, blessedly, that our store of contraband clothing had got through, it had been so skilfully hidden that it would take a couple of weeks at least to refurbish and make it presentable. This would carry us into mid-November at the earliest. Clearly the grand gate scheme planned at Warburg was not now practicable. It was getting too late in the season for cross-country running; the season for that would end with the first snowfall. Arrangements for a much-reduced scheme involving mainly German speakers were just getting underway when Lance, Terence, Tony and Bill were hauled off to serve a three-week spell in cells held over from Warburg. This was bad; the urgency of the situation was intensified when, a few days before they had served their time, Terence and Lance learned 'informally', so to speak, that there was talk in the *Kommandatur* of moving them to another camp.

To cope with this crisis the plan for the attempt on a gate was further refined. Winter had unmistakeably set in and all travel would have to be by rail. That reduced the number to the German speakers in the team. A 'friend of the management', Henry Duff, who had been out twice but had no German, had observed that small parties of French p.o.w.s were occasionally brought into the camp by the little used lesser gate, under German guard of course, for dental treatment by one of our Medical Officers. This they received in the camp hospital, the second of the buildings from that gate on the upper level street. Henry very handsomely gave this scheme to Hector, after checking that the Dental Officer always received a couple of days' notice of such visits, which routinely took place before midday.

Hector decided to replicate the second half of this process. He would send out a *Sonderführer* and a German soldier with three French prisoners of war. They would emerge from the hospital while the real Frenchmen were in the dentist's care, but after the guard who had let them in had been relieved at 10:00. Hector named his players: Lance for his flawless German would act the *Sonderführer*, Stewart Walker the soldier. Stewart was a natural ham actor who, along with a good honours degree in German from U.C.L, commanded, when he chose, a really common Bavarian dialect, *ganz gemein!* Terence, Tom Acton and I would play the Frenchmen. Although I must have been outside the camp a good number of times in the last stages of both the Laufen and the Warburg tunnel it was always underground. I had never been outside the wire. Tony Rolt would tell me about this as we walked the perimeter of the sports ground to work off our impatience over the arrival and readiness of our escaping costumes. He had been outside twice, from Biberach and from Warburg, and it crossed my mind that he might have been put up to coaching me in the fieldcraft at which he had shown great skill. We got on well; like me he was a freak in a regiment of polo-playing, foxhunting Etonians. His father manufactured automobile parts in the Midlands, and Tony's sport, developing out of this, was to test them in the big-league motor races. He once told me how it was only after he had appeared in the Sunday papers as having won the big race at Brooklands the day before that he felt accepted into the Regiment. Of course he came into his own when the Rifle Brigade was motorized in 1940

From Lance Pope, whom I asked to coach me in 'how to do and say' in Germany at war, I learned a great deal about many apparently trivial points of behaviour, nonconformity to which attracts notice. We spoke German for my benefit; I learned the colloquialisms that went with buying tickets and ordering beer, when to say *Heil Hitler*, how much to put into a *Winterhilfe* collector's box. He passed my German for correctness and fluency, but confirmed what I had always suspected, that my accent had a faint but unmistakeable North American trace.

Not that I had any intention of trying to pass myself off as German. For an escaping p.o.w. travelling by train there were two critical principles. The first was not to attract attention, whether from fellow passengers or officials. The second was to be able, if need be, to account for oneself as an able-bodied male of military age in civilian clothes in a country at war. Our forgers were wonderfully skilful, but they had virtually no information about *Kennkarten*, identity cards, for German nationals. And any cover story an escaping p.o.w. might offer, in whatever guise, would be vulnerable to checking and dismissal in five minutes of telephoning. It had better be superficially good.

What foreign nationality to choose was much discussed in our room. My firm preference was for Finnish because of the excruciating difficulty of that language, which I rapidly discovered in 1940 when I bought myself a *Teach Yourself Finnish* in preparation for going to war, as I thought, in the Scandinavian peninsula. Contrary to popular opinion the Germans number among them many excellent speakers of what one might call the main European languages, and the police were used to interrogating foreign workers on the run. But far from providing foreign workers, Finland was at that time fighting on the left flank of the *Wehrmacht* in Northern Russia. As to the cover story, the police might find it hard to find a fluent interrogator in Finnish. The Escape Committee accepted my argument, and along with Tom Acton who would travel with me, I carried Finnish papers. We were forestry students sent by the Finnish government to study German forest economy.

Much of the crucial planning had been done when Terence and his mates were carried off to the cells. The objective would be the Schaffhausen salient on the northern Swiss border. It was no great distance from Eichstätt and we could easily have reached lying-up-and-reconnaissance positions on the day of a successful escape but for one security consideration. There were three kinds of train in wartime Germany, the *Schnellzug* or express train, where inspectors rigorously checked all passengers after each stop, a second, the *Eilzug*, not so fast notwithstanding its name, and the *Personenzug* or local, which stopped at every station. The *Eilzüge* were not systematically checked. We would simply not take the *Schnellzüge*, sacrificing time to security. Terence and Lance, Tom and I planned a concerted border crossing effort from the east; we would detrain at Tuttlingen just over 20 miles from the frontier. We would leave from Eichstätt Junction some four miles walking to the south; the main town station was too risky because there we might run into a German who recognized one of our faces. Travelling in separate pairs we would be in Munich by early afternoon. Terence knew his way around a little there; he and Lance would spend the night there and come on to Ulm the next day. Tom and I would kill time in a cinema, take a late night train to Augsburg, get through the night there, and take an early train to Ulm. Here, in the late morning we would board a local, bumbling *Personenzug* for Tuttlingen. Lance and Terence would take the same train and we would meet at Tuttlingen. Stewart, who was keen to try the west side of the salient, would lie up in the woods for a couple of hours and catch a 2:00 *Eilzug* to Ingolstadt, travel from there to Ulm and on to Neustadt, where he would take to the road and the woods. There was an unknown factor, the weather: the big winter snowfall might begin any day.

Lance, Terence, Tony and Bill had gone into cells at the beginning of November to serve their three-week suspended sentence. They were returned to camp on the 18th. A party of French dental patients had been booked for the morning of the 24th. Our dress rehearsal was set for the 22nd, and on the day before that Lance came down with what the doctors quickly diagnosed as acute appendicitis.

This was a wicked blow for Hector and the team, the third cruel setback. Lance's 'officer class' German, Hector's trump card, was irreplaceable. Terence had been 'out' twice but, as he describes in his book, his German was not up to an argument at the gate. Stewart's German was fine, and many German officers spoke *Landessprache*, regional dialect, by choice. But, small and dark complexioned, he did not look like a German officer, and could not have been made to look like one. Tom's German was correct but his vocabulary was limited. My handicap was that I had no gate or outside experience. I was nevertheless promoted to *Sonderführer*, and I am bound to admit that after a haircut by a camp orderly who had been a ladies' hairdresser in Glasgow and removal of my moustache I looked like a Kraut; friends and acquaintances failed to recognise me on my way back from his chair to my room. The vacancy in our party was filled by a fine man, James McDonnell, with fairly good German; he had been outside twice and had travelled by train. James had to be clothed and kitted from scratch. I was much the same size as Lance, and my costume needed little alteration. Meanwhile it had begun to snow.

We passed the test of the dress rehearsal. Bill and Tom had devised diabolically ingenious means of concealing civilian clothes for Stewart and me on the Frenchmen. There was a day to wait. John Mansel himself brought our various documents: they looked pretty good. Friends in the know called to wish us good luck. I do not recall much of 23 November, only a general sense of being much cosseted and grossly overfed. I suppose I was too nervous to be hungry. One of my limitations, I have come to realize over the years, is that while I am a very serious person, I find it hard to take myself seriously. So here, having had responsibility 'thrust upon me', I could make nothing of it except to be embarrassed.

To get this right: a gate scheme was unquestionably the least dangerous form of escape attempt. There was almost no likelihood of any physical violence in the course of one: the gate opened or it did not. In a tunnel you could be electrocuted as John Dupré was or trapped by a fall of earth as I almost was; on a through-the-wire scheme there was a good chance of being shot by a nervous sentry; on our spectacular ladder scheme the air was full of hot metal. I suppose what I feared in anticipation was making a fool of myself and — in the army this was a very serious consideration — of 'letting the side down'. I am ashamed to confess that as I lay awake the night of 23 November I gave no thought of what might happen to the sentry at the gate if we were successful.

At long length it was the morning of the day, the sky grey but not sombre, a continuous light fall of snow. We were up early. Hector and Terence made the final decision: the scheme was on; how else at the eleventh hour? It was too good to risk losing it by postponement. Shave, shower, sit down to a huge breakfast — Stewart, who had slept that night in our block helped me eat mine. Then the serious dressing began. Because timing was crucial, and *Appel* might drag on, I was partly dressed in my German rig before it, and was counted in a British army greatcoat built for a six-footer. *Appel* seemed endless; actually it took little longer than usual. We five made our way singly to the hospital where the team finished dressing us. We met the deadline and were ready before 10:20 when we had to be ready to start, so as to be in good time for attempting the gate before the French dental patients were ready to leave camp, but not too much before, so as to give the gate and tower sentries who would have come on at 10:00 time to get cold and bored. Our dressers were experts; we were ready not long after 10:00 and sat waiting while Hector, eyes glued to the window over the street, watched for the signals that the change of sentries was completed and their part of the camp road clear of Germans.

They came about 10:10 and down the stairs we went, *Sonderführer* Kane in the lead, the Frenchmen in train, Stewart the natural ham chivvying them in bad French or profane German for being out of step. As for myself I was bucked when someone who knew me tolerably well but knew nothing of our scheme clearly failed to recognise me. The sentry began to unlock the gate while we were still some way off and came to heel-clicking attention as I passed through it. I turned left with my party and up the rude steps of the path to the Eichstätt-Ingolstadt road that ran along the camp wire.

I sit now more than 60 years later searching my resources of language to describe my state of mind in those first minutes. It certainly had a huge component of exhilaration. And I remember a sense of unreality. Amateur drama, play-acting, has never interested me. But this was different, a game with stakes not far short of the highest, and at the same time — wearing enemy uniform and my pistol holster charged with a mix of chocolate and oatmeal — a serious theatre of the absurd. Our act had looked good! Terence writes in his book, 'George cut out a rattling pace.' I do not recall intending this; in fact as we marched along the side of the camp my eyes were on the wire I had escaped from and (it relieves me to be able to write this) my mind on my many good friends still inside. I was aware, too, that our getting through the gate without a word spoken was the work of the tailors and planners, a result of their skill and timing. But the dominant awareness was that I was 'out' and on the way

We passed our own barrack building, then presently the *Kommandatur* and the main gate where the sentry came to grudging attention. No one else took any notice of us and we were clear.

Just short of the fringes of Eichstätt we turned off the main road to a lesser one heading southwest by south in the general direction of the Junction. We were now about three miles from this, with broken, occasionally wooded country between that would provide us with cover to change into civilian clothes. Just as we were taking the turn a woman in uniform passing on a bicycle blew a long shrill blast on a whistle. We were within an ace of running which would have been madness when someone, I think Stewart, said 'It's the post woman delivering the mail!' She ignored us, and as soon as she was out of sight we made for cover. We had been out of camp about forty-five minutes, and were not much more than two miles from the Junction station, when we came to a little gully between ridges where we made ourselves into civilians.

Of that process I can report that changing clothes and footgear in November snow is a cold, awkward business. James and Tom and Terence had only to strip off their French uniforms and the items of civilian clothing they had been wearing under them for Stewart and me. Jackboots, I can confirm, are ideally removed by a bootjack, rather than sitting on a German uniform tunic in the snow, but I managed. So that we would not arrive at the station together Terence and James set off before us. We stripped the insignia off our uniforms and buried the latter as best we could in the snow. Then, leaving Stewart to catch his later train after an interval, Tom and I set off for the station.

There we kept clear of Terence and James whom we saw at the far end of the platform. There was no difficulty about buying the tickets. The train was full but not crowded; this was ideal. Tom found a seat between two well-upholstered *Hausfrauen*; I sat in a corner. Nobody seemed talkative. Not long after 2:30 we pulled into Munich. We did not look for Terence and James, hoping to see them in the late afternoon the next day at Tuttlingen station.

Finding a cinema to fill in the afternoon was easy enough; they tend to cluster near railway stations. The programme looked pretty dismal, but in our total ignorance of Munich we were both nervous, needlessly I think, about going too far from the station and decided that this one would do. I recall no detail, but the main film was badly conceived and directed, the supporting comedy unfunny, the newsreel crass propaganda. We sat through it three times, which took us to about 10:00, when we made our way back to the station where I bought our tickets to Augsburg and we sat down to watch the Arrivals and Departures board until our *Eilzug* came up.

The distance from Munich to Augsburg was not much more than 80 miles; we were there all too early for our liking. Our *Eilzug* to Ulm was not due until about 6:00 am and it was barely midnight. There was still something of a bustle of travellers in the main hall at Augsburg Station and again we sat down before its Arrivals and Departures board. This established us as travellers rather than loiterers, but only for a short while. For it was losing entries one after another as the last late-night trains departed, and presently we began to feel ourselves conspicuous.

So we took to the streets. We had expected to have to pass the night by that means, but like almost all escaping train travellers before us we were not long in finding how slowly time passes when one walks without a destination, or how hard it is to walk briskly as if for a purpose on broken, half-frozen snow, and how depressingly desolate blacked-out residential streets can feel at night after an hour or so. I thought of the following night when we would have no option and a good distance to cover, and how we would feel by then. I put it to Tom that we would be better advised to go back to the station and trust to our luck. He agreed: I remember sensing that he seemed relieved.

Back in the station the main hall, no longer abustle with comers and goers, seemed huge and felt almost empty. There were a few little clusters of people, obviously families and from their appearance sitting out the price of a night's lodging as they waited for one of the very early trains that had begun to appear on the departure board. Somewhat apart sat a couple of nondescript young men. Here and there a soldier slept where he sat. Fairly well dressed and of military age we felt alarmingly conspicuous, but we would try to carry it off. I tried to doze, but succeeded only in pretending with half-open eyes.

But not for long: presently a pair of *Bahnhofspolizei*, railway policemen, came into the hall and strolled their way about it. Not surprisingly they picked up the two young men; they were on their way out when one of them apparently had second thoughts and came back, straight to us. I suppose we looked respectable, for when he asked 'Was machen Sie hier?' he was using the courteous plural. 'Waiting for our train' was the obvious answer, but I added 'Schon langweilt es', 'we're already bored'. Again quite civilly he asked us to come along and took us to an office where an evidently more senior policeman was sitting behind a desk. This man, again civilly, asked us to sit down. I played the continental and did so with a slight bow; out of the corner of my eye I saw Tom do the same. We passed over our ID and travel permits as a matter of course and I told him our cover story while he studied them. I tried to give an impression of recognizing a need for this procedure but finding it boring. Presently, having sat silent for a couple of minutes, he reached for his phone and spoke quietly into it. I could just make out that he had picked up a couple of young men who seemed not to know their way about, and were, in a police sense, 'loitering'. To my surprise when his interlocutor, a rank or so senior I suppose, answered I could hear what he was saying clearly: 'Do they look respectable?'. Our man answered, 'ganz anständig', 'Yes, quite respectable'. 'What are their papers like?' 'They look official (*amtlich*), but I have never seen anything like them.' 'What do they claim to be?' 'Finnish forestry students.' There was a pause; then Senior Voice said 'Das ist schwierig', 'That is tricky. We don't want to cause any trouble with Finland. I leave it to you. Use your judgement.'

During that conversation I was as much on edge as ever in my life. The four of us sat silent for a good three minutes; then the man behind the desk stood up and gave us our papers without a word. The policeman who had brought us in asked us to follow him and took us where, with a long wait before us, we should have gone on arriving in Augsburg. It is what is called a *Wirtschaft*, a cosy old-fashioned station barroom with beer pumps, a few bottles of spirit on the shelves, and what looked like a food counter. There were tables and chairs, a dozen or so civilians and a few soldiers. 'Here you can wait in more comfort for your Ulm train. If you ask the barman he will make sure you don't miss it.'

I reckon that before that day I had not spent five minutes alone with Tom Acton, except possibly at Calais where he seemed very much my senior officer, or indeed any social time in his company until we found ourselves in the same room at Eichstätt. I have seldom met anyone who, with no evident reason for it, was so reserved. He was, I later learned, an only son of a widowed mother, with two sisters, had been to Eton and Sandhurst in both of which he shone, and was in 1940 the youngest battalion adjutant in the British army. Not many months older than me, he may have found the job hard at Calais. There are occasions when an adjutant must speak with the colonel's voice, and in our battalion all the company commanders were 40 or older with great war service. I learned after the war that at Calais in the dunes on the evening of the 25 May he had been unable to persuade Vernon Knollys to withdraw his men to the inner perimeter that Alex Allan, in command after the colonel was wounded and out of action, was forming. In the bag I messed with Tom for more than two years and we reached a point where we were at ease with each other, but I never in all that time found him an outgoing person. On the occasion he impressed me by knowing instinctively how to behave. If either of us had shown any sign of anxiety or nervousness we would have been held while our papers and story were checked. One telephone call to the nearest Finnish consulate or government agency would have exposed us.

We found ourselves a table, treated ourselves to a litre of beer, put our heads in our arms and tried to sleep. I can sleep sitting up, but I have never been good at sleeping head on arm, and used to envy fellow students in the library making up for a night out in front of a pile of books. But it was without question better than sitting in the cold, draughty main hall, and vastly preferable to tramping the night streets. In the *Wirtschaft* we could probably have bought food of a kind without ration cards, potato salad and vegetable soup, better than camp fare, but were not confident enough or hungry enough to try. Lance Pope did not tell me about these snuggeries; probably they did not figure in his posh, pre-war Germany.

The barman did not have to wake us to catch our Ulm train. There was no difficulty with tickets or checks, and we were in Ulm, 50 miles from our ultimate destination, when its citizens were hurrying to work. We had the morning to fill in, but the day was fair as yet, and we had been off our feet long enough. Ulm figures large in German history; nevertheless most of the part we wandered in was featureless and dull, as yet untouched visibly by the war. Remembering Calais after the first two days I was glad. We made for the Cathedral as soon after 9:00 as we could assume that weekday morning services would be over. An aged but shrewd looking verger welcomed us, assuming that we meant to go up the exceptionally high tower. 'I'm an old man, but I will gladly take you up and point out the sights.' I declined the offer as politely as I could, but with a wicked lie: we had come for a moment of pious meditation. I tipped him the price of a struggle up the tower and more; then moved up the nave with Tom at my elbow. We stopped about halfway to the high altar, made obeisance, entered a pew, and adopted the half-kneeling, half-sitting posture of most males in church, our hands before our faces. The old man recognized the ritual attitude and returned to his cubby-hole.

When we thought he had settled down we reckoned it safe to carry out our real purpose, eating some of our concentrated chocolate and oatmeal ration, which eaten publicly would have excited curiosity and suspicion in much-rationed Germany. But after the first few bites we found that we could eat only a little of it without water, of which we had none: it was simply too sweet.

So back to the station hall, now peopled enough for us not to be stared at. Tom agreed that it was imperative to get something to drink, and that the beer, being pretty thin, would do. We soon found a station bar, not as *gemütlich*, that is homely, as the Augsburg *Wirtschaft*, but otherwise just right with a mixed clientele of civilians and soldiers. I ordered two litres of *Helles*, the pale beer. It was certainly refreshing and answered our immediate need well enough; how it would have gone with the chocolate mix is another matter. It did not take long to drink, and we decided to have another half. After setting our refilled mugs down on the table the barmaid lingered, gave the table a swipe with her napkin and said amiably, 'Sie sind Ausländer, nicht war?', 'You are foreigners, aren't you?' Without thinking I said the first thing that came to my mind, 'that was clever of you! However did you know?' 'Oh, I can always tell', she answered, and went smugly back behind the bar. Watching her go I recovered my balance, so to speak, and said to Tom, not quietly, 'Da hast du Eine!', 'There's one for you!' Nobody in the bar took any notice of the exchange. Terence tells a similar story of himself and James in Munich.

Our train was not due to leave for half an hour when it appeared on the Departure Board, but I bought our tickets and we went through the wicket to our platform without any sort of check. It looked as if our absence had been covered successfully for two *Appels*. There stood our *Personenzug*, steaming and fizzing in anticipation as trains do. We boarded a carriage with a long centre aisle and, instead of compartments, the seats four a side of this in facing groups. We sat apart but facing each other over the backs, on the arrival side so as not to miss the station signs. Sitting together would have been bad fieldcraft; two young men of military age together are more than twice as conspicuous as one. As to conversation, we had no German small talk that would have been safe in our circumstances. We did not look out for Terence and James.

It was fine when we pulled out of Ulm, but very soon it began to snow. For the first hour or so I let myself doze, invariably waking as we slowed down to a stop, subconsciously afraid, I suppose, of missing ours. Terence and James had to be on this train; otherwise Tom and I would have to rethink the last stages of the border-crossing plan. As the snowfall persisted, thickening, I began to worry about movement once we left the road, whether as a four, or if they proved not to be on the train, as a pair.

Simply to approach the salient and the patrolled border area would call for the utmost stealth. The cold was not a problem. We were warmly dressed under our town clothes; we had high calorie rations, and for thirst there was the clean snow. The problems created by the snow were of movement and camouflage. Walking in soft snow over a certain depth is exhausting, laborious and slow. Our timetable, predicating a certain distance achieved the first night, was generous in dry going, but would be hard to keep to in the fresh deep snow after we took to the woods. And in snow-covered country a man in dark clothes would be starkly visible anywhere if he made the slightest movement. We would be penetrating a heavily patrolled zone. On the train to reassure myself I nursed the thought that the frontier post commanders on duty might, thinking that only fools would attempt a crossing in such conditions, be a little less vigilant, but against that, my mind continued, they might order particular vigilance because, a clever evader might, with that possibility in mind, set out to exploit those conditions. All he would need would be a white overall. But that kind of thinking was like playing the ancient game of scissors, stone and paper. In any event, we were committed and we had no white overalls.

Stop by stop the train shed its passengers and the evening drew in. it would be almost dark by four, about when our train was due in at Tuttlingen. The names I had memorized as warning of our approach to it were beginning to show on the station boards. Presently there were not more than half a dozen people in our carriage. Now my eyes were glued to the window, and at the expected moment the train stopped at Tuttlingen Nord, the last stop before ours. I glanced across the seat backs dividing Tom and me and saw him stand up as if planning to leave the train. I managed to catch his eye and shook my head once. He got the message.

Not many minutes later we trundled in to our destination. I took my time getting off the train, had no problem at the barrier and found Tom and Terence waiting for me. A moment later James turned up. We shook hands like good Europeans. The square in front of the station led directly to the road out of town to Immendingen that we planned to take. We were not alone; a number of other passengers, commuters to go by their briefcases, took it as well and we did not feel conspicuous. A mile out of Tuttlingen we left the main road for a minor one that led up into the hills. Here we were alone, and finding good cover destroyed all our travel papers, keeping only the identity cards, and got rid of the money we had left as well as any railway ticket stubs,

We waited for half an hour, eating chocolate mix washed down, so to speak, with mouthfuls of snow. The quiet was absolute, and one had a sense of violating it in speaking. Then back to the main road and to begin our serious walking.

Now we entered an ascending valley that looked like managed forest. Our road here appeared to have been ploughed; beyond the banks left by the plough the snow proved almost a foot deep, damp and heavy. The temperature must have been around freezing all that day. In favourable conditions we would be leaving the road about now and moving by compass across country. As things were it was out of the question; we would have to sacrifice security to make time and distance on the road. Without much discussion we agreed that we had no real option: to keep to our timetable we had to stay on the road.

We were approaching Riedhof, a village about five miles beyond Tuttlingen when we came upon a couple of milk cans of the sort I had found in the Calais farm, evidently for early morning collection left by the roadside. The temptation was extreme, and in turn each of us drank deep out of the inverted cover of one of them. I found some change I had not got rid of in my pocket, and disregarding food hygiene dropped it into the can I had opened. That would make a story for someone.

We were walking in an unusual light where the sky was cloudless and somehow not pitch dark and an absolute contrast between the unspoiled snow and all the solid objects threw these into sharp definition in an illusion of silver half-light. Any noise was sinister. Once we thought we heard the distant wail of an air raid warning siren; for a moment or two we thought we caught the distant droning of aircraft. It was the kind of setting in which a man imagined things. Once we were reminded that we were in a frontier area by the sight of a *Hochstand*, a wooden observation tower covering a forest ride. Nine miles beyond Tuttlingen we came to the outskirts of Biesendorf, a long, straggling village; we had no option but to pass through it. Beyond the village we came to a poorly signposted fork in the road; while we were trying to read it a man came out of the right-hand fork wheeling a bicycle. He took no notice of us; in retrospect this should have put us on our guard. Presently this road began to meander bewilderingly. Had we misread the sign? That we were bearing away from our intended lying-up position seemed certain when, about an hour out of Biesendorf, we came upon what had to be the Immendingen-Engen railway and a main road. As we stood discussing sotto voce whether to go cross-country now, another man, on foot, came up from behind and passed us, again taking no notice. We decided on the road, passed beneath the railway, and after about half a mile came to the skirts of a village. Just inside this was a crossroads where, if we turned left and took it, we would be on course again.

We never got to take it. Almost as we turned there was a great clamour of shouts; I recall the two dominant ones, 'Hände hoch!' and 'Wir ha'n se!' 'We've got 'em!'. There was no point in hesitation or debate: no papers, however good, or cover story, however plausible, would legitimize four men in town suits walking in the snow of a winter night so close to an international frontier. Our captors, with sporting rifles and shotguns and (he really scared me) a youth with a pitchfork, were the local *Landwacht*, the home guard. They had had warning of our approach; the countryside was on the alert for airmen from the raid we had actually heard. This was at Talmühle, about eight miles from the Swiss frontier.

My recollection of subsequent events does not always tally with Terence Prittie's, differing in some details from his account in *Escape to Freedom*, the second edition of his 1946 account, and in important matters from that in another book, *Through Irish Eyes*, published in 1977, which I did not come upon during his lifetime. I never took the earlier ones up with him; they did not seem to matter then and do not today. In what follows I shall lay down my own recollection.

When our captors were satisfied that we were not armed they took us into the local *Wirtschaft*, not much more than the room in which the owner of the house served beer to the community, and guarded us while one of their number fetched a man who, to go by his bearing and their deference was of some importance. Terence took him for a Gestapo officer; I would judge him not to have been of sufficient intelligence for that diabolic elite. He sent someone to fetch the *Grenzpolizei*, the state frontier police, then set about searching us. He barely glanced at our papers, dismissing them as rubbish; our maps, evidently camp-drawn but very accurate he set to one side. So far he was doing well. The chocolate mix of our marching ration, carefully packed but unlabelled, puzzled him. But his questioning and threats were trivial; unequipped as we were we could scarcely be saboteurs or intelligence agents. He tried all those. At length he came to the essential question, 'Was sind Sie eigentlich?', 'What are you actually?' Terence had enjoyed egging his questioning on with provocative answers. I glanced at Tom and raised my eyebrows; he gave the merest of nods. So I said 'We are British officer prisoners of war. We were attempting to get home and rejoin our regiments.' I gave him my name, rank and p.o.w. number; the others followed on.

With that he turned to detail. What camp had we escaped from? By what means? On what date? To go by our appearance we must have travelled by train. Who had supplied us with clothing, money, and the master-maps we had copied? Who had forged our papers? When he got no answers of us he began to rant. 'You are not officers you are spies! You will be sent to a civilian prison where they will get the truth out of you!' He paused, as if spent, and I said, 'Ich bin so frei', 'I take the liberty of asking you whether we may have a drink of water? It is very hot in here.' He refused without giving a reason, but I suspect he hoped we might offer to talk if promised a drink. From then on we sat in silence until some military police arrived and took us with much brandishing of weapons by truck and train to a civilian prison in Singen where we were 'handed over by signature'.

We had become counters now, in the game of denying your opponent a fighting man, but stacked by the side of the board, no longer in play. In the civilian prison we lost status altogether. A grizzled veteran with a huge bunch of keys clinking at his belt took us along a dismal corridor to a tiny cell that stank of urine and vomit. As he threw the door open it struck me that he had said nothing abusive or threatening, and that his crustiness might mean no more than irritation at being interrupted while snoozing on duty. I still wanted that drink of water, so I tried an oblique approach. In the most stilted formal German I could command I said, 'Forgive me for expressing an unsolicited opinion, but that is not the kind of accommodation we would have expected as officers.' This did nothing to improve our accommodation, but he actually apologized, he had nothing better. He was probably telling the truth. I sensed an advantage: we were parched with thirst and longed for nothing so much as a long drink of water. He locked us in, went off and came back with a bucket and a mug. Then he left our light on briefly while we came to terms with our lodging.

This was a cubicle mainly occupied by a wooden platform about two feet off the floor, with one small barred window near the ceiling. The other furniture was a bucket, evidently a gesture toward sanitation. There was no palliasse, or pillow, or blanket. The bed platform was about as wide as the desk where I sit to write, about five feet. Whether my reader believes this or not, the four of us actually slept on that 'bed' until about 7:00 when our jailer roused us, not because it was time to turn out but to take formal leave. He was going off duty.

An hour or so later we were collected by four military police and driven to Singen station. There, while we sat on a platform bench staring into the muzzles of the rifles of our vigilant escort, we were amazed to see Stewart Walker come limping onto the platform under guard.

He told us the following day what had happened to him. He duly caught the 2:00 train from Eichstätt Junction for Ingolstadt, but then, for whatever unfortunate reason, experienced traveller though he was, got off at Ingolstadt Nord and thus missed the one *Eilzug* of the day to Ulm and thus also the connexion for Neustadt 21 miles from his chosen lying-up place for the final attempt. The only other Ingolstadt-Ulm train that day was the *Schnellzug*, the express we had been warned to avoid. In his situation I think I would have chanced taking this. Not so Stewart: he learned that from Donauworth, 38 miles to the west, he could get a 9:00 *Eilzug* next morning that would get him to Ulm in time to make the connexion to Immendingen in the Schaffhausen region. Very well: he would walk to Donauworth. It took the madman 18 hours, but he made his connexions and was then picked up, barely able to stagger, no great distance from Switzerland. Poor Stewart!

Our escorts were understandably vigilant: we were still in civilian clothes, not yet too disreputable to lose ourselves in a civilian crowd if we made a break. In the course of the morning I became very familiar with the look of the muzzle of a firearm. Generally we were not allowed to look out of the window, but once, when — I suppose — we were as close as we would get to Switzerland they invited us to do so. It was a glorious morning, and the unattained looked very beautiful.

Soon after midday we detrained at Villingen. This was a punishment camp designed to discourage the many French conscript labourers caught attempting to get home through Switzerland. Here we were joined by Stewart. Terence writes of us being well treated. To be sure, an officer who interrogated us here gave us a cup of 'tea'. But after the inevitable search we were ordered to take off our civilian clothes and to put on Polish private soldiers' uniforms deliberately chosen not to fit. I was vain and foolish enough to protest, but to no avail: I was left with trousers made for a smaller man and designed to be worn with high boots; my tunic meanwhile was much too large. 'That's what you're getting. You don't have to wear it; go naked if you want.' Then for a couple of hours we were penned, individually, in cages of chicken wire roofed just low enough to keep a man from standing and too small for him to lie down. Eventually towards evening we were trucked to the station and spent the night and much of the next day on a slow train to the French Oflag at Weinsberg, a standard p.o.w. camp. Our interrogation on arrival was pretty much of a formality: our ritual answers were accepted. We were locked in single rooms, virtually cells, but they were clean and warm. The wooden bed had a palliasse with pillow, covers for these and a blanket. A soldier took us one after another to wash and clean up. An orderly brought a tolerable supper of soup and bread. The lights were turned off early. But within minutes I heard a mysterious French voice, which I traced as coming from the heating system; it belonged to my neighbour in the next-door cell. If he was a 'plant' he got nothing from me that the Germans did not already know, but he confirmed that the R.A.F. had indeed raided various towns in South-western Germany two nights before.

There was bread and drinkable *ersatz* coffee for breakfast; trust the French to do themselves well. The French officers sent in food and newspapers, and we luxuriated in warmth and relative comfort for a day and a night. We were in Weinsberg more than 36 hours before a guard party, n.c.o. and three soldiers, arrived from Eichstätt to take us back 'Nach Hause', 'home', they called it. You could see they were shocked at our turnout, though they made no reference to it. They never raised the question of how we had escaped, though they must have known that it was by one of the gates and therefore by a comrade's error. They seemed to bear no malice towards us for this.

On the contrary, they were very friendly. The Weinsberg people had given us travel rations; our guards had brought theirs with them. We messed together, so to speak. Pictures of their families and sweethearts were brought out and admired. When we changed trains, at Heilbronn I think, they apologized for not being allowed to buy us a drink in the station bar. These, one remembered, were frontline troops on rest leave, and of course not from fighting a British enemy. Not long after dusk our train pulled in to Eichstätt station from which we moved briskly to the camp where, to our surprise, there were few formalities. Our guard delivered us to the duty officer who happened, not surprisingly, to be Hauptmann Klau. He affected not to notice our grotesque appearance and neither mocked us nor crowed over our recapture. No search; the interrogation was a formality. As we were about to leave the office he stood up and saluted us with the quiet obser-vation 'Pech!'. 'Bad luck!' Without more ado we were taken not to the guardroom and cells, which would be usual, but to the inner gate, where we were turned loose into the 'big pen'. This was the evening, I believe, of 28 November 1942, marking in my world of that time the swiftest of transitions from the crest to the trough of my morale. It did not bear thinking about what we had had almost within reach.

It was already known that we had been retaken. Our roommates, when we came into the room unannounced, welcomed us warmly but without drama and waited for our story until we had cleaned up and were back in uniform. Tom went off with Hector to report to the escape committee. We learned that we had been covered for *Appel*, which accounted for the absence of checks at Augsburg and Ulm and above all at Tuttlingen. Our room and James's and Stewart's had pre-dictably been searched. The German security staff could not know, within a day, exactly when we had escaped since for all they knew we might have used *Schnell-züge*. There had been no visible change of procedure at the gates. In the camp peo-ple were at a loss to say why we were back there and not in solitary as would have happened at Biberach and Warburg. When I climbed into my clean bunk and the past few days flashed through my consciousness I had to shut my mind to the ugly self-reproach that if I had spoken up in favour of putting off our attempt until the spring we might have got home. We might, to be sure, have lost our escaping cos-tume in a search before spring, but in that game, wherever you looked, you took a risk. And we had lost it as things were.

We never did divine what subtle motive Klau and his team may have had for putting us back in the camp without a cooling-off spell. It is even possible that, being the sort of man he was, he wanted us to have the chance to reorientate our-selves and to have a good night's sleep. Be that as it may, the next morning at *Ap-pel* the S.B.O was told that we had an hour to get ready for a spell of solitary; we could bring shaving kit, a towel, a spare shirt and smalls, and one book. We were not told that this was for the statutory permitted 30 days of 'punishment', only that it was a formal security requirement because it was not known how we had escaped. In that case we were unlikely to be put away indefinitely; someone was bound to come across the clothes that, in the snow and without spades, we had not been able to hide effectively.

The cells were in the guardroom block, eight of them ranged along one side of a corridor. In the middle of the range, between numbers 4 and 5 stood a small cast iron stove, lit at midday. Opposite the stove a door gave onto the guards' quarters, washrooms, showers and latrines. The cells were bigger than the ones at Singen, and boasted a wooden bed about 30 inches wide, a palliasse and a pillow, calico covers for both, a sleeping bag of the same material and a blanket, a stool and on this a mug, plate, fork, spoon and crude table knife. There was a small heavily barred window just below the ceiling with no view but the sky. There was no light in the cell. I rejoiced in my choice of book, Richardson's *Pamela*, which had been long on my conscience.

That first day Terence produced drama for our entertainment. While serving his previous sentence he had picked up from the guards that a renegade Walloon Belgian officer was living in comfort in a luxury cell in another part of the *Kommandatur*. Now this morning one of the guards had given him a cryptic 'Psst! Strangers!' warning. Terence also knew the layout of the cells, and once we were locked in and the guards were gone checked our location by shouted communication. At one end were Tom, Terence and myself, in cells 5 and 6 James and Stewart, in 7 and 8 British p.o.w.s with short sentences. If there were a plant, as the guard's warning whisper seemed to imply, he would be in number 4, and might well be the Belgian. There was a plausible reason for the warning: the plant would be there to pick up any information about the means of our escape we might give away in shouted conversation, and it was in the interest of the guard company, out of loyalty to their guilty comrade, that Security should not have such information. Indeed it might even have been the unlucky culprit sentry himself who gave the warning. Terence could command a penetrating, somewhat high-pitched voice that carried remarkably. Assuming this, for most of the morning he shouted in tolerable French a succession of outrageous threats to Monsieur l'Officier Belge, of what would be done to traitors after the inevitable allied victory. These succeeded in alarming the 'Man in Four' to the point where he asked to have himself moved. In the next cell I heard him. Cell 4 remained unoccupied for the rest of our time in solitary.

Later that afternoon we were interrogated by the *Lagerkommandant*, Oberst Blätterbauer. To go by the drama of his performance he fancied himself at the job. Terence writes about him at some length so I will not. It was clear that the security staff had no precise knowledge what day, what time and by what means we had escaped. From the trend of Blätterbauer's questions he was looking for a lead. I found him easy to manage. If I looked patronising and mildly bored he became rattled and lost focus. We never had a chance to discuss him at this stage. To communicate between cells we had to shout, and we were never alone together as a group. He had us up a second time, and then passed the problem to his second-in-command, Maior Nikoll. This man's manner of proceeding was altogether different, formal rather than dramatic. Nikoll likewise saw us singly. I was fetched from my cell by a *Feldwebel*, a senior n.c.o.; this in itself, doing honour to me, when my usual escort as a subaltern would have been a soldier,[9] was clearly meant to indicate the seriousness of the occasion. Nikoll asked me to sit down. The *Feldwebel* clicked his heels and left. Nikoll assumed that I spoke German; fair enough: that would be obvious from our having travelled by train. But I did not answer

---

9. A subaltern in the British army is an officer holding a military rank below that of captain, esp. a second lieutenant.

him in that language until he quietly accused me of discourtesy for not doing so. I apologized; that had never been my intention; I was embarrassed by my poor command of his language. Whatever opening gambit he might have planned, this put him off, and he came straight to the point. 'We know the soldier who helped you escape. He is under arrest and awaiting court-martial. As you may imagine his sentence will be very severe. It distresses me to have one of my men in such a situation, especially if, as in this case, he has a wife and children. For you young gentlemen, escaping is a sport — if you will be honest with yourselves. But that man will have to pay a very high price for your diversion. Do you want to have him and his family on your conscience for life?' A pause here; then, 'That can be avoided. Tell me the means of your escape, the day and the time and — I give you my word of honour — I will intercede at his trial and ask for leniency. He is a simple soldier, you are an officer'. Then, in English, 'Play fair!'.

Nikoll was good. As he continued in that vein I felt more and more of a swine — until what I should have spotted immediately dawned on me, that if they knew what sentry had 'helped' us to escape, they had to know when and at which gate he was on duty, and at what time or times in, say, the three days before we were retaken. And they would have grilled him in the first instance. As with Blätterbauer's performance we had no chance to discuss Nikoll's interrogation as a group, but since we continued in cells we assumed that all five of us had steeled their hearts or seen through him.

As I wrote earlier, Lance and Terence had established good relations with our guard company on their previous visit. Now James found that one of them, in peacetime a skiing instructor, was a friend of a skiing instructor friend of James in the Bavarian Alps. Such a meaningful connexion, and the fact that they were combat troops from an evidently crack regiment, led to some relaxation in our treatment and improvement in our lifestyle. We could now, 'informally', when we sent our laundry back to the camp include a note with requests for books, chocolate, cigarettes and soap. There was no outdoor exercise (Terence is mistaken about this), but our cells were opened for the half hour or so before lights out and we congregated with our guards by the stove in the corridor. Their unit would be going back to the *Ostfront* in due course; we did not talk about that feature of their lives and they did not often raise the subject. The future was better forgotten. They could not fail to know that one of their number had opened the gate for us since there was no physical trace of any other means of escape such as a wire job or tunnel would leave. And they certainly knew what could not harm our relationship, that we had given nothing away in the interrogations. Because of the successful cover-up none of them except for the actual sentry who opened the gate, and possibly the sentry in the tower box above him, can have know exactly when we escaped. As for the man at the gate, he showed his face, which I recalled very clearly, only once and that only for a moment at our gatherings. As it happened

I was standing facing the door when he appeared in it I saw him quickly scan our five faces and his face whiten when it came to mine. Poor devil, he did not stay for a chat. But to see that face in the door was a great comfort to me.

It was a curious relationship. I do not believe they had any sense of treasonable complicity in covering up for a comrade; they may even have admired our feat a little. Terence writes of establishing a line of communication to the Escape Committee and sending back useful information. The fact of the matter is that we had gathered only two pieces of that commodity. The first, hardly a novelty, was that weather of the sort we encountered most gravely handicaps escapers. Thus, even if we had escaped the ambush at Talmühle our tracks in the new snow would probably have given us away the next day. The second, that the *Wirtschaft*-type bars in big railway stations were relatively secure places for well-dressed fair-haired German speakers to kill time between trains. To go by his book Terence never took that in. For these soldiers a *Kameradschaft* such as they evidently enjoyed displaying was not disloyal. We had 'turned' enough p.o.w. camp staff, buying dyes, bleaches, civilian hats and once even a Berlin telephone directory, to know the signs and degrees of venality.

We began to feel settled in. For Blätterbauer we constituted a dilemma. Since his security staff had not established the detail of the escape he could not return us to camp; this would cause trouble when the Swiss Red Cross commissioners next visited Oflag VIIB. But if he wrote to a higher authority requesting our move to another camp, giving failure to establish the means of the escape as the ground for the move, then he was, as a reservist, risking job, rank and pay. Not that we lost any sleep over this.

Our daily routine was simple. We were roused at 7:00. After a shave and a wash or cold shower, there would be 'tea' or 'coffee' and bread at about 8:00. Soup and potatoes came at 12:00, coffee and bread at about 5:00, but all these meals were 'improved' by Red Cross parcel foods sent by our comrades in camp and 'not noticed' by the *Kommandatur*. During the day if you needed the latrine you shouted for a sentry and were escorted there. Your door had a judas, but I don't recall mine ever being used. On a clear day there was light to read until about 4:00. After that boredom set in. The social half hour was a great relief. After this the dismal hours in the unlighted cell until sleep finally came afforded plenty of time for examination of one's life in the Socratic sense, but I cannot recall having any dazzling insights about myself. This was the worst of the day in solitary. Terence passed the time by singing, which did not help.

During reading hours *Pamela* was sustaining fare. The story enabled boredom in the grand style. What intrigued me in the experience was not so much the narrative as the general tone. I admired, also, Richardson's staying power, and beyond that, was delighted by what the book proclaimed about the difference between the mentality of his readers and my own. As I neared the end, rewarding to me as to the heroine and of course Mr. B., I sent out not for *Clarissa* — one can have too much of a good thing — but for *Tom Jones*. This, from what I had heard tell, might be an antidote. Reading it was a romp rather than an improving experience. Then I sent for *Joseph Andrews*, not knowing at the time that this was written before *Tom Jones*. I read it with a strong impression of a skit on *Pamela*, but there was no one handy to talk to about Fielding and I put the thought aside for years. When at length I found some confirmation of this it was clear I would have been a blockhead to miss the parody.

The days when the sky was overcast and it was too dark to read even at high noon were bad. Above all they drove home the realization of what we had lost by our failure. This led to foolishness. I found myself thinking that here, in the guardroom, we were actually outside the camp perimeter wire. Chancing that no one would peer through my judas I attacked a floorboard in the corner of my cell with my 'table' knife. Even with that instrument, more suitable for spreading margarine, the wood proved soft and workable. I calculated that within ten days at the outside I would have access to the space under the floor of the guardroom from which, since the building was a standard army pattern, there would certainly be a means of exit. Luckily, before I got myself into trouble for damaging *Wehrmacht* property, my reason recovered command with the question, what would I expect to do in enemy uniform, in winter, without a map or papers or provisions, and so on. I had merely made the taste of defeat more bitter.

There was one occasion of comic relief. Three or four days before Christmas Blätterbauer decided to have one more try at interrogation. Terence describes how he pulled out all the sentimental stops, even referring to *die heilige Weinachtzeit*, the sacred season of Christmas. What he did not realise was that for the majority of the p.o.w.s, the more of us assembled at Christmas the deeper the gloom.

When it came to the point our friends looked after us handsomely, even to the extent of enabling us to give a token Christmas party by the stove in the corridor for those of our friends among the guard company who did not live nearby and could not get home on leave. A dismal feature of this period was that we knew little about how the war was going; the BBC news from the camp wireless did not get to us.

We had just passed the Geneva Convention's thirty-day limit when our uniforms were found. This happened in the course of a weeklong countryside hunt for a pathetic group of Russian prisoners of war from a nearby labour camp who, maltreated to the point of frenzy by their guards, killed several of these and escaped. In the course of the hunt a tracker dog had come upon our imperfectly hidden German and French uniforms, which gave the show away. After Blätterbauer had subjected us to a speech combining homily and congratulations on our release we were returned to the main camp.

It was naturally a great relief to have freedom of movement there and to be with the many good friends who, far from reproaching us, seemed to think we had done well. For myself, I was anxious; I knew I had better construct some sort of programme or system to live by: I had discovered that I was temperamentally incapable of drifting with the slow movement of time to the war's end. At the same time I was not interested in committing myself to another winter scheme supposing opportunity offered. It would have to be a programme of organized reading, then; but even that, in my state of mind, went against the grain, always supposing the camp library resources were adequate. Had I know that a grand camp tunnel project was being planned I would certainly have applied for a place on its team. Such a tunnel was actually undertaken and completed, and the following June enabled the escape of 65 p.o.w.s. But had I applied and been taken on I would not have gone with them.

For we had been back in camp little more than a week when an order came for us to prepare to move next day. Our packed luggage was taken into the *Kommandatur* to be searched. We ourselves would duly follow. A day and a night passed. Our friends among the guard company thought we might be for Oflag IVC, Colditz, about 40 miles southeast of Leipzig. If that superstition was initially correct, there was a change of plan; we were definitely for Oflag IXA, 15 miles south of Kassel, where the more senior and the older p.o.w.s had gone from Warburg in the previous September.

Midmorning of 15 January 1943 we set off with an escort of four soldiers and an officer, Hauptmann Braunsberger, a genial soul who had been a p.o.w. in England in the Great War. He and the guards seemed to regard this duty as an enjoyable outing, and we drank each other's health in the servicemen's bar of Würzburg Station where we changed trains. Oflag IXA in Spangenberg was divided into two: an *Unterlager*, a lower camp in the midst of a pleasant old town called Elbersdorf, and an *Oberlager*, the upper camp in an early sixteenth-century castle on a sugarloaf mountain about a mile away. The camp authorities, German and British, had had almost no notice that we were coming. We arrived in the morning, and spent most of this day waiting for a decision by the former which camp to assign us to. We were comfortable but bored in a room of the German officers' mess in Elbersdorf, after a search, of course, and interrogation. It was all very civil, but by the time we knew we were for the Upper Camp and had made the long climb of steps up the sugarloaf it was dark, about 7:00, as I recall. I suspect there had been delay in the Upper Camp too, about where to accommodate us. Here, at length, we crossed what must once have been a drawbridge over a dry moat that relentless searchlights made to seem pretty deep. The place gave me an ugly sense of finality: here you are, here you stay.

Rereading this section after coming to its close I find it unduly preoccupied with our attempt to escape, as if I and the team with me had become wholly self-centred, the wellbeing and state of mind of more than 1,000 brother officers many of whom one knew by their given name and considered one's friends of no account. All of us in the bag were unquestionably self-centred in one sense, some more, some less so; this was a matter of individual temperament. But if you were in a scheme intense preoccupation was inevitable because of what was at stake. Certainly things did happen that took a man out of himself.

One such was the arrival of new prisoners in camp. This happened twice in the weeks just after we settled in at Eichstätt. The first lot were from North Africa, caught in the course of the surrender at Tobruk. A dozen or so were Afrikaners, big, tough-looking men who did not seem likely to take to captivity easily. I had, thus far, met only two South Africans in my life, a deliciously Rubens-type young woman at a Victoria League dinner party and a dry droll surgeon, at London House while he worked for his fellowship examination. We got on well. These from Tobruk were sullen and bitter and said so openly, for which they came to be disliked. I was sorry for them because they had not seemed to realize that almost everyone in the bag was there because of some sort of higher level mismanagement and could have had a grievance; that most took for granted. The few Australians who came with them, for instance, profanely critical of their senior officers, were found to be amusing and were liked.

Then there was Michael Alexander. One November evening, with the BBC news, came an order for anyone who knew an officer of that name to report to the camp adjutant next morning. The two names are not uncommonly combined in Scotland, but I thought I had better form up, thinking of the Michael Alexander I had served with in the 5th Scots Guards. This one was a solitary officer introduced by the Germans. Such persons were always subjected to checks, and his story, though not impossible, was of the kind to need some sort of confirmation. The adjutant told me it before he sent me to the hospital where the man was in care. He had been captured in the Western Desert after the reconnaissance unit he belonged to had been shot up, walking eastwards alone, wearing a khaki German peaked cap because he had lost his own and the sun was almost unbearable. The Germans who took him treated him as a spy because of that headdress, in some circumstances understandable, and sent him to Berlin where he was grilled until his interrogators at length gave up. After that he was kept in poor conditions in a civilian prison for some months. 'Check that, please, George.'

The man was in bed in a room by himself; he looked in a bad state, sunken-eyed and hollow-cheeked, skin grey from being long indoors. I did not see the Michael Alexander of Chamonix there. He seemed browbeaten, as a maltreated dog does. Straight questioning, it struck me, would do no good. So I came to the point obliquely, as if there was nothing questionable at issue: how it would be good to hear first hand about the desert war; like a bloody fool I had missed being posted there by volunteering for that ridiculous Norway adventure; how I had been wise only after the event when, during the embarrassing disbandment, Stirling's cousin, Andrew Maxwell, had tried to recruit me for his next project. As I rambled on he dropped his guard: 'You had sense; he talked me into it and look at me!' After that it was easy and we were doing a tour of the Chamonix bars. I have not seen him since Eichstätt, except in a television programme about the Colditz *prominenti*: the Field Marshall was evidently his uncle. I asked Charles Jansen, who had become by then by marriage what he called a 'bogus laird',[10] whether he knew Alexander. He shook his head disapprovingly: 'A sad rake!' Be that as it may, what might have happened to him had he been turned away from camp or even not identified took my mind off myself for a day or two.

One event at Eichstätt changed the mood of the whole camp. A group of Canadian officers, survivors of the misconceived attempt to establish a bridgehead at Dieppe in August, were sent to our camp in September. They had little to say about the fighting there although it was evident that the loss of so many comrades had left its mark on them. They were much liked, and respected for showing no sign of self-pity; their grumbling about the stupidity of the Canadian General McNaughton responsible for the operation was accepted as understandable. Our room, probably because one of the most pleasant in the camp, had the two battalion commanders as 'guests' for a few days while accommodation more appropriate to their rank was arranged. Youngsters barely into their thirties (a new feature of the army for us), with a V.C. and D.S.O. to come, they were quite without starch, affable and genial. The camp was shocked into deep outrage when on 8 October a *Führerbefehl*, a direct order from Hitler, came that all Canadian p.o.w.s were thenceforth to wear manacles in reprisal for an incident when a commando reconnaissance party in kayaks tied the hands of their prisoners in a raid on Sark and one of them struggled to escape and was killed. The order had a single good feature: it shocked the guard company as much as it outraged us, and they went to great dramatic lengths to conceal the leniency they had been especially ordered to refrain from. The order was quickly rescinded in spring when the *Afrikakorps*, captured in Tunis, was sent to Canadian camps.

By and large Eichstätt was not a lucky camp. In June Hector, with uniforms still to spare, and his team made another attempt, this time at the main gate. Somehow in the fifties, Terence managed to lay hands on a snapshot of the party after its failure. There was Lance, of course, looking grim, another 'German officer' a Lieut. Col. Broomhall, who would look a Colonel Blimp in any uniform, Tony Bampfylde as a weedy, bespectacled desk n.c.o. and two very smart civilians, Tony Rolt and Hector himself. I did not know that Broomhall had any German and would have thought not; he used to kibitz when I translated the communiqué for Alex Allan. But he was not stupid and might have been working at it.

<hr />

10. Charles Jansen (1917–2006) married Elizabeth, Countess of Sutherland.

The tunnel scheme I mentioned earlier was a sensational success as a means of egress. It broke ground on 2 June and according to Foot and Langley sixty-five p.o.w.s passed through it and got clear of the camp. But their very number, ruling out any possibility of a cover-up, ensured that before midday every ticket collector and railway policeman in southwest Germany would have been alerted: so much for the travellers by train. As for the night runners, again the number would have turned out the male population of the countryside against them. Foot and Langley report that the authorities fielded the amazing number of 50,000 police, troops, home guard and *Hitler Jugend* for the hunt.

As if that were not enough, during the collapse of German resistance in 1945, when the occupants of Oflag VIIB, Eichstätt were being marched northeastwards by their captors, they were strafed by American fighter-bombers, which, even though it was night, took a heavy toll. It was grim to learn from survivors what friends one had lost that night.

12
OFLAG IXAH SPANGENBERG
JANUARY 1943 AND AFTER

Spangenberg Castle held about 190 officer p.o.w.s in January 1943, mainly the elderly and the field officers who had been sent there from Warburg the previous Autumn, but also, notably, Major General Victor Fortune, and from another source the commando troop and an accompanying R.E. officer who had gone with the naval force in March 1942 in the highly successful attack on the German submarine dry dock base at Dieppe. The general and the most senior field officers were housed in small rooms in the castle tower, the rest but for the subalterns and the quartermaster captains in larger rooms on the first floor; these latter were lodged in the largest room on the same floor, called the Arab Quarter by its inmates in ironic disparagement. In the sixteenth century this room would have been the great hall of the castle; at that time the room below would have housed the garrison.

Here our party was accommodated. It had the single saving grace of not being crowded. The bunks were of two tiers only and did not mask the tall windows on one side. But on the other side from these there was a permanent wooden screen about ten foot high concealing a long row of hand washbasins that served all the rooms on the first floor, so that all day for the occupants of the Arab Quarter there was the noise of human traffic from other rooms. The quarter had one fine feature, a vast renaissance fireplace at the end that gave into the room from the staircase. Down the middle stood four or five long tables with accompanying long stools.

The 'room commander', British appointed, was a Captain Alexander Bardwell from a Highland regiment and emphatically kilted, with the Scottish prefix 'Master of' (I forget what) before his surname. He assigned our bunks, putting Tom Acton, an acting-captain, along with James McDonnell and Terence, both what the Mitford girls called 'hons', up at his end of the room where already the two 'full', that is two-star lieutenants, were housed. Stewart and I found bunks among the commando subalterns along the window end. There was a free top bunk and I made for it, under the amused eyes of surrounding young men who when I had claimed it informed me that my tier-mate below was the most formidable snorer

Card sent to mother from p.o.w. camp, front side.

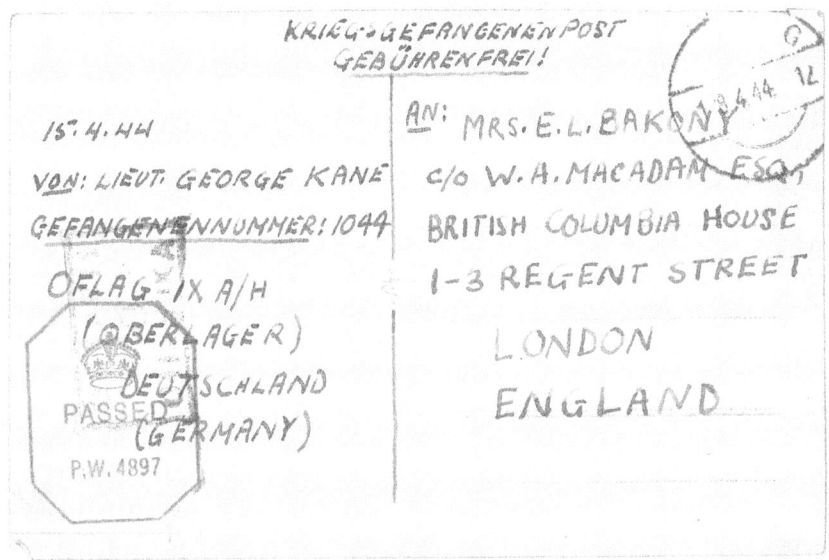

Card sent to mother from p.o.w. camp, reverse.

in the British army. Never mind; he proved to be a charming man when awake, and I kept a loose bed board along the side of my palliasse to check him by banging the bunk when he woke me at night. We became good friends.

As we were settling in Alex Allan called to say 'Good show!', as did presently Peter Brush; they were dear people both, with the gift of the right blend of commendation and sympathy. I was tired, and while we must have been fed somewhere I do not recall supper. At 8:00 Bardwell, inevitably called Sandy, read the BBC news summary to the assembled occupants; at 8:55 a German corporal and two soldiers came for the nightly count. While I sat on my bed waiting for that visit and lights out a very youthful-looking person from another room, toothbrush in hand, came up to congratulate and commiserate. We exchanged the usual information. He had been taken at St Nazaire, but no, he was a sapper, not a commando. He had come along with another of his kind who had been killed to blow up the pumping station that served the submarine dry docks. I dwell on this meeting because, a little more than three years later, I married his sister. His name is Bob Montgomery.

The Arab Quarter, after the escape clubrooms I had lived in at Warburg and Eichstätt, was a comedown; such authority as Sandy Bardwell exercised did not extend, as Ed Ree's had done, to seeing that it was kept tidy. But everyone was civil and otherwise considerate and within a couple of months I had moved to an upper bunk by a window; and in any event I spent very little of my day in the room.

In all other particulars Spangenberg was the most comfortable camp in Germany. It had central heating, which was, very fairly, turned up in the depth of winter. And it was the best run, not surprisingly with General Fortune to lend weight to whichever lieutenant colonel was S.B.O. at the time. Below our room was the dining hall in which every p.o.w. sat at his mess table three times a day. The kitchen was relatively modern, and by general consent some of the standard contents of the British Red Cross parcels were pooled, notably bully beef, spam and tea. This last was served in standard mugs at breakfast, where the mess in most cases shared its bread and jam, also margarine when this was not rancid on receipt. The German ration was honest and for whatever reason more varied and palatable than in other camps. You could tell that the soups were made with pulse, not powder, that meat had played a part in their cooking; on occasion there was even meat such as the German variety of Bologna sausage for the meal. The chocolate and biscuits in the parcels were issued individually, but many messes shared these. How the composition of our mess was determined I never found out. Tom and Terence and I were together but James and Stewart went to other messes, possibly by request. I sensed that James sometimes found Terence tiresome; I liked James and could wish to have got to know him better. Then there was Sandy Bardwell, necessarily by his choice as room commander, and a subaltern in the Royal Sussex called Alan Leake. Then, surprisingly, a Major Walter Clough-Taylor in the Welsh Regiment. Add a quartermaster, Captain Parsfield, and you have our mix. Sandy was, to my taste, garrulous and conventional to the point of being dull but otherwise easy to live with. Clough was in his middle thirties, I suppose, a regular soldier, a man of strong likes and dislikes and little patience for the latter. With us he never once pulled his rank or greater age, and seemed to find us as amusing as I, at least found his dry, somewhat sardonic humour. He could be very sharp about anyone he disliked, but we did not enquire why he chose to mess with junior officers. Alan Leake was a sweet-natured, simple soul with no finesse whatever. Parsfield was a loner with some kind of grievance against life; the other quartermasters could not bear him. We tamed him. When the mess was first put together he was very prickly, ready to take offence, but without any prearrangement we never made fun of him or treated him otherwise than as a messmate and as we did one another, and we included him in all our treat sharing. He responded by becoming, very gradually, less crusty. Watching this process with interest as an alien over two years I found myself increasingly impressed by my messmates.

I spent little time in my room. If it was fine there was the moat to walk in with good company and conversation always available or, in season, the parapet to lounge on. Otherwise I lived in the library, a fine oak-panelled room which got the sun on winter afternoons and, but for two tables of inveterate bridge-players who broke the silence at intervals with post mortems, was quiet. As to the books, our librarian, Major Charles Shears, in peacetime a senior figure at Hutchinsons, seemed to have arranged a steady supply of new publications as they came out. The Germans permitted book parcels from England, and since most people who received these had no bookshelves, they tended to give them to the library when they and their friends had done with them.

Within days I was taken down the camp's show tunnel by the Lieut. Col. Hugh Swinburne who with James Murray-Grant had escaped by way of the island from Laufen in 1941. It was in every way a formidable project. It started from the 'Music Room', so called because it contained a decrepit upright piano. Here, as in our Warburg project, access was by a trap under a stove. The shaft began with cutting through eight inches of concrete sub-flooring. It was four foot by five foot wide and about 10 foot deep. When I was taken down work on the chamber had just begun. This was to lead, well below floor level, under the castle wall to a nearby bastion. Beneath this bastion a second shaft was planned, to descend the 40 feet and more needed to take the second chamber under the moat. This in turn would join an ancient passage, itself believed to exist and to run from the cellar of the castle to the side of the castle mount and the free world. The tools were, for hammer a broken cannonball about three inches in diameter, for chisel a spike, and for good measure a small hand axe. Leaving aside the scale of the project, it did not need a geologist to tell that all the digging would be through bedrock.

This was January 1943. The *Afrikakorps* was in retreat; Paulus had been checked at Stalingrad and the German pressure on Moscow was being contained. A man could see a possible end to the war in Europe after another winter, but no such end to this tunnel. At best a two-pound hammer and a supply of good chisels would have helped to pass the time of waiting. But there was no joy in the futile punishment of one's hands with the broken cannonball and the spike.

The team — all, in their turn, had been shown over the tunnel — was of one mind about this, and we turned our thought to the gate. This was formidable. From the courtyard you reached it by passing under its guard tower to what had once been a drawbridge over the moat. This was out of bounds to p.o.w.s. At its immediate end was the gate. The sentry in the box there did not have its key. If called upon to open it for a German, however senior, he had to telephone from his box to the n.c.o. on duty in the guardhouse some 5 yards back from the gate. This man in his turn was required to keep record, in his duty book, of the comings and goings of all German personnel in the camp. Except during *Appel* and on special occasions like searches the number of these was never very large.

We spotted one weak point in the system. For about five minutes each evening, at a time determined by the weather, the light and the season, the duty n.c.o. and the guard commander of the castle detachment, with two soldiers, came into camp to clear the battlements and, that done, to lock the gate that gave onto them from the castle courtyard. Because of the variable time of this activity there was a second time factor: the sentry, meanwhile at the main gate, the man with the rifle slung over his shoulder, had to have come on duty not long before the battlement clearing if he was not to know there were no strange German officers in the castle. Otherwise no amount of either blarney or blustering would have induced him to allow passage through the gate or to refrain from pressing the alarm bell. The one thing we did know was the time when new sentries came on duty.

This was a long shot but not beyond range. Anything was better than inactivity, and almost anything better — given the state of the war — than that Chateau d'If tunnel. So the team moved into action. Ironically in this small, almost unbreakable prison, the Escape Committee was highly organised and very efficient. With a little pressure from the Greenjacket mafia (this included Col. Euan Miller and Major Jack Poole of the 60th, the latter a seasoned and ultimately successful escaper in the Great War), Tom had the pick of the camp's fine fabrics for his German officer tunics, in particular camel hair dressing gowns, without exception 'donated' by senior officers. Shame on me! Only one was given grudgingly. James along with Major Rupert Christie, a recruit to the team, did the unstitching and most of the stitching, as well as most of the sewing, after Tom's skilful cutting. Terence, against — according to him — all likelihood, became skilful in the fine embroidery of badges and silver braid. They made me responsible for the elaborate officer cap badges and the 'silver' buttons. I have little skill in such fine work, but there were people in the camp who could carve out the moulds for me, and just barely enough tin foil for melting down available from cigarette packets (it was going out of use) to finish the job. Stewart had had enough escaping; who can blame him?

Before we got to the point of putting the plan I have just described to the test what seemed a better one took shape. The keen amateur drama element in the camp had, one fine evening the preceding summer, put on a very successful Shakespeare play on an open stage with the inner gate on the battlements for a background in the castle courtyard. This had attracted half a dozen strange German officers. This year's production was to be *Henry V.* Terence and I would be ready, if any came to see this rousing show, to leave halfway through the performance, fed up with pro-British jingoism. It seemed very promising.

Everything was, regrettably, not all right on the night. Only two Germans came to the play, n.c.o.s, one well known to the guard company. After waiting almost an hour for possible latecomers we gave up the project and changed out of our costumes, which, the pockets crammed with papers, maps and money, were put back in the hide, ready for early use in the original plan. But, with what might well be called hubris, we decided that since a third uniform, intended for James, was almost ready, we would wait and take him with us. Within a week, for three successive days we were turned out into the moat after morning *Appel* and held there while the camp was subjected to the most rigorous search in its occupants' memory. Each day the Germans combed a particular area, and found, in succession, the camp wireless, two major hides containing the camp's escaping stores, and worst of all, a hide we had thought impenetrable, containing our team's wardrobe of uniforms, civilian clothes and tailoring kit. In each case they seemed to know an area was sensitive and persisted there until they succeeded; in the case of our cache, which none of the team would have known how to open, they as good as dismantled the wall of a room before success. Evidently they had general information of the whereabouts of the hides.

How they came by this is circumstantially indicated. A couple of months after we were sent to Spangenberg the Germans introduced a solitary p.o.w. into the camp, as they had done Michael Alexander at Eichstätt, a second lieutenant Pollock. He was predictably accommodated in the Arab Quarter. He was quiet and unremarkable, as I remember him, neither prepossessing nor otherwise. He tended to appear beside one and initiate a conversation, as often as not about the person he was addressing. The uncharitable expression 'gave me the creeps' comes to mind. The team quietly decided to avoid him. Some days before the disastrous searches he was transferred to Rotenburg, another element of Oflag IXA about a dozen miles away. And not long after his transfer a tunnel there, on the point of breaking ground, was discovered. I don't have any doubt he was a plant. And what he can have reported, from the nature of the searching, suggests there was no individual breach of security by anyone in the camp community. The castle was a very small structure, and any unusual coming and going such as during the disposal of tunnel spoil, or a stooge on duty regularly at a given point, was bound to be noticed. I do fault the Escape Committee for not vetting him, which would have been easy. Simply 'What service, what unit, what regiment were you in? Where were you taken? What camps have you been in?' Occupied Europe was full of strays, of whom a good number were found to have impersonated officers in the hope of better treatment in captivity; found out by the Germans, they often proved easy to turn. Whatever the explanation we cursed our luck.

It looked now as if our team had no future. For one thing Terence and I were unquestionably compromised: the size of the two uniforms with loaded pockets pointed to us, and Nikoll's interrogation report, if it came with us to Spangenberg, would have pointed to me as the first German speaker. Certainly Hauptmann Seibold, the Security Officer, found us interesting. If he happened to be in camp and encounter one or the other of us he would salute with some ceremony, and then would say, as if turning it over in his mind, 'Prittie oder Kane, Kane oder Prittie?', the wrong name always first. He was a very effective security officer, and a civil one to boot. We did not know at the time that he had been an English master in a *Hochschule*, and was definitely pro-British. In April 1945, I learned after the war, during a lull before repatriation, three of our Spangenberg security people hired a German car and driver and drove back to Spangenberg to see how our belongings left behind had fared. They found the castle, which had been defended, a smoking ruin, but the *Kommandatur* offices in Elbersdorf were intact, and rifling through Seibold's desk they found in a bottom drawer an order that our five, individually named, were to be held covered by the notorious *Führerbefehl* of 1944, and must not be allowed to leave the Oflag alive. In the summer of 1945 Seibold was finally located in a somewhat rough American p.o.w. camp and moved to West Kensington where, with other similarly 'rescued' Germans, he lodged for a while in comfort. I wish I had known of this; I would have called on him. He was, from that disregard of an order, evidently brave as well as upright.

Back to my story: it looked as if gate schemes were out of the question. More rigorous control procedures had been put into effect and our faces were too well known. The moat wall was smooth and its 40 feet looked unscalable. The moat itself had, before we came, been found too wide for any bridging scheme with the timber available. A Falstaff act with a large laundry basket had been tried once and failed. In effect we accepted defeat.

For this we were twice shamed. The first time was when two R.E. officers did indeed get over the moat wall and away. That wall afforded no foot or handholds, but between its top and the sentries' walk outside it there was a simple iron fence with three stout rails. The escapers made a rope ladder with the requisite ropes from hempen parcel string and somehow an iron grapnel fitted with a ring to serve as a pulley at one end. The grapnel, a long loop of rope through its ring, was thrown from a bastion opposite the point farthest from the gate where the two sentries beats ended. The grapnel caught in the uppermost fence rail. The ladder was hauled up from the moat. The escapers slid down another rope from the bastion, went up the ladder and over the fence, threw the grapnel back and were away. If that sounds easy my reader must realise that during all this while the two sentries had to be held by chatty German speakers at the points in their beats farthest from the bastion. All this apart, some 40 feet of rope ladder and 120 feet of rope had, for days before, to be kept in readiness and safely hidden until two sentries known to be talkative were on duty. It took three tries, at times when that condition was fulfilled, to get the rope over the top rail. Once the grapnel caught on a lower rail and could not be dislodged; its loop rope was pulled free and it was left there. The sentries must have seen it, but evidently did not see fit to report it. There were plans for a second attempt, but before conditions were right for this the Germans increased the barbed wire along the sentry's walk. I had, I suppose, the least crucial job in the operation, to take the ladder and ropes up and down the chimney to a space behind the grand fireplace in the Arab Quarter. The fireplace was of course not in use, but the chimney served the camp kitchen as well and I would come back down black as a Moor. Luckily the sweep's access was just opposite the shower room. But I never did get the rims of my eyes clean during this operation and was mocked for unnatural propensities by my friends.

The two escapers had a good run for their money but were retaken in the end. For the preparation and planning in their scheme they deserved better.

The second successful break from the castle was a solo effort by Captain Bill Edwards of the West Kents, one of the unsung heroes of escaping. Upon capture, once settled in an Oflag, he learned German from scratch for escape purposes. On this, his second successful escape, he was caught on the actual Swiss frontier. He got away while walking down to the Lower Camp as interpreter with our pay officer and a sentry by a brazenly simple contrivance. About halfway down the mountain he said to the sentry, 'Ich muss schiffen', 'I have to pump ship,' gave him a cigarette, and as if in modesty moved off a little distance while the pay officer, clumsily offering the sentry a light, stood so the latter was facing away from Bill. When he was caught my signature on his papers, deliberately indecipherable, came close to getting him imprisoned by the Gestapo. Here, if one remembers Henry Coombe-Tennant and the other two innocents who, in uniform and with no German between them got home, you have the absolute demonstration of the importance of luck in the escape game, not that everyone who swarmed over the wire that night did not deserve to get clear and home.

We cannot have been more than a month without a wireless. The replacement was homemade, so to speak, by a quiet little Signal Corps Second Lieutenant; it was necessary to 'buy' only one component from a tame sentry. In the second half of that fourth summer there was some comfort in the course of the war, which I often found myself discussing with Alex Allan on days when the German communiqué looked of interest. He had, albeit sometimes mocked by officers of his own rank for testiness, a very good, if not a cool head. We would sit side by side while I translated the communiqué, amazed at Hitler's orders to Paulus to hold a manifestly untenable position at Stalingrad, observing with fascination how the Soviet forces outweighed and outfought the *Wehrmacht* in the tank battle of Kursk, biting our nails after the Sicily landing, rejoicing in the Italian surrender.

After that surrender a considerable number of the 1000 or so British personnel captured by the Germans in North Africa and guarded for them by the Italian Army in Italy, who ought to have walked out of their camps and southward to join the allied forces landing there, were, in consequence of a foolish order emanating from Higher Command, recaptured by the Germans and moved to existing camps in Germany. Among the small number that came to Spangenberg were two Rifle Brigade subalterns, one of whom had during his Italian confinement set himself to learning his jailers' language, and to good effect. He was ready enough to pass on his knowledge. The camp *Sonderführer*, a lecturer in *Anglistik* in a nearby university and, I will write without discomfort, a friend with whom I wish I could talk to today, found us a *Heath's Italian Grammar* which, *Lagermarks* being useless to him, I paid for with soap and coffee (Seibold shut his eyes to this), and we set to. I didn't advertise the class; it consisted of Ronnie Swayne, a

St Nazaire Commando, James McDonnell, Terence, the other R.B. subaltern from Italy and myself. We were keen to learn and brought out the best in our teacher, whose name — I confess with shame — I have forgotten. By the end of the winter I had a reading knowledge of contemporary Italian along with some military slang not in Heath. It was a distinct advantage to have struggled through the Italian of Longfellow's print of the *Inferno* with its facing-page translation. My friend the *Sonderführer* presently found me Ulrichus Hoepli's one-volume edition of the *Commedia* and a *Heath's Italian-English Dictionary*. There was no modern Italian literature in the library, and when we had worked through Heath's grammar the class dismissed itself. Ronnie and I both felt it a poor thing to stop there, and began a practice of preparing a certain number of stanzas of the *Commedia*, then meeting and translating to each other. Ronnie had a classical education at school and soon learned the trick of getting back to the Latin etymons. Moreover, James McDonnell had been sent Forbes's three volumes of Russian grammar and, plying the needle with Rupert Christie, had learned in casual talk that this man had, then a fledgling subaltern just touched by the war, during 1919 prepared for and passed the army interpreters' examination in Russian, having studied it under an émigré countess in Riga. James nobbled Rupert as a teacher and I invited myself to be his second pupil. By such means I regained a little of the sense of purpose that I needed.

Possibly because I spent so much time in the library, Charles Shears asked me to become Assistant Librarian. Since my only duty would be to catalogue accessions, and this would enable me to read those that interested me at once, I accepted. By Christmas I had read all the English books new to me in the library except the technical volumes. I must confess that soon after coming to Spangenberg I had received a huge book parcel from Professor Chambers containing Skeat's E.E.T.S. *Piers Plowman* volumes, Jusserand's *English Wayfaring Life in the Middle Ages* and Owst's *Literature and Pulpit in Medieval England*. This kindness, unquestionably so intended, should have directed me to examine my life constructively; all it did was induce a guilty awareness that I owed the Imperial Order of Daughters of the Empire a doctorate. I did not care at all for the thought of not honouring that debt, but with the best will in the world I could not force myself to be interested at that time in Jusserand's sturdy beggars and Owst's delinquent religious and mercenary friars. As for the *Piers* texts, these were not accessible without the sort of concentration I was unable as a p.o.w. to bring to bear. I salved my conscience a little with the thought that these books would be handy to have the moment I got out of uniform; I would make sure they got back to England somehow.

At least, I thought, I will read for a little more than amusement; I will read French books, and systematically. I started with *Candide*, which had interested me at school, but then, limited by availability, I followed with *Manon Lescaut* and *Les Liasons dangereuses. La Dame aux camélias*. Then there were *Le rouge et le noir* and a good collection of de Maupassant's short stories. Had there been any Balzac or Zola I would have read on and greatly improved my understanding of the history of the novel. Had there been any Proust in French I might have been able to force myself to read him as a discipline, but there was not, and I have never been able to abide him in translation. The next work in chronological order was *La rôtisserie de la reine Pédauque* which soon had me dozing. So much, I thought, for my good intentions.

The French reading was, however, rewarding in another way. I had been admiring Katherine Mansfield's short stories; in Maupassant there was a narrative logic absent from her mood pictures, of its kind, for instance in *Boule de suif,* just as sensitive as her elegant sketches of episodes. I had been playing at writing the Mansfield kind; I would try to intermesh the two excellences. I managed to finish enough of these, for better or for worse, to want to try the combination on a larger scale, and for the rest of my time in Germany laboured away at a novel in which I tried to combine sensibility with inevitability of outcome. I even carried the manuscripts back to England. Luckily when I tested the products on the market they came back invariably with the message, 'We regret etc., but would like to see your next book.' The message was clear enough.

I was not the only scribbler in the winter of '43/'44. A surprising number of people in that small community took to putting words together as a refuge from tedium. I particularly remember two captains in their late thirties who went straight from morning *Appel* to the library, broke only briefly for lunch and afternoon *Appel* and supper, and put pen down only when we were turned out of the library. If they published after the war it was certainly not under their own names. Ronnie, who had a respectable second in Greats from Oxford and talked of the Foreign Service, read nineteenth-century history and took extensive notes. Terence, who had an amazing memory for the data of cricket and had somehow acquired a copy of Wisden, generally treated by the German censors as a code handbook, wrote a number of essays on the game later published. Presently, encouraged by Charles Shears, he began an account (names and other giveaway data omitted) of his experiences as an escaper. Carefully hidden when not actually under his hand, he carried what he had so far written home to finish, and Hutchinson's brought it out as his first book. He had asked me to look at light verse which he wrote for the diversion of his friends; luckily it was technically adequate and I could commend it for this truthfully. Later he showed me the first half dozen chapters of what became his escape book. Here there was room for improvement, and I risked our friendly relation by telling him what was wrong. But he wanted to learn and accepted criticism and did indeed come to write an easy style. He was not ungrateful; he included me in the dedication of this book, and much later in another set down that I taught him to write. It was not so easy when dear Alex Allan very shyly asked me to read part of a draft of an account of our battle at Calais, which as surviving senior officer he would be required to submit on return. He was unquestionably literate and his spoken language was always clear and logically assembled. But his writing was amazingly stilted, and fossilized into conventional formalities, as if plain English was not to be used. I could not bring myself to tell him this in so many words. Luckily the officer who put together the history of the regiment in 1939–1945 from any number of reports acknowledged his debt to Alex handsomely and repaid it by translating him into easy English. All this took me through the winter of 1943–1944. The experience was good for me. I knew at heart that I could not write unlaboured fiction; I was not a 'natural' writer; in due course I 'got that novel out of my system'. And as the Russian lessons went on into spring I was just beginning to read Tolstoy's *In the Caucasus* in the original. I never finished it, because James was moved to another camp and his grammar went with him. But I knew the story; there was a translation of it at home. And it passed the time.

During the latter end of 1943 and early 1944 we had news of the war beyond that of the BBC bulletins from officers, several quite senior, recently taken in Italy, who told us that England was swarming with American military forces. The long-awaited assault on the European mainland was a matter of no more than months away. Speculation about dates became feverish. I found myself once more going over the German communiqué daily with Alex, gauging German morale by the distance of its report from that of last evening's BBC bulletin. Ronnie and I stepped up our *Commedia* reading to two days a week. This was very good for us and sealed a friendship.

Another circumstance that made the waiting more tolerable was a directive received by the British camp authorities that officer p.o.w.s need no longer consider it their duty to escape and might give their parole for recreational purposes. The reason behind this relaxation was not good. On 24 March 1944 seventy-nine RAF p.o.w.s escaped from Stalag Luft III. Of these, three got clear away and eventually to England. The rest were captured, and fifty of them shot dead by Hitler's express order. At the time we did not know the atrocious detail, only that the Germans had ceased to observe the terms of the Geneva Convention about recaptured escapers. Some of us in any case had not been impressed by their understanding of parole. In military language it meant 'word of honour', an undertaking to be observed. But in Spangenberg, as doubtless in other Oflags, you handed in a parole card with a forty-three-word signed statement to that effect, and on 'parole walks' there were armed sentries in attendance.

What 'turned' me was an invitation from General Fortune to interpret between him and the local forestry officer, Herr Schuhart, whose domain was a sizable *Reichswald*, that is, National Forest, a couple of miles from the castle: the General for his part owned wide acres of managed forest in south-western Scotland. When I told him that my German vocabulary did not extend to forestry terminology he reached for a book from a nearby shelf and said, 'This will take care of the problem'.

I confess to enjoying the job, which lasted until the hot summer months confined the General, whose rank prevented him from stripping to the waist as we junior officers did, to his tower room. He was as charming as I had found him on our first meeting, which he remembered. *Herr Förster* Schuhart was initially stuffy; I fancy he thought me too familiar with my *very* senior officer. The vocabulary came fast enough, and I found that forestry management was of absorbing interest.

With the General away, Schuhart was less enthusiastic about the wood walks, but by chance I hit on a means of reviving his interest. Noting some sign of neglect I asked him how many people he employed in his *Reichswald* in peacetime. This set him to deploring his lack of labour; the forest could not be kept tidy, and he could not realize any of his plans for paths and rustic benches, let alone keeping down the undergrowth. There were one or two younger and more active lieutenant colonels among the wood-walkers, notably Hugh Swinburne of the tunnel project. He agreed with me that making forest paths and building rustic benches could not be considered helping the German war effort, and that he would countenance our offering to do this for the forester. It would in any case be more interesting than merely 'walking in the woods'. So the programme of a day in the woods became a couple of hours of very welcome exercise in the fragrant shade during which we cleared enough paths and built a rustic seat or two to keep Schuhart happy, and an afternoon exploring the woods, our armed escort meanwhile dozing in the shade with a packet of Virginia cigarettes to keep them happy. Often, returning to camp, if it was at all hot, we went by way of a hillside spring with a stone basin and a silver cup chained to this; the water tasted good beyond belief. I have a snapshot of our mess at the forest gate (without Parsfield of course), about to return to the castle. We do not look pitiful or deserving of sympathy.

The fourth of June was such a day. As we came into the courtyard at about 5:00 it was possible to feel the suppressed excitement; then we learned that there was a rumour of the allies having landed in Normandy. It had doubtless originated in the kitchen or canteen where the Germans were 'tame'. Evening *Appel* was tense, and the wait for the BBC bulletin was nail biting: we had read so much of the Atlantic Wall in the German papers. Once this was manifestly broken Ronnie and I decided that we would finish the whole *Commedia* before we were liberated. Now that we could be sure of liberation in a foreseeable future the question *when* remained just as teasing. It was a good decision. Our friends thought us mad, but we had come to love the poem. This occupation took our minds off the fluctuations of the campaign to some extent.

The first low was the check of the Anglo-Canadian advance at Villers-Bocage a couple of weeks after the landing. But then at the end of July there was a peak when the Americans broke out of the bridgehead with the consequent fall

of Caen and the rout — there is no other word for it — of some of the most famous
regiments in the *Wehrmacht*. An ironic consequence of the rout was a pleasant
addition to our mess, a fresh-faced twenty-year old second lieutenant in the regiment, Edward Rose, who with his platoon corporal pursued the fleeing enemy
with more zeal than caution and was caught up in the flight. The chase that began at Caen did not end until the river Maas was reached in western Belgium and
the high Ardennes to the east. There was talk about being home by Christmas,
but this was muted by the setback at Arnhem. At the end of November our camp
received a dozen or so Airborne Division officers from hospital. They had been
beaten in the end because the ammunition and heavy weapons they should have
received were dropped among the Germans: the planes carrying these had the
wrong crystals on their wirelesses. Some of us old lags, remembering 1940, had to
suppress the thought that nothing had really changed.

But the worst check to optimism came on 20 December with the German
thrust, designed to cut off Antwerp and Brussels, into the Ardennes. It was no immediate relief from disappointment to be aware that this had to be a last desper-
ate gamble by German High Command to create a setting for a separate peace.
To our immense relief it spent itself on Christmas Day when the allies went over
to the offensive. In a matter of weeks they had cleared most of Europe west of the
Rhine except for enclaves where the Germans still stubbornly denied access to
the great Rhine bridges, determined that their last man should get over before
these were blown.

On the *Ostfront* the German situation was manifestly hopeless. This was having an immediate direct effect on the thousands of allied prisoners of war in eastern Germany of all ranks. It was *Wehrmacht* policy not to allow occupied prison
camps to be overrun by the enemy. Even in the depth of winter this was put into
effect as the Soviet armies approached. We heard in late February what this was
like from a Medical Corps captain who had been in charge of a *Stalag* and, having made the march, was sent to Spangenberg. What he had to tell about the mis-
ery in the snow, as often as not without food or shelter at night, was not good to
hear. In our case as yet there was to our knowledge no *Kommandatur* gossip about
moving us eastward, but we assumed that it would certainly happen.

Since September our food parcels had been infrequent, understandably because although they could now more easily be got to Switzerland their priority on
the Reich's railway system cannot have been high. We read this as an indication
that liberation was imminent. But then came an order, apologetically given, that
our considerable camp reserve of Red Cross food must be disposed of and could
no longer be stored. If we did not use it, it would have to be confiscated. The reason for this, I find in Foot and Langley's book, was that German intelligence had
picked up or got wind of a high level discussion — it was no more — about the possible need to arm p.o.w.s by some mean for their self-protection in the last stages

of the war. The notion never got off the ground. Our response was not to grossly overfeed ourselves but to cache the reserve supplies, sure enough in the chimney where, ironically, the rope ladder was still hidden. Sure enough I was asked, as good as ordered, 'to arrange the disposal' of the reserves. Since I did not want to lose my friends, I took up the bully beef, biscuits, etc., myself.

On another plane Ronnie and I had finished the *Purgatorio* and were well into the most difficult book, the *Paradiso*. Life in the mess continued genial. Young Edward Rose fitted in very neatly. Life became, but for *Paradiso* readers, a matter of waiting, and as far as possible preparing, for a walk.

German resistance, hopeless though the soldiers must have know it to be, was still very stubborn, especially in defence of the bridgehead enclaves of the Rhine. One after another, as these enclaves were reduced, the bridge to which it denied access was prepared for demolition and would be blown only when its enclave could no longer be held and was on the point of being overrun. On 7 March that tactic failed at the Remagen bridgehead about 100 miles southwest of Spangenberg. An American advance company broke into its enclave, surprised the German sappers in the act of preparing it for demolition and got enough men across the bridge before they could demolish it to fend off German counterattacks while reinforcements were rushed to its support. The Germans never succeeded in dislodging it.

The location of this bridgehead determined the strategic direction of the first great Allied advance into Germany. And if all went well we were in the line of this. When we left camp it would be to march eastward, and this would be before long. How long we marched would depend on the speed of the American advance.

As soon as it was evident that the crossing was secure I took Tom by the elbow one evening and walked him into the courtyard where we could talk privately. I told him my assessment, and that I did not propose to go one step further east than I could contrive. I hoped this would be the team's attitude, but if not I would go alone. I added that it might be a good idea to test the S.B.O.'s position, but that I could not believe he would rule out escape from the march. Tom was not a man for instant decisions, but he agreed immediately about my last point. The S.B.O. at that time was Euan Miller; he ruled that leaving the column was permissible as long as the action did not put fellow p.o.w.s at risk.

The middle of March was very full. Ronnie and I resolved to finish the *Paradiso*; with considerable effort we achieved this. For 200 cigarettes I bought a wooden crate big enough to hold my Hoepli's Dante, the Heath *Italian Grammar* and the *Piers Plowman* books from Chambers. There had been no open notice from the *Kommandatur*, but it was taken for granted that we would be moving, and we were told that if we packed and labelled our possessions they would in due course be sent to England. I put together a sort of knapsack big enough to hold a change of small clothes, my wretched novel and short stories, rations and a quantity of cigarettes in lieu of currency. It had been hard to concentrate on high theology to the distant sounds of artillery fire; in compensation this was an incentive to preparing to move.

I should explain the references to cigarettes. Until now these had been something of an embarrassment. After Dieppe one of the Canadian tobacco companies undertook to send 1000 cigarettes a month to every Canadian prisoner of war in Germany for $1, and, to match this, Canadian Customs and Excise waived the tax. My stepfather had been sending these to me since the arrangement was published. Once the *Afrikakorps* was behind wire in Canada the *Wehrmacht* could not refuse to cooperate, and my parcels began to arrive in early 1944. I smoked in those days as most males did, but not 1000 a month, so I banked the mess surplus in the communal camp store to be put to such good use as the British Parcels Officer saw fit. When at length we left camp they were shared out.

Although it must have been clear to our captors, if only because of the increasing volume of the gunfire, that we would be moving any day, nevertheless they gave no formal notice to the S.B.O. until the 29th March, when we were ordered to be ready to move at 12 hours notice; probably that is all they received themselves. For me the immediate consequence was trips up the chimney to fetch down the camp food reserves. Then that evening there was detail: we would move off at 3:30 next day. The camp guard company would be coming with us as 'escort'.

The team reformed itself on Terence, Tom and myself, joined by Clough, Sandy and Eddie Rose. We paired off the German speakers, Terence with Clough, Tom with Eddie and Sandy with me. He would not have been my first choice as a running mate; he was a deliberate thinker and probably not in training. But he agreed to let me make the 'Let's go' decision; if he did not follow I would go alone, and he accepted that. It was in my mind to break away as soon as possible, with Schuhart's forest as a hideout.

We did not, in the end move until dusk next day. Our Germans must have had a second order, to march by night, which made sense. By day the Americans might have taken us for German troops withdrawing, as they would do with the p.o.w.s marching out of Eichstätt next month. At about 6:30 we trailed off down the long stairway to Elbersdorf where we picked up the occupants of the Lower Camp and set out on a road that trended, allowing for bends and curves, east by northeast. Our guards, the men with the rifles slung over their shoulders, comprised the sentries and n.c.o.s of both camps, all told more numerous than we liked. The soldiers, mostly middle-aged reservists, were in fact not disagreeably officious, but because of the n.c.o.s' presence kept their intervals at our side carefully, not more, as I recall, than 30 feet. This was closer than we had expected, and might make slipping away more difficult. We moved at no great pace. I suppose the mean speed for the night, allowing for halts, was about two miles an hour. Some of the older men were anything but fit, not because they had neglected their walking in the moat, but because their age and the scanty diet since September had reduced their stamina. Moreover the road ran through rolling countryside; the climbs put an added strain on the many who had overloaded their shoulder packs. Young and all, I was glad I was travelling light.

The road ran through unfavourable terrain, either arable and fenced pasture or mature evergreen plantation with very scanty undergrowth. In the open stretches a clear, starlit sky shed a kind of half-light; in the forests we were in the dark. One incident afforded a chance. An older prisoner who had overestimated his carrying power stumbled, fell, and found it hard to get to his feet. This threw the sentry system into momentary confusion while arrangements were made to take care of him. I was reaching to touch Sandy's arm with 'Let's go!' when I caught a glimpse of the beam of an oncoming vehicle's headlights topping a rise not far ahead. The chance was gone. Moments later there was a commotion a little behind us and a shout of 'Kommt züruck oder Ich schiesse!', 'Come back or I'll shoot!' From where I stood I could just make out a couple of shapes, now clearly silhouetted in the approaching headlights, getting up from the ground and stumbling back to the column. I did not learn until later that the unlucky pair had been Terence and Clough. Terence reports that the sentry rebuked them for taking foolhardy risks.

Presently we plodded on, our pace decreasing as we went. Not long after first light we reached Waldkappel, a village 18 miles from the castle. Here we were penned in the compound of a very substantial and prosperous looking farm, what would in earlier English have been called a grange, very likely before 1918 part of a larger estate. There was a courtyard with a well, and for our accommodation, almost certainly by arrangement, a large barn, its floor covered with clean wheat straw, not, in March, hay as Terence wrote. By daylight, having staked out our bedding territory in a far corner of the barn, washed and shaved by the well, we were ready for a fine meal that Major Bob Winders, the messing officer, and his cookhouse orderlies had somehow contrived to prepare. They had trundled a commissariat cart along throughout the march. The day would be for sleeping; we would be marching again come night.

But before we turned in there was entertainment. We had barely finished our meal when literally out of the blue a pair of American Mustang fighter-bombers appeared and set to strafing the village railway station. This was immediately cheering for it meant we were certainly in the line of Patton's advance. But after the planes' first run it was disconcerting, for the bomb fragments came clattering down on the barnyard roofs. We took cover.

I was not sleepy; the raid had wakened me and made me want to explore. Arming myself with a couple of packets of cigarettes in case of unexpected need, I told the lads I would be back and set out to look over the grange. It was escape-proof; byre and stables and machine sheds, as of course the barn, had all windows securely barred. A main courtyard gate and its wicket gate were guarded by a couple of our sentries, who grinned at me knowingly and put their backs to it. There was bound to be a way into the street through the sizable house that constituted much of the same side of the courtyard as the gate. Having nothing to lose I opened its door and went in. The room I entered was evidently both the farmhouse kitchen and a place of assembly, but unusual in the long table being counter-high. On one side of the room half a dozen men, some in German army uniform, stood about in conversation. A middle-aged woman was busy at a large kitchen range along the other wall, and behind her, by the counter, stood an attractive girl of about 20, with bronze-to-russet coloured hair and a fine complexion. No one took any notice of me or asked my business there. It crossed my mind that apart from railway ticket vendors and the barmaid in Ulm I had not spoken to a woman, let alone an attractive one, for almost five years and that this was the time to remedy that condition. So I went up to her and addressed her with 'Guten Tag'. She looked oddly at me and my uniform and asked what I might be. There was no point in pretending so I told her. There had been something about her accent, so I added, 'And where, may I ask, do you come from?' She was, poor thing, a Russian slave labourer, lucky, to go by her looks, in her employers. I tried some of Rupert's Russian; this produced a puzzled look. So I reverted to German. But what with pity for her situation and that dash to my ego the magic was gone. To save face I wished her a safe return to her own country in German. Many years later when my son brought a BBC Russian language-learning disk back from school I learned that there was little resemblance between the Russian of the émigré countess and that of the girl's generation and class.

I don't doubt that I could have walked through the house and out into the street without being checked or challenged. But just as surely there would have been a couple of sentries there and it would have taken more than a packet or two of cigarettes to get past them. A hundred at that stage might have done it. But if I were to go back to the barn and come back with my pack on my shoulders that would certainly have interested the men in uniform in the kitchen. So I returned to the barn to make the best of it by sleeping.

There I found it impossible to get to my friends in the far corner. Every square foot of floor between the door and them was covered by a sleeping body; to reach them I would have had to wake any number of people. Luckily for me to one side of the door there was a pile of straw that had not been strewn and because it looked precarious had no sleepers on it. I could have done worse; I would sleep on top of this and rejoin the team in due course.

That evening we set off for the night's march a little after 8:00, this time for Wanfried about 20 miles to the east. Clough had had enough of trying to leave the column; Sandy and Tom were out of action: Tom had pulled a muscle in his leg and Sandy had found himself too badly out of training to do more than keep up.

Terence and I were still resolved to go if the chance came, he with a proviso that this was only for the first three hours. After that, he said, he would be too tired to trust his judgement. This would not bind me.

There never was a chance. Our route was through open country all the way, at the bottom of a valley at least a mile wide, and what with the stars and a clear sky visibility was simply too good. We were straggling along even more slowly than the night before, and it was almost 5:00 on the morning of 1 April before, having skirted the substantial town of Eschwege on its south side, we approached our destination, a large barn in a field about 500 yards to the north of the road. Here we were to lodge for the day. We were all weary, and chastened by the one incident of the night's march. Some time after midnight we saw approaching us a large open-backed truck loaded with heavily armed German troops; we got off the road to one side pretty fast. When it was halfway along our column an officer old enough to have known better shouted a term of abuse. The truck slowed down, halted and reversed to where the hero was standing. The p.o.w.s around him drew back and as if in unison all the weapons converged on him. He threw himself to the ground. There was a burst of derisive laughter from the soldiers in the truck, which started up and drove on. I am glad I was not near enough to hear what the men near the fool said to him.

In the barn the straw sloped from more than half the height of the wall at the far end to a couple of feet high at the door, not ideal for several hundred men to sleep in, and the timber of its walls had shrunken so it was draughty. A thicket of brushwood just to the north of the barn had to serve as latrine. Until morning, when water was fetched from Wanfried, we could not drink or wash. Otherwise the place had much promise. Come daylight, I would scout it. Meanwhile, to sleep. I scrambled up the sloping straw till I was well clear of people coming and going at the door, levelled a nest in it, and did not wake at daylight. I suppose I slept until high noon, as most did. When I emerged from the barn a meal of sustaining soup and bread was being served from the kitchen cart.

There were a good many sentries about, but they did not seem very alert, rather dozing on their feet. The place had distinct possibilities. There were open fields of stubble to the west and north of the barn; in front of the door a level space of untilled ground the size of a tennis court. From the far side of this, likewise un-tilled, the ground rose in a clear slope of about one foot in three as far as the eye could see. At a point on the north side of the tennis court a gully overgrown with brushwood ran up the slope. This, I decided, was the way for me. There was bound to be some disorder and confusion when the Germans, come dusk, would try to muster us into a marching column to continue on our way, and the sentries would be even wearier, their morale low.

As it turned out we did not march that night. Our excellent Camp Medical Officer declared a number of the older officers in absolute need of a rest, and the

S.B.O., Euan Miller, with support from the other very senior officers, persuaded the German officer in charge of the column to break the march at Wanfried one day longer. I put off my departure for twenty-four hours. Here was food and shelter, and the sound of combat was getting louder by the hour. I slept like a log again that night in the straw.

Next day, 2 April, the gunfire came to sound steadily closer, not in long bombardments but at intervals, as if in a succession of local engagements, not always, because of the conformation of the ground, from a determinable direction. There was talk of not marching any farther, another 'night's rest', in effect waiting for Patton's armour. Had there been a German officer to be seen I would have asked him. But the question was resolved for me another way. About 6:00 one of the castle guard detachment, a *Feldwebel* whom I had never seen unbend in my time there and did not much care for, took me aside and said to my amazement, 'Herr Oberleutnant Kane, I wish to surrender the guard company to you', and began to unbuckle his Schmeisser holster. I looked hard at him and said, 'I am surprised to hear this from you! What does this mean?' He pointed southeast; 'My home is just over there in the next valley.'

Several considerations should have passed through my mind but did not. Why did he not simply make off over the hill? Was this offer agreed by the guard company? How would his officers react to this? What I did think, crudely but also correctly, was, 'This is fabulous, but I had better get sanction from above.' By a fluke, just then, one of the younger lieutenant colonels, Gabby Gamble, passed. I asked the *Feldwebel* to excuse me a moment and told Gamble. His reaction was not surprising: 'Splendid, George, but I had better tell Euan. Ask the feller to give me five minutes.' Gamble was back in less time than that, crestfallen. 'Sorry, George, no go. Euan says, tell George it's too dangerous.' I told the *Feldwebel*, he buckled his holster up and made off. As I watched him go it came to me that we would be marching that night.

So I called a team council, although not in those peremptory terms, and proposed slipping away up the wooded gully while we were being mustered to march that evening. Terence, Tom, Clough and young Eddie Rose were of one mind with me. Terence thought he would reconnoitre the gully beforehand; I did not think it necessary, but he was after all the senior escapist member of the team.

As I had expected it proved easy to break away.[11] A little before nightfall the Germans, without much zeal, began to muster our hundreds on the level ground outside the barn, and in the milling confusion, having moved to the edge of the crowd, we five slipped off one by one up the gully. Terence makes drama out of this in his book, but the going was not too bad; there had evidently once been

---

11. Foot and Langley, *MI9: the British secret service that fostered escape*, 294–95: 'When finally the Third and Last Reich foundered in a cloud of putrid dust, some 250,000 British, Commonwealth and American prisoners marched briskly out of the ruins.'

some sort of path, possibly a cattle track, and the brushwood was not thorny or impenetrable. It was not possible to go wrong. We soon found that we had company: Ronnie Swayne, Bruce Shand and another desert capture, Richard Dendy. The ascent was about 1000 feet, I would guess, but by no means steep. We emerged from the gully onto the edge of an open, gently rounded plateau about half a dozen acres in extent, much of it carrying a plantation of deciduous saplings about three feet high. There was enough starlight to see that to the east the plateau fell away and that this slope was covered by a more mature plantation; to the west it fell more gently into what looked like open fields. To the south the slope was clear and we ought, come daylight, be able to watch the Bebra and Eisenach roads, by one or the other of which we might expect to see our first Americans. For that night the hardwood of the saplings would have to serve as cover; we could not go floundering about in denser woodland in the dark.

Our one problem would be water. I had no water bottle; they could not be got for love or cigarettes in camp. And the water cart had not come up from Wanfried that evening. In open country in that half light it was possible to see one's feet, so Terence and I set off down the west slope of the plateau to find water, through what felt underfoot like farmland. It was pretty countryside, and being loose and unburdened after many years we were exhilarated. After about a mile of this we came on a farmhouse snugged up against a wood, but not a light showed. My instincts told me that a nocturnal visit would not be well received, and Terence agreed to mark it for a visit next day. So back to the plantation where we bedded down on the ground, spoiled after three nights of luxury on straw.

Nevertheless this would have been one of the best nights of my life had it not come on to rain not long after I fell asleep, a gentle, persistent, penetrating rain. I wish I could write in honesty that the exhilarating awareness of being free kept me warm, but I was stiff and sodden when day finally broke.

Come morning the five of us decided we had best move down into the plantation on the east side of the plateau. The trees were some sort of conifer, about 20 years old, I would guess, and in poor order for not having been culled and their lower branches cleared since 1939. We found a spot where the slope was not too steep, built a fire-trench, and with a discreet flame made cocoa with the last of someone's water, then breakfasted on this and bully beef with Canadian Red Cross biscuits. If only one of us had been carrying a camping knife we could have built a waterproof shelter against the intermittent rain. We did our best with the half-dead lower branches we could break off, but their needles were sparse and it was not by any means rainproof, more a visual comfort than anything else. Tom's leg was giving him trouble again; Terence was visibly tired but claimed not to be; Clough for a man approaching 40 was in good order; Eddie was full of bounce. When the sun came out, I determined to get dry. I broke cover and went back up the hill to watch the roads to the south. All day there were sounds of heavy gunfire, but the land formation made it hard to determine its direction. Members of Ronnie's party were about on the hill and we exchanged notes. One of them, Dick Barclay, swore he had seen Sherman tanks on the Eschwege-Wanfried road. We learned the next day that the Americans had on 3 April in fact attacked and overrun Eschwege and the Luftwaffe fighter base there. So the movement Dick saw had been part of the main thrust. As for our situation, we reckoned we were unlikely to encounter German troops on the hills, but we had better keep clear of the valley until we were in shouting distance of our own side. This meant another night in the wood. We did what we could to improve our wretched shelter. Someone found a half-rotten straw stack in the open and we helped ourselves to this for bedding. Terence writes of us achieving a waterproof shelter with windproof walls and a door; that is fiction, fantasy. After nightfall I went with a mixed party led by a Lieutenant Cleasby from the Airborne division to fetch water for the dozen or so castle people who turned out to be lurking on the hill. Our five must have been lent vessels; I recall carrying several. Cleasby's fieldcraft, leading us by compass in the dark across rough terrain, was superb. But he would stop during our return at every change of direction to give us a short talk on compass-marching technique. We were all tired, and the men up the hill were very thirsty. I pointed this out to him and after that we made better progress. Before we left the riverbank I drank deep. My uniform had dried out in the course of the day, and it did not rain that night.

Next morning, in the wood, we could hear gunfire but it seemed more distant, and where we were on a wooded hillside its location was again not determinable. Tom's leg was better, and he went up the hill to our observation post while we set about making a fire for breakfast cocoa. It never got made. Within half an hour of going off up the hill Tom was back, breathless with excitement: American infantry had been seen on the road south of the plateau. We threw our things together and made for the top. There, sure enough, at the foot of the long slope were a dozen or so foot soldiers, probably a section, moving east in extended order on the road, by their walk as much as by their helmets unmistakably not German.

We gave great yelping shouts of excitement and bounded off down the hill. The only race I ever won at school was a sack race, but this day I ran level and finished level with Terence. By this time there must have been a dozen of us, but we appeared unarmed and otherwise cannot have looked warlike. The G.I.s unslung their rifles but did not bring them to bear. The man nearest me raised his free hand and beckoned with his index finger, 'Mitkommen, Kraut!' I said 'Actually I am a British officer', and he replied 'Well, Gawddam!'. For me that was a warm welcome.

They were support troops of an armoured element of Patton's army called Colonel Carraway's Combat Group which had overrun Eschwege the previous day before pushing on to Wanfried and beyond, on a reconnaissance patrol while the armour waited for petrol and munitions. What could they do for us? Somebody said, 'What I really would like is a bath and a shave!' The answer was, 'Leave it to us.' Then for two or three miles we were marching east again, but this time with comrades, not guards. In Wanfried, where they seemed to know their way about, they took us to a small *Gasthaus*, led us in, said, 'We'll be back,' and left.

A couple in their fifties emerged from a back room, visibly terrified. I used soothing language, 'Keine Angst, keine Angst'; the woman was on the verge of tears; 'Wir sind britische Offiziere'. Then the tears really did flow, but mingled with many exclamations of 'Gott sei Dank!' I wondered what they had been led to expect of the American soldier.

They had barely calmed down when three of our G.I. friends returned, laden with a huge can of coffee, another of Klim, the excellent Canadian powdered milk, a can of jam, several loaves of bread, a whole side of bacon, and for the perfect anti-climax, a packet of K rations. We were to let them know if we wanted anything else. Our host and his wife were ready and happy to cook breakfast for us, and made no difficulty when I mentioned the possibility of eggs.

Washed and shaved, our party sat down almost formally to breakfast which, but for an oversight of mine, which I do not recall confessing to at the time, went down well. I had forgotten that this bacon would be brine-cured like that on my grandfather's farm, and needed to be parboiled before frying. It was simply too salty to eat. Never mind, the coffee was excellent, the eggs a treat, white bread toast and peach jam, after camp fare, delicious.

What with the food and the civilized setting the relief of tension after breakfast was great. Terence was dead tired and had 'booked' a room. No doubt he was right; but there was no way I could have slept. Clough was in the same state; we decided to explore.

We found the headquarters of the combat group that had welcomed us. Yes, it had fought its way up from the bridgehead; at that immediate moment it was the spearhead of the advance. Clough very properly reported us to Col. Carraway, after whom the group was named. After a very civil congratulation he turned us over to his Intelligence Officer, a captain of my age who before enlisting had been a graduate student in the English Department at Harvard. I wish I had not forgotten his name; he was very engaging, and appropriately intelligent.

We got on very well, and as we were taking leave, for he had, obviously, work to do, I said 'I wish I were coming with you!' 'Why not?' he said; 'I'll talk to the Colonel about it. Come back about midday.' Clough thought he would like to come too.

This in retrospect was a madcap notion, in the first instance cruel to my mother, in a second, likely to get me into trouble in the army. But it would have been immensely exciting. I suppose I was lucky, in the final assessment, that it came to nothing. When Clough and I went back 'about midday' the Colonel had just had an order that all liberated prisoners of war were to be treated as Displaced Persons, and delivered to assembly points for return to their country of origin.

This process in our case turned out to be not as forbidding as it sounded. Our collection point was the *Luftwaffe* base at Eschwege, to which we were taken within the hour, leaving our host of the *Gasthaus* and his wife with the rations. We found the *Luftwaffe* barracks already occupied by our Spangenberg comrades and the p.o.w.s from the Lower Camp — Terence's account of our being put to work on arrival to organize the accommodation for them is fiction; I tell myself that he was very tired at that time, and was filling in the blank in his memory when he wrote his story later. We found a room and settled in; two-tier bunks, to be sure, but this time with springs and a real mattress. Word was that our transport home would be Dakotas expected with petrol cargoes for the armour.

There was even a welcoming bottle of Spanish brandy awaiting each of us from an apparently inexhaustible supply in the *Luftwaffe* officers' mess cellar! To my surprise I was not much interested in it or in the hearty meal that the American army cooks had put on for its presumably starving charges. I was distinctly queasy, the only time in captivity apart from the rotten potato attack in Laufen when I was at all unwell. I could not account for this except for the quantity of tainted River Werra water I had drunk the night before. I did not want to go in search of our castle Medical Officer, Jimmie James; I would try violent measures. I forced down a large dose of the Spanish 'brandy', more like grappa at its crudest, and turned in. Next morning after a shower and a shave I was myself again, all the more for learning that we were to be on standby to be flown back to England at short notice.

Terence's account of that and the following two days in his *Through Irish Eyes* differs substantially from my recollection of them, and since we were together much of the time I conclude he was writing 'creatively' at that point.

Coming out from breakfast in the *Luftwaffe*'s huge mess hall we came upon Tom Acton, standing on the edge of the parade ground with a rifle slung over one shoulder; by 'bearing arms', he told us, somewhat embarrassed, he was qualifying for any campaign medal that might be struck. Well, he was a professional soldier, and we wished him luck. We admired the rifle for its exceptionally long barrel; it was Polish booty and looked as if it might have seen service in the Great War. Terence and I agreed that there were other ways of qualifying for the medal than standing sentry, and decided, meanwhile, to explore Eschwege.

We began with the officers' mess, very different from the one I had known in Tidworth; we noted what neither of us had seen before, a row of china furniture of type called *vomitorium* in a room of convenience, designed to facilitate the oral disposal of beer drunk to excess. The station kitchens were amazingly elaborate; even the U.S. army cooks who were manning them during our stay were impressed. We found an auditorium evidently designed for training purposes, where there was a continuous cinema show of American films, but not from Hollywood. They were an unbroken succession of motion pictures taken by the cameras that were activated by a pilot's trigger finger firing at an enemy plane, all, of course, successful. Half an hour of disintegrating Messerschmitts was enough for us. Not far from the actual airbase was an impressive building with an American sergeant at the door. This looked interesting and was. The building, he told us, was the local *Partei* food depot; would we care to be shown over it? What we saw was shocking, one chill-room after another stacked or packed with the kind of food that was supposed to be scarce in Germany, fat chicken, quarters of beef and pork, hams. I wonder what happened to it. We moved on. There was virtually no damage in this part of Eschwege, but the shops were shut and there were few people about. Then surprisingly we came upon a barrack-looking structure from inside which bursts of not unmelodious singing could be heard. This was intriguing, and having pushed the door open we found ourselves in a room with a couple of dozen Italian forced labourers celebrating their liberation. We paid for this intrusion by having to drink toasts to peace and democracy (fair enough) in a synthetic *vino* they had combined their chemical skills to concoct. They had a great vessel full of the stuff to dispose of; I hope they survived to enjoy the peace and democracy we toasted.

When Terence and I returned to the station for lunch we learned that there would be enough empty Dakotas to carry most of our Spangenberg party to England that afternoon, leaving only a small number of senior officers to wind up the affairs of the two camps. I found myself not quite ready to go, subconsciously afraid, I now suspect, of losing the sense of orientation and stability conferred by a known environment and membership of a close group with shared values. To my surprise Terence was similarly disinclined. After very little consultation we formed up to Euan Miller and offered to stay behind with the rear party in case they need interpreters. Although this must have seemed unlikely, since there were no Germans to be seen, they agreed. We took leave of our Spangenberg messmates and friends, swearing to meet again soon, and set off once more into the town.

The reason we gave each other, which may indeed have had some force, was interest in the effect of the disintegration of an arbitrary central authority, unmistakably in process, at the level of a town like Eschwege that had been overrun without street fighting and little bombardment. Having decided that to cover ground we needed cars we made our way on foot to what in England would be called the Town Council Offices where we would see how the structure of government might be functioning without an effective higher authority. On the first floor we found its main office, large and well-lit, with about twenty desks of various sizes, all occupied by clean, neat, composed-looking persons, mainly women, busy seeming busy; as we came in the typists typed harder and the paper-shifters shifted a little more briskly. Saying nothing at first, we walked up and down the room: neither of us swaggered; I tried to walk like an invigilator in an exam. After the first few moments you could feel the relief that we were not Americans.

I identified the *Hauptbeamter*, the chief clerk, by his very large desk and an expression that combined apprehension and indignation, and told him that we were there to observe the processes of administration during transfer from one authority to another. We needed transport and for that purpose were commandeering two automobiles. Then I confess I behaved badly; I sat on the corner of his desk and waited. After a moment he got up and went to confer with what seemed from the size of his desk to be the next in authority. He returned with two car keys; I asked him to make out receipts for us to sign, which surprised him, but he obliged. I could not decide whether his expression was sceptical. We drove the cars back to the airbase, collected rifles and two willing volunteer drivers from among the orderlies, and set out to investigate, having agreed to meet after half an hour or so. The result was disappointing. The town was pretty well shut down, with few people on the streets. As in most German towns there was an old centre, intact; the growth was relatively modern and dull. The town had evidently not been defended, and the main damage by the bombing was to operational buildings serving the airport and the anti-aircraft battery positions. The runways appeared intact and were in use, undamaged as far as I could tell. Come the time of meeting, Terence and I decided that we had seen enough of Eschwege; so we returned our drivers and drove back to the Council Office. Here Terence minded the cars while I took the keys up. I asked the Chief Clerk whose cars we had taken. 'Mine for one, his', nodding towards his Number Two 'for the other'. I laid the keys on his desk for him to choose. The other man, when I gave him his key, looked as if he would burst into tears. I got out of the office as fast as I could.

It was actually more interesting to walk the Eschwege streets than to be driven about. The American presence was not at all emphatic, only the occasional jeep with a G.I. driver and one passenger on some errand, no strolling G.I.s; the attack had undoubtedly moved on and we heard no gunfire. Glass front windows were intact, only a few boarded up. There were no signs of looting. The few bars were closed; Eschwege was evidently not a tourist centre. This was too bad. We would have liked a glass of beer.

Not far from the *Luftwaffe* barracks we noticed what looked like a large vehicle shed with a closed door and an American sergeant on guard, apparently in front of this. A senior n.c.o. on sentry duty was unusual enough to be interesting, so we asked him what he was guarding. In reply he opened the door for us on a jumbled pile of Nazi banners, Storm Troopers' military insignia, officers' ceremonial dirks, and firearms, these latter all recognizably civilian. He supposed there had been an order to hand that sort of thing in. What would happen to it? 'We'll run a tank back and forth over it once or twice and it will be scrap.' Then, reading our minds, 'Help yourself.' Terence found a double-barrelled shotgun that fitted him. I chose a beautiful Mauser sporting rifle in an elegant canvas case, thus fulfilling a boyhood dream. I carried that object in and out of England and across North America without being questioned, and, when it comes to the point, have never fired it. Two of my brothers used it a few times; neither however was much given to killing animals. As far as I know one of my nephews has it, without ever having fired it.

While we were chatting to the sergeant a jeep with a single American occupant, a lieutenant, pulled up to ask for directions. The sergeant was able to tell him. It struck me as unusual for him to be alone and I took the liberty of asking him what he was doing. He was, he said, a sort of forerunner, of a body I had never heard of, the Allied Control Commission, his assignment to find a man who had never been a member of the Nazi party as temporary *Bürgermeister*, mayor, of Eschwege. This was intriguing and I shamelessly asked him whether I could come along. He was about to stop 'work' for the day, but he would pick me up next morning at the barracks.

Next morning the word was that the rear party was likely to be flown out at 4:00 that afternoon, but to be standing by at 2:00. My mayor-maker was as good as his word. As we drove he briefed me. It had been very difficult to find anyone who was not, or had not been, or was not accused of having been, a party member, and the one man he had found with an apparently clean record was reluctant to take on the job. Today's business was to persuade him.

We found him sitting in the *Stube* above his place of business, with his wife, both well over fifty, rather pathetic and distinctly apprehensive. His reasons for not wanting the job were sound; he had no experience of administration; by temperament he was not suited; his health was indifferent; in any case he was too old. I found myself increasingly embarrassed by the blustering, almost menacing manner of the lieutenant, and when from the accent of his German it dawned on me that he was Jewish, I was ashamed for my Jewish friends. I had not yet, of course, seen the newsreel of the liberation of Belsen. We left the matter unresolved, the lieutenant telling his man that he would return next day in expectation of a favourable answer.

Back at the *Luftwaffe* base I found that the 4:00 departure was confirmed. Indeed we boarded our Dakota punctually. The hold stank of petrol, and for seats there were wooden racks of a sort, but I managed to get a 'window seat'. We flew low; the plane was unarmed and there seemed no concern about German aircraft. Except when we flew over the Rhineland and the Ruhr there was little or no sign of bomb damage, but the sight of Cologne was horrific. While we were in flight it turned out that we would stop over at Paris and on to England next day. I do not recall what airport we put down at there; it was about half an hour by coach to the city.

Our hotel was a rather pretentious Edwardian structure — I forget the name — doubtless in its time very fashionable. The room assigned to Terence and me was grandiose, but the beds looked comfortable and the bath big enough to drown in, and there was hot water aplenty. Dinner was an anticlimax; we should have known better than to expect *haute cuisine*; it was unmistakably spam, albeit served with a wine sauce. The night city was very quiet and we awoke next morning in a much better frame of mind.

There was real coffee for breakfast, and enough butter in the baking of the croissants. As we lingered over this breakfast in a lonely state word came that our coach would pick us up at midday: three hours to kill in Paris! We both looked what my grandmother would have called a disgrace, in uniforms that had been rained on and slept in the best part of a week. A blinding insight came to me, to assert my nationality. The next jeep with military police in it that we met, I raised my hand and stopped with a shout. Large formidable men, indignant at first, until they saw we were sober. Where was the Canadian Officers' Club? Again we were lucky; it was an easy walk away in a street we both knew. The receptionist there looked oddly at us, but my accent was our pass, and he went to fetch a quartermaster sergeant major who, when I told him our history, gave each of us a complete change of underclothes and uniform and stood by while we changed. That done, I asked him for the loan of a scissors or knife, and having cut one of the buttons off my discarded battledress jacket I showed him how it functioned as a compass; he was very happy to have it. Our midday coach carried us with most of the rear party to a vast American staging camp, a veritable city of tents, half an hour's drive somewhere to the west of Paris. Here we learned how to lunch American army style, moving down a line of serving tables with a many-receptacled tray into which cooks ladled whatever you might ask for. The food actually tasted good and was hot. The drink was coke, if you wanted it, or water. About an hour later we were driven to another airfield, where we waited in agreeable sunshine until about 5:00 when a Dakota that 'had room for us' became available.

That description was apt; the plane only had a half-cargo, at most, of empty petrol drums; you had a choice of standing, or sitting on one. I don't recall much talk during this long-awaited flight. Looking back I realize that it was at the heart of a prolonged individual rite of passage into a world different from not only the one that we had just left, but also that before captivity. We were not in the Dakota well suited for peering out of its little window and I did not see the 'White Cliffs of Dover'.[12] Presently we landed in what seemed the middle of nowhere, at RAF Bovingdon in Hertfordshire. Here we were welcomed with a piece of cake and a cup of tea by bright young women in RAF blue, and driven by coach to a wire-enclosed collection of army huts a mile or so north and west of Beaconsfield in

---

12. The inverted commas show that the reference is to the popular wartime song recorded by Vera Lynn in 1942.

Buckinghamshire on the Jordans road, which our driver told us was a reception centre.

Being received did not take long and was pleasant enough. A young ATS officer took my name, rank, number, regiment, place and date of capture, address of next of kin, and that was it. She would be seeing me again in the morning, after breakfast; meanwhile I was to make myself comfortable in the anteroom until dinner. There would be beer at the bar; here were vouchers.

Dinner, as we knew to expect, was plain and simple, but the setting felt right. There was, however, no ceremony and nobody had much to say. Nobody lingered in the anteroom after the meal; those who could telephoned their families. Terence and I were the only ones for London apparently, and agreed to meet for breakfast; our train from Beaconsfield to Marylebone would be at about 10:00. My room was small and simply furnished but the sheets and pillowcase were dazzling white and the mattress was soft. To my relief my new trousers had survived the journey with the petrol drums unstained.

Breakfast was symbolic, without question: one rasher of bacon and one egg. But the toast and marmalade were unstinted, and there was even a pat of butter. You're back now, but things are a little different. In the interview my first question, arising from my Vancouver next-of-kin address, was for an intermediate address; in due course I would be going to Canada on leave, but meanwhile the War Office must be able to contact me. For a moment this was a problem; I had no fixed abode in London. Commander Crofton, the Comptroller of London House in 1939, had then already been on the point of retiring and my name would mean nothing to his successor. If I named my bank there would be at least a day's delay. The best choice, I thought, would be British Columbia House; having been in contact with my mother the Agent General might be said to have a personal interest, and it was central, at the Mall end of Lower Regent Street. Luckily I had made a courtesy call there in 1938, at Dean Bollert's suggestion to be sure. Next, there was a travel warrant to London and there would be transport to Beaconsfield station. Then, to my relief, 'I don't suppose you have any English money; here is, let's call it, a travel allowance, and you need not be grateful; naturally your pay will be docked.' Then she gave me a ration book with the injunction always to let my hostess use it if I was a houseguest. And finally, 'You'll be hearing from the War Office about your leave. Welcome back and good luck!' Terence's account of making his way back to County Tipperary without a penny in his pocket is romantic fiction. He had his travel warrant and allowance, Irish Republic and all, just like the rest of us.

For all his sometimes-assertive manner he was insecure, at least that time. We scarcely spoke during the journey from Beaconsfield to Marylebone. It was as if, at that moment, neither of us wanted to talk about past or future. As to the past, for each of us it had, since 1940, amounted to a series of failures, of high anticipation and anticlimax, until the last evasion, and that had been too easy.

About his future, I knew he was anxious. Coming out of school he had been apprenticed in a snob merchant bank in the City. He was shrewd enough and might have done well there, but he understandably did not want to go back now, with his draft of a book of cricket essays and at least half a book about his interesting escaping adventures. His dream was a career as a writer or newspaper correspondent, but he knew how long the odds against him would be. As for me, there was my half-finished thesis on a subject not my primary interest and vague suggestion of an assistant lectureship at University College which, Chambers had said with embarrassment in 1939, was 'probably less than your scholarship'. Neither was immediately attractive, and to be wholly honest with myself I had come to enjoy the active life outside academe. Neither of us on that occasion seemed to know the appropriate language of parting; it would have been easy if one or more of our group had been there as well. We shook hands; he said, 'You must come and stay in Ireland', and we went our separate ways.

To this day I do not understand our relationship. I suppose our backgrounds, assessed in terms of our common situation, were as different as could be in almost every particular; yet from the time we began to work together in Hector's team we almost always agreed on the appropriate course of action. Although we were in the same regiment we had hardly spoken before I played the gate sentry for the project at Warburg. In the mess he could be irritating. Except for Parsfield, whom like the rest of us he treated with exaggerated courtesy, and for Clough, whom his instinct must have told him not to tease, all were victims. Tom Acton had chronic catarrh: Terence called him 'Gobber'. James McDonnell, from the shape of his head, was 'Bullet'. I don't think James cared for this, possibly for an underlying social reason: he was the younger son of the Earl of Antrim, the first Irish peer,[13] and Terence's family title went back, to use ascendancy terms, to 'one of Cromwell's corporals'. I got off lightly with 'Geowerge' for my Canadian accent. He repeated the invitation to come and stay in Ireland a number of times; for various reasons I was never able to accept. But one way or another he became and remained a part of my post-war life.

At British Columbia House I was warmly received by two of Mr MacAdam's secretaries, both very pretty, and told that I was expected. He was indeed very welcoming, and when I thanked him for being kind to my mother he brushed the gratitude aside; it had been a pleasure. He told me of the Canadian Officers' Club in Carlyle Place just off Victoria Street where he would book me in if I had no other plans. I would be welcomed and looked after there. All this, and the excellent cake and ice cream that the girls pressed on me, were very reassuring. You could say I was out of my element.

---

13. The earldom of Antrim, created as recently as 1620, is certainly pre-Cromwell; in Gaelic traditions the family has its roots in legendary times.

Promising to be back later in the day I set off for my bank in King William Street by bus. Riding upstairs I saw with horror the damage, increasing as we drove east to the City itself. But my bank was intact, as were the manager, Mr Percival Huffman in his frock coat, and the senior clerk Miss Jennings, both with beaming smiles. On hearing of my capture he had changed my account from current to savings, and written to my mother how pleased he was that I had survived. I left the bank with a sense of being valued, money in my pocket, and a chequebook. From the bank I went to Bloomsbury and London House in Guilford Street to check my belongings in the luggage room there. The Comptroller was a new man, as I had anticipated. He had moved my belongings, trunk, typewriter, books and all, to the house of the uncle of a friend of mine in Muswell Hill which, regrettably had been firebombed and then looted; storage space for servicemen on duty had been very much in demand. The 'friend of mine', in fact, was another Canadian graduate student at University College on whom I had no particular claim. I found it hard to be civil to him. At the time it was the books and typewriter I grieved for; had I known about clothing coupons I would have been even angrier.

At least, I thought, my *Piers* collations were safe in Aberystwyth, thanks to Chambers's solicitude. Still, I had better go to University College and check it out. Here there was another shock awaiting me, the sight of the central structure of the College reduced to first floor level, the fine dome gone, grass growing on the floor where the English Library had been. Still, the wings were intact and I made for the one that had housed the Registry. This was not only intact but open and staffed by three tired looking, elderly men.

One of them, seeing me enter, got up and came to the reception counter. He stepped back a pace, peered at me hard, and after a moment said, 'Mr Kane from Canada!'. He had news: the English Department was returning from Aberystwyth in September, but Professor Chambers had died in 1942, having been ill again and never really recovered. I had a twinge of guilt here; the books he sent me became a farewell present, not admonitory. At least I had written to thank him. Professor Sisson would be coming back with the Department. Dr Smith was in the RAF, a Wing Commander.

It was mid-afternoon by then and I had had enough of being 'home' for one day, of the grim streets outraged and ravaged by blast and flame, the tired faces of the people in the streets. So I made my way back to British Columbia House. Mr MacAdam had time for a chat; I think he was surprised to find me looking so well. It was about breakfast time in Vancouver, and I asked about the possibility of telephoning my mother. He discouraged me: very few private lines were available, and I might have to wait days before getting my turn. But he would be cabling his weekly report next day and would include a message to her from me. And, oh yes, he had booked me in at the Officers' Club. When I tried to thank him he brushed my gratitude aside; it was part of his job. Having taken leave of him

University College after the blitz.

and his charming assistants I set off for Carlyle Place. In the bus it occurred to me that I had not eaten lunch. Not to have noticed this was, I suppose, another stage in the rite of passage — or a symptom of emergence in the process.

This London Canadian Officers' Club, unlike that in Paris which was run by the army, was staffed by civilian Englishwomen of middle age, kind, sweet natured and pleasant to look at, but distinctly motherly. The rooms were plain but spotless, the bathrooms efficient and clean, the beds comfortable. I quickly perceived that it was primarily for RCAF pilots stationed in England, designed to provide a setting reassuringly dull in which the stress-relieving rest that would be their first need on leave was afforded. The food was excellent and you could buy duty-free cigarettes and unrationed chocolate, but there was no bar. If a man, once rested, wanted to go on the town, there it was ready to take his money. I saw this work. Some RCAF personnel on arrival slept two or three days.

That day the Club was what I needed. Some of my experience had been warm and reassuring, some of it distressing, even harrowing. I was, I suppose, emotionally tired. In the sense of being unconstrained by barbed wire I was free, but immediately encountering other constraints I had forgotten, of circumstance. For the moment the Club with its kindly staff whose mission was to pamper me and demand no return was right. By the time I had booked in and settled into my

University College after the blitz.

room it was 6:00; the Club kept Canadian mealtimes and I was ready for dinner. There was even a childhood treat, apple pie with ice cream! Early to bed, I thought to plan my war with circumstances the next day, my first action, to replace the distinctive Rifle Brigade lanyard that I had mindlessly discarded as damaged in the Calais hospital. Without it I had been improperly dressed for almost five years. I fell asleep before getting any farther. This was 10 April, and I had been seven days, in the one sense, a free agent. What none of us knew at the time was that our Spangenberg party was among the first, if not the very first, substantial element of the 160,000 British and Commonwealth p.o.w.s to be liberated and returned to England by a good three weeks. That statistic does not make its way into Foot and Langley's book. Neither is our camp credited with its two fine escapes.

Breakfast next morning was eggs and bacon: note the plural. I asked the manageress how this could be done and she said 'Thank the Canadian Government'. I could make a hearty breakfast with a clear conscience. At the regimental tailors they looked me up in a huge ledger; the regiment had expanded to seven battalions over the past four years, and deduced that I must have been an 'old First' officer. There was no problem about replacing the lanyard, but to replace my service dress uniform I would have to have clothing coupons: here was the War Office address where I should apply for these. But they warned me that because of labour shortage and demand I would have to wait at least five weeks for a fitting.

Writing and waiting seemed to me accepting avoidable delay and I set out for Whitehall to make my application in person. But half an hour of hunting for what proved a wholly arcane address induced me to accept another constraint, and having equipped myself with stationery, pen and ink, I sat down in the Club and made my formal application for application forms. But there was a benefit from this setback in that it reminded me to write to my mother, and to Dean Bollert as well, my first uncensored letter in five years.

Very few details stand out in my recollection of the next few days. The most prominent is an official confirmation that I had been granted sixty days leave in Canada: 'You will be notified of dates as soon as transport becomes available. You will meanwhile ensure that the Department has an effective address until such time.' I was surprised not to have been ordered to report to the regimental depot, wherever that might be, but felt no responsibility to enquire why not. Another surprise was a remarkably quick response to my request for clothing coupons, accompanied by a form of application for reimbursement of expenditure for lost kit. But the tailors' warning was inflexible. Special case I might be, but they did not dare begin to make exceptions.

There was plenty of coming and going in the Club and I could easily have found companions to 'do' London with, but I felt no inclination for this. I was both lonely and wanting to be alone, sorry for myself — I realise as I write — at having lost the easy, taken-for-granted comradeship of friends like Charles Jansen, Pat Sherrard and my messmates. I was afraid of intruding on their homecoming; in retrospect I realize that I would have been welcome. I walked the London parks and streets till I was footsore, and read what was readable in the Club library.

It must have been after mid-April when I was called to the 'phone one morning, to be agreeably surprised by Bob Montgomery's voice: what was I doing? 'Kicking my heels waiting to go home on leave to Canada.' Would I come to dinner at his parents' flat in Chelsea? He brushed aside my excuse that I had nothing but the battle dress I was standing in to wear, and named a day. I was surprised and pleased that he had gone to the trouble of hunting me down; we had been on friendly terms in the castle, but his particular friends were Major Bob Winders and Jimmie Johnson, he who snored, and a cavalry major, Charles Peel, who was Clough's *bête noir*, and just as eccentric as Clough. I was actually senior to Bob by date of commission, but for his job at St Nazaire he was ranked acting captain, and I did not put up my second pip until 1943. His parents were charming to me; the father, a reservist Colonel in Signals, called back from the reserve in 1939, the mother a Red Cross Volunteer, in her day the belle of Newcastle. They seemed to enjoy listening to Bob and me telling stories and the dinner was excellent. I left their flat in Chelsea to the sound of 'You must come again!' in a much better frame of mind.

Not many days later Bob 'phoned again. His sister who was in the W.R.N.S. would be coming home on weekend leave, and what about going to Manetta's in

Clarges Street for dinner and dancing on Saturday night?[14] We would meet for sherry before at the home of the girl he was bringing. I wanted to accept, remembering Bob's picture of her beside his bunk, but was embarrassed by my battle dress; 'Nonsense!'. As I put the 'phone down, I realized that I had no shoes, and that army issue boots would not do on a smart restaurant dance floor. It took me almost a day to find a pair of black shoes my size in a shop willing to sell me them without coupons.

From the beginning I enjoyed the evening. For a start, Bob's girl's parents actually lived in Carlyle Place, a good omen; and they were most friendly and welcoming. For another thing his sister was all the photo had promised and more, attractive, straightforward, easy to talk to, and graced with the quality I have never found a better word for than 'style'. She was a petty officer in the Admiral's Signals Office of H.M.S. Daedalus, a 'concrete' ship, that is naval shore base, in Lee on the Solent, having declined a commission because out of consideration for her parents she did not wish to be posted abroad. Her name was Bridget, but she suffered from the childhood pet name 'Bunty' which she disliked. So I called her Bridget, which pleased her.

Hugh Smith tracked me down and telephoned; we met and drank beer in a pub in Victoria. He had had a lively and interesting war in a mysterious RAF Intelligence unit working among others with R. V. Jones, a young physicist who had had to do with the electronic air defence of the south of England against German night bombers. Hugh had evidently been very much in his element in that world; his gift, of a very high order, was technological rather than literary or even linguistic. About the Department he seemed less than happy. Chambers, he told me — as I knew — had taken it for granted that Hugh would succeed him in the Quain chair. But Sisson seemed to have no notion of this. I knew something of London University procedure in making appointments and failed to sense the implications of trouble to come here. As for me, Hugh seemed to assume that I would come back to finish my degree, and that an assistant lectureship awaited me.

Bob Montgomery 'phoned again. He was going down to stay a long weekend with his Aunt Mary Bell-Davies and she had suggested he bring me along. The Bell-Davies house, Dormers, was at Lee on Solent, where she was Chief Officer of the W.R.N.S. detachment that his sister belonged to; her husband, a V.C. of the World War, had been one of the founders of the Fleet Air Arm, and had retired as a Vice-Admiral there to grow roses. He was away on Atlantic Convoy duty. Their house was big and hospitable, a rendezvous in particular for Commonwealth officers on leave. They had a daughter Bridget's age and a somewhat younger son, a sub-lieutenant in a submarine somewhere in the Indian Ocean. Bunty/Bridget was billeted there. The house glowed with 'Aunt Mary's' hospitality, and she

14. W.R.N.S. = The Women's Royal Naval Service, alternatively known as the Wrens.

Bridget Montgomery.

treated me as she did Bob from the outset. The daughter, Anne, married to another submariner also in eastern waters, was expecting a child sometime in the
summer. She seemed to like me.

Back in London I had one of the most horrifying experiences of the war,
indeed of my life, the newsreel of the first concentration camp liberated by British

troops. At Warburg, in a pen adjacent to the main compound, we had seen how the Germans treated Russian prisoners of war and shuddered, finding it hard to imagine a hunger that made men fight like dogs for the loaves of bread we threw over the wire to them. But these were soldiers, and would probably have treated German captives much the same. Some of the living skeletons in the newsreel were women and children and old people. If I ever had any self-pity about captivity it ended there.

The following weekend, as I recall, was the occasion of V.E. day, which I celebrated soberly in British Columbia house with cake and ice cream; we watched the crowds from the first floor balcony. I was disappointed not to have been asked down to Dormers, until, later, I learned that Bridget had been on duty for the weekend. But I was asked down for the next, during which I extorted from her a copy of the picture Bob had on his bookshelf in the castle. I wanted to show it to my mother; but I did not tell Bridget this.

All that was fine, but I was finding the waiting for my movement order more and more irksome. Here it was almost June and I had been in England almost six weeks. At the Club the RAF officers were beginning to be replaced by army people, from Germany and then from Italy where they had fought a hard war against a superbly led enemy with every advantage of terrain to his defence. Among them, to my surprise, was Bobby Allen, with a captain's three pips, as boyish as in 1938. I was unreasonably envious; they would be going home after a week of celebration in London. It was too easy to forget who would not be going home, John Logan and Ken Macalister, for instance.

On Monday morning a few days later I was called to the telephone soon after breakfast to hear the voice of Alex Allan, whom I had barely seen at Eschwege. 'What the devil are you up to? What are you doing? Why haven't you got in touch?' Feeling like a delinquent younger brother I made excuses; I was waiting for my movement order to go on home leave. 'Never mind that! Pack your toothbrush and get on the train to come down here!' He named my destination, the time of the train and which station it went from and said, 'I'll be there.'

He was indeed waiting, at the very rural station of Great Bedwyn in Wiltshire, in a dashing pre-war sports car, which he drove in matching fashion to a pleasant house, Wexcombe Manor, on the eastern edge of the Wiltshire Downs that he had taken for his family during the war. His wife, Cecile, welcomed me as warmly as Aunt Mary had done. She had a grown daughter, and Alex two sons, in each case by a previous marriage. The sons were away in the army, the daughter at home. Not long after my visit she married Tony Rolt. They made a handsome pair.

During our five-mile drive Alex had quizzed me about Terence and my return to England, learned that I had lost my civilian clothes, and developed a considerable indignation about my having to wait so long for my passage home. His practical reaction was immediate and typical of the man. When the introductions had been becomingly performed he took me upstairs to his dressing room. Looking me up and down he said, 'We're about the same size'; and opening a wardrobe door, 'Suits, jackets, trousers for you to wear while you are here. Wear what you feel comfortable in'. Then, having shown me my room he left me to change out of my uniform. He had a 'phone call to make. There were deck chairs in the garden and he would be with me in ten minutes. I changed into flannel trouser and a jacket and made for a deck chair in the garden. The weather was glorious. Within minutes the daughter, whose name I cannot recall, brought me a long cool drink and sat down companionably, as pleasant a person as her mother. And not much later Alex emerged, drink in hand and looking like a man who had scored a point. He had been speaking to a fellow Greenjacket in the War Office, and I could expect my movement order within that week.

He was right. After an idyllic three-day visit I returned to the Club on Thursday morning to find that my orders had come by the first post. I might have had to wait a long time for them without his applying pressure. He was as good a friend as a man could wish for, crotchety in his way and for that reason possibly not as much respected as he deserved among his contemporaries in camp. But he unquestionably deserved the D.S.O. awarded for his performance at Calais, where his formation of an inner perimeter of defence on the Saturday night held up the two German armoured divisions engaged there for another day, priceless for the defence of Dunkirk. My recollection of how his persistent questioning at Laufen about Vernon Knollys's tactics had irritated me is coloured by realization that he would have valued me less had I told him what I considered the reason for them. He was a complex personality but I valued his friendship all the more for that.

My orders were to report to the Transport officer at Southampton Docks the following Wednesday, and to travel to Vancouver by way of New York on the Queen Mary. My warrant and travel allowance would be in tomorrow's post. At long length I was going home. But I had unfinished business in England. Having observed English social custom I telephoned 'Aunt Mary' that evening and proposed myself for the weekend. Her answer was, 'Of course', and by good fortune Bunty was not on duty after Friday midday. Doubly ensuring my welcome with a carton of Cadbury's milk bars I arrived at Dormers after lunch on Friday. It was a fine weekend, much of which Bridget and I spent weeding the rose gardens and walking along the Solent shore. In due course I asked her to marry me. She neither refused nor accepted; if I still felt so inclined I could ask her again on my return from Canada. This was so obviously sensible that I was in no position to debate and had to be satisfied.

The Queen Mary, designed to be a luxury passenger liner for the Atlantic trade, was barely finished at the outset of war in 1939, and was instead fitted as a troopship. This crossing she would be carrying several thousand G.I.s home to the States for demobilization. In a sense I 'worked' my passage: I was in command of muster on A Deck Starboard, and would be taking my turn as ship's orderly officer. But I had a cabin to myself. One of the experienced ship's officers warned me that the G.I.s would make life hard for 'deck officers', seeing themselves as good as out of the army already. This was useful knowledge. At my first ship's inspection I found 'my' men lounging on A Deck Starboard, more or less properly dressed but chewing gum and smoking, sergeants and all. I made a fair guess at how soon the captain with his party would appear around the bow deck and said, 'Men, we have to put up with this; the sooner it's over the better. Those of you who have to smoke stand on the back row (note, not "rear-rank"), and gum-chewers freeze your jaws for thirty seconds while the captain passes you and stare straight at him.' When the moment came I did actually call them to attention; to have said 'Stand up straight and take your hands out of your pockets' would have given the show away. They performed creditably, in fact, and we got on well enough. Whatever else they had suffered for their country they were not luxuriously accommodated. The ship's cooks did them well, but the crowding below decks put me in mind of what I had read about slave ships. As for me, since my first sight of the Pacific in 1934 I have loved oceans, and with them sea travel. That crossing was just rough enough to be exhilarating, and I enjoyed it, musters, orderly officers and all.

We were four days at sea. About midmorning of the fifth day, when we were at a guess about three miles off Brooklyn and Staten Island and had just turned north for the Narrows a veritable fleet of small craft, harbour tugs, New York and New Jersey fireboats, even a yacht or two, bore down on us to the sound of sirens, ships' steam whistles, hooters, foghorns and brass bands, the fireboats shooting great fountains what seemed hundreds of feet straight up into the air. Presently as it became possible to make out detail you could see, on the tug decks, what looked like patterned groups of girls in cheerleaders' tutus, dancing a dance new to me, which I was told was the jive, and singing to the music of their bands a catchy tune I did not know of which the theme appeared to be, 'Waiting for the Yankee dollar'.[15] On our deck the G.I.s were beyond themselves with excitement and delight. The clamour, essentially cacophonous but curiously moving, differed absolutely in character from the rejoicing of the London V.E. Day crowds, but was similarly beyond doubt joyous. The celebration accompanied us until we were set for mooring.

It would be almost true to write that I was met on arrival in New York. But what actually happened is that before general disembarkation a stylish American matron wearing a badge that I was too polite to peer at came aboard and announced over the ship's Tannoy that she would like to meet any British passengers before they went ashore. She gave me a note of a downtown Manhattan hotel

---

15. The song 'Working for the Yankee dollar' was particularly popular in the recording made by the Andrews Sisters in 1944.

reservation made for me, and an invitation to a reception and buffet supper from an organization I supposed to be the American equivalent of the Victoria League.

My hotel was no great distance from the docks. I booked in quickly, excited by the prospect of exploring Manhattan. But first I ate a ritual lunch, one of the food dreams of summer 1940, a hamburger with a milkshake; my younger readers should know that both those terms had different meanings then. I did not have the sense to buy a map, merely wandered about in the streets I would come to love. The reception was very friendly and welcoming, but fruit cup is not an ice-breaking drink, and the conversation was anything but lively. By their shyness I guessed that the younger females had been dragooned into helping entertain; I could sense 'You must get out, darling and meet people!' What struck me as I walked back to my hotel, remembering Chicago and Vancouver and even staid Toronto, was how quiet the streets were.

After breakfast I checked out and made for Grand Central Station. My train was not due to depart until midday, but the station itself was rich in interest. The route prescribed by my travel warrant was unusual. The quickest would have been north to Montreal, and thence west by express. I would go by way of Chicago, around Lake Michigan, and then north through Michigan and Wisconsin to the Canadian border. I was comfortable enough with a Pullman car reservation, but very bored by the time we reached the border, in the middle of nowhere, next morning. The Canadian Customs and Immigration Officer, hard up for conversation, wanted my story. At length he remembered his duty with 'I don't suppose you have anything to declare'. He seemed not to notice the rifle. Without thinking I, who had often stood, pockets loaded with contraband, chatting with German security staff, declared the two cartons of duty free cigarettes in my knapsack. Afterwards I felt a great fool; evidently he wanted me to answer that I had nothing to declare. His reaction had been, 'Too bad, I'll have to confiscate them'.

At Winnipeg, late that afternoon I boarded the Continental Express. About noon the following day we halted for forty-five minutes in Saskatoon to service the locomotive and the dining carriage. I telephoned my stepfather from the station to tell him that I was safely back and would see him in Vancouver; he usually spent some time there in the summer. But this year, he said, he could not get away. Had I known of this in England I could probably have arranged a Saskatoon stopover on the way west; I don't think I could have arranged this in the station in Saskatoon during the lunch hour. With the pressure off in August it would be easy to do this in Vancouver. I promised that I would see him in August.

Arriving in Vancouver on the evening of the third day I was met at the station by Mother and four large persons, two of them in uniform, whose faces were familiar. I would have to get to know them again. I was home, but with a difference. I would have to learn to live in this new world.

13
HOMECOMING

It does not even seem worth attempting to convey the quality or depth of emotion in such a reunion. In this instance it was clearly my mother who, having been most sensible of loss, was most moved. For me the dominant pleasure was in being with her and enjoying her relief. I found her as beautiful as ever, albeit aged and marked with anxiety. For my two elder half-brothers the reunion must have involved reappraisal, our getting to know one another in an adult relationship; Edward was just now 24 and Leo rising 23. The younger children, Stella not long 20 and Charles rising 19 would not remember much of me from 1938. At their age seven years is a very long time.

It was hard to convince Mother that I had not suffered or come to any harm from going to the wars, indeed was in excellent health. Both Macadam and my bank manager had written to her of their pleasure at my return and she was full of how helpful the Red Cross and Mrs Enid Murray's team in Victoria had been about personal parcels for p.o.w.s from distant British Columbia. Edward and Leo, private soldiers in the Canadian Infantry Corps, had been allowed to complete their economics degree courses at the University before being called up, and now were in the final term of a course in a small Canadian Services Japanese Language School. The Director was an orientalist from the University with the rank of major, their favourite teacher a *Nisei*,[16] that is a Canadian Japanese, a very beautiful woman, they reported. Stella was building Flying Fortresses in the local Boeing plant and Charles was in his last year at high school a cadet sergeant-pilot in the RCAF. It was some comfort to Mother that I could reassure her that neither of the older boys would be allowed anywhere near a combat zone; as Japanese speakers they were simply too rare and valuable. My first day or so home, I sensed, or imagined I sensed, a certain stiffness of attitude on their part. If indeed there was, it disappeared after each had beaten me roundly at golf and tennis. Indeed I regained my elder-brother status, such as it was, only when I took the car to a petrol station and found that the oil in the sump was dangerously low: each had been leaving it for the other to see to.

---

16. *Nisei* = someone born to Japanese immigrants, i.e. second generation.

Vancouver 1945 with half-sister Stella.

Sometimes it seemed to me that Mother was finding it hard to get used to not having to worry about me; here too it may have been my imagination that occasionally she was looking at me as if I had come back from the dead. To please her I let her show me off to some of her friends; they too seemed to think that I had been subjected to an 'ordeal', had 'suffered'. Sedgewick had surmised that I would be coming home on leave and had been telephoning Mother regularly to check whether I was back yet. I found him rather pathetic, with an intensified sense of being out of things. Dean Bollert was as affable as ever. She did not seem to take my forsaking scholarship and joining the army amiss.

None of my particular friends was in Vancouver. John Harrison was still in the Maritimes, where he had been flying Catalinas on anti-submarine patrol and convoy protection; Leonard Grant was in Naval Intelligence in Ottawa, Rodney

Poisson on a cruiser in the northern Pacific. I failed to make contact with Ivan Niven or his parents. It was a hot summer, and I envied my brothers their light-weight khaki denim uniforms; I ought without delay to have made for the nearest Quartermaster's stores and begged, bribed or bought an outfit for myself instead of sweltering in serge. I tried to find civilian clothes, at the very least flannels and a sports jacket off the peg, but with little success. As for tailors, they had long waiting lists. Even the beach was a disappointment, my beloved Pacific no longer limpid blue but an oily brown swill littered with flotsam and jetsam, the latter mainly plastic containers.

I do not think I was consciously bored. It was wonderful to be among my family. But now at this distance I perceive that I was in danger of becoming sorry for myself, and that without grounds. I had no right to be disappointed: I was home and in good health. My mother's mind could at last be at ease about me. I had many good friends, and although none might be immediately at hand to talk to and drink with they were there for the future. I have since learned that many long-term prisoners of war experienced this sense of disappointment on homecoming. I suppose this was mainly because we were in the process of rediscovering that 'freedom' is a relative term in a cruel practical sense: there is no life without constraints.

This was brought home to me very sharply when, less than ten days after my return there was a telephone call: my stepfather had suffered a severe stroke and was in hospital at Cudworth, about ten miles from Wakaw. The doctor held out little hope of his recovery; would Mother come immediately? We put her on the eastbound express that evening and drove back to the house in a sombre state of mind. For my part I knew that this would be very hard for her; they were a devoted couple. As for their children, these had not yet experienced death in the family, but I had in conscience to tell them what Mother had told me.

He was alive and conscious when she reached the hospital, and lived a day and a night with her by his bedside. To this day I do not know whether I am at fault for not disregarding my army travel regulations and stopping over to see him on my journey west. Was it too easy to say, when I 'phoned him, 'I'll see you on my way back to England'?

It was clear when mother telephoned me of his death that she needed support and that I must go. But there was more bad news: his health had evidently been failing for some time and, his manager told her, he had not filed an income tax return for at least three years. No doubt that omission, preying on his mind, worsened his condition. Here was something I could not cope with; my ignorance of income tax was total. It came to my mind that both his sons had read economics at the University; they must know something about tax returns. One of them would have to come to Saskatchewan with me. There was no point asking for a volunteer. Both were nearing the end of a course they loved. Edward was his father's eldest son.

This was very hard for him. He was, it appeared, a very apt student in that difficult subject, and another month or so would have equipped him with an unusual and valuable qualification. After a struggle with himself he agreed, bitterly to be sure, but recognizing there was no alternative. There was also urgency, with Mother in mind. So I undertook the boldest action of my military career. I telephoned the Major, the Director of the School, identifying myself as a subaltern in the British Army on home leave, half-brother of his student Private Edward Bakony, and asked for indefinite compassionate leave for Edward, giving him grounds. In retrospect it seems incredible, but without verification of my identity or meeting and questioning me himself, he agreed. The only formality was that Edward must report at the School to collect a leave pass. I can think of only two plausible reasons for his compliance, one that he was only a soft academic in uniform, the other that he had read and recalled articles in the local broadsheets some days before reporting the homecoming of Vancouver p.o.w.s from Germany, notably Lieut. Col. Cecil Merrit the Dieppe V.C., and incidentally lesser fry among whom I was named, in a *reductio ad minimum*.

In any event three days later Edward and I were in Wakaw where we found Mother, very brave and wretchedly unhappy. She was living in a flatlet, no more than that, which my stepfather had occupied unless in the summer he slept in the Cottage, still in good repair, albeit somewhat sparsely furnished. There was a car, and the three of us drove the two miles to the lake to inspect it. I elected to sleep there rather than take a room in the hotel in town, which Mother accepted on the undertaking that I would breakfast with her. There was a restaurant, which, although its menu was not imaginative, had an excellent cook. Edward opted for a camp bed in the flatlet.

Evenings were long and sunrise early at that time of year; the two periods of solitude were good for me. The lake was as lovely as ever, but different in detail. The big black poplars that had been at the peak of their twenty-year life cycle in my boyhood were gone, including the one by the veranda door where the hummingbirds had nested. The new growth was elegant and graceful, and created a different, shimmering and broken light effect in the early morning. After twelve years of drought the lake, spring-fed, was sadly down, but still clean and clear. And my boat, waterlogged but otherwise intact, was tied to the pier. I was glad to learn that in 1970, when my cousin Evelyn took Bridget to see Wakaw and the lake, its level was well up.

My stepfather's affairs were indeed in disarray. When I last saw him in 1938 he looked his age, but no more, at 51. He drank little, and played golf regularly, but he smoked, and much as he tried, could not stop. At that time his businesses, a large garage and petrol station and a 'general store', both run for him by managers, were doing well. But evidently, come the war, petrol rationing with a reduction in private motoring, and the transfer of manufacturing to military needs, resulted in the garage ceasing to be profitable and the store becoming impossible to stock adequately. Moreover his friends told me, over the past two years or so his health had been deteriorating. This, doubtless to save Mother anxiety, he had kept from her.

When Edward and I appeared on the scene and took over the office the manager, who had worked for him for years and known us as boys, was both relieved and dubious of our competence to handle the situation. Luckily for us the first step was obvious, to sort an accumulation of miscellaneous, unfiled paper, the content of his desk drawers and filing cabinets. His solicitor, who also remembered us, established our *bona fides* at the bank, and we set to work. I assigned to Edward sorting and calendaring all paper that had to do with buying and selling, profit and loss. It was quickly evident that he owed the Inspector of Taxes three years' returns. It was hard to see how we could prepare these from the information we had. But at any rate the manager was reassured when he saw that we were working to a system.

Meanwhile I was also concerned with arranging for my stepfather's funeral. We are not a religious family. My mother, when I was not much older than 12, had shocked me by observing that my father had thought French Canada 'priest-ridden'. My stepfather, Catholic by birth, was openly agnostic. On summer Sunday mornings he would drop us three elder boys outside the parish church and make for the golf course. Nevertheless he could be persuaded on special occasions to sing, usually solos, with the choir; he had a fine tenor voice. It would sorely grieve the largely Catholic Hungarian element in the community if he were not buried in their churchyard.

But the parish priest, French-Canadian and not much older than myself, was dubious about this and seemed ready to make difficulties. With, probably, as good a theological education as he, I could have given him firm grounds for a Christian burial, but if he were to refuse to conduct the service I would be foxed. As we spoke, however, I sensed an ulterior motive, and presently it showed. One of his parishioners, whom I recalled as a friendly young man with pretty younger sisters just too old for me, had assumed that Mother would be selling the store and hoped he might be considered the preferred bidder. This was not problematic; his parents were solid Austro-Hungarian citizens of the Old Empire, eminently respectable. I could honestly tell the priest that I would speak to Mother about this. But, I cautioned, the business was not mine to dispose of. I was only a stepson and she was the outright heir of the estate. Like all funerals this one was melancholy, on what seemed like the only cold and windy day I recall from that summer.

Mother's youngest sister, Aunt Mary, recently a widow, lived in nearby Cudworth, and Grandma Kopp with her, having finally conceded that she could no longer live alone. This had been a blessing for Mother when her husband was dying in the hospital there: they gave her the loving sympathy that only close kinswomen can provide in such situations. For my part I was delighted to see Grandma again. It might have been impossible for me to break my return journey. On most matters Grandma's mind was as sharp and lively as ever, but on the war and my captivity it was blessedly vague: I did not try to enlighten her; better so. Aunt Mary was as darling as ever, and her daughters very pleasant, growing up.

Mother was left the whole of her husband's estate; this we would now have to prepare for probate. It was small but not contemptible. The business, even inadequately stocked, would sell without too much of a notional loss, for the Canadian economy was bound to improve with the German war now ended and a beginning of a return to peacetime conditions. But before all there was the income tax problem to take care of; probate would have to wait.

Here Edward came into his own. He recalled a teacher in one of his economics courses describing and illustrating a formula used by federal tax officials to check returns submitted with inadequate data. He would apply this inversely to his father's situation and thus establish a succession of acceptable figures for the missing successive returns. I cannot pretend to have understood it, but it seemed our only recourse. His father's physician would readily vouch for his progressively declining health to account for the absence of documentary support.

Edward's plan was to submit the overdue tax returns thus-prepared, with such documentation as we had, the medical certificate and a covering letter drafted by me under his direction — he knew the terminology — by mail. I did not care for this at all; it might lead to extended correspondence and possible investigation, and for what it was worth, my time in Canada was limited. I made a hard decision, both in taking responsibility and in assigning it. Edward must submit the returns in person, as the late taxpayer's eldest son representing his mother, the beneficiary of his estate. As such he was the obvious agent. Moreover he was very presentable; his uniform set him off beautifully. And he could provide immediately such answers as the Inspector would ever get; he knew what to say whereas a single technical question would have floored me. He did not like this assignment, but to my relief accepted the arguments and agreed. Before he could change his mind I telephoned Saskatoon and made an appointment for the following day. Mother and I crossed our fingers when we had seen him onto the train.

His visit was successful. The returns were accepted and the business of probate could now go forward; the pressure was off. There was one melancholy document among my stepfather's miscellaneous papers, a letter from a newly formed combine called General Motors Corporation offering him, as the owner of a commercial garage, twenty-five shares in the Corporation at $5 a share. The letter was dated in the spring 1930 before the Great Depression hit the Winnipeg Grain

Exchange. Simply the bonus issues on those shares would have made him a rich man by 1945.

Mother had been reluctant to sell the business. She was right, of course, in believing that, poorly stocked as it was, it would not fetch its real value. But to keep it as it stood until it could be stocked would need 'hands on' management. Her notion was that Edward should take this on. Without doubt he had the acumen, but, even to my small knowledge of him as an adult, neither the temperament nor the inclination. And he was used to city life; he would never be happy in a small town. In any event he was still in the army; there was no assurance that he would be demobilised on compassionate grounds before his number came up. And he was passionate to get back to his course. I think Mother sensed this. She did not put pressure on him and accepted that she would have to sell.

Before she sent him back to Vancouver we had a most agreeable surprise. It was a Saturday morning, and we were at the lake with a substantial picnic lunch and a fine summer day to enjoy, sitting on the veranda or in and out of the lake, when a strange car appeared containing, to our delight, Grandma and my cousin Josie, now Father Philip, whom I had last seen in 1939 in London where he made a short stopover on his way to the Benedictine College in Rome. His Abbot had lent him a car; he had driven to Cudworth, stayed the night in the rectory where my erstwhile history teacher was on parochial duty, picked up Grandma and driven on to us. He bore good wishes from all my former teachers and the Brodner brothers, also now ordained. I have a snapshot of Grandma with her three eldest grandsons taken that day. She looks serene, even proud, her features at 78 still remarkably fine. That day was not long enough. I never got around to asking Philip for the story of his crossing France in 1940.

Soon after that visit Mother sent Edward back to Vancouver. He had unquestionably done his filial duty in settling his father's affairs, and there was nothing more for him to do. Before he left we swam my boat out into deep water and sank her honourably. I would see Edward again when I myself went back to Vancouver to collect my travel warrant and my kit for the return trip to England.

My stepfather had belonged to a general merchants' trade association. He and its Saskatchewan representative had been good friends; Mother and I decided that we would put the sale of the business in his hands. With probate accomplished there was not really anything I could do, and in any event negotiations might extend beyond my leave. Meanwhile I finished tidying up my stepfather's affairs. There was a surprising amount of correspondence, formal or courteous, to deal with.

I was in his office one day when there was a 'phone call for me from a man who identified himself as Professor John Lothian of the University of Saskatchewan, whom I had never heard of, inviting me to come and spend a day there. I did not want to leave Mother alone unnecessarily and tried to put him off. It was, he said, about a teaching post. As civilly as I could I told him he was wasting his time. I was in the British Army, as he must have known, had no notion when I would be demobilized, and had an obligation to the Imperial Order of Daughters of the Empire to complete a half-finished Ph.D. course in London University. He persisted: this would not be a junior appointment. I would take over the English Department and build it up. Here was sales talk at its richest. At length, largely out of curiosity, I agreed to come.

On the day he walked me proudly around the Department and the Arts Building. The University was evidently set upon a course of major growth and development. Its standards, I knew from St Peter's days, ultimately in the Scottish tradition by way of Nova Scotia, were high. In another life and different circumstances I might have been tempted. But in any case the absurdly inappropriate rank of the initial appointment was, if anything, a disincentive. Elementary common sense brought to mind my total inexperience of administration, lack of teaching experience, the half finished doctoral project. When I started telling him this he did not listen.

He took me to his pleasant house on campus (another lure) for lunch; his wife was charming and there was a presentable daughter. We sat over the meal well into the afternoon, when quite out of the blue Mrs Lothian said, 'The President's wife is expecting you to tea. I am to bring you over.' I was certainly being looked over, but in my mind nothing was at stake. The President was there too, evidently no academic, but knowledgeable about university matters. His wife was gracious; again there was a presentable daughter. Just as I was getting restless — there was only one train to Wakaw of an evening — Mrs Lothian came to reclaim me and take me back to their house for an early meal. They would call up a taxi for me in good time. When it was time to leave ten minutes of frantic phoning failed to produce a taxi. I set off on foot at a rifleman's pace, but without much hope of catching my train. I think I would have missed it had I not flagged down with a policeman's hand signal a private car containing two stylish young matrons who, amused by my plight, broke all speed restrictions: I was the last person to climb aboard. Mother was amused by my day and the extravagant offer, and agreed that I was right to decline it, which I did in plain but civil terms by letter the next day.

There is not much more to write about my leave. I stayed on in Wakaw with Mother as long as I could. For the first time in my remembered life I was alone with her for days on end. We got to know each other a little as adults, and apart from having to fend off overfeeding I enjoyed every moment of her company. She was a very courageous woman, and intellectually remarkable. Ahead of her time in asserting the parity of the female intelligence, with unusual finesse she retained an elegantly female style. Her cruelly bad luck in the health of both her husbands seemed to have strengthened her. And indeed she would need this, with two immature children to care for. Luckily she got on well with both.

George Kane with Charles, Leo, Stella and Ed Bakony.

She understood that I could not say how long I would be away this time. But I could assure her that I was unlikely to be posted to Burma, since all battalions of my regiment had been engaged since 1942 in the desert or Italy or Germany and would need extensive retraining to be of any use in jungle combat. Moreover the Burma campaign was going well. She understood that I might not be demobilized for some time and that I had a residence requirement at the University to complete. I had told her about Bridget. Toward the end of July when it looked as if the process of selling the business would drag on beyond my deadline she sent me back to Vancouver, with an injunction to report how the young were getting on in her absence. For my part I would collect my travel documents, say my few goodbyes, and put myself together for the return to England. The young seemed in good order; I reported this. And they saw me off on the train.

As far as Montreal the journey was comfortable and scenically new, the only one of the four Canadian transcontinental lines I had not yet travelled by. The Cordillera was spectacular and the prairie quite different in landscape and appearance from the North Saskatchewan of my youth. But the last lap, from Montreal to New York was a letdown, a third class carriage without air conditioning.

I did at least have a reserved seat, but almost every other passenger seemed to be a mother with a child that cried all night, not that I could blame them. Luckily my New York hotel was cool and comfortable.

I awoke to VJ day. I had known it was impending, but had not had a chance to buy an evening paper in Montreal. This put paid to my plan to extend my exploration of New York, for by the time I had breakfasted the streets were crowded to the point where that was no longer possible. So I drifted aimlessly with the crowd or stood gawping at the flashing headlines in Times Square. People were friendly, but here was nothing like the sheer joyousness of the Londoners on VE day, or the wild, rousing welcome given to the troopship as it approached the New York docks in June. American casualties in the Pacific war zone had been cruelly heavy, and the mere concept of the atomic bomb seemed to hang over the day like a dark cloud. The only shared emotion I could sense was one of relief.

Next morning held another disappointment. It was about 9:30 and I was setting out to walk to the dock, no great distance, and embark. As I passed the door of the all-night bar of my hotel half a dozen American servicemen poured out into the street. I was not paying attention, and was surprised to hear one of them call out to me. They were Col. Caraway's Intelligence Officer and his team, who had been celebrating their very recent return to the States, and now VJ day. They were not what I would call drunk, but certainly elated. Where had I been all this time! I must come and have at least one drink to celebrate our meeting! The excitement of that morning in Eschwege came back to me in a surge of recollection. The inclination to accept was powerful, but a cruel inner voice cautioned me that if I did I would probably not make the 10:30 deadline of my embarkation order. I think he understood my situation, and I took his address; I did not at that moment have one to give. I lost his address, and over the years have even forgotten his name. I have only myself to blame.

This time I crossed in the Queen Elizabeth, also fitted as a troopship, sharing a cabin with a British captain in one of the technical corps. He was affable and mannerly but no great conversationalist. I had only a couple of books, the ship had no library and the seascape was too calm to be interesting. One thing became clear to me during that crossing: I would have to make a number of decisions, and they depended on interacting contingencies that would not necessarily be resolved in convenient sequence. Thus, what would I be doing for what remained of my time in the army? When could I expect to be demobilized? Where would I live after I was out? How soon could I expect to register for my second year of university residence? Would Bridget still be interested in me? Because of my preoccupation I had scarcely written to her while I was in Canada. If, as I hoped, she still was interested, how did I plan to support her?

My generation was taught that a man did not marry until he could support a wife. Dean Bollert had told me that my tenure of the second year of my scholarship was secure, but that would not begin to maintain a household even for that year. There was that assistant lectureship at University College that Chambers had talked about, but Chambers was dead. In any event I did not intend to stay in England. The job would have to be in Canada or, failing that, the States.

Some of the uncertainty was dispelled soon after we landed. In the Movement Control Office at Southampton Docks I was handed an order to report to the Regimental Training Battalion, now at Ranby Camp near Retford in Nottinghamshire. After picking up my now ready service dress in London from the regimental tailors I duly reported. The Adjutant was a busy man. Having welcomed me, he informed me that my demobilization number would come up in late February and summoned an orderly to show me my quarters and take me to the Officers' Mess. It was as good as deserted at that time of day. It was comfortable enough, but drab, clearly a wartime improvisation. I was beginning to get an impression that as far as the Adjutant was concerned I could vegetate here, that he had no duty to assign me to. There was one bright moment: the n.c.o. in charge of the Officers' Mess bar was 'my' Sergeant Headley of C Company. He had heard that I was alive and appeared pleased to see me in the flesh. With great relish he told me that in the latter part of our little action among the dunes the Company-Sergeant-Major, with a follow-up party, had 'taken care of' the machine gun team that I had failed to capture. I thanked him, but derived no pleasure from this information; it simply made me wonder who, in the end, got my binoculars and pistol. I lasted only a few days at Ranby, bored to excruciation, nothing to do, nothing to read! Then I broke into the Adjutant's peace and demanded a posting. He barely looked up from the paper he was pushing, said 'Take some leave', and returned to it. He may have thought me mad.

Back in London next day I made my number at the Canadian Officers' Club, from which I telephoned Dormers; Bridget's Aunt Mary told me to come down at once. Before making for Waterloo I called on Mr Macadam at British Columbia House to give him Mother's thanks, and indeed mine, for all his kindnesses. There was a letter awaiting me from Woodhouse offering me an Assistant Professorship in University College Toronto at a salary of $2400, to begin in September 1946.

This seemed to resolve all problems except the date of demobilization. That could probably be arranged. The Imperial Order of Daughters of the Empire, I had no doubt, would accept the surrender of my second scholarship year in the circumstances. And I would register as a doctoral student under Woodhouse while teaching.

But Bridget, while she seemed very pleased to see me again, would not even consider emigrating to Canada. If I wanted to marry her we would have to live in England. I could sense that neither pleading nor debate would be of avail, so I played for time: I wrote to Woodhouse how proud and honoured I was by his invitation, but that I could not come in September 1945. I was still in the army, had a second year of residence in London University to fulfil, and needed to be near my primary sources in the great libraries to finish my dissertation. His reply was prompt and cool. Should I at any time wish to come to Toronto I would have to write enquiring whether there might be a vacancy for me. Fair enough, but evidently he was not used to receiving negative answers.

One certainty emerged from this: yes, Bridget would marry me, although for the time being this would have to remain an understanding. She did not wish to become formally engaged until after her demobilization in December. I could scarcely object, since it was very much in my own mind that I had no more than the possibility of a job in sight. However the 'understanding' was common knowledge in her family who seemed, without exception, pleased.

It now became of immediate importance to ascertain where I stood with the University College London, and, for that matter, fulfilling my residence requirement in uniform. I got in touch with Hugh Smith. He anticipated no difficulty with the registration, but with Sisson now Head of the Department that matter rested with him, and he would not be back in London until October.

Early in September, while I was kicking my heels and waiting for his return, a job came up that would have solved the finance problem. This was a post in AMGOT, the Allied Military Government in Occupied Territories. It would mean immediate demobilization without loss of my bounty, and very handsome pay and allowances. But it would have been in Germany or Austria, and I had no stomach for this. I did not know at the time that Terence had had a similar offer and rejected it.

More for something to do than with any hope of success I got out the manuscript of my novel and scanned it — without pride or pleasure. But I needed to know once and for all whether I could write fiction. I invited myself to Dormers, borrowed Bridget's typewriter (the looters took mine) and hammered it out. Not unexpectedly it came back, from two publishers with the same courteous negative topped by the bromide, 'we would like to be permitted to see your next book.' I needed to be told that I did not have the fabling gift in any form, that my mind refused fantasy, the composition of fictional patterns. I could neither assemble in cold blood a story that I found plausible and interesting myself, nor lose myself in the imaginary experience of one. I could, obversely, tell a poorly wrought story from a bad one. It had amused my friend the Camp Librarian at Spangenberg, when I was his assistant, that I had a considerable 'What shall I read next, George?' following.

He and I had talked about publishing in a general way. On our return to England he had given Terence good advice about his escape book and about publication of a book of cricket essays Terence had written in camp. I would sound him about a job in the 'book trade', in publishing; he could do nothing worse than discourage me. Dear man, he seemed delighted when I made contact, and in the course of our conversation predictably asked what I would be doing after demobilization. I told him of the unfinished degree work and the possible assistant lectureship, which latter did not seem to impress him. Presently, after a pause he asked, 'Have you ever thought of going into publishing?'. It was clear he had sensed why I had come to see him; I did not have to answer. He closed the topic with 'I'll look into this, George. Keep in touch.' I still remember my surprise at the outcome, an offer of a job as a manager of a subsidiary branch of his firm, to begin after completion of my Ph.D. work, and a salary of £800 a year. Of course I accepted.

At the end of September Sisson was reported back in London, and I made an appointment to see him. Apart from civility I needed to know for certain about registration and when I might expect my thesis materials. He seemed pleased to see me, and readily undertook to support my application for 'resumption of residence', as he called it, while still in the services. As for Chambers's precious College muniments and my books with them, they would be returned to London when a suitable repository for the former had been prepared. He would let me know.

We talked about Chambers, who had died in April 1942. On an impulse of what must have been curiosity to see Sisson's reaction I mentioned Chambers's assumption that I would be staying on in College after getting my doctorate. Sisson did not reveal whether he knew of this. After a moment's silence he said that he would 'look into it'. I cannot to this day think why I did not tell him that I had other plans, unless it was that I did not take his undertaking seriously.

There was one more matter to arrange, a place to live in London immediately after demobilization. With luck I was able to book a room in London House beginning from that date. All I needed now was something to occupy me until then, so back to Retford, where I badgered the Adjutant. He was no longer as harassed; within a week he found me a posting as Welfare Officer on an Army Medical Board concerned with former prisoners of war of the Japanese. It sounded interesting.

Before I was due to report Sisson summoned me, to tell me that I would be appointed Assistant Lecturer in the English Department from October 1946 at a starting salary of £425 per year paid quarterly in arrears, to teach 'Medieval Literature'. Meanwhile he would appoint me Departmental Assistant (unpaid) for the session 1945–1946. This would enable him to recommend me for an increment in 1946 and legitimize my registration.

Now with two jobs in prospect I was in a new predicament, a dilemma of choice between them and a very uncomfortable sense of obligation not to put off the decision and of informing the friend whom I had permitted to waste his time on my behalf.

Publishing would pay better, both immediately and, if I did well, in the long run. The work, turning my critical responses into a financial commodity — to put it crudely — would be a sustained gamble with two stakeholders, myself risking a career and the firm its money. I was pretty confident of being up to this. But a lifestyle went with it, office hours, three weeks holiday a year, the umbrella and bowler hat, and reading more bad or indifferent than good books in typescript.

I suppose that precise recall of one's reasons for making a major decision sixty years ago is likely to be shaped by the nature of the sum of consequences of that decision. But the fact that I cannot, today, envisage myself as a personality after, say, thirty-five years working and living in that milieu, seems to indicate that in 1945 I had some sense of apprehension of being, if not a failure, then a misfit there. I do not recall consciously weighing against a life in publishing the sense of community in a college or university, the flexible timetable, being one's own master in the long vacations, as Todd was, for instance, able to take a couple of afternoons a week off simply to read Greek poetry with a former student for pleasure, the variety of company in the Senior Common Room of a large college, intellectual give and take.

Unquestionably each job meant a new beginning. It was starkly clear in my mind that I was just as inexperienced at preparing London University English Honours students for their final examinations, which is what Sisson's 'teaching Medieval Literature' meant in the end, as in managing a publishing business, however small. For instance I had not read, or heard, except as sources of instances of phonological change, of *Ancrene Riwle*, or *Handlyng Synne*, or *The Ayenbit of Inwit* or even *Havelok the Dane*; I found *Gawain and the Green Knight* very difficult, as for that matter I did many passages in *Piers Plowman*. I had never had a good course on Chaucer. I did not then know of R. M. Wilson's *Early Middle English Literature* (1939) or Renwick and Orton's *Beginnings of English Literature* (1940). Ironically the looters who had made off with my civilian clothes and typewriter had left me my notes on Spargo's course, Klaeber's *Beowulf* (the unrevised edition) and a *Chanson de Roland*. I did know the difference between good and bad or indifferent teaching, and the importance of organization of material, in class and course. The devil was in the material, the knowledge I did not have. How I survived the decision to stay in the university world is another story.

Charles Shears was understandably vexed when I told him that I would not be taking the publishing job. He had, he said, evidently understating, 'gone to a certain amount of trouble to arrange it for me'. I could only say that I was abjectly sorry for having wasted his time. But he was a man of understanding and did not hold my letting him down against me; before long we were good friends again.

The Nottingham posting proved disappointing. The Board consisted of a Lieut. Col. in the RAMC who would take care of our clients' physical welfare, an ATS corporal to keep the records and myself, there to ensure that their material wellbeing was cared for in such matters as coupons for extra rations, disablement pensions, even accommodation; in these matters the p.o.w.s from the Far East were handsomely treated, as was right and good. The challenge for me would be to overcome an instinctive fear in the ex-prisoner of anybody in uniform, especially an officer. In a Japanese camp to make any sort of request, however reasonable, was to risk a beating. My qualification was that I too had been a p.o.w. and must therefore seem less of a threat. The disappointment for me (I can't speak for its other two members) was that the Board had very little custom. The rush was over; we rarely saw more than two or three clients, and as time went on, somedays none.

My billet was disappointing too, a room in a private house in a terrace, no elegant country rectory or genial Essex pub this time, let alone the luxury, however chilly socially, of the Hambro mansion. It provided a solid breakfast and a substantial dinner, plenty of hot water and a comfortable bed, but the bedroom had no writing table or armchair or even an adequate bedside reading light. I suppose that previous occupants simply made for the nearest pub of an evening.

That, it appeared, was also expected of me. The Colonel and his secretary had a favourite pub, which made me welcome enough, but beer-at-the-bar-till-closing-time was not my favourite diversion; in this I disappointed the Colonel, who blossomed out there.

The Board sat from Monday to Friday, and since I was detached from my unit I could give myself leave, which I did every weekend. When Bridget was duty petty officer, every other weekend, I would make for Dormers; other weekends she came up to London to her parents' flat. They could put me up as well, and we got to know each other doing the dishes, so to speak. My billet landlady had my ration book as regulation required, but I could still pick up a carton of Cadbury's best and one of duty-free cigarettes at the Club to make up for that. As I had been led to expect I was invited to spend Christmas at Dormers.

That left only a bleak January and part of February in Nottingham to which I had not been looking forward, but those weeks turned out better than I could have hoped. Within days of being back on duty after Christmas I was telephoned by Pat Sherrard, who had got my billet 'phone number from Ranby. He had a car, and we spent the best part of that weekend and most others together sitting over meals or a drink, or walking in the countryside and talking.

The future seemed to be taking shape. I would have a job. I had assurance of a place to live while I finished my dissertation. My *Piers Plowman* materials would certainly be accessible by the end of February and I would be able to finish and type the thesis in the very handsome, generally empty library of London House.

14
THE DEEP END

On the first of March I was at length once more a civilian. My engagement to Bridget had been announced in the *Times* in January. I shared a room in London House with a Canadian of my age who was studying to be an ophthalmologist, as agreeable a man as I could wish and hardly ever there by day. I was an 'Assistant' without duties or pay in the English Department at University College London; in October I would be an Assistant Lecturer, teaching 'Medieval Literature'. I had almost no civilian clothes beyond such essentials as I had been able to find in Vancouver on leave the preceding summer and a green trilby and an unwearable suit bestowed on me by a grateful sovereign on demobilization. I had the hard core of my doctoral thesis, at length back from Aberystwyth but needing an introduction. Ideally this would be completed, submitted and examined by the beginning of the long vacation. Bridget would lend me her typewriter.

Curiosity sent me to College. The Departmental Secretary, its strong backbone I was to learn, Miss Winifred Husbands, remembered me and was very welcoming. She took me to see the 'office' that I would share with a Miss Elizabeth Sweeting, who happened to be in College that afternoon.

She was a most engaging person of about my age. The first thing she did after we exchanged civilities was to express pleasure and relief at my arrival. She was restive in her job and would be leaving as soon as I was ready to take over in October '47; her real interest was stage management and she had a job waiting for her. I was relieved in my turn; there would be no resentment at being replaced. I wondered a little about a 'career' in stage management. A couple of months ago, fifty-eight years later, I was reassured by an obituary in the *Guardian* which sang her praises in that career.

To my question about what she taught the answer was Middle English prescribed texts and some Anglo-Saxon. Before I took my leave I borrowed her copy of the University English Honours Examination syllabus, to see where 'Medieval Literature' fitted in. The answer appeared to be 'Nowhere in particular and therefore everywhere'; it was evidently to be taught as part of the explication of texts.

In the meanwhile there was no time to worry about this. I had not merely to produce what seemed to me the archetypal text of those three last passus of

Piers Plowman, and to justify my decisions where variation was not simply an evident matter of manifest error. I knew very little about the history of textual criticism. Chambers had told me about Griesbach and Housman and Moore and the Westcott and Hort team. Having no German he evidently did not know of Maas's 'Einführung in die Textkritik' in Gercke and Norden's *Einleitung in die Altertums-wischenschaft*. Worse still, determining the archetypal text of those three passus seemed too easy a way to earn a doctorate. Of necessity I managed to put together an introduction of sorts and such notes as the few real problems warranted, but I was not easy in mind until I had passed the oral. And to this day I think that if I had been the external examiner I would have sent myself back for more. My thesis was slight and I am not proud of it. Certainly my external examiner, Dorothy Everett, gave me a thorough going-over, and that excellent person was not given to compromise; since a couple of years later she mercilessly turned down for publication an essay on the *Parlement of Foules* I submitted to the *Modern Language Review* I suppose I can assume that the thesis was 'not all bad'.

When Bridget's father was retired a second time in 1946 he and his wife bought a house called Beechcroft near Botley in Hampshire large enough for an anticipated extended family. Bridget and I were married from there on 1 June 1946 and lived in a wing of it while we househunted in London for something we could afford within reasonable distance of the College. There was very little in our reach to be found; rents were controlled by law and tenants disposing of accommodation very often exacted a large premium as a consideration of transfer. We did not have that kind of money, and one day when Bridget's mother found a maisonette on the boundaries of Kensington and Fulham advertised for £200 a year, which was about our limit, it seemed too good to be true; the occupants were bound to want five times the rent as premium. But she persuaded me to court disappointment by telephoning. I was overjoyed to be mistaken. A well-spoken woman answered my call. Yes, the rent was £200 a year, no, there was no premium to pay. But there was one condition: we would have to buy a ton of coke in their cellar under the street; this would cost £15. Her husband, a very successful London surgeon, had been thinking of retiring in 1939, but had joined the R.A.M.C.;[17] now demobilized he and his wife were moving to the country and they wanted to let to young persons just out of the services. The maisonette would be available at the end of October. Of course we took it. We would manage the month somehow. We had even been lucky in getting the ton of coke which kept us snug during the bitter winter of 1946/47. And our luck held. Not many days later, in London to consult Elizabeth Sweeting about the courses I would be taking over from her, I mentioned our problem. Her face lit up; one of her friends who lived in West Hampstead had to be abroad for October and had spoken of letting her flat furnished if she could

---

17. R.A.M.C. = Royal Army Medical Corps.

find a suitable tenant. If we were interested Elizabeth would recommend us and undertake the negotiation.

This was fast and furious action over a few days. Most of the summer I had spent writing the article 'ENGLISH LITERATURE' for a children's encyclopaedia to be published by Charles Shears's firm, revising my *Beowulf*, trying to come to terms with a wretched edition of *Ancrene Riwle* and with *Gawain*, and learning to garden English style from my father-in-law the Colonel. The encyclopaedia article brought in £100, a handsome sum in those days; the teaching preparation brought home to me uncompromisingly what I had undertaken. In a very real sense I was going to learn to swim by jumping off the deep end.

What I recall most clearly of the first time I faced a class at University College in October 1946 is a sense of almost absolute isolation from the young people, expectant or merely curious, facing me. This was a very different matter from reading a paper at a table with fellow students and our teacher in a graduate seminar, which I had come to enjoy. These were strangers, finalist honours students who had studied at Aberystwyth until called up. It was quite different too, from the May morning in 1940 when then platoon sergeant, I had marched smartly from the Company Office to take over command of it. For one thing the riflemen were trained to wear wooden expressions while standing to attention; for another I knew my job, short of combat experience which these men did not have either. Moreover I knew from Winifred Husbands that Chambers, very sentimental about such matters, had talked to his students about my enduring the ordeal of a p.o.w. camp in Germany. For the soldiers I was just another officer in a regiment that traditionally treated its members well.

It would not be truthful to suggest that I enjoyed my first two or three years of teaching. The students were invariably kind and responsive, but I never ceased to be aware of my very limited acquaintance with the subjects I was teaching and of Middle English literature in general. Some fifty years later I asked Kenneth Palmer, in his second year in 1946/47, how they had been able to endure my early teaching years. His answer was doubtless true, but not very comforting for my ego: 'George, we knew even less than you did!'

University College had a very high score of firsts in the July 1947 English finals. I cannot claim the slightest credit for this, only that I never broke my resolution to answer 'I don't know' to any question where it applied. This could be embarrassing. At the faculty Christmas party in 1946 Sisson introduced me proudly to the Provost's wife as 'Our new appointment; his specialism is medieval literature'. She said, 'Splendid! Now at last I shall learn who Robin Hood actually was.' I had, of course, no notion and said so. It is a small retrospective comfort that to this day no one has.

My first and second long vacation I spent in the Main Reading Room of the British Museum. Since Middle English Literature was to be my field I was determined to read it all. Of course I did not achieve this for many years. But I did read enough to discover a culture which *Piers Plowman* and what I had so far read of Chaucer both belonged to and were sharply distinct from, as in other features these poets were distinct from the French culture where they found their models. I sensed that this was a field worth working in; I would master the language as I went. There would be no more regret for the unattempted study of the Renaissance epic. During those summers in the Round Room I took copious notes, and wrote them up, first as a course of lectures by which I recovered something of my self-confidence, and presently as the little book of lyrics, romances and *Piers Plowman* that, with some exaggeration, I called *Middle English Literature*.

As literary criticism the book is elementary and impressionist, but it seems to have caught the interest of teachers and students for it sold out two editions. To the best of my knowledge at the time it was the first book to have paid extended attention to early English writings apart from Chaucer's as of literary value in themselves, rather than sources of phonological information. I was, of course, unaware as I wrote, that I was part of a movement of reaction, and that this would in my time come to frustrate itself through losing sight of its objective. A history of all modes of writing in the degraded language of a conquered people, describing their development and assessing the products, in its own, not today's social and cultural setting, has yet to be written. I would like to have attempted such a book, but by the time I had anything like the knowledge to give me the needed scope I was otherwise committed.

Back in the 1940s it really was a matter of sink or swim: I had to learn to teach, both in classrooms and as a tutor, and how to get on with a highly individualistic set of colleagues. It was as well that Elizabeth Sweeting stayed on for my first year, and I was given a 'light load' of two courses, *Beowulf* and some prescribed Middle English text of which I recall nothing except that its glossary seemed almost designedly cryptic. *Beowulf* I could cope with as long as the class asked me no philological questions, but for the Middle English, it must have been *Ancrene Riwle*, I needed the small print entries in *O.E.D.*, and the College English Library, those few books that had gone to Aberystwyth, did not include one. As to being accepted by my colleagues, I left that to the processes of time; they would cease to be interested in me as someone 'marked by his experience' in due course.

The Department's premises on the first floor of a grim structure that ran the length of the east side of Foster Court were pretty squalid. My room was about ten feet wide and eighteen deep, with a good window at one end. The room sorely needed redecoration; the paint on the window frame was peeled and faded; its glass had evidently not been cleaned for many years. There were two tables, three or four hard chairs, and a small free-standing set of bookshelves with what I took to be Elizabeth Sweeting's books. After she had taken leave, just before the Autumn term of 1947, Bridget came up to College with me one day; we washed the window and painted its frame, which made the room feel better. With Elizabeth's departure I acquired a new roommate, Randolph Quirk, who had been appointed Assistant Lecturer upon graduation. He stayed with me only a year: the following session he moved to a room of his own, a luxury I never enjoyed at University College. Sharing a room one made a joint timetable with one's roommate, reciprocally accommodating tutorials and lectures.

In due course I found that I had learned to swim and was enjoying the 'deep end'. In 1948 I was made a lecturer with tenure. The next year I was delighted to be relieved of teaching Old English texts, which should never have been assigned to me; my colleague Hilda Hulme was much better qualified and my ego did not suffer. Moreover she became friendlier henceforth. I was allowed to offer a course named Middle English Literature. Methuens accepted my book, which came out in 1951; this was favourably reviewed in *TLS*, and dismissed in *Scrutiny* as having 'nothing in it' by John Speirs, just as much a distinction, apparently. In 1951 Sisson offered me an examinership on a University board designed to give access of more mature students to matriculation. This was strenuous. We collected the answer papers in the late afternoon of Day One, graded them overnight, and examined those candidates orally the next day. It cost sleep, but paid very well, if you could stand the pace. Moreover it was interesting to watch the scientists and historians and economists on the Board in action. Many of the candidates were Polish ex-service men with the peculiar difficulties of people born to a Slavonic language, many others young Iraqis sent to England by the Iraqi Petroleum Company. The challenge was to set a paper in which no knowledge other than of English as a language was called for. I collected much information about oriental food, the innumerable varieties of dates, the escape of the Polish army from Soviet Russia.

By this time, as I recall, the University had made me a 'recognized teacher', that is a member of the Board of Studies in English. In some ways University College had been enjoyable from the outset, the easy democracy of the Senior Common Room in particular, where an assistant lecturer might be joined for coffee after lunch by an internationally known professor of history or a 'name' from the Slade School. Within the department, regrettably, there was tension, suppressed but to be sensed, between Hugh Smith and Sisson. This may have been more apparent to me than my colleagues, for I knew that Chambers, in the past, had spoken of Hugh succeeding him in the Quain Chair, and there it was, unoccupied. How Chambers would have gone about setting Hugh there had he lived to complete his tenure I had no notion. The faculty had grown since 1945. But whatever the procedure, now with Chambers dead, the College's Professorial Board would have waited for a first move from Sisson, at least for a courteous interval. My surmise, at this distance, is that Sisson did not regard Hugh as an 'obvious' appointment. The University would require advertisement of the chair. Hugh was not yet a strong candidate on paper. He was a brilliant philologist, but had published very little and with a monster project, a comprehensive study of the common elements in English place-names in hand, was not likely to produce his great work in the next while. All this changed, however, when Sisson retired and James Sutherland succeeded him in the Northcliffe chair. Within a year Hugh was Quain Professor. Whether because, or although, Hugh and James were radically different personalities, they got on very well, probably because James was not interested in College politics and was happy to leave departmental administration to Hugh.

James was a delightful colleague, genial, even-tempered, with a fine wit and a sense of mischief. One instance of this I must record, since I set it off. We had just acquired a new colleague on the medieval side, a student of Wrenn's from King's,[18] traditionally the 'enemy' for U.C. undergraduates. During one morning coffee break he came and joined two or three of us, Randolph among them. A wicked impulse came upon me, to test him by the question that legend has it was customarily asked of every newcomer to the British school in Athens: what was his opinion of a non-existent Greek poet. The name 'Crabtree' came to me. The King's man passes the test: 'Never heard of him; what are his dates?' At this moment James appeared on the scene, sensed sport, and asked what we were laughing at. After a moment's pause his face grew very serious. 'We have a duty to see that the poet Crabtree is henceforward fittingly honoured.' This duty was fulfilled at University College by the institution of a Crabtree Foundation,[19] and an annual Crabtree Memorial Dinner at which a distinguished speaker delivered the Crabtree Memorial Lecture. I lost touch with the ritual in 1976, but was delighted, after returning to England more than a dozen years later, to see a review of the collected Crabtree Memorial Lectures in a respectable broadsheet's Sunday supplement. The reviewer, if he knew it was a spoof, did not let on.

Tutorials were the one element in my work that I enjoyed from the beginning, and even more after I had by great good fortune chanced on I. A. Richards's *Practical Criticism*. Here too I found the students responsive, and understanding when I answered a question with 'I don't know'. As the College English Library and the University Library in Senate House began to acquire stock it became possible to be confident of having the answer at the next meeting. Again by chance I picked up Robert Thouless's *Straight and Crooked Thinking* in a rummage bookstall and learned from it how to correct a potentially good essay for a student in a few sentences instead of laboriously recasting it.

University Board of Studies meetings, which I now attended, were interesting, other reasons apart, as occasions for the study of personalities. I went to my first with Hugh's counsel, 'Keep your mouth shut for a year and you'll learn how to get what you want from the Board' in mind. Better expressed it would have been

---

18. C. L. Wrenn (1895–1969) had by then moved on to become Rawlinson and Bosworth Professor of Anglo-Saxon in Oxford,

19. See < http://www.ucl.ac.uk/crabtree/officers>.

worded 'and you'll learn what you can reasonably ask for.' Another new duty was serving on the University Board of Examiners for honours finals. This paid well, but it involved a month spent in careful reading of scripts and three very taxing day-long meetings, as well as a loss of vacation research time. I was very lucky in my first year at this, in being teamed with a wonderfully proficient and wholly amiable woman, Professor Willcock of Royal Holloway College. Each read half the scripts; we then exchanged them and read the other half. At the second meeting the Board considered all grades and decided which papers must be read once more by the External Examiner from another university. I was much relieved to find that my grading was almost always accepted by Professor Willcock.

Chores seemed to multiply. In 1952 (as I remember) James became chairman of the Board of Studies. Between them he and Hugh dragooned me into being his secretary. The actual work was exacting rather than burdensome; I too had a secretary, one of a number of very efficient women on the University administrative staff assigned to Boards of Studies to ensure that their agenda went out on time and contained all the routine business dictated by the calendar, to take back-up notes at Board meetings and type the academic secretary's minutes. My problem was James whom, deep in writing the *Restoration Literature* volume for Oxford University Press, I could never manage to persuade to do his homework properly. He was nevertheless a very smooth Chairman. I would prompt him with a sotto voce sentence or two and within a minute he would set the discussion deftly on its way. It was interesting, several chairmen later, to watch Geoffrey Tillotson having to be rescued by his secretary Barbara Hardy. I could see Kathleen Tillotson's mixture of embarrassment and sympathy and was sorry for her. She knew better and flatly refused to take on the chairmanship when her turn came.

It was not long before I was put to another chore when London University lent its lecture halls in Senate House to an international congress of linguisticians. One of its organizers was the Professor of German at King's, Frederic Norman, a friend of Hugh's. Norman was complaining to Hugh that, because attendance was proving to be unexpectedly large, the conference secretary, albeit erudite in ancient Indo-European philology, was quite unable to cope and was swamped with unanswered letters, in fact had thrown up his hands. What should Norman do? Who would take over? I have never fathomed what prompted Hugh's answer, 'Get George Kane to take over.' Of course I declined. I had a large programme of work that vacation; I could not afford the time; linguistics were not my line. Hugh exerted pressure: 'You can't afford to refuse.' It occurred to me to make impossible conditions: I would need my own telephone line in College, two secretaries during the run-up to clear the correspondence pile, the same two at the conference administrative table, two telephones there, and petty cash for unforeseen taxi errands. To my dismay Norman accepted these terms. The School of Oriental and African Studies provided two proficient, and moreover decorative, secretaries;

between us we cleared a really huge backlog of correspondence in a couple of days, and I continued friends with the overworked College switchboard. At the actual conference we coped with a range of crises ranging from loss of luggage to an emergency hospitalization. I suppose it cost me eight days at my own desk.

By now I was comfortable with teaching. These students, many of whom had had to do national service after the war, were no longer intent only on examination success like the ones 'back from the war', many with a wife and child. This new lot was more challenging, more critical, and at the same time more responsive. I had mastered the Middle English of the *Gawain* poet and the *Ancrene Riwle* and the crabbed syntax of Mannyng's *Handlyng Synne*, and I had even tempted some students to range beyond the set texts with synopses of the tales in *The Seven Sages of Rome*. Dillon's University Bookstore,[20] by now well stocked — a stone's throw from the Department — and the Senate House library under John Pafford's direction growing by the day were easier to use than the British Museum Library, where one might still have to wait an hour for a book.

In 1953 the University made me a Reader. Since the favourable reception of my book Hugh had occasionally mentioned 'putting me up' for the promotion when I was 'ready.' Of course promotion was desirable for a variety of reasons, but I fought off letting it become a preoccupation with the reflection that the University Board of Appointments and Promotions might well find a couple of lightweight articles and a single book insufficient ground for elevating me to its upper level of academic status. Typically of Hugh, he did not tell me when College did put me up or when the Board would meet. But on that day he and James looked in on me and said 'We are just off to sit on your Readership. We shan't be long.' Luckily the tutorial essays I was reading were clever and interesting and so did not need much concentration to grade. And the meeting did actually not take long.

Of the rest of that I day I can recall only a sense of relief. Hugh must have had an engagement, for he did not keep me at his pub, the Marlborough Arms, beyond the ceremonial pint, and I was home early enough to read *The Hobbit* to my two children of three and five before they were put to bed, and then sit quietly with my wife beside me and a drink in my hand savouring the relief and the thought that I had learned to swim almost anywhere.

There would be money, now at last, to buy the books I badly needed, of which the first was the *OED*, second-hand, of course. For this Dillon's would be no help, but in Store Street there was an International University Bookstore, managed by a quietly efficient Dutch bibliophile named Jan Bijl, set up in business by a wealthy biscuit-manufacturing uncle in Holland. He could not recall a second-hand *OED* on the market in his time, but undertook to look out for a set. My luck was in: within weeks he had found one, moreover of the 1933 edition, which he let me

20. Dillon's, Dillon's University Bookshop Ltd from 1956, is now a Waterstones' bookshop.

have absurdly cheap. This was a time, too, when one put one's name down for the *Middle English Dictionary*, and I sealed my commitment to that language and celebrated my promotion by becoming a subscriber.

About this time I began to find students interesting rather than formidable. Postgraduates were straightforward; the good ones needed only guidance. My pride was Stanley Hussey who produced with more encouragement than direction a survey of *Piers Plowman* scholarship. A masterpiece of its kind, it would be a standard work had he published it. The undergraduate honours students afforded a different sort of interest. Each year, between thirty and thirty-five strong, developed its distinctive character, generally imprinted by a few personalities that stood out for one or another reason. The serious students, from good nature or so as not to waste time on unessentials, tended to let them have their way up to a point, but could exert influence if they took a stand. And most 'years' had a misfit or two. Often the only problem of these latter was that when enrolling they had not appreciated the heavy language component of the London honours syllabus of those days. One tried to help them but they could make difficulties.

In one of my *Gawain* classes there were two men like that who more often than not came to class unprepared and so shirked translating when called on, which I had found a necessary part of teaching that poem. At length we reached a point where I judged that this had to be stopped, and told them that if they failed me another time I would exclude them from the class. The day came; first the one and presently the other, when called upon stated without excuse or evident embarrassment that he was not prepared. This was a challenge I could not refuse. The other students were absolutely motionless; there was no shuffling of paper or moving of feet. My standing with them, I realized, was at stake. So I addressed the two men quietly: 'Please leave the room.' They assumed wooden expressions and continued to sit at their desks. Some instinct told me to wait this out; I closed my *Gawain*, left the lectern desk, and went to a window where, by happy accident, there was a fine November morning to admire. The room was absolutely quiet. After what seemed like an age there were shuffling noises, the sounds of footsteps on the bare floor and of a door closing. It was probably my imagination that made me feel a sense of approval. More likely that the other students had mutely signalled to the two to leave. The two men neither came to see me afterwards nor complained to their tutors; they turned up the next time the class met and when in due course I asked them to translate they had prepared. Indeed their grades on the Middle English Texts finals paper — I was an examiner — were not discreditable. I was lucky that day.

Of some students I could be proud. One such whom I tutored was John Dodgson, a man with many friends drawn to his exceptionally agreeable personality. I found him a competent rather than brilliant student: he would have agreed. So I was surprised when, during the autumn term of his final year, the quality of his work fell off. At our last meeting before the Christmas break I asked him bluntly why, and the answer, which I should have deduced from occasional remarks, was that he rowed stroke oar in the University of London eight and that during the vacation a championship would be decided, in Holland, as I recall. He readily acknowledged that he had neglected his work and was sorry not to have done better. It was hard to know what to say to the excuse which by Student Union values was good. To gain time I counted off the number of weeks between the beginning of the Eastern term and finals. Then I asked him what he had read during the term just ending aside from the set texts; as I expected the answer was almost nothing. All I could say was, 'John, go win your race and when you come back in January remember that you have less than five months to do a year's work in.' As for John, he cannot have slept much during that Lent term, for in finals he achieved a very creditable upper second honours degree. After graduation Hugh Smith kept him on as a departmental assistant; in due course he became Secretary to the English Place Name Society, and after Hugh's death he was made President with a titular professorship.

David Lodge I can claim no credit for, not having been his tutor, but I was sufficiently involved in his student life to read with interest recent reviews in praise of his biographical novel about Henry James. David was not, as I recall, especially interested in the medieval side of his course, although he did its required work conscientiously enough. His earlier novels I found no more than mildly amusing, but those reflecting the postmodernist trend in the English-speaking world showed his real quality, and I believe I know who was the model for his egregious Professor Zapp. The student context in which I recall him is to his credit. I had occasionally noticed a student whom I tutored named Mary Jacobs in his company, a young woman as intelligent as she was good to look at. A time came in her final year when her tutorial essays began to seem less thoughtful, less well put together than usual, and while on principle I studiously avoided getting involved in women students' lives outside the study of literature, the time came when I was anxious about her work. I had to tell her this; I can recall my language which may not have been as gentle as it should: 'Miss Jacobs, I would not have expected an essay like this one from you.' She burst into tears. My handkerchief was no longer folded, and in those days one did not keep a box of tissues in a desk drawer. So I said, 'Why don't you go and wash your face and come back when you feel better.' 'Please,' she pleaded, 'Don't send me out there looking like this.' When she had rallied we went over the essay, and as she left the room I thought the matter concluded. From then on, however, during all her tutorials, I thought I heard in the corridor outside a sound as of a patroling sentry or policeman on his beat, a plodding heavy footstep; the floor was uncarpeted wood. One day I asked her if she could hear it. 'Oh, that's David waiting for me'. Well, they are still married as I write in 2004. As a successful novelist and sanely balanced literary critic David has been a force for good in the English-speaking universities of the world.

In the late forties and the fifties University College was a good place to begin a career. Its English department was large enough to ensure a considerable variety of personalities among its staff, and attracted student applicants of high quality. In its Senior Common Room and on social occasions as for instance the Professors' Dining Club, academic rank was ignored. My two professors attracted interesting visitors from universities in the UK and abroad. A junior teacher could propose someone from abroad in his own field as a 'Visiting Professor'; such an invitation as good as ensured the American nominee of a Marshal or Guggenheim fellowship. So I had Morton Bloomfield and Donaldson as rewarding colleagues. Hugh Smith, who before the war had spent a year in Uppsala, had a succession of more senior Swedish visitors, some of them highly congenial and interesting, attracted by his place-name studies. One of them, Dag Strøhmbek, with Hugh's support offered me a place there, family and all, with a handsome honorarium, but there was a catch. A notable folk-lorist, Dag was as good as recruiting me to specialize in that subject. Sweden attracted me, becoming a folk-lorist did not.

Being near the centre of things can be gratifying, and I suppose I was experiencing such gratification in 1953, as well as enjoying the absence of the stress that had driven me in the earlier postwar years. That is probably why, when Hugh and James — the combination was always a little ominous — came to me with the news that Royal Holloway College would be advertising for its departmental chair of English and that I must apply for it. I said I was not interested; I was happy where I was. The chair was vacant upon the retirement of the Professor Willcock with whom I had examined a final honours paper not long ago.

Royal Holloway, founded in the late nineteenth century as a college for young gentlewomen, was an architectural gem, a superbly executed imitation of a chateau in the best baroque, set in its own park about a mile south of Egham in Surrey. Bridget and I had been there once, in the summer of 1947, invited by its Principal, Dr Edith Batho, whom I had known before the war as one of Chambers's staff at University College. But I did not want to move and said so. Hugh and James between them could exert considerable influence, and did so to the point where I thought they might be wanting to get rid of me, so I capitulated and put in an application, tiny list of publications and all. As I recall I did not take much trouble preparing my c.v., and I put James and Hugh down as my references without consulting them.

I do not recall being especially pleased when I received a letter from the Academic Secretary calling me before the University Board for interview. In long retrospect that seems remarkably perverse; of course I would have been very dashed not to be shortlisted. My interview was quite brief and Dr Batho, the only member of the Board whose face I knew, asked me the only difficult question: would I be

Royal Holloway College.

able to give a course of lectures on sixteenth- and seventeenth-century poetry? There was only one possible answer: I had never taught one, but I reckoned I could learn. I came away with a strong impression that the Board was not much interested in me, and regretting that by letting myself be talked into applying I had exposed myself to disappointment. The man who followed me — we had exchanged names — was called Kermode. There was all the rest of the alphabet to come! So I was relieved when I received a letter of appointment from the Academic Secretary, to commence in October 1955. Meanwhile I taught for the best part of three terms at University College as if nothing had happened.

Not much later I had a letter from its Convenor, Professor C. L. Wrenn, to a Congress of the Association of University Professors of English in Paris that November. This puzzled me, both by the short notice and because I was neither a professor nor a member of the Association, until I recalled that there was to be a general strike of French railway employees; attendance already registered must have fallen off. Hugh and James, again, advised me to go; College would fund me. It was only three or four days, and I had loved what little I saw of Paris in 1938 and in 1945. Moreover there was a bonus. Hugh Smith, having built two replicas of Moxon's seventeenth-century printing press, one before the war and the other to replace it, was planning a book on early presses of the time and wanted photographs of pictures in European books to be found in the Bibliothèque nationale and that of l'Arsenal, and libraries in Amsterdam, Utrecht and Haarlem in Holland. I could play truant from the congress one afternoon to order those in Paris and then fly on to Amsterdam, which would be my base for ordering the photographs in the other Dutch libraries.

The Congress took place in the Cité universitaire, and I learned to use the Métro in the course of my visits to the Paris libraries. In the Bibliothèque nationale I was, so to speak, policed while I looked up my illustrations to be photographed, but in the Bibliothèque de l'Arsenal procedure was genial, as if the staff seemed glad of something to break the monotony of their day.

At the Congress, which I found heavy going, I made the acquaintance of Piet Harting, the professor of English at the Amsterdam Staats Universiteit, and we flew to that city together. The flight was direct, and Dutch Customs and Immigration formalities were dealt with on the plane soon after takeoff. I was surprised to find that from the moment I showed my Canadian passport the stewardesses made a fuss over me. This was, Harting explained, because it was the Canadians who had liberated Holland in 1944/45. Harting was very helpful about a hotel and my three library visits. These went smoothly, again at different tempos in quite different settings. Next morning I went first to Amsterdam where everything was smooth and efficient, then on to Utrecht, the farthest afield. Here people managed to combine civility with the bureaucracy proper to that city. But finding my books took longer accordingly and it must have been late afternoon when I got off the train at Haarlem. Until that moment I had not met anyone who did not speak English, but on the station platform at Haarlem not one person did. Very foolishly I switched to German. The answer, in Dutch, did not sound friendly, and within minutes there were a dozen people around me with scowling faces, and a huge man in uniform wearing a sabre, a policeman evidently, who looked anything but friendly. By that time I had come to my senses; I reached for my passport and said, still in German, 'You can see that I am not German.' The scowls became smiles, and I was escorted almost ceremonially to the municipal library, where, I was relieved to find, the staff spoke English.

There was one more uncomfortable moment in store for me that trip. My return flight next morning was to the City of London Airport in a two-engine low wing plane with about forty seats, most of them unoccupied. Because I like to see where I am going I made my way to the front of the plane with a good view forward and to one side. There was disappointingly little to see on the flight; the excitement came when we landed. 'Touchdown' was not the word for the process on this occasion. By some error the pilot put us down too fast and too abruptly. We must have bounced four feet, and as we rose I was horrified to see the tyre of the wheel in front of me, as distorted as a squeezed balloon. I had a second's vision of us coming down on a flat tyre and slithering askew. But by the next second, the tyre had resumed its shape and this time we bounced no more than a couple of feet, after which we taxied sedately to a stop.

In due course Hugh Smith received his photographs, but to the best of my knowledge the book was never written.

My last term at University College ended with a farewell party given after finals by the students of the English Department for two of their teachers, Terence Spencer and myself. Terence, pretty well the same age as me, a product of King's College, was one of Sisson's last appointments, made some time before his retirement, to teach Shakespeare. He was very versatile, moreover something of a Hellenist who, able to speak Modern Greek, had spent his war in an Army Intelligence office in Alexandria. We got on pretty well; he was a fine raconteur, enjoyable company. I secretly relished having a slight edge over him: although he was appointed to a lectureship I had been elevated to that grade a few days before that appointment. And he had lost interest in his PhD thesis subject and found it hard to finish. But at length he had managed this, and was going to a professorship at Warwick University. At our farewell party the English School had invited us to a picnic on a Thames steamer cruise. There was a catch: they also invited each of us to give a formal public lecture before we set out for the Westminster piers. There was no option: like the lion in the Colosseum we must pay for our meal. I was not greatly perturbed by the requirement: in my desk drawer at home I had a half-finished article on *The Miller's Tale* as a comedy that conformed to the definitions and models of the eighteenth century, and I would write it up without a single 'bad word' in my text. Terence lectured first being my junior; I do not recall his subject, only that it was learned and a little dull. The students seemed to like mine, speculating that its delicate euphemisms might refer to a book filled with Shakespeare's bawdy being written by Hilda Hulme, a sedate modern lady colleague of about my age.[21] I never got round to publishing that article, which years later was virtually replicated except for the euphemisms, by Charles Muscatine in one of his excellent Chaucer books.

The entertainment on the river boat was lavish; I have often wondered whether James and Hugh, who pleaded other engagements, did not help to fund it; students are traditionally thought of as hard up. It was a remarkably enjoyable occasion even though I had to pay twice: toward the end someone mischievously set afoot a clamour for me to sing. I have no gift for this but the pressure was extreme; I managed to get away with chanting the dirge about the 'Old Woman Who Swallowed a Fly'. They had drunk enough beer by that time to applaud.

A cruel feature of life as one grows older is the loss of friends; a time comes when the subjects of broadsheet obituaries begin to seem shockingly young. All

---

21. Hilda M. Hulme, *Explorations in Shakespeare's language: some problems of word meaning in the dramatic text* (London: Longman, 1962); the phrase 'Shakespeare's bawdy' was popularized by Eric Partridge.

George Kane with Hugh Smith.

my senior colleagues, and too many of my contemporaries at UCL are gone. Hugh Smith I lost early; he died suddenly in his beloved Uppsala. James lasted longer; there was time enough for me to take him for a day's fishing on the Wiltshire Avon, where he outfished me with both larger and more trout. And another time, when he was older he came to Beaconsfield where we lived then and I drove him up to London for an Academy dinner. We were back home by 11:00, but he was a fabulous raconteur, and we did not turn in until 4:00. Breakfast was late that morning.

15
ROYAL HOLLOWAY COLLEGE 1955–1965

In a strict sense the chapter heading is not applicable, for it does not immediately correspond to the changes in the life of my family and myself. This apparent discrepancy reflects my concentration, in the preceding section, on learning the trade after seven years absence from academe. I shall put that right now with family doings and an account of how, at University College, I acquired a commitment that would as good as prescribe my scholarly activity for many years.

The first exciting change came about in summer 1951 when a great stroke of luck enabled us to move into a 1700 square foot flat in a stately Edwardian block on Battersea Park Road named York Mansions with controlled rent, a room for each child (one serviceable as a playroom by day), even a guest room, partial central heating, and the lovely park across the street. We learned of it by chance from Ronnie Swayne, a managerial trainee for an international shipping firm which had housed him and his family there during the first stage of his course. At dinner there he told us what we could not conceivably have known otherwise, the name of the owners of the flat and their letting agent's telephone number.

I called the agent the next day. He was civil but brusque: the waiting list was yards long and it would be pointless of me to nurse any expectation of a letting. However I managed at length to persuade him to put my name down; when he finally gave in he added 'Expect nothing!'. Nevertheless about a year later when by further good fortune I was working at home he called. There was a flat vacant and for rent on the fourth floor; it was not in good condition. If I wanted it I must take it as it was. I could see it immediately; the caretaker-manager, Mr Estcourt, would show me over. Here was his phone number. It was a long taxi-ride from Fulham but I was there within the hour.

Mr Estcourt, a retired naval petty officer, told me the story of the flat as he showed me over it. It had had the same occupant since the Mansions were built, a young man who brought his bride there. When in due course she died he stayed on, never remarried, and withdrew as a recluse from the world and indeed his family. When after his death his kinfolk came to remove his belongings there was crested china encrusted with the dirt of ages, corroded silver; the rooms were dark with cobwebs as thick as curtains, the carpets had to be taken up with spades. It needed intensive professional cleaning when I saw it, and complete redecoration.

I had neither the skills nor the time to undertake making it liveable, and told Mr Estcourt this, adding that to have the work done professionally was likely to be beyond my resources. He came to my rescue: he knew of two reliable young men who could do such work. How much was I able to spend? As it happened I had just been paid £200 for a bout of examining and named that figure. Mr Estcourt undertook to find out what that would buy. Next day he reported that for that sum they could clean professionally throughout and redecorate as far as the money stretched.

Even a short spell in the services teaches a man to recognise a good n.c.o. (called 'petty officer' in the Navy). Mr Estcourt seemed one such; as for the two young men I surmised that they were demobilized naval ratings setting themselves up as painters and decorators. I would take the chance: the sheer size of the flat, room for the children and for me to work at home, and of course the lovely park, were too good to miss. The young men also proved good and true. It took time, but when they finished the flat was as clean as one could wish, and decorated but for the spare room. We were installed by the beginning of the autumn term and lived there until the summer of 1956.

Luckily the kitchen was big enough for family meals and the dining room was big enough to take my large desk in the window, bookshelves along one wall, and a massive trolley with my *OED* and a slowly growing stack of *MED* fascicles, and still leave room for a table big enough to have people to dinner. For I was by now committed to editing *Piers*. I have not described how this came about in 'The Deep End' (Chapter 14), largely because it developed while, during my time at U.C.L., my immediate preoccupation was to reorientate myself in the academic world. Once I began to teach, and then to write the Middle English literature book, there was no time to think about editing. That was the case until well into 1947 when the book was with the publisher, waiting out the postwar paper shortage.

I knew what I wanted to write next, a book of deeper penetration and broader scope on the same subject, but I also knew that I was not ready to do it justice. In the Department I was not under pressure to publish, but I sensed that I was generally thought to be 'working on *Piers Plowman*'. The only creditable way of correcting that notion was to show by results that I was 'working on' something else, which with my inclination would take unduly long. I was 38 years old and very much aware of the time lost in the army. So I decided to finish editing the B text. That would not take too long; increasing familiarity with the poem would be a teaching, and later, a writing asset, and my duty to the memory of Chambers, if I had one, would be fulfilled. The A text was, after all, Grattan's problem, and from reports Mitchell was active and making progress with C. It looked like a safely limited commitment.

At the outset everything seemed straightforward. The College Secretary, who had known both Chambers and Grattan, made over the B photostats to me. The obliging stationers in the City had survived the War. My British Museum passes to the Library and the Manuscript room were cheerfully renewed. I set about collating the B Prologue–Passus X with Grattan's A text in mind; he would need exact information about the B manuscripts if not for any other reason than to establish the shape of the A form of the poem in the first instance.

Except for the absence of physical hazard, collation was like tunnelling in that a man's sense of progress, if he paused to think, was slow. But unlike tunnelling in good soil it was never monotonous: its diversity lay in the response by scribes to the text as it passed through their heads and hand. 'Experts' in the theory of textual criticisms with no experience of large-scale collation have pooh-poohed what they call the 'profiling' of scribes, which I take to mean identification of patterns of individual idiosyncrasies of unconscious or subconsciously induced and deliberate substitution. They have obviously not experienced identifying a change of scribe in the exemplar of their immediate copyist. I admit to having enjoyed collation at that stage. There was time for it in the long summer vacations, and during term time on Wednesdays except when it was my turn to give a course of intercollegiate lectures.

Once underway I could fairly approach medievalist colleagues in the Modern Language departments about 'further reading' on textual criticisms in the fields; I came away from French with Fourquet's work as a corrective to Bédier, from Italian with Pasquali's *Storia*, from German with Maas, and as a bonus, direction to *Der Akermann aus Böhmen*. By midsummer 1947 I had finished transcribing my basic manuscript of the B text for Prologue–Passus X and collated enough of the B copies to make it clear that I would need the text of A to edit B. For that A text I assumed I could depend on Grattan who, to go by his having published an important article in January, appeared still active, though none of his contemporaries at College had heard from him for years. I knew Chambers had told him of 'recruiting' me, and now I had something to offer in return for access to his A materials.

Luckily Hugh Smith was not shy about approaching him, and after an exchange of letters the two of us called on him (he was lately retired) at his house in Liverpool. His housekeeper served tea and sweet biscuits, and the visit was a success in eliciting a suggestion from him that I should spend a couple of days as a guest of his in his University in one of the nearby campus halls of residence to enable the two of us to discuss the editing situation at leisure, which I did in the last week of the long vacation.

Grattan did not conceal the fact that he had never made substantial progress with his edition of A, which had begun as a collaborative project with Chambers and indeed been so announced. That information confronted me with a decision that could be neither escaped nor, indeed, deferred. For to edit the second form

of *Piers* I needed full information about the first form, of which it was clearly a
revision.

Grattan and Chambers had, by and large, collated separate sections of the
poem, but apparently not throughout: each had collated some manuscripts on
one base text and others on a second. Grattan admitted that he could not always
be confident, in his own papers, which manuscript a particular variant came
from. It was quite plain from such work as I saw in his possession that to get the
information I needed I would have to help Grattan edit the A poem. That was
one option; the other was to give up the editing of B. For a mixture of reasons
I chose the former option. One was probably obstinacy, having put my hand to
the plough, etc., another doubtless vanity, a wish not to be seen as a 'quitter'. But
in candour I must, I suppose, have become intellectually engaged in this poem,
which stood out monumentally among other Middle English alliterative writing,
in itself and as a major literary work of art in process of growth. The price has
been high, thirty-five years of preoccupation at the expense of time that would
otherwise have gone to more lively and exciting literary engagement.

Grattan was delighted, indeed openly relieved when, having made my decision, I asked him whether he would like me to help him complete the editing of A,
but cautioned that he 'would not be free to resume work on it until after Christmas'. He was in fact seeing his important article on coincident variation, which he
called 'the substitution of similars' through the press. But he never did get back
to editing as such; his last activity to do with the edition was to arrange a loan
of a photograph of the Chaderton manuscript of *Piers* to me by his University's
Librarian.

Within days of returning to London I had a letter from the College Secretary
authorizing my access to the Chambers papers in its archives. There was much
more here than Grattan had shown me. My session 1947–48 was very full, and
I did not have time to assess the extent of Chambers's progress until the spring
term. I sent Grattan a detailed report on Chambers's *Piers Plowman* papers on 7
June 1948; I have a carbon copy in my files.

It contained, for a start, a large folder labelled 'Introduction to PPL I–IV' of
undigested notes, by no means all relevant to editing. Then, I quote my letter,
'Text and apparatus in various stages of finality...for Prologue to Passus VII', then
'Collations...for the remainder of the work...in various stages of completion.' Of
this material three copies were collated on a base of R(awlinson), the remainder
with three exceptions, were collated on T(rinity), but not systematically or indeed
completely. There were no collations from the three exceptions. After outlining
my notions of what would have to be done I put it to Grattan that making this
material serviceable would not be much quicker than recollating from the outset,
and that if he accepted this I would undertake that recollation. I have no copy of
a reply to that proposal and no recall of having received one. In one of his 1947

letters he had written, 'I speedily get tired. Probably I need a complete change; I have not had a holiday since 1936(!).'

I found him easy to like, and wish I had got to know him better. It was impossible not to respect his candid self-criticism; in wry mockery of his failure to get on with Chambers's project he told me why there are so many books with some title like *Geschichte der englischen Sprache: Lautlehre* with no *Zweiter Bandt*. In fact the notion of doing no more research once you have your chair did not apply in his case, for his time as professor on the medieval side went in maintaining a philological element in a department where the dominant professorship and accordingly appointments were aggressively literary. It was still strong in Liverpool in the 60s when I was external examiner there; I recall James Cross complaining that under Kenneth Muir the language side was very much the poor relation. Grattan died in 1951, before I could show him any of my work on A.

For in the absence of word from him I had decided to recollate rather than attempt to introduce system into the information Chambers and Grattan had left, and before I undertook that, to finish collation and checking B Prologue–Passus X. When at length I began editing A it seemed to offer more of a challenge than B. For a start, what actually constituted the A form? Of the copies Skeat had classified as such, four consisted of a prologue and eleven passus, three of a prologue and twelve, this last at best only partly authorial, two of a prologue and eight, one of a prologue and seven, the last passus incomplete, five of a prologue and eleven with a conclusion from Skeat's C version attached, one of a prologue and eight passus similarly concluded, and one of A V 106–XI attached to B Prologue–V 105. I found Skeat right beyond question in identifying these as more or less complete copies of an ancestor with a prologue and eleven passus. His argument was simple. Where the shorter copies were represented they exhibited the same treatment of key topics or developments of narrative as the copies with eleven passus. Moreover in the copies ending with Passus VI and VIII the discourse at the end is broken, interrupted; at the end of XI it comes to a crisis point that can be read as terminal.

There was an eighteenth copy of the short form of *Piers* in MS Bodley 851 consisting of a prologue, seven passus and 88 lines added in a somewhat later hand, and CX–XXII added to all this in a third hand of similar date. Skeat in his 1888 survey of the *Piers Plowman* copies had dismissed the A content of Bodley 851 as 'written from recollection'. To me it looked more like an attempt to restore a defective unbound copy of A from memory by a scribe who had copied A and copied or read B and C. The text in the first hand differs markedly from that in all other A copies in organization and formal division of content, in lacking some 300 lines of content, in reading some 200 lines peculiar to itself, and in the presence throughout to A VIII 88, of single B or B/C lines and readings. To go by his contributions the restorer's response to the poems was enthusiastic rather than sensitive. His voluble, sometimes grammatically incoherent additions stand out starkly by the crudity of their style. His memory served him best in pastiche, as in a vehement twenty-nine lines at the end of an incomplete Passus III. Ironically this addition registers both his acquaintance with the last passus of the longer form of the poem and his crass misunderstanding of it.

It seemed to me beyond question that Skeat's assessment of that text of A in Bodley 851 as of no use for recovering the ancestor of the surviving manuscripts was correct. Between them the evident circumstance that it was at least in part a reconstruct from memory, and the density of its contamination from the longer, later versions, reduced its value as a 'witness'. I decided not to take it into account or to include its variant readings in my critical apparatus. I am still confident after fifty years that this was the right course. But I ought to have stated the omission with my reasons for it in the edition; I can only plead ignorance of editorial protocol at the time. It did not cross my mind that anyone at all well acquainted with the *Piers* poem could seriously propose that the sorry A text in MS Bodley 851 was an early form of the poem.

How I set about editing A is described in detail in my Introduction, not — I will say — as a manual of textual criticism but to account for my results. It will be seen that the character of the A tradition dictated my objective. What the Introduction does not tell is the variety of skills I had to master in the process. There were new hands from a century and a half and more of copying, and almost a similar range of Middle English dialects from various regions. I would be expected to date the manuscripts, that is to say, the hands. If aids existed to do that — this was well before the rise of Ian Doyle and Malcolm Parkes to authority — I did not, with the exception of Richard Hunt, find them, and I could not in conscience plague him unduly. Neil Ker professed ignorance of vernacular usage, as did Francis Wormald. As for the copies on paper, those of which the watermarks had been dated afforded a *terminus a quo*; in the other instances I had no option but to describe the watermark and plead ignorance. As to codicology, I had learned a little about the structure of books as forced labour during Hugh Smith's printing on the Moxon hand-press that he had built to replace the one destroyed when the College was firebombed. And after all that there was attempting to establish the provenance of the copies; this was an exciting game in itself, but as Kenneth Sisam pointed out to my publishers, to print anything other than definitive results of searches was an expensive extravagance.

The staff of University College's English Department was large and my teaching and tutorial duties accordingly light. By the summer of 1951 I was deep into editing the A version. Collation and the first check were completed. It was already looking likely, from manuscript grouping of agreement in manifest error, that recovering the family history, that is the line of descent, of the surviving copies would not be possible. This proved to be the case; recension as a system of determining the text was 'out'. As a compensation, however, the undebatable scribal errors were proving remarkably similar in character to those in the patterns identified and handed down by classical editors over the centuries. As to the text confidently restorable with that information and the application of Maas's *discriminatio,* at best this would be the text from which the surviving copies were immediately descended, their exclusive common ancestor. And taking account of the date of the earliest of the surviving copies, this would be at least a generation removed from the *ipsissima verba auctoris.* Anything beyond that would be conjecturable and assessable as such.

By now I was deeply involved. I was finding this exciting in the immediate sense, but from a longer perspective, bleak. I would, for one thing, eventually have to type it all, text, apparatus, introduction, notes; then there would be proof-reading of a book consisting almost wholly of detail, set in monotype, more often than once, no doubt. I knew of no-one whom I could ask for help. And when all that was done there was B to edit, which I was aware, after reading and digesting, was a much more complex operation. I suppose that if I had applied for a grant to employ an assistant to finish the collation of B I might well have been successful, but I sensed that what I needed was more, in fact a collaborator, a co-editor.

Morton Bloomfield came to mind, but when I raised the possibility with him his answer, albeit sympathetic and understanding, was clear: he did not see himself as an editor. He named Talbot Donaldson at Yale as a possibility; an agreeable personality as well as the fine scholar his book on the C text had shown him to be. Indeed Morton went so far as to arrange a meeting over lunch when I passed through New York in September 1950 on my way to a month's immersion in the files of the *Middle English Dictionary.* We three hit it off immediately, and when Morton, still at Ohio State, had to leave, Talbot and I talked through the afternoon and dinner, from which I came away with an invitation to visit him at New Haven on my way back to England. To that end I sacrificed a day with the *Dictionary* files and in return acquired a collaborator as well as a lifelong friend. On the strength of his book he had applied or was about to apply for a Guggenheim Fellowship; with the collaboration as a further item in his c.v. He was sure of and in due course received the award. He had never worked with manuscripts before; his induction would be to collate and check B Passus XI–XVII under my eye. But before that we collaborated in decorating that spare room at York Mansions.

He was a quick, apt pupil and made good progress with the collation during that leave. But on his return to New Haven his career and his university took most of his time. To assure his promotion to associate professor he wrote, on the strength of the year's collation, a substantial paper on the status of the two B copies which constituted one branch of the bifid stemma of the B manuscript tradition; from 1953–57 and 1958–63 he was Director of Graduate Studies in English at Yale; and during the first of those periods he produced two excellent student

Talbot Donaldson.

texts, a translation of *Beowulf* and a Chaucer anthology. But on the credit side, during summer vacation he would come to England and stay with us for at least a couple of weeks for discussion, of which I kept detailed notes. I found him in every sense a reasonable man. We never once fell out in more than thirty years of association, and in a sense collaborated until the end; even in his final illness he would not publish his *Piers Plowman* translation until I had read it to the very last line.

As it turned out, our timing was neatly matched. In February 1956 the Board of Athlone accepted my A text for publication as submitted, giving me discretion with respect to a suggestion by Dr Sisam, that the descriptions of manuscripts might be reduced by omission of detail in the matter of provenance.[22] He was right, of course; hunting down manuscript survival history is good sport, but printing accounts of inconclusive searches is an extravagance. At the same meeting the Board recommended inviting me to become General Editor of what had, without deliberate promotion by me, assumed the character of a 'project'. It was still the day of monotype for books of this sort. Here I was lucky in the Assistant Secretary of the Press, Arnold Dewey, who saw the edition of A through the pitfalls of 'old language' printing over the years with meticulous efficiency, through a printers' strike and one near-calamitous occasion when a junior print-setter was given critical apparatus to set up. The stress was Dewey's; I merely read and checked and rechecked galleys and page proofs as they were put into my hands. He had his laurels in due course when the A edition was a prize-winner at the Leipzig Book Fair. I was still checking, for the second time, page proofs of the critical apparatus during Donaldson's presence as a visiting Professor at Royal Holloway in 1957–1958; I put him back to work at collating B, while, in spare time, I checked away at A.

Almost as if by accident, it was not my teaching that made undue demands on *Piers*. I first formally met my new departmental colleagues there, not long after my actual appointment, at tea one September afternoon in 1954. I had scarcely balanced my cup and saucer safely when Miss Green, one of the two older women, said, 'Well Dr Kane, we are waiting to know what you propose to do with us.' The wording is engraven deep on my memory. Taken aback I said the first thing that came into my head, 'I have no plans to make changes.' This assured the ladies, as, evidently, did my pleasure in the list of Professor Willcock's courses which I inherited, Middle English except Chaucer and — this was new — English verse from Skelton to Herrick, a vastly explorable two-year course. There were good Middle English college texts by this time, and the sixteenth and earlier seventeenth century offered an opportunity I had longed for. As Head of Department I would tutor the finalists, usually ten to a dozen of them. Customarily the Department met for tea at 11:00 Thursday in the study of one of my colleagues; this was the occasion

22. The Athlone Press, founded in 1948 as the press of the University of London.

'The Good Queen'.

Founder's Building, North Quadrangle, Royal Holloway, University of London.

for discussing individual students' learning difficulties, not to mention Board of Studies issues. Conforming to the existing practices seemed to pay off: our proportion of first and upper second honours degrees continued to be high.

As long as we lived in London I made good progress with *Piers* A. But after the move to Englefield Green a Board of Studies meeting or session with Arnold Dewey at Athlone meant no *Piers Plowman* that afternoon; the Egham trains did not lend themselves to close work. In College there were the Academic Board meetings unquestionably important and not designed for speed; discussion was interrupted by the arrival of tea and biscuits. The College was that kind of place. My study could have passed for a middle-class sitting room except that it looked out on a baroque quadrangle dominated by a statue of the Good Queen. There was a sofa under the window, a good rug on the floor. My furniture was a table, not a desk; bookshelves ran along one side of the room.

Next door a smaller room, sparsely furnished with a table that would hold a coffee urn in one corner every weekday morning at 11:00, was a place of assembly for the male faculty. Tradition had it that the room's real function was to accommodate the royal patroness's chauffeur, originally coachman, of course,

on the ceremonial occasions of her visits. I found my colleagues lively and interesting and made a point of never missing morning coffee — except, of course, on
Thursdays.

I recall particularly Hugh Tredennick the Professor of Greek, for his wit paradoxically but evidently sharpened by having edited Aristotle's *Metaphysics, Prior
and Posterior Analytics*, not to mention translated Plato's *Last Days of Socrates* for
Penguin. Robert Latham, the Reader in History, was deep in annotation of what
was to prove the definitive decipherment of Pepys's *Diaries*. For the sentimental
there was Allan Cunningham his young colleague, a specialist in Turco-Byzan-
tine history, who had recently come back from leading a climbing expedition in
the Colombian Andes. Regrettably our science colleagues, whose departments
were housed in new buildings some hundreds of yard north of the original College, usually turned up only when they wanted to discuss or sound us out about
College business.

Then there was High Table in the Great Hall. I was taken there on the first day
of my first term, introduced all around and given to understand that I would be
expected to lunch there whenever I was in College, by my Reader, Dr Joyce Tompkins. This was no hardship; the menu was not elaborate but Cook knew her job.
As for the conversation, it was invariably interesting and the range of topics was
wide. It embarrasses me to recall how radically I had to change my original notions of teaching in a women's college. Certainly the intellectual calibre of my colleagues in Egham matched that of any university in my experience.

After lunch, unless people had an early meeting in London, they resorted to
the Senior Common Room. Like that of University College this had a sense of vitality, but it differed markedly in its expression. The decor was agreeably femi-
nine, chintzy in the best taste, and the room had been designed with windows
that caught the midday sunshine at all seasons. People tended not to bury themselves in corners with the *Times* crossword; we stood or moved about amid light
domestic chat. Not even the *Lady Chatterley's Lover* trial (Helen Gardner, now at
Oxford, a main witness, had been a member of the College) could affect the mood.
Principal took pride in bringing her luncheon guests to coffee. This could have
consequences. One such was a senior Turkish government official to do with the
education of women; Principal having introduced me, he asked for a half-hour of
my time. But our interview took less time: we went straight to the point. On Principal's recommendation he invited me to accept a hugely remunerative post as
advisor in his department. I felt no obligation to Principal to accept.

At U.C.L. before the war Dr Batho had a name for Wordsworth scholarship; in
that aspect she was remote from me. But I had sat in her Old Icelandic course and
become aware of the warmth of her personality. At Royal Holloway as I watched
her in action I became increasingly aware that, as much as any single person,
she was responsible for the good feeling in the College. Its administrative system

was remarkably cumbersome for such a small institution. There was a Council of twenty-two members: the Principal *ex officio*, fourteen invited members chosen from various august bodies, three from the Academic Board and the remainder local worthies. On critical matters this chairing body could call for deftness. In popular terms she was 'good with people'. This mattered particularly in relation with the College Secretary, Miss Hustler, who was also Secretary of the Finance Committee and thus the real centre of power, for in that capacity she knew the limit of the possible, namely the financially practicable. Miss Hustler was greatly respected; she had no close personal friends among the teaching staff and thus no departmental bias. Dr Batho's unquestionable contribution to the success of the College was to ensure that its Secretary's unquestionable shrewdness and general ability were channelled to its best academic advantage.

Edith Batho was Principal during six of my ten years at Royal Holloway College. She was also formally a lecturer in the Department of English. I suppose I must have been aware of this, but I do not recall it coming up with my departmental colleagues until the early sixties when, one November Thursday morning, over the ritual tea, Dr Tompkins spoke for her colleagues: Dr Batho had come to be so much in demand at University level that she was actually cancelling more lectures in her course on the Romantic Poets than she delivered. This, Dr Tompkins pointed out, was not fair to the students or the colleagues who had to sub for her. Would I put it to the Principal that for the good of the Department she should resign her lectureship and make way for a full-time replacement? My colleagues were evidently right and I had no option but to take the matter up.

On the Friday afternoon I made an appointment with the Principal's secretary for Monday. Already by Friday I had discarded the notion of approaching Miss Hustler with a formal request for an addition to my departmental staff. This would have had to have been supported by a written statement in which, unavoidably, Principal's inability to carry out her job would have stood out. Moreover it would have gone behind her back, which was ugly. A weekend of brooding left me with the single conclusion that I must ask Principal to resign that lectureship.

In retrospect I am inclined to think that we two were bonded by the sentimental consideration or subconscious awareness that we had both been 'Chambers's people', had known each other, however slightly, in a different world. She must have been at least ten years older than me, but we took unusual pleasure in each other's company. On one occasion together we brought off a remarkable prank; her readiness to take part in it tells something about her. This happened before we moved to the Green, and was set off by the circumstance that our Battersea 'phone number had been incorrectly assigned in a classified directory to a maternity nursing home. One night in the small hours, making my way to the other end of the flat to answer it, half asleep I walked into a tallboy and dealt myself what, by morning, was a many-splendored shiner. That same night Principal, after working late in her office, gave herself one stumbling on the staircase from her office to her apartment above it. About midday next day we met in one of the long corridors where by chance the daylight fell on our good eyes. The mischief occurred to me while we were being sorry for each other. Did she, I asked, have a guest for lunch? She did not and when I suggested that she keep a place for me her face lit up with mirth as she cautioned, 'Mind you don't be late!' Only the students I had taught that morning knew half the explanation, and they evidently did not publish that: the effect was all we could have wished. It was going to be hard to put it to this woman that she ought to give up the academic status she evidently cherished.

On Monday, in trepidation and as gently as I could, I asked her to consider that she was so much in demand at University level that her effectiveness in the department was being reduced. Would she consider making way for a replacement? I knew her well enough not to expect an emotional reaction; even so the plain common sense of her answer dismissed my concern: she should certainly relinquish the lectureship and indeed ought to have done so without prompting.

Two of my departmental colleagues stood out as the stalwarts, both superb teachers, and with markedly different personalities. One was Miss Hilda Green, a Senior Lecturer, who had put the 'What do you propose to do' question, a woman of strongly held views, most of which, luckily, were sound. On my arrival she took over the Chaucer course, presumably because it seemed unseemly for a male to teach 'young gentlewomen' (the Founder's expression) a subject where coarse language was involved. This did not seem to me a matter serious enough to make an issue of it, and when our final honours grades in the Middle English paper of the final honours examination continued high, was pleased with myself. One could not help feeling sorry for her; she wore an unmistakeable and unbecoming wig; I was told that as a child she had witnessed her missionary parents being massacred in Shanghai. She was fond of children and pampered ours when occasion offered, and they did not find her odd. What our students thought of her I do not know, but they unquestionably responded to her as a teacher.

The other pillar was the Reader, Dr Joyce Tompkins. She had a South Midland background; a cousin, a major in a TA infantry regiment,[23] had been a p.o.w. in Spangenberg with me. Dr Tompkins was unreservedly extrovert, and was known to say that her generation of women had been denied husbands and children by the Great War, unconcerned that for all its truth the statement raised eyebrows among her maiden colleagues. She raised mine, once, at least internally, when out of the blue she said, 'Professor Kane, you awaken both the bride and the mother in a woman.' Miss Green had no books to her name; Dr Tompkins had published with authority on the eighteenth century novel and was still active in the reha-

---

23. TA = Territorial Army.

bilitation of William Morris as a poet, and of Kipling. Of the two I got to know Dr Tompkins better. We were able, occasionally, to persuade her to visit after she retired in '65.

From the time of my appointment we had known that we would be moving to Englefield Green and that the moment would be dictated by education. It came in August 1956. Michael, born in January '48, was in his last year at a preprep school across the river; Mary, born in autumn 1950, and taught to read and write early like her brother by Bridget, would be ready to begin formal schooling in September 1956. Schooling apart there was the environment: Battersea was pleasant enough in summer, but come November there would be five months with impenetrable green fog as often as not, and at all times the chimneys of the Power Station a quarter mile east and the Polytechnic fifty yards north of our block of flats.

As for the A text, the time spent travelling to London and back for meetings would set me back. But to go by my correspondence files, by September 1956 I had submitted a draft copy of A's introduction, Text and Critical Notes to Athlone and had had them accepted. In my old age I find this hard to believe, but the dates are not debatable, and I can only suppose that my last year or so at U.C.L. the department made no demands on me beyond my teaching and that I must have worked like a beaver.

We moved to Englefield Green in August '56. There was no problem about Mary's schooling; a girls' boarding school named St David's that was on land adjoining the College's broad acres took a small number of day boarders. Michael was harder to place. The nearest boys' grammar school was some distance south of Egham and thus the Green, a long, unsupervised journey, and, at least at the outset, among complete strangers. Having been teased myself I could imagine what that could mean. A mile or so in the Windsor direction there was a prep school to which the Lathams had sent their son. There was a demand for the few day boarder places there, but they took Michael after some pressure.

As to housing, here we were lucky. Professor Willcock, dear creature, was moving with a sister to deep country, but though her house was with an agent she kept its sale in abeyance until I had had a chance to buy it. The house was engaging, but too small and had little ground. She was able to sell as soon as I told her this, which comforted me. Meanwhile Robert Latham's wife had heard of a recently vacated apartment, a 'quarter' of a large house about a mile from College. It belonged to a Miss Schroder (yes, the bankers) and was available for lease. I located her agent, liked the look of the house and its setting, and we took the lease.

The apartment occupied about two-thirds of the ground floor of a two-storey structure built as a charity home for orphan children; upstairs was evenly divided. It stood in King's Lane, which ran from the little cluster of shops that constituted Englefield Green to the roughly east-west road that serves as northern boundary of Windsor Great Park. Its setting felt rural rather than suburban. Our apartment, evidently the original custodian's quarters, had an entrance hall, three bedrooms, one of them double, a good sitting room, bathroom, larder and kitchen. The fireplace in the sitting room looked promising; one wall was long enough to take my oak bookcase, and another had a window wide enough for my five-foot wide desk. Most of the garden belonged to this apartment. For the children this was vastly better than Battersea Park, for they could play unsupervised. Both quickly learned to ride the bicycles that came with the move. There was little traffic during the working week on the road along the Park, and before long Michael was cycling to school (with the Headmaster's sanction). Regrettably this was never possible for Mary; St David's, like the College, was separated from the Green by a major north-south highway, and there was no traffic light within a mile. I took her to school on my way to College; on afternoons when I had to be in London or late home Bridget would fetch her.

By the end of August we were settled. Mary did not like school; the boarders, especially those who were from overseas, appear to have been cliquey. And she was twice at a disadvantage: she was somewhat plump, and considerably brighter than the other girls in her form. This affected my life: to minimize the teasing by getting a front row desk Mary had to get to school before nine o'clock; to avoid the embarrassment of running into tardy young females with heads wrapped in towels I had to arrive at College after the hour. Guess who won. I developed a habit of reading the morning paper in the parking lot for a quarter of an hour. Meanwhile, Mary received excellent teaching.

We lived in St Agnes Cottage until the spring of 1961. Luckily there were no bad winters during our time there, and what with the excellent fireplace and electric heaters we were tolerably comfortable. Our fellow tenants, three commuter couples, were good neighbours. Bridget, years later, remarked that she had not been happy there. This puzzled me at the time, but in retrospect I can see that it was for lack of something worthwhile to do with the children off her hands all day. She never showed boredom at the time, probably because the Egham Public Library was well stocked. And when the occasion arose she was the ideal faculty wife, entertaining with dexterity and finesse in our cramped quarters. But as a group the faculty wives did not figure largely. Perhaps that is the way in women's colleges?

As for myself, I had settled in comfortably and was often able to find an hour or two of a term-time afternoon checking A proofs. Taking account of the vast amount of detail to be covered and of delays when the printers went slow or actually struck, A was making good progress at this stage.

It was by no means finally checked when Donaldson came to the Green for a year's leave. In the summer of '56 he wrote that in 57/58 he would have a year's respite from directing graduate studies in English at Yale and was planning to apply for a Guggenheim fellowship: would I support him? Of course; further, I would arrange a Visiting Professorship for him at Holloway; that would effectively ensure the success of his application. We found a furnished house for him and his wife and daughter; College provided a study and Common Room rights. Once he had found a car for his wife in England and to take back to the States for himself he settled down and put in a good year's work.

On his earlier leave I had set him, as yet unaccustomed to working with actual manuscripts, to collating the Bodleian Rawlinson and Corpus Christi B copies against Bodley's Laud Misc. 581 which Skeat had used as both base and copy text: undebatably it had fewer unmistakeable scribal errors than the rest. Donaldson's collation confirmed the conclusion of Chambers's student Elsie Chick (Mrs Blackman) that the two copies he had collated (with sigils R and F) constituted one family of a bifid stemma of copies of the B version. But unlike me, whose Middle English was self-taught, he had earned his doctorate under one of the outstanding philologists of his time, Robert Menner, and was highly critical of the spelling and grammar of Laud, indeed considered it unsuitable as the linguistic vehicle of a great poem. There was the Trinity College B copy in best fourteenth-century London English: *Piers Plowman* would have been more easily accessible and, for all we know the poet might have written in that dialect, whatever regional form Langland had learned in childhood. I could not match his argument. The changing of base and copy text mean rearranging all collation up to date; but Donaldson had a year free, and he soon made up the time the transfer took. He learned very fast.

While he worked on B my priority after teaching was to see checking A to the finish. Even so our proximity made daily discussion effectively a routine. We stopped work in College at 5:20 and in my car resorted to the Fox and Hounds at the gate of the Park, conveniently on Donaldson's way home. There we had an hour in which we were almost always the only customers. The landlord, both quiet and genial, had no objection to our using the darts scoreboard for diagrams and we worked mainly on the stemma of the larger B family. I was scribe and kept notes of any decisions we might take, and indeed of any lively issues that would need discussion. The landlord at length broke down and very nervously asked us if we were atomic scientists. Before the Donaldsons returned to the States in later summer '58 we were in a good position to establish the B stemma as far as that was feasible and I had a good-sized 'shoebox' of notes by the time I began to focus my research on B. Meanwhile checking the final A proofs as they arrived from Dewey had priority.

The rich intellectual engagement I enjoyed during my twenty-five years of collaboration and association with Donaldson is, in retrospect, some recompense for the unquestionable drudgery of much of the editorial work. Over the years nonsense has been written or implied about our relationship, above all the fatuous notion that I domineered him. The unlikelihood of my doing so should be evident from his succession of notable controversies, for instance about Chaucer's metre or the rôle of patristic studies in our discipline. The appendix to his *Piers*

Plowman: the C text and its Poet and my *Autobiographical Fallacy* lecture represent wholly opposed positions. He was, if rationally approached, altogether reasonable.

In editing B we worked from the same position, that 'editing' is an activity of which both the theory and the procedures are determined by the nature and quality of the text in question, again in all literary senses of that word, above all as this was observable in the small details of the writer's manner of expression. Having come to *Piers Plowman* by quite different approaches, we found ourselves in remarkable agreement on such detail. By similar coincidence, although our personalities differed radically we found each other uniformly congenial company.

There were other interruptions to my work of another order. Luckily the first proof-checking of A was well forward in the early summer of 1959 when my sister Stella appeared on the scene with an English friend married to a Canadian husband. Stella's story was that the two of them needed a short break from being wives and mothers and had made the trip on impulse. I soon uncovered Stella's real purpose: Mother was not very well and I ought to visit her; she had wanted to convey this without alarming me. There were no obstacles; I would go as soon as the schools went into vacation. Bridget's parents would be delighted to have her and the children during my absence.

So I flew to Vancouver. Mother was unquestionably not in the best of health. But when I quizzed him her doctor did not seem to think her dangerously ill and she was very lively during my visit, which peaked soon after I arrived when Leo and Charles, each with a very acceptable newly acquired wife, appeared on the scene. But clearly my next visit must not be too long put off. I made contact with my more senior friends of graduate student days and found one of them Head of the English Department. It was no problem to arrange a summer school job for 1960.

When the formal invitation came it was to give a course of three lectures a week on the *Canterbury Tales,* notionally for second-year undergraduates. Luckily I recalled from the hearsay of my undergraduate years that many students in such summer schools were actually graduates with teaching experience making up requirements for an M.A. in English, so I dug out and furbished the notes for my last year of Chaucer teaching at U.C.L. And just as well, for in July 1960 all my students were keen graduates.

Summer school at U.B.C. began some time before the children's schools broke up, and I flew out in advance of the family, to find Mother a different person with the prospect of meeting the grandchildren. At the University my study in the new Arts Building was roomy and cool. The Library was larger by a handsome new wing, but at the Main Desk, to my delight, there was Miss Lanning, still in charge, and with scarcely any grey in her hair. Her greeting was a happy 'We were expecting you!'. What is more, after we had exchanged warm sentiments and I had (outrageously) borrowed a spare *Oxford English Dictionary* from the Library, when I mentioned that my next task was to find a place for my family for the summer:

she happened 'to know of a friend with a furnished house that could be let for the summer months'. I went to see it that afternoon, knew that Bridget would like it and closed the deal then and there. As for transport, Bill Robbins had recommended the garage where his own car was serviced and using his name I bought a Chevrolet there, somewhat advanced in years but, as it proved, a sound machine.

Mother and Bridget took to each other at once, and the children loved her. She did not drive, but Edward was living at home then, and took pleasure in showing them Vancouver and the dramatic coast northward as far as the highway ran in those days. Our house was at least 1000 feet above sea level on a slope that ran gradually down to a beach uncrowded, clean and with no undertow. For drama, at its west end there was a hangar that housed an aging Catalina flying boat which, once a day, flew a ritual patrol up and down the eight miles of open harbour.

My class of graduate students were all bright and strongly motivated. Two were nuns with faces of seraphic innocence; Miss Green came to mind. Of my student friends I saw John Harrison, now in charge of labour relations for the British Columbia branch of the international timber firm Weierhauser. His personality was made for that kind of 'good relations' job and he seemed to be enjoying it. He was married to a Vancouver girl whom we had met in Toronto and they had two sons of whom he was evidently very proud, but his wife was not in evidence and I formed an impression, later confirmed, of a relative coolness in the marriage.

Rodney Poisson, married to a musically brilliant wife and with two gifted daughters, was teaching in Vancouver. One weekend he drove me up into the Coast Range mountains to fish for the legendary steelhead, the seagoing rainbow trout of the Northwest Pacific but our timing was bad and we caught nothing.

Leonard Grant, now very senior in the Classics Department, was not teaching that summer, but came in to college one afternoon which we spent in talk. He puzzled me, for the free-style wit that I remembered him for was quite absent from his attitude; I sensed constraint in him and an underlying bitterness that I could not account for. It was some time before I learned the reason. During a postwar leave in Oxford he had married a German woman. I seem to recall that they had a son, but in any case she left him for another man. It appears that a year or so after our meeting he took his own life by deliberately crashing the barrier on the old coast road just south of the Canadian border, where he and the car fell hundreds of feet into the breakers pounding the foot of the cliff. To this day it grieves me to remember him; I am much in his debt for the confidence he built up in me as an undergraduate.

It was no surprise, but still disappointing, to learn that my two favourite teachers, Robinson and Todd, were no longer alive. However, Thorleif Larsen, younger than them, who had opened my eyes to the Renaissance, was alive. Although his speech had been impaired by a stroke his mind was evidently still in good form; he recognised me without help and was clearly delighted to see me again after fifteen years, bless him! The Faculty of Arts staged a reception for Bridget and me, a formality that made me, briefly, feel important. And the Dean of the Faculty took me salmon fishing offshore up the coast. He caught the only fish of the trip.

We did not leave British Columbia until the children's school calendar required it. There was time to enjoy my chief pleasure of the visit, observing Mother's delight in Michael and Mary and the evident affinity between her and Bridget. As something of an adventure we drove in my elderly car some 400 miles inland to Kelowna on Lake Okanagan where Stella and her family had a house on the shore. The last three or four days we stayed with Charles and his family in North Vancouver; their first son, Roderick, was a babe in arms: more joy for Mother, I could see.

Our return flight was a spectacular experience and comfortable to boot; I had flown by the Air Canada transcontinental route the preceding summer and found it exhausting; this time we flew by Canadian Pacific Airlines. The plane was piston-jet propelled and accordingly much quieter than a propeller-driven craft and roomier as well. It was uncrowded as well and the crew were children-friendly. We took off at about 9:30 and in the course of the morning crossed the Cordilleras, silhouetted throughout in the eastern light. After a brief stop to refuel in Edmonton we set off with a northerly bias across the tundra, a setting for an exquisitely varied tracery of lakes, this at length replaced by the brilliant blue vastness of Hudson's Bay, thereafter the stark rock of Labrador, briefly the Atlantic, and before expected, Greenland, its mountains already white. There, it seemed almost immediately, we came down to about 500 feet and were picked up by a pair of USAF fighters that closely shepherded us, by way of a deep and crooked fjord, to a US air base where we would again refuel. Here my family, disembarking to stretch their legs, having disregarded my injunction to put on their jackets, showed a fair turn of speed as they experienced what 'thirty below' means in Canadian.

In the spring of 1961 we moved to Beaconsfield in the Chilterns, about half an hour's drive from the College. Michael had passed his 'eleven plus' exams creditably, and Mary, not yet eleven, had completed the work of the top class at St David's. We found that sending them to local schools from the Green would have meant long, unsupervised bus journeys for each. Mary was in plain terms too young to travel alone, without an elder sister or companion. As for Michael, his Scaitcliffe teachers pressed me to send him to Sherborne in Dorset; he had shown some aptitude in the classics, for which Sherborne teaching had a good name. Having been impressed by the grammar school product during my ten years at University College I would have let him make the social adjustments of the bus journey, but there was Mary to find a school for as well. This was problematic in that she refused flatly to be a boarder. After much searching we found Oakdene in Beaconsfield, with a good name and a custom of taking day boarders. With her

St David's record they were willing to admit her at the beginning of the summer term. So I gave in about Sherborne. I would rather have sent him to Winchester.

We were lucky to find a house in Beaconsfield big enough, affordable and with possession conveniently timed. For unrecoverable reasons it was called Shandon Cottage. It stood on Stratton Road, a part of the then most northerly development of New Beaconsfield feasible in the local terrain. The 'Road', gravel at the time, was in effect a ledge or shelf cut by machine in a 150 yard, north-facing slope that levelled off about twenty yards short of a steeper rise. The view south from the uphill side of the house beyond the road was of a beautifully kept wild garden hillside. There were two magnificent beeches, at least eighteen inches in diameter, on our ground on the uphill side of the house; the downhill view was, to one side, of a superb horse-chestnut, on the other, a little farther down, a lovely stand of about twenty silver birches, very likely planted by the first owners, and down on the flatland to one side, a splendidly shapely oak of very great age and dimension. One lateral boundary, to the east, was a mixed hedge that could do with attention; the other, on the west, natural brushwood. There were problems: down the slope four huge willow stumps that had been pollarded in their time and three patches of ill-kept kitchen garden, doubtless going back to the 'Grow Your Own Food' slogan of wartime.

The house had one freak feature, its living room, which ran the whole length of the downhill side and took up rather more than half the north-south dimension. What remained here was a good entrance hall with the stairs, a small room with windows on two sides and a corner fireplace — guess what! My study to be!, an adequate kitchen, larder and lobby, and a hatch from the kitchen to the east end of the long room. We could live in the house as it stood, but there would have to be changes.

My first move, once the sale was concluded, was to find a competent builder-carpenter. I was lucky in this, and in being able to engage him immediately. His first assignment was to do away the corner fireplace in the living room. The second was to partition off the east quarter of the living room; the dining room this produced was big enough to hold a round dozen. The third was to replace the ill-fitting wooden French doors that gave onto the terrace on the north side with close-fitting windproof metal ones. In due course but without delay came rewiring the house, more cupboards in the kitchen, and with the onset of autumn chill, a new boiler and a laborious removal of tar deposit left by years of burning wood and failure to clean the chimney as this required. That summer was sometimes hectic and often noisy, but by September the house was snug and ready for winter.

I was lucky in having nothing of stressful urgency in hand that summer; I had no qualms about delaying reviews of Morton Bloomfield's *Piers Plowman as a Fourteenth Century Apocalypse* and David Fowler's *Literary Relations of the A and B Texts*; I owed myself this summer of taking time off for my family; until I was shed

Shandon Cottage.

of the A text they had had less of it than I would have wished. Shandon Cottage would be their home until they flew the nest, and so it was for almost fifteen years. As for the A text, which finally came out in early 1960, my friends and colleagues were lavish with congratulations. I was, of course, delighted, but I do not recall any particular sense of relief at delivery from what I had at the outset seen as a burdensome obligation, with myself as the Muggins of the *Piers Plowman* project. Certainly none of that resentment shows in its *Introduction*, which I have recently scanned. It reads to me like an account of a learning process in the course of which the learner becomes increasingly involved in his subject.

Thus, already at the stage when, having collated and checked all the copies of the B text I was collating A, I was satisfied that the two forms of the poem were by a single author. Both my ear, in which — I will arrogantly assert — I have confidence, and the constant, half-subconscious analytical scrutiny of the language and style of the text being collated proclaimed a single author, the arguments for several coming to seem ill-founded or inconclusive. The next lesson was a bonus of familiarity with what Skeat had called the A copies: the evident fact that their content and condition are best explicable on the assumption of their descent from a common ancestor. To this was appended a third conclusion: the state of preservation of a number of those copies precluded the reconstruction of their line of descent, that is diagram or stemma. This last conclusion, I recall, took some courage, for it ran clear counter to the Knott-Fowler argument. What I had, without

Dinner at Shandon Cottage: Mary Chapuis, George, Mary and Bridget Kane.

becoming aware of it come to think of as 'my' A text, would have to be edited without benefit of Lachmann.

By the time I reached that position I had read, to the best of my then knowledge, everything of significance available on editing medieval texts, and indeed on editing the New Testament, except Havet's *Manuel de critique verbale*. When at length I laid hands on a copy in the seventies I found the reason: it was too elementary for people to recommend! I could accept Bédier's argument as applicable to the thirteenth century French romances, but wholeheartedly agreed with Jean Fourquet's position, that Bédier's notions about editing were not valid on the fourteenth-century texts. There was confirmation of this position in Pasquali's *Storia della Tradizione e Critica del Testo*. As for German literature on the subject, there was Kantorowicz's *Einführung in die Textkritik*, largely concerned with medieval legal literature; its importance lay in his expression *lebende Texte*, that is, texts particularly subject to change because of developing in substance. It was quickly evident that other texts than books of law, among them *Piers Plowman*, had lives, that their texts were likely to be affected by changing contemporary issues. Paul Maas in his *Textkritik*, writing from the position of a classical scholar, assumed respect on the editor's part for the text in hand as his first requisite, and his close knowledge of it as an indispensible qualification. I came to see that his two terms, *discriminatio*, exercise of editorial judgment between rival readings, and *divinatio,* scrutiny of readings unchallenged by variants but in some way discrepant, or uncharacteristic of the grammar of the poet's style, comprise the essential process of editing. Griesbach's *durior lectio* took its place as a component of this type of reasoning, an element of *divinatio*. When I had finished the collation and checking of A and began to put the Introduction together I became increasingly aware of the range of meanings *durior* carried in this approach. Editing had in practice become a demanding lesson, a long one indeed. But in retrospect I cannot deny that I was finding it interesting.

A was generally well received. Sir Walter Greg had not found fault with the Introduction, which he read for me in typescript in the summer of 1955; Dr Sisam read it for Athlone and commented only that the account of manuscript hunting was too long for the results it reported. He was right, of course, and I reduced it accordingly. Donaldson read it in typescript and expressed regret that he had not seen it before he published his study of the B text Rawlinson and Corpus Christi copies. As for the description of manuscripts and dating of hands where I was almost wholly self-taught, Ian Doyle, whom I did not know of until I read his review, found serious fault with only three of my seventeen datings. Best of all, the outstanding Middle English scholar of the time, Jack Bennett, whom I had not yet met, and Norman Davis, whom I had met just once, liked the book. Indeed Norman used intemperate language in his review, describing a part of the introduction as 'epoch-making'!

I saw my A text as an experiment, a venture, an attempt to reconstruct the exclusive common ancestor of an accidentally preserved and propagated copy of something the poet may never have intended to publish as it stood. There are about three dozen points where it would have been possible to go back beyond that exclusive common ancestor; many are trifling; others stand out as against the grammar of the poet's style in B and C; still others are authorized by the now completed *Middle English Dictionary.* All are listed at the end of the 1988 reissue of A, which, incidentally, the University of California Press was *not* authorised to call a Second Edition by me.

In 1961 I viewed the prospect of editing B comfortably, with no particular sense of urgency. The Department as good as ran itself. I could escape the time-consuming summer chore of serving on the Final Honours Examination Board with the excuse that my younger colleagues needed the money. When in 1961 I was coopted to the College Board of Governors I took comfort in the thought that this meant no more than a quarterly visit to London where it met. Moreover I had a collaborator in editing B, and we would soon be making progress with it.

Of course that is not how things went. For a start such time as Donaldson had after teaching went largely to his post as Director of Graduate Studies in English at Yale. And beyond that he was domestically driven to writing for the pot. In due course he would have another year's leave; meanwhile there was plenty of work that, as the more experienced, I could put in hand. I would begin on description, dating and provenance of the B copies; here living in Beaconsfield would be an asset: even in those days it was only a 45 minute run from my house to Bodley.

But when I opened Fowler's *Literary Relations of the A and B Texts* I was checked again; this book was not lightly to be dismissed. David Fowler knew his two texts and wrote with the confidence which that gives. That he was misreading them *and this poet* might well escape the inexperienced student reader. A review would have to take the assumption of two poets as Fowler's radical primary consideration, not merely as an opinion to be noted and dismissed. As I read on I found my notes on the authorship issue outgrowing a review; this needed a monograph. I wrote to Jack about my predicament and he was very good-natured, even though the ultimate review was about four years late.[24]

I suppose I must have enjoyed writing the little book,[25] for there is unquestionably a touch of smugness of tone in its making of the points. But the only part of writing it that I remember enjoying is the search in thirteenth/fourteenth century 'dream vision' poetry for conclusive evidence of the force of the convention of cryptogram signature by its poets. It did not take long to assure myself that, as Chambers had believed, 'I have lived in land, my name is Long Will' was an author's signature beyond doubt.[26] But the genre has an engaging quality, and I spent much more time reading its verse than was needful for my project.

There was excitement as well. At breakfast the very day I planned to deliver my typescript of the authorship book to Dewey I had a letter from a Mr Corbett of Much Wenlock in Shropshire, evidently an amateur antiquary, asking for my advice about what to do with three Shropshire land documents recording transfers of named pieces of land in which the surname Langland appeared, either as interested or as witness. This land was in the parishes of Kinlet and Highley, no distance from Cleobury Mortimer in Shropshire. Beaconsfield is on the Marylebone to Birmingham line: I was in Birmingham well before lunch, and the City Librarian, Mr Woods, put before me not just Corbett's three findings but two more of his own. Together they ranged from 1399 to 1581, and between them they established the existence of a family of some substance named Langland with branches in both Shropshire and Buckinghamshire, Eustace de Rokayle's county. I will write no more than I was permitted in my *Oxford DNB* article on Langland, that the hunt for the poet is not ended.

Another distraction from the major editing project was less creditable: I allowed myself to be talked into becoming the University's Public Orator for a

---

24. *Medium Ævum* 33 (1964), 230–31; Jack = J. A. W. Bennett, who was editor of *Medium Ævum* from 1956 to 1980.

25. Piers Plowman: *the evidence for authorship* (London: Athlone Press, 1965).

26. See *Piers Plowman: The B text*, ed. Kane and Donaldson, B XV 152 'I haue lyued in londe, quod I, my name is longe wille'. This modernization was used by Kane in 'Langland, William (*c*.1325–*c*.1390), poet', *Oxford DNB* (2004).

George Kane, Public Orator, University of London, *c.* 1964.

five-year term to begin in 1962. I was thus persuaded by the Principal of the University, backed by Edith Batho ('It will be good for the College'). When Bridget and I were invited to the 1961 Foundation Day Ceremony (the occasion when the Orator performs) and I watched James Sutherland whom I would succeed in action, I realised what I had let myself in for. It added up to delivering, over five years, three dozen three-minute commendations — the time limit was absolute — of persons whom, except for Benjamin Britten and Peggy Ashcroft — I had never heard of before my assignment.

One enjoyable occasion in which I had to perform was a meeting of the Congress of Commonwealth Universities, when the 'Mother' institution conferred doctorates to mark the occasion.[27] The delegates were accommodated in two of the University's new halls of residence in Bloomsbury and Principal Logan asked Bridget and me to be formal Hostess and Host in one of these; we would be put up in the Senior Tutor's apartment on the top floor. Her duties were shepherding and keeping happy the accompanying wives; the spouse of one West African delegate was notable for her gorgeous costume but she had not a word of English. My duties were much easier and mundane to boot: seeing that breakfast was ready on time and the bar was well stocked and closed on time. I had, actually, a fine team of graduate students who happened to be 'living in' during vacation, headed by a charming economics student from India, Ashok Bansal, whom we kept in touch with for some years. Logan's programme of entertainment for the occasion was impressive: a reception by the Lord Mayor and the City Companies, the Russian Ballet, fortuitously in London, a night at Glyndebourne, a fabulous symphony concert in the new auditorium on the Embankment and a Buckingham Palace Garden Party. For the amusement of my unborn great-grandchildren I record that along with the other host, a professor of engineering from Imperial College, I was an equerry, closely rolled umbrella, grey top hat (hired from Moss Bros) and all! Bridget and I had been asked to a Garden Party before, goodness knows why, when it was largely a matter of jostling for a cup of iced coffee to reduce the boredom.

A spinoff of this Conference Meeting was that Dr George Hall, the President of the University of Western Ontario, invited me to be his representative on the Congress Standing Committee. This did not meet too often, and seemed to involve little homework, so I undertook the job. To my agreeable surprise I learned that the Standing Committee had the disposal of very substantial research fellowships, and I had no compunction about arranging, in due course, one for Professor George Russell, whom Alex Mitchell, now Vice-Chancellor of newly founded Monash University, had recruited as a collaborator in editing the C text. Russell, a New Zealander, had an exceptional record: a travelling scholarship to Cambridge, where he studied under Basil Willey and David Knowles, a year as

---

27. 1963. The Association of Commonwealth Universities (ACU), the world's first and oldest international university network, was established in 1913.

assistant lecturer at King's College London in 1948–9, then a succession of Australian appointments that brought him, in 1961, to the Chair of Early English Language and Literature in the University of Sydney; I was going to need his C text
for my own long haul. Thus far I had had only occasional information about C,
and — when I asked for them — C readings.

Only as I write about this Standing Committee does it occur to me that my
acquaintance with George Hall might have had some connexion with a letter I
received some weeks after the Congress, enquiring whether I would allow myself
to be considered as a candidate for the presidency of Victoria University. This was
a new foundation, subsuming Victoria College where Leonard Grant and Rodney
Poisson had studied, itself founded in 1902 as an offshoot of McGill University in
Montreal, and since 1920 when the University of British Columbia was founded,
a junior college of that institution. Now, in July 1963, it had by statute become an
independent university. The letter was signed by someone I did not know who
had subscribed himself as the secretary of a committee to elect its first president.
It contained no detail of that officer's duties, but held out an intended carrot: the
sum of $5,000,000. was available for the 'first phase' of its development and an
equal amount would be so for the second.

I do not recall hesitating about answering in the negative. The new university's situation on Vancouver Island was beautiful and the fishing on the Island
among the best in the world. But I evidently could not see myself being happy in
the job, and I suppose that I had without awareness collated the sort of tedium
that heads of universities live with. Just now, forty years later, with a little reflection I came up with a list of the problems innate in such a situation: placating
existing staff passed over, that is the local hopefuls; keeping academic and struc-
tural expansions at a matching pace; recruiting high-quality faculty; funding student accommodation; the cost of new departments. As for my ego, I did not delude
myself that I was on a short list. I could name half a dozen Canadians of my age
who would be in the running.

My ego did get a huge boost in early winter 1964, putting the finishing touches
to the authorship book at home on a Wednesday morning, when the telephone
rang. 'This is Norman Davis; I am calling to ask whether you would like the Cambridge chair.' It took a moment to recover my mental balance: this had to be the
chair that H. S. Bennett had gone to great lengths to get established, with himself
in mind as the first occupant. But it went to C. S. Lewis who, presumably from
Norman's enquiry, was on the point of retiring. As for Norman telephoning, I supposed that he was on the Board of Electors for it. I did not want to go, though was,
of course, chuffed to be asked. But my ego was boosted even more over the next few
years by invitations to serve on both Oxford and Cambridge boards of advisors.

I had one more approach from British Columbia while I was at Royal Holloway. A third university, named after the notable explorer Simon Fraser, was to be

established from scratch in what were virtually the foothills of the Coast Range of the Rockies. Would I like the job of founding its English Department? This was a straight offer and there are circumstances in which I might have accepted it, but a combination of reasons made me turn it down.

One of them was the difficulty, general at that stage in the development of English Studies, of recruiting first-rate staff. One of our promising younger teachers on the language side, Margery Morgan, was lured to Australia. I knew of only one possible replacement of her quality, Eric Stanley, then a lecturer at Queen Mary College. I sounded him out and the next thing I heard was that he had been put up for a readership at his own college. On the modern side a youngish member of staff with health problems needed indefinite leave. We had only one especially good applicant for her post, Inge-Stina Ewbank, but my two senior colleagues did not care for the notion of a foreigner in the Department, and we had to gamble among the less striking applicants.

The sixties were not proving as generous with time for my B text work as I had hoped. Too much was happening in College, so to speak. For a start Edith Batho's term of office as Principal came to an end. So, about the same time, did that of the Secretary, Miss Hustler. 'We' were able to make good appointments to both posts, but the process involved special meetings of the Academic Board and Council, the latter in London.

The new Principal, about my age, was put to the test from the outset, for about the time she was appointed, as if this had been deferred until Edith Batho's departure, the topic of College becoming coeducational was seriously mooted. As far as I know the possibility was raised in the Science Faculty. I had no part in the initiation, for I was, so to speak, comfortable in my work. Coeducation was no novelty to me, and my reaction when it came to be seriously considered did not, as I recall, go beyond curiosity about how the change would be achieved.

Taking the decision was a process that began at Academic Board level; I do not remember us discussing it seriously in the Department. I do recall the gravity of the discussion in the Board (tension, not conflict or even disagreement, but concern at the seriousness of the decision). The vote was by ballot, not the usual show of hands, and there was relief when the votes were counted. There was further business, but we stood up notwithstanding this and the new Principal (I watched her) pressed a button that brought in not the usual tea and biscuits, but trays with glasses and a decanter.[28]

There was no escaping being on the Council's Planning Committee but this was a scale of performance out of my depth and I can write as an observer that the transition was wisely planned. To be sure, the resources were considerable. College owned ninety-five acres of ground, playing fields, parkland and an arboretum,

28. Marjorie Williamson became Principal of Royal Holloway College in 1962.

the latter developed by the Professor of Botany over the years. There did not seem to be any money problems; Council engaged Sir Leslie Martin, then Professor of Architecture in Cambridge. Accommodation was the first consideration. As to bodies, College would admit 150 men in 1965, the same number in 1966, and 200 in 1967; admission of women would be scaled to realize a mainly residential college of 1000 students. My Department was immediately involved, as was French, in the first move to gain space in the original building. The College bought two large mansions nearby, to be converted and ready for academic use in October 1964. The new home of English was across the main highway, directly opposite the main College gate. Planning the redesign of its interior into an independent element of College and keeping an eye on the builders took time from the B text.

When the Planning Committee decided to issue a brochure I was, I suppose by reason of my subject, asked to prepare it, a document addressed to headmasters and tutors describing the resources, potential and amenities of the College. Such data were readily forthcoming from the heads of Departments, and the Finance Committee gave me carte blanche, except for photography, where my limit was £1000. The original College building, much admired by Nikolaus Pevsner, was splendidly photogenic, but I used only three pictures of the main structure, and used photographs of departmental subjects where available as more to the point. But I spent on paper, printing, layout! As to written content, all I did was to put the various departmental contributions into a single style. In my opinion the most effective visual recruitment was the cover photograph, supplied by the Professor of Physics, Sam Tolansky, its subject 'triangular hollows on the natural surface of a diamond, revealed and emphasized by a precision optical interferometric technique invented and developed at Royal Holloway College'. As science, I was given to know, this technique was notably advanced. As art, it would have put the Tate Modern at its best in the deep shade. There were paeans of praise from all departments when the brochure 'came out', a reward in themselves for the good vacation month preparing it had taken. But I could not not in decency have refused it, for I was on the point of resigning my chair at Royal Holloway College from June 1965 and to use this as excuse for not preparing the brochure would have been ugly behaviour by my standards.

My reasons for moving to King's were not simple. The dominant one was practical. I was finding it very time-consuming to take my car to the Green for a morning of teaching, then down to Egham Station and a train for a meeting in London and, at the end of my London commitment, repeating the process in reverse, especially because by the time I got to the northward road through Slough it was rush hour. Another was the accessibility of Senate House and its Library, the Institute of Historical Research, the BM and of course the bookstores, all half a day from Egham, in effect, and a short bus or taxi ride from King's.

George Kane with colleagues, 1960s.

Another reason, which I realize only now forty years later, was that I craved male companionship and that the ambience at Royal Holloway was not conducive to it. There was Robert Latham, a scholar of fine quality and a fine wit; we played squash together and went to each other's house for drinks, but I was a professor and he was not and unlikely to be made one; the history chair had gone to a very erudite and temperamentally disagreeable female; this situation embittered Robert's wife and thus himself. Sam Tolansky the physicist of the brochure cover and I got on well but he lived in London; his wife and son were charming professional musicians but they inhabited a different world. Rafe Tymmin the German chair was amiable and charming but uncomfortably shy. Actually the person in College whom I had most in common with was Dr Tompkins in my department, and she would be of retiring age in 1965.

How I came to move to King's College London can be quickly told. During the session 1962–3 Hilda Green had a leave of absence, and on her recommendation we asked Professor Norman Garmonsway of King's to teach her courses. He and I were already friendly acquaintances from service on the Board of Studies and examining Boards; during his time at Royal Holloway we got to know each other as much as anything by my driving him to Egham station at the end of his day at College. Thus when he told me he was being retired by age in July 1965 I felt able to ask him, perhaps impertinently, whether King's had chosen his successor. The pause before he answered was not too long, and his answer was, 'Would you be

George Kane with with Joyce Tomkins.

interested?' It seemed too easy: a letter from the Principal of King's asking me to call on him, an interview by his sole self, another by Geoffrey Bullough who had the senior chair at King's. And so to a new chair.

That easy translation did not imply severance. I can still enjoy remembering the idyllic setting and the smooth succession of the academic seasons of my time at Royal Holloway College. As for my departmental colleagues there, I did not lose touch as long as we lived in Beaconsfield. At some time or other during my last while there I must have mentioned that I was preparing a surplus piece of my garden for planting fruit trees; as my farewell present each gave me an apple tree sapling. It is gratifying to recall that they thrived and bore fruit early enough to offer their visiting donors this in season. We were always glad when Joyce Tompkins came for a weekend. She and Bridget's mother got on especially well.

On one occasion not long before we left Beaconsfield I went back to the College. Marjorie Williamson and her governing body had decided to institute an annual Foundation Dinner and she invited me to deliver the inaugural address. The second contact occurred about fifteen years later, at the Senate House at sherry after a formal lecture which I had attended from a sense of duty. I was addressed by a goodlooking, smartly dressed woman in her thirties with a couple of somewhat older, bearded men in tow whose faces were familiar.[29] She claimed to have been a finalist in my last year at Holloway. The men I recalled, beards and all, as my two male appointments. But as for the woman, they told me with evident pride and pleasure in the fact, that she was the Head of the English Department at the College.[30]

29. Katie Wales (now an honorary professor associated with the Centre for Research in Applied Linguistics at the University of Nottingham).

30. Kane wrote no more. There is a sense of pride in this last sentence: pride in the success of one of his own undergraduates, now Head of Department.

AFTERWORD

The more I learned about my father, the easier it was to deal with what at times could be a very difficult relationship. Typing his memoirs gave me, Felix, Chloë and Tony a much better understanding of how to contend with him over the last ten years of his life.

He was an honest and honourable man with a strict moral and ethical code. But he was not an easy or comfortable father to have and we were probably not easy children, being similar to him in some ways.

Like most men of his generation he was not a hands-on parent; and because he had never experienced life with his own father, he parented in the style of his own grandparents, which could be harsh. Michael found that particularly difficult and they clashed frequently. If we made mistakes he gave no quarter; he expected us to be the best, even where it simply was not possible. He had difficulty expressing emotions and was extremely strict with us as adolescents (understandable considering his moral code was instilled by people born in the 1840s).

But my friends adored him since he treated them as his students and took their ideas and opinions seriously. He was generous with his time, always willing to discuss their degree subjects and give advice. When my friends in the small sixth form expressed dissatisfaction about our lazy and fairly incompetent English teacher he held classes for those of us doing the English Literature exam in his study every week. Everybody laughed a lot, learned more, passed and got good grades. And this carried on in later life when he financially supported a friend of my daughter through her degree at UCL, knowing her family could add little to the basic grant and disapproving of student loans. We were very proud of him but found it hard as children to tell friends what he did. 'He writes' was the best we managed. I still remember him winning the 1963 Israel Gollancz Memorial Prize. It resulted in a boudoir grand piano. And his being Public Orator gained us a new fridge!

I tried to read *Piers Plowman* but failed. Not surprising as a degree in law does not teach one to read Middle English. In contrast, his study on Chaucer was read avidly by all the family.

He and I were at King's together for three years, but almost no one knew of our relationship, which made us both laugh although I was constantly anxious that someone would mention my student behaviour to him.

George Kane.

His great loves were his immediate family, Canada and fishing, probably in that order.

I value three aspects of his parenting enormously.

He instilled in both of us an immense love of reading and books, together with good grammar and a love of language, which my children have certainly inherited. He read Tolkien to me when I was 4 and I have reread it cyclically since

Front row: Bridget Kane, Ellen Wittig, Felix Kane Gott, Chloë Kane Gott, Mary Kane, George Kane; behind: Haydn Gott, Joe Wittig. *c.* 2000.

then, let alone seen the films which Pa would have hated. I read whenever I have a moment, 'there's life and then there's reading'.

He insisted that I had a profession (most unusual in my school in the late 1960s) based, obviously, on his mother's situation even though he did not encourage my mother to qualify as a teacher, which she wanted to.

And he encouraged Michael and me to debate. Although he did not like to be contradicted; we could question everything except his views — a habit I have encouraged in my own children (who contradict me all the time).

He had strong opinions about what we should or should not do, even when we were adults but he was proud that we both became professionals, although he was never comfortable with my working areas of divorce, mental health and prisons. I sometimes think he preferred me being quoted in the monthly journal *Commercial Motor* (after a case in one of my quasi-tribunals) than hearing about all my other work!

He was more relaxed with his grandchildren and was immensely proud of all of them, no matter what they did. He loved reading their theses and essays and they could do little wrong in his eyes.

His years in Chapel Hill were happy ones for him and my mother, who blossomed in a different country where the wives of academics were involved far more than in England. She set up and ran many projects in the local hospital, including the library and a helpline for patients and appeared in the newspapers and on local radio. They followed the university football team avidly and she travelled around the USA with Pa when he was going to conferences, nearly being arrested in New Mexico when she trespassed into a reservation without realising. They made good friends who remain close and were a source of generous help, guidance and comfortable accommodation for Chloë when she travelled in the US for three months.

After Michael's death he became very close to Rod, Charles's son, who, working as a pilot from Dubai, used to fly in to Gatwick to gossip about Canada and the Canadian side of the family, and Pa enjoyed having extra young members of the Canadian branch to spoil and have fun with.

He mellowed a great deal in his seventies, particularly after his double hip operation, which made us realise how much pain he had stoically endured. He and Michael fished and indulged in genealogy together, which gave them both a focused task when Michael was diagnosed with terminal bowel cancer. Michael's early death just before his 50th birthday was a terrible time for him and my mother but Michael's two daughters and Alison, his wife, remained very close to both of them.

He was unhappy about my divorce but became very fond of Tony and valued his discussions with him as well as the high quality of Tony's cooking.

He was delighted that Felix read medieval history for his degree and was amused by Chloë's choice of religion for hers, knowing her views very well.

How he would have loved to know that she ended up doing her Master's degree at King's and doing so well. Three generations of Kanes there would have thrilled him.

Michael and I always said that we gained everything intellectual and tough from our father, including the ability to deal with difficult situations, and that if there was anything kind and gentle in us it came from our mother. Looking back I know we gained far more from both of them. He was a father who was hard to like at times but always easy to love, respect and be proud of.

Mary Kane
Sussex 2016

Lightning Source UK Ltd.
Milton Keynes UK
UKOW06f0739221216
290627UK00002B/116/P